THE

WILLARD J. GRAHAM SERIES

IN ACCOUNTING

BOOKS IN
THE WILLARD J. GRAHAM SERIES IN ACCOUNTING

CONSULTING EDITOR   ROBERT N. ANTHONY   *Harvard University*

ACCOUNTING MEASUREMENTS
FOR
FINANCIAL REPORTS

ACCOUNTING MEASUREMENTS FOR FINANCIAL REPORTS

WILLIAM J. VATTER
Professor, School of Business Administration
University of California, Berkeley

1971 · RICHARD D. IRWIN, INC.
HOMEWOOD, ILLINOIS   60430
IRWIN-DORSEY LIMITED, GEORGETOWN, ONTARIO

Library of Congress Catalog Card No. 71–141390

Printed in the United States of America

TO ROSE

*This book could not have
been written without her help.*

PREFACE

This book grew out of a need for the kind of materials that would serve to bring beginning MBA students (without previous acquaintance with accounting or accountants) to a level of reasonable competence in understanding published financial reports. It has thus far served in one form or another to teach a good many such students what accountants do to prepare published reports, and why they do it.

To be able to accomplish this within the time constraints (an MBA program is not an academic country club), such a task requires that mechanics be minimized and that essential relationships be stressed. There is little time for drill and reiteration; ideas must be built into the structure directly, in logical sequence, with maximum coherence. Whether or not this has been fully accomplished, the results of use and development over ten years and several mimeographed editions now seem to have use-potential for other students in other circumstances. Hence they appear in this present form.

The approach is a bit unconventional; there is no "balance sheet equation." The concepts of accrual accounting are perceived by starting with cash transactions, augmenting and refining the measurements as the desire for better analysis becomes apparent. Chapter 1 presents the functions of business measurements, the usefulness of dollar measures, the idea of business entity and its relation to the market, and cash flow as a surrogate for resource conversions. The notion of an account as a device of record—an item of accountability—is used to show the need for better information. This is partially met in Chapter 2 which uses double entry and a set of accounts to classify, and summarize, cash flows in a trial balance which can be converted to a statement of receipts and payments. A recognition of the difference between restricted and unrestricted receipts serves to distinguish proprietorship from revenue in Chapter 3, and the fact that costs may apply to the future, as well as to the present reporting period establishes the concepts, asset and expense. The simple work sheet used to handle data to fit these concepts produces the position statement as a logical consequence of timing costs and revenues. Chapter 4 introduces the journal entry as an easy way to write transactions, and it is used to write out the entries needed to make the ledger agree with the work sheet. Then the cut-off needed to set out short period operations from cumulative records suggests ways of disposing of one year's operating data without interfering with current data collection. Chapter 5 brings out the impact of credit upon accounting measurements, thus extending the accrual pattern. Receivables and payables become the basis for recognizing revenue and cost. Payrolls and related taxes provide application of the accrual idea among the various equities involved; loans and interest, taxes and service-cost accruals provide for equity classifications that round out the position statement structure to encompass nearly complete accrual presentation.

Revenue determination is then refined in Chapter 6; it deals with the criteria for revenue recognition via extant practice, as to approval sales, consignments, and long-term contracts. However, the conventional revenue-adjustments for uncollectibles, discounts, and the like are discussed in Chapter 7. Chapter 8 extends the expense concept, dealing with criteria for cost assignment and transfer, write downs for inventory and other losses; it introduces the concept of operating charges and the flow of manufacturing costs (through inventories to expense) with some recognition of the "normal-cost" concept. Long-term asset accounting appears in Chapter 9; various methods of amortization are related to depreciation and depletion, and the accounting for investments, leaseholds, and goodwill are presented. Chapter 10 concerns itself with short- and long-term financing via notes, loans, amortized mortgages, bonds, and sinking funds. An appendix to this chapter considers capitalized leases and compound interest amortizations, including not only the annuity and "rate of return" methods, but also a time-adjusted production approach. Chapter 11 presents the Statement of Funds as an essential element in financial reporting, and shows how this statement can be prepared from basic data. Business Combinations (Chapter 12) comprises poolings and purchase (by exchange of shares as well as for cash) and also an elementary view of the preparation of consolidated reports. As a general summary, Chapter 13 includes a review of several published reports, and outlines the methods of ratio- and index-analysis.

The last chapter examines the problems of changing prices with respect to inventory procedures, appraisals, and specific price shifts; it also presents the way to reflect changes in the general price level in a full set of financial reports.

The materials are arranged so they can be used in different ways. For a minimum prerequisite to managerial issues of accounting, the first eight chapters would be sufficient background for effective use of basic cost accounting or budget procedures, as conventionally presented in such texts. The appendix to Chapter 10 may be ignored if one is not concerned with uncommon depreciation methods and the capitalization of leases. Chapter 14 can be omitted if the aim is to stay out of "valuation" issues such as LIFO, appraisals, and index numbers. But the book as a whole attempts to give a comprehensive view of what accounting is, with some implication of what might be done to improve it.

Questions and problems appear at the end of each chapter as is expected; these are regarded as applications of the text rather than exercises. They range from quite simple ones to comprehensive and challenging types; the instructor can pick as he chooses. I have never found it necessary to use more than one or two problems to a chapter, and I have never had to repeat an earlier list of problems exactly in a subsequent course.

It is customary for an author to acknowledge debts of various kinds in the preface to his book; but to me it seems abundantly clear that such a task could be discharged—so far as this book is concerned—only in broad statements. Many of my present and former colleagues have (sometimes without knowing it) had a hand in clarifying my ideas and helping me see some of the errors of my ways. Several hundred students have contributed by trying to work with earlier drafts of this material; they have put up with many errors, confusions, and inadequacies in my writing; some of them were brave enough to tell me the things I needed to know about my work. The University has been patient with the allocation of my time to this, rather than to other projects; and some of the office staff have devoted many hours to preparing copy (for use in my classes) from which this book has emerged. Above all, there are those who helped me most by their continuing encouragement, and their confidence that what I wanted to do was worthwhile. To all of these I am grateful; my hope is that they will not find the result marred by too many of my own errors and misjudgments.

March, 1971   WILLIAM J. VATTER

CONTENTS

Effect of Price Shifts on Depreciation. Errors in Past Depreciation. Over-all Changes in the General Price Level. Basis for Measuring General Price Level Changes. Summary of Price Level Changes. Conclusion.

Chapter 1

MEASURING BUSINESS TRANSACTIONS

Introduction

Accounting is a systematic method of measuring and reporting business transactions. Every business firm has some kind of an accounting system; everybody makes some use of financial records and reports. The use of accounting is so widespread and the purposes served by accounting records and reports are so far-reaching that it is safe to say that accounting is *the* generally accepted means of recording, reporting, and interpreting financial information.

Managers rely on the accounting system to obtain information about what is going on in the firm; they use accounting data to help make decisions, to plan and to control operations. Present and prospective investors or creditors use accounting reports to form judgments about the position and the progress of the enterprise; this use of accounting is universal throughout the business world. Accounting is also used in many situations which might, at first glance, appear not to be "business." Nonprofit organizations such as hospitals, schools, foundations, and the like make use of accounting in much the same way as business firms. City, state, and federal government agencies use accounting records and reports to obtain and present financial information and to help maintain control over the operations that are carried on. Indeed, there are few if any financial activities that are not closely related to accounting methods and techniques.

The uses made of financial data in various enterprises may be quite different. Banks, insurance companies, department stores, factories, construction companies, and other enterprises are individual and different—each has its own special problems and its own plan of collecting and processing data for records and reports. Nevertheless, every one of these different accounting systems is built upon certain basic ideas common to all of them.

We shall begin the study of accounting by examining these basic ideas. The story of accounting and its uses will develop logically from this framework; as each new procedure or method is developed, we shall relate it to the basic structure of ideas. In this way, the reader will be better able to understand why, rather than merely how, accounting methods are used. We begin by raising the question, why do we measure business transactions?

Uses for Business Measurements

Everybody has some interest in the measurement of business events. Each of us has the problem of living within his income, and we must have some plan or pattern for managing our financial resources. If we try to operate without such a plan, we get into confusions and difficulties. Anyone who has a bank account does a certain amount of accounting because keeping the "running balance" straight in the stubs of a checkbook is one form of accounting. A person who operates without a bank account, making payments only from cash, will often be annoyed by his inability to remember the amounts and kinds of expenditures; his uncertainty as to where and how wisely money has been spent makes it difficult for him to plan for a better future.

Everyone who saves any part of his income has an interest in the firm or enterprise to which he entrusts his savings; he needs to know what that firm is doing and what effect this has upon his situation. Therefore, banks and other enterprises that use other people's money in the form of loans, mortgages, stocks, or shares are required to make reports of their financial operations and position at regular intervals.

Every employee has good use for financial information about his company. A company must be successful if it is to provide steady work; the company must grow and prosper if it is to provide satisfactory opportunities for advancement. The worker is interested in the affairs of his employer because the future of both the employer and the worker are tied together; neither can succeed very well without the other. Accounting reports can only tell what has happened in the past and what the present situation involves; accounting does not deal with the future per se. But often the best way to approach the future is by way of a careful analysis of what has happened in the recent past. Accounting can provide such an analysis in the form of financial reports. By making possible a better understanding of what has happened, accounting makes the future easier to understand and to provide for.

Customers of a firm are interested in the financial success of their suppliers. The satisfactions obtained from a product or service often depend to a large extent upon the dependability and reputation of the maker; one of the factors used in establishing the dependability of a supplier is and should be his financial records and prospects. On the other hand, sellers need information about their customers. Certainly the whole field of credit operations, on which so large a part of our lives depend, would be greatly handicapped without some means of collecting and analyzing financial data. There is a general and widespread need for financial information even among buyers and sellers who are otherwise independent.

Communication by Numbers

To convey information to the many people who wish to have it, we must put that information in terms that will mean something. One of the most effective ways to convey information that means something is to use numbers. To say that a room is large or spacious is not nearly so definite as to state the length, width, and height of the room in standard units. When the size of a room is given in feet, anyone who knows what a foot is and can count, can reconstruct the size of the room in his own mind, even though he has not been in, or even seen, the room. The idea of size is conveyed positively by measurement in a way that mere words cannot do.

Not all ideas or situations lend themselves to numerical expression; it is quite difficult to state such things as wisdom, pleasure, or ambition in terms of numbers because we have no universally recognized units of measurement. However, we can report in numbers the scores made on tests that indicate knowledge or understanding; and we may measure the amount of money spent on certain hobbies, thus reflecting the pleasure gained by individuals pursuing these hobbies. We may also measure the time devoted to self-improvement as an indication of one's ambition. By such means we convey ideas more concretely, even though our measurements are not direct and precise counts of the qualities under consideration. Although some things are hard to measure, a great many other things can be measured, expressed in units familiar to our communicants, and thus may be better understood.

There is still another advantage in using numbers to express ideas. It is possible to compare and to extend number data so that the data can be put to many valuable uses. A car traveling 30 miles per hour will ultimately overtake one going 25; if we know how far apart they are, we may even predict when they will reach a certain point and in what order. If the relation between two variables is really understood in a way that can be expressed numerically, we may use this information not only to understand but to analyze, generalize, and predict. The whole field of science depends upon this property of number data; scientific laws are often expressed in number relations because the validity of the law basically depends on its use in prediction. There are many business and financial situations that can be predicted in a similar way. Even when the laws or relationships are not entirely clear (as is the case with some business situations), it is still true that we can handle problems better by trying to extend and apply observed number relationships between the factors and variables of these problems.

Money Measurements

Colloquially, business is often thought of as a process of making money; we tend to express business transactions in their money amounts because so many business transactions involve money. We think of a purchase in terms of the amount to be paid (the cost). Employment is thought of in terms of the compensation agreed upon. Other business transactions are thought of in terms of money because they are expressed in, or are effected by, exchanges of money. But why do we measure transactions in financial terms? Money is not the only unit in which transactions or events may be expressed. We can measure the output of a mine in tons, the work of an employee in hours, the output of a machine in product units, the use of electricity in kilowatt-hours. There are many measurement units that can be used to convey information about business events. There must be some reason why money should be used to measure business events.

Additivity.   A business measuring unit must permit the addition of things or amounts for reporting purposes; this is what actually happens in the business process. A typical product is a combination of materials, personal services, and the use of equipment. We could state the details of manufacture in pounds of material, hours of labor, gallons of water supply, yards of thread or cloth, kilowatt-hours of electricity. To put such varied units all together into one summary statement would be confusing, because the units that have gone into the product are of different kinds; pounds, hours, gallons, and yards do not appear as such in the final product. Although such a report of the operations of a business would be entirely correct from a descriptive point of view, there would be no way to add these different units in a numerical sense. In terms of the kinds of decisions and activities that are involved, it would be much more meaningful to convert the product components into dollar values, which may be added together, to state the production cost. Granted that there are some limitations on the substitution of costs for other measures —and we shall consider some of these later—still the addition of monetary amounts is a useful and worthwhile process.

Comparison. Many business decisions involve the comparison of one thing with another. For example, we may have a possibility of substituting one material for another. Even though we may be able to measure that material A weighing three pounds is the equivalent of material B weighing only two, the real question is what kind of equivalence we are talking about. The difference between the materials may be more clearly seen if the effect of substitution is stated in terms of transportation cost, the effect on the product selling price, or the savings in maintenance. The materials are merely contributors to the economic result, and the effect of the substitution can be best evaluated in financial terms. Only when the savings and advantages of a more expensive material over an inexpensive material is expressed in terms of money, can it be readily determined that the expensive material will save electricity, worker time, or storage space.

Again, if we want to see the effect of general trends or aggregates, we can get a better view by comparing sales of this month with those of last month, or to compare the costs for the same periods. Even though this may raise more questions as to what has occurred, it at least provides a firm starting place for further analysis.

Analysis and Extension. Business information can be used more effectively if it can be analyzed and manipulated mathematically. We may divide the aggregate of costs by units of output to establish unit costs. We may calculate relations between the various items— such as the amount of unpaid bills compared to the amount of cash on hand. We may add the amount of materials acquisitions to the amount already on hand and subtract what we have used to establish what should be on hand now. We may combine or relate financial data in various ways to establish bases for interpretation, comparison, or forecasting future results of operations.

There is no unit other than money that can be used in all these ways. To decide whether one method of making a machine part is better than some other method, there is no point in trying to work out whether or not an hour of time of a worker is equivalent to an extra pound of materials if we can express them both in comparable money terms. Since every business event is more or less directly related to some receipt or expenditure of cash, it makes good sense to systematize a method of business measurements in terms of money units. We begin to measure business transactions when we start keeping track of cash transactions.

Meaning of Cash. Although cash is the term ordinarily used to describe money in a general sense, it should be noted that cash is a somewhat broader notion than money. Strictly speaking, only coins and bills issued by government agencies or banks are recognized as legal tender. Cash includes legal money plus undeposited checks, bank drafts, money orders, and demand deposits in banks. The test to determine whether an item is considered as cash is its *immediately* available purchasing power—the fact that legal money may be obtained for these items by demand on a bank or other financial agency. Thus postage stamps or government bonds may be certainly worth their face value, but they are not cash because they are not spendable. They can be used only for a specified purpose, unless they are sold to provide cash.

Recording Cash Transactions. We shall begin our measurement and reporting of business events in terms of cash receipts and payments as if these were the only things to be noted. This is of course not true; we shall have occasion to recognize a great many other kinds of events in the operation of a really effective accounting and reporting system. However, there are some businesses (small retail stores and even some parts of the federal government) that actually do their accounting on a cash basis, recognizing only the receipt and payment of cash in their records and reports. In any business there is always some cash record-keeping, for cash collections and payments are inevitably present to some degree.

Cash accounting consists of something more than merely stating the amount of cash on hand at a given time. What we really want to know about the cash situation is how or why the cash arrived at its present state; that is, we want to identify the *sources* from which cash has come and for what purpose or object it was expended. By reviewing the cash inflow and outflow pattern, we can establish how much cash *should* be on hand, and thus we can "control" the cash situation. This is important in every situation, for cash is a volatile thing which can drain away or disappear quite easily unless it is brought under some kind of control by maintaining records of cash transactions.

Such records may be kept in a number of ways. One approach is to keep in chronological order a simple running list of the various transactions which produce increases and decreases in the cash on hand. The balance carried in a typical personal checkbook is such a record; it shows the amount of cash in the bank after each transaction, adding the deposits and subtracting the checks as they happen to be drawn. It is possible to arrange such a record in a slightly more formal sense, keeping receipts in one list and payments in another, the balance being found at any time by merely subtracting total disbursements from total receipts. Such an arrangement is sometimes found in cashbooks with one page (usually the left side) reserved for receipts and another (the right side) for payments. This might also be done on a single page, divided in the middle to separate increases from decreases. Such an arrangement is the basic form of an account.

Cash Accounts. An account is a clerical device for keeping a systematic record of transactions; an example appears in Figure 1–1. Cash accounts are conventionally arranged so that increases appear on the left side of the sheet and decreases on the right side. The rules which make up the form are standardized to show for each transaction the date, an explanation, and an amount. There is also a reference space between the explanation and the amount to identify the source of the data that has been recorded, such as the document number from which the information was obtained. We need not be concerned with this now, but standard account forms always contain this space.

This form has certain advantages. The location of an amount automatically labels it as an increase in cash if it appears on the left side, or a decrease if it appears on the right side. The entries appear in chronological order within the columns, and a total may be had by adding either column at any time. The rules make it easier to add the columns of figures. The balance of the account can be determined by subtracting total expenditures to date from total receipts to date. The account in Figure 1–1 shows the penciled-in totals and the balance, in italics, inserted on the side with the larger total. The account as shown indicates total receipts to date of $1,627.68, total payments $858.00, and the balance is written ($769.68) on the left side which has the larger total.

FIGURE 1–1

An Account Form

CASH ON HAND

Jan.	1	Total forwarded			625	40	Jan.	1	Total forwarded			50	00
	5	Salary			814	48		2	Rent			200	00
	17	Interest on Bonds			50	00		18	Insurance			143	75
	24	Dividends			74	30		20	Miscellaneous Ex-				
	29	Tax Refund			63	50			penses			300	65
								22	Clothing			40	00
			769.68		1 627	68		30	Furniture			123	60
												858	00

Such a record could be maintained over a considerable period of time to show the individual transactions—with totals and balances written in as needed, carrying the accumulated totals forward from page to page. Note that dollar signs are omitted.

Formal Ruling and Balancing. Sometimes it is desirable to separate the transactions of one period from the ones following and to stop the cumulation of amounts that otherwise would continue indefinitely. This may be done by formally ruling off the account, and carrying forward the balance of the account at the appropriate point. Figure 1–2 shows this. The balance of the account was determined and entered on the right side as if it were a transaction; this amount if shown as "carried forward" and the totals are then written in. Since they are the same, they can be ruled off, and the forwarded balance entered in the new section of the account. The rules have specified meanings: a single line under a list of figures indicates that the list is totaled under the rule; the double line indicates the end of a series of data; in effect, it signals "that's all!" Thus, at the end of an appropriate period the account may be terminated, and only the balance carried forward.

In practice, accounts do not show as much detail as appears in Figures 1–1 and 1–2. Often, transactions are accumulated in blocks

FIGURE 1–2

Formally Ruled and Balanced Account

CASH ON HAND

Jan.	1	Total forwarded			625	40	Jan.	1	Total forwarded		50	00
	5	Salary			814	48		2	Rent		200	00
	17	Interest on Bonds			50	00		18	Insurance		143	75
	24	Dividends			74	30		20	Miscellaneous Ex-			
	29	Tax Refund			63	50			penses		300	65
								22	Clothing		40	00
								30	Furniture		123	60
								31	Carried forward		769	68
				1	627	68				1	627	68
Feb.	1	Brought forward			769	68						

or totals by using other summarizing devices. But for the present, we shall deal with transactions one at a time and will write out the details so that it will be easier to follow the recording process.

Debit and Credit. These terms are merely the accountant's shorthand way of referring to entries made in the accounts. They mean simply entering an amount on the left or right side of an account. Thus, "debit Cash on Hand, $814.48" means place an entry for $814.48 on the left side of the Cash on Hand account; a credit entry would appear on the right side of an account. This applies to all kinds of accounts that we shall use—now or later. By convention, all cash accounts have debit balances; they are increased by debits and decreased by credits. As we shall see, there will be other kinds of accounts; and the associations of debit with increase and credit with decrease will not apply to some of them. But debit always means an entry on the left side, and credit always means an entry on the right side of the account mentioned.

In the early days of accounting (many hundred years ago) the terms debit and credit had other meanings as suggested by their Latin origins, but those meanings were lost long ago and no longer have much significance. There is an advantage in the shorthand expressions to substitute for "place an entry on the left (or right) side of the account," but the only meaning of these terms is merely "left" for debit and "right" for credit.

Additional Cash Accounts. A small business or an individual could operate fairly well with only a single cash record; but usually it is advisable to have separate records for different kinds of cash. A retail business will almost always have some actual cash on hand from its regular sales operations; but usually it will maintain a deposit account with a bank. Cash not actually required for immediate use ought to be deposited, and payments should ordinarily be made by check. This reduces risk of loss, and it serves to preserve a record of cash transactions that is useful if not essential to control cash. But some small business firms do make payments out of the cash drawer, and keep a systematic record of such payments.

The use of a bank deposit account requires that a record be maintained of the deposits and withdrawals. Otherwise we would not know the balance of the account when this was needed. Thus, we usually have a separate account for bank transactions. The Cash on Hand account would serve to control the handling of transactions within the day-to-day, hand-to-hand area, and the bank deposit account would serve to control or report the transactions with the bank. A deposit would require two entries: a debit to Cash in Bank account, and a credit to Cash on Hand. We shall see later that *every* transaction really requires two entries to record it properly, but for the moment this may be ignored until the reader is ready to deal with those issues.

Summary

Accounting is a systematic measurement method applied to business transactions. It emphasizes money measurements because such measures are more generally useful than those made with other units. We begin our study of accounting by working with records of cash transactions.

The basic form of accounting record is an account, a form which shows increases and decreases in the item that is being accounted for. Cash on Hand or Cash in Bank accounts show increases on the left (debit) side; decreases in Cash on Hand or Cash in Bank appear as entries in the right-hand (credit) column of the related account. The balances of these accounts indicate the amount of Cash on hand or in the bank. From these ideas, we shall proceed in the following chapter to develop a more extensive and informative set of records, to keep track of different kinds of transactions and more complicated situations.

QUESTIONS

1. Is accounting the only systematic method of measuring and reporting business transactions? Indicate some other methods of measuring

and reporting business data. Do these serve the same functions as accounting?

2. Is it really true that everybody makes some use of financial records and reports? What kind of financial records do people keep as individuals for their personal use? For other uses—such as tax returns? In what form are these "other-use" records kept? Why are they not systematized in the form of accounts and complete record keeping?

3. Why are employees and customers interested in the financial success of the firm? Creditors, of course, have a stake in the firm's activities, but do employees and customers have such an interest?

4. Accounting is a basic source of business "numbers" useful for decision making. What is the advantage of using numbers for such purposes? Do numbers tell the whole story of business enterprise? Why or why not? Why don't we use a system which includes those things which cannot be expressed in numbers?

5. What important properties are available in a "money" unit which make it useful for establishing and reporting business events and situations?

6. Contrast the accounting definition of "cash" with the economist's notions of money. What economic attribute is the important criterion of whether an item is to be included in the accounting concept of "cash"?

7. Nearly every state or condition is the result of some prior event or chain of events. Put content into this, indicating the scope of accounting for cash. Does this mean that the amount of cash on hand is a mere secondary statistic? If there is more or less cash on hand than the accounting record indicates than should be, what has happened?

8. The emphasis upon a chain of events as a part of reporting a given state or condition implies some form of record-keeping. One such form is an account. Indicate the way in which a cash account is used to record transactions, explaining the use of the various columns.

9. What is a *balance* in a cash account and how is it determined? Need an account be ruled to determine its balance? When and why are accounts ruled off formally using double lines?

10. Could an account be kept in a form other than the arrangement illustrated in the text? What about using a slip of paper, one for each transaction, on which appears the date, amount, and explanation of a transaction; could we not put all these into two boxes, then periodically use an adding machine to obtain total receipts and total disbursements? What about writing the slips on separate printed forms—using two colors of paper to isolate additions from subtractions? Consider the use of slips of paper from the viewpoint of in-

tegrity of the record. What would you do to make sure none of the slips were lost?

11. Suppose we did our writing by other means (a) holes punched in cards indicating amounts or other data by positioning the holes in columns, (b) similar holes punched in paper tape, or (c) magnetic effects on plastic or mylar tapes. Aside from the difference in readability, is the record keeping any less effective? Assuming we could use machines to read such records electrically, what advantages would be gained?

12. The text suggests that a business firm might have separate records for different kinds of cash. What would that mean in a fairly complex organization like a hospital or a university? Would one need as many bank deposit arrangements as there are different kinds of cash? On the other hand, would it be at all advantageous to open a separate bank deposit account for each weekly or monthly payroll in a large firm? Note the kinds of control that might be effected by separating the cash accounts for different operations, assuming that the records are kept by someone other than the persons who make deposits or write checks.

PROBLEMS

Electro-Radio Shop I

The following transactions involving cash occurred during the first three days of operation of this business:

(1)   Proprietor's investment deposited in the State Bank, $5,000.
(2)   Rent of store paid for six months in advance, $1,200, Check No. 1.
(3)   Deposits made for utility and telephone service, Check Nos. 2 and 3, $20 each.
(4)   Fixtures, shelves, etc., received and installed, paid by Check No. 4, $985.
(5)   Initial stock of radio tubes and supplies delivered, Check No. 5 issued for $179.40.
(6)   Merchandise—lamps, appliances, etc.—delivered; payment of half the invoice made by Check No. 6 for $1,215.
(7)   Electrical supplies and parts received paid by Check No. 7, $169.24.
(8)   Sale of toaster for cash, $11.60 plus 4 percent sales tax.
(9)   Electric iron and bathroom heater sold for $21.79 plus sales tax.
(10) Check for $165.36 received as full payment for new washing machine.
(11) Parts purchased to repair old washing machine traded in on preceding transaction, $17.30 plus 4 percent sales tax Check No. 8 issued for this.

(12)   Collected for repair work on radio set, $7.38 cash. This includes 18 cents sales tax on tubes installed.

(13)   Received down payment on new dishwasher, $30. The price of the dishwasher was $199.50 plus 4 percent sales tax, payable $10 per month for 18 months.

(14)   Sold the traded-in washing machine, (10) and (11). Customer's check for $69.50 includes sales tax.

(15)   Checks and cash deposited, $306.96.

(16)   Sales of small parts (switches, fuses, lamp bulbs, etc.) amount to $33.70 including sales tax.

(17)   One pair of table lamps sold for $23.60 plus tax.

(18)   Help-wanted advertisement inserted in the *Daily Clarion* paid for out of the cash on hand, $3.50.

(19)   Purchased a used pickup truck for $250, paying $50 down by Check No. 9; balance due $50 per month with no interest charges.

(20)   Paid carpenter for building partitions and installing new door locks, using Check No. 10, $78.50.

(21)   Washer-dryer combination sold for $437, taking an old washer in trade at an allowance of $47. Four percent sales tax on $390 and interest at 2 percent per month to be added. Down payment of $30 in cash, balance to be collected over 18 months.

(22)   Made service call to repair customer's TV set. Charge for service call, $7.50; parts and tubes replaced, $4.20 plus 17 cents sales tax; total, $11.87.

Required:

1.   Set up two ledger accounts in proper form and record these transactions.

2.   Indicate the deficiencies of this two-account system by pointing out the kinds of information that would be required that is not made available in those accounts. How would you deal with these deficiencies?

This problem is continued in Chapter 2.

Ed's Cycle Mart, Part I

At the end of the first year's operations as a dealer for Imperial Bicycles, Ed started to make up his income tax return; very soon thereafter, he decided that he should start keeping better records of his business operations.

When he started the business a year before, he had invested the entire balance of his savings account of $6,000 by opening a checking account for Ed's Cycle Mart; in addition, when his wife received a small inheritance in July, she had also invested $2,000 more in the business. Looking at his bank passbook, he saw that the list of daily receipts deposited in the bank was a total of $21,570 in addition to the two invest-ments. He had no clear idea as to what had happened to all this money. The bank balance at the end of the year was $3,716, and there was $50 change in the cash register drawer; what had happened to the other $25,804?

In his desk he found the most recent checkbook, but this covered only the last quarter's transactions. The bank statements and cancelled checks had been "put away" somewhere in the shop, but it would take too long to try to trace things that way. But he found receipts for the monthly utility bills, totalling $472 for the year. There were rent receipts for each month, and for the next month's rent in advance ($300) paid only a day before. Various other receipts and paid bills established that parts purchases and miscellaneous expenses had amounted to $833. Sales tax reports showed the payment of $460 of sales taxes. An insurance policy issued at the beginning of the year showed a two year premium charge of $800 had been paid. Ed remembered that he had "occasionally" cashed a check for family expenses and bills, but he kept no record of this, because, after all, it was "his own money."

In two boxes kept in the bottom desk drawer were the "service record" cards, one for every bicycle received from the manufacturer. From the model number and descriptions on these cards, the standard selling price of each bicycle could be determined. The cards were sorted into two piles—those for the bicycles still on the floor of the shop, unsold, and the others presumably sold for regular prices. Ed admitted he sometimes "threw in" an extra accessory or two (taken from inventory) to make a sale. But he was certain that he did not ever sell a bicycle without col-lecting the full purchase price within a relatively short period of time. There were no amounts still owing for bicycles sold, and no unpaid bills from the manufacturer. The selling prices of the bicycles sold was $13,552 total. From catalogs and discount schedules, it was determined that the cost of the bicycles sold was $8,980, and the cost of those still on the floor (unsold) was $1,296.

Continuing the inventory of the shop, Ed found tires, tubes and accessories on hand which would cost $465 to replace; these were all new, in original packing. The cash register had been acquired from a used office equipment dealer; $150 had been paid for it. Tools and equipment in the repair area were listed, and priced from catalogs. The total of these costs was $2,250. Ed was quite sure that these prices were substantially the same as those he had paid for these things. 16 used bicycles were on hand; a separate sheet was written up for each one, showing the parts needed for making them salable, the time required to recondition them, and their selling price. But Ed had no clear idea of where these had come from. He recalled making a few trades, but he had never allowed more than $10 on an old cycle, and even then this allowance was only made to cover the accessories not included when the new cycle had come from the factory. He thought he had not sold more than one or two trade ins, because he had never found time to recondition more than this. However, he guessed that these 16 trade-ins might altogether bring about $200, if he could find 40 hours of time to put them in shape. The parts needed would cost $35, and the going rate for mechanics was $2.80 per hour.

Set up an account with Cash in Bank, and enter the transactions that may be inferred from the data given. Some of the data have no bearing on the cash flow, but you should find transactions to arrive at the balance of $3,716. State your assumptions, if any.

This problem is continued in Chapter 2 and in Chapter 3.

CLASSIFICATION AND DOUBLE ENTRY

The introductory discussion of accounting measurements established a systematic means of recording cash transactions—the account. It also set up a way to obtain better information by separating out-of-pocket cash transactions from those to which a bank was a party. Such a system is adequate for its purpose. Even when a business is large and complex, it will still use accounts like these to control cash on hand and to keep track of transactions with individual banks.

Most people as individuals are willing to get along with only limited records because their needs for such data as a formal system would provide are quite limited. Many keep no record at all for out-of-pocket payments; often, they may rely on the bank to keep track of important receipts and payments. Checks and deposit slips may provide all needed detail, and the bank will do the adding and subtracting necessary for one to know how things stand. If the transactions are not too numerous and complex, this approach may give reasonably adequate ideas of what has happened; but when a tax return is prepared, we need to know the amounts of medical costs, or other deductions, as well as the amounts of income from various sources. Such needs may be met by saving various memoranda during the year; but there is an advantage in doing this in a systematic way.

In managing a business enterprise, however, it is not enough merely to have a good idea of what has happened. We must have definite measures of events so that we may from time to time decide whether to continue or to change our procedures. There is often a need for much detail about particular situations, and such data must be readily available and reasonably complete. Therefore, there is a real need to collect information in some systematic way, so as to be sure that we have positive and complete information—readily available when it is needed.

On the other hand, information about receipts and payments need not always be detailed to be useful. Although it is important to maintain records, the business manager is seldom concerned with the exact amount paid for every single item on a given date. Usually, he would rather know the total amount of payroll cost than the amount paid to each employee. This is because the sales, payrolls, purchases of merchandise, taxes, and other such items are really better understood if they are compared in total for given periods of time or with regard to specified operations. For instance, it might be quite interesting to compare the sales made in a given department with the payroll and other costs incurred, or to compare both of these figures for the current period with similar results of a past period. We thus need a *classified* record of important summary totals so that we may readily obtain "breakdowns" of cash receipts or cash payments by source or object involved.

This may be accomplished by using additional accounts: one for each of these separate classifications. There will thus be an account for each major kind of cash receipts and an account for each class of disbursements, such as payroll, merchandise, and so forth. The system will then encompass many accounts. One or two of these will record the effect of transactions upon Cash on Hand or Cash in Bank, but there will be other accounts to show what kind of transactions these were; they will show the amounts of different kinds of cash receipts or payments—sales, purchases, payrolls, and other such things. These additional accounts will give additional information about the business—not to show the effects on cash or bank balances, for that is already done by the cash accounts, but to indicate the amounts of cash that have come from various sources or have been expended for various purposes. These *source* and *object* accounts will show the kinds of transactions which have occurred; they will give a more complete picture of the ebb and flow than would the cash accounts alone. Those events which accompanied and produced the receipts and payments will be more clearly seen by the use of accounts to record them specifically.

At this stage, we have set up two kinds of accounts related to the business, as shown in Figure 2–1. The cash *position* of the business is represented by Cash in Bank and Cash on Hand accounts; the other accounts (as many as needed) reflect the various flows of cash related to those transactions which brought money in or took money out of the business.

The accounting system will thus contain a number of accounts, each one used to show the accumulated data concerning some "item of accountability." An item of accountability is the thing or condition which is the subject of an account, as shown by the account title. Thus cash on hand, cash in bank, sales receipts, rent payments, are all items of accountability—things we want to keep track of. Some of these reflect the status or position of an item, for instance,

FIGURE 2–1

Cash Position and Cash-Flow Accounts

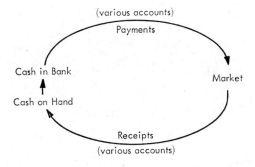

cash on hand or cash in bank. Others deal with flows, such as the *inflows* of cash from various sources, or *outflows*—payments made for specified purposes such as rent, or purchases of merchandise.

To keep things straight, we shall put all the accounts into a loose-leaf book or *ledger;* the loose-leaf feature will make it easy to add or to remove accounts as needed. This book is called the *summary* or *general ledger* because we shall have other kinds of ledgers later. The summary ledger will show on its pages the effects of all the transactions, with each transaction traced to the items of accountability which it affected. Each page of the ledger will show the summary effect of the transactions with regard to one item of accountability—as specified in the account title on that page. Thus there will be accounts for Cash on Hand, Cash in Bank, Sales, Merchandise, Payroll Cost, and as many other items as may be required to yield appropriate information.

Double-Entry Procedure

The additional accounts we have added to our system have increased the available information but made the system more complex. For even a simple business, such as a small retail store, we might have as many as 20 or 30 accounts to record the various effects of transactions in such a way as to give the manager the needed information. In keeping these accounts we would have to record each transaction *twice:* once in the appropriate cash account to maintain the record of cash position, and a second time in those other accounts which are used to record sources of cash receipts and objects of cash payments. This is likely to cause errors in recording; for example, we might forget to enter a sale, as it should appear, in both places. Such an omission would probably be most noticeable in the cash record; it would certainly be caught when the amount of cash actually on hand or on deposit was compared with the record. But the omission would not be so obvious in a sales account. Even if we knew there were some errors, it might be difficult to establish just which items had been entered incompletely. We therefore need some way to check clerical accuracy, as we record transactions.

This check is provided by the very fact that we *do* record each transaction twice; the dual record is both necessary and convenient. The double record is necessary because every transaction has at least two elements; but it is convenient to use the double record to provide a check on clerical accuracy.

The necessity for a dual record may be seen by noting that cash cannot be just "received." The increase in cash has come from some source, and the sources of cash are items of accountability in which we are interested. Similarly, cash payments are not just "made"; the object of the expenditure is again an item of accountability in which we are interested. Every transaction is of this nature; even when we consider very complex situations, there will always be at least two items of accountability involved. This requires a dual recording—a *double entry*.

The check of clerical accuracy may be established quite readily if we systematize our use of left and right sides of the accounts. In Chapter 1 we called the left side of an account the *debit* side; the right side was called the *credit* side. But accounts may themselves be differentiated by using debit or credit characteristics. All Cash on Hand or Cash in Bank accounts are increased by debits and normally have debit balances; but accounts for sources of cash are handled in an opposite fashion—they are increased by *credits* and normally have *credit* balances. Accounts in which we accumulate expenditures by object classifications are the reverse of source items and are set up with the debit side reflecting increases and credit side showing decreases. The "balance" character of an account thus indicates its nature. A Sales account will be increased by credits, decreased by debits, and will have a credit balance; a Payroll or Merchandise Purchases account will have a debit balance and will be increased by debits and decreased by credits. This makes a neat logical package, because the accounts used to describe and summarize transactions involving sources of cash are opposite in sign to those accounts which record expenditures. Now we have three classes of accounts in our system, represented schematically in Figure 2–2.

The accounts in the summary ledger may be increased to any desired number. However, no matter how many accounts we use to

FIGURE 2–2

Relations between Various Classes of Items of Accountability

Sources of Cash		Cash or Cash in Bank		Objects of Expenditure Items	
—	+	+	—	+	—
Debit	Credit	Debit	Credit	Debit	Credit

record cash transactions, they will be of only three kinds: those in which we record sources of cash receipts, those in which we record objects of expenditure, and those which show the cash position. Every transaction will affect at least two accounts and will involve equal debits and credits; for instance, a cash sale will be recorded by debiting Cash on Hand and crediting some sales account.

If there is more than one kind of goods involved in a given sale, there may be corresponding credits in a number of sales accounts and the combined entry might involve, for example, a debit to Cash on Hand for $20.07 but credits to Sales of Groceries, $8.29; to Sales of Meats, $7.16; and Sales of Produce, $4.62. The record is complete and correct only when the total debit elements are equal to the total credit elements: $8.29 + $7.16 + $4.62 = $20.07. Thus, the analysis of each transaction may be checked for clerical accuracy when it is recorded.

It is possible to make another, more general, check by applying the idea of double-entry to the system of accounts as a whole. What applies to a given transaction in the way of equality of debit and credit items also applies to the entire aggregate of *all* transactions. The entire summary ledger will balance—add up to equal debits and credits—whether we total all individual entries, the totals of columns in all of the accounts, or the balances of accounts. Thus, besides being able to check each transaction as it is recorded for equality of debit and credit amounts, we can check the whole set of accounts in the same way.

The Trial Balance

A formal procedure to test the entire summary ledger for debit-credit equality is the preparation of a *trial balance*. This is a list of the accounts in the summary ledger showing the debit weight or the credit weight of each account in corresponding columns. These columns are totaled for the entire list; the debit total should equal the credit total *exactly*, or some error has been made. This check is, of course, only negative evidence; even if the trial balance shows equal debit and credit aggregates in the ledger, we can only say there is no evidence of error. However, if the trial balance shows an inequality of debits and credits, the tabulation cannot be complete and correct. The use and the content of the trial balance is best demonstrated by example. But before we attempt this, it would be well to summarize what has been done thus far.

The basic accounting system has grown very rapidly, even in the very simple circumstances we have considered. We have described in theoretical terms the nature and uses of elementary records designed to accumulate data with respect to individual items of accountability, and we have noted the relations between them. This discussion has brought out the need for logical methods and systematic procedures to provide wanted information with a minimum of error. These ideas constitute a basic structure from which more extensive systems may be built. We shall be doing just this in each succeeding chapter of this book as we examine the different situations to which accounting is applied. However, to summarize and clarify our present position, let us consider the following example.

Illustration

Mr. Ross James has been a pharmacist for a number of years; he has accumulated $4,000 in savings and he decides that at last he will start a retail drugstore of his own. His first act in this direction is to set up a separate bank account for his business. This is important, for if we are to measure the transactions in the business separately from those of Mr. James' personal affairs, we must keep records for the business as an entity entirely separate from other operations. The bank account is under the name of "James Pharmacy, Ross James, Proprietor," not merely in Mr. James' own name.

To start off our accounting records, we set up an account for Cash in Bank in which we record an increase of $4,000; to show the source of this cash, we set up another account labeled Ross James, Proprietor, and we credit this account with $4,000. The ledger appears as follows:

Cash in Bank		Ross James, Proprietor	
(1) 4,000			(1) 4,000

Note that in this illustration (as well as in later ones) we abbreviate the account form to a "skeleton" of its typical appearance. The accounts now show the effect of the first transaction, an increase in the Cash in Bank and the source of that cash increase. The use of an account with "Ross James, Proprieter" makes sure that we will not confuse Mr. James' inital investment with other sources of cash. As we shall see, this account may also reflect other things concerning Mr. James' relation to the business as proprietor, but these need not concern us yet.

Now James rents a store and writes a check for the first month's rent amounting to $200. This is recorded by crediting Cash in Bank and debiting an account entitled Rent for $200. The accounts then look like this:

Ross James, Proprietor		Cash in Bank		Rent	
	(1) 4,000	(1) 4,000	(2) 200	(2) 200	

The cash balance is now only $3,800, and the disbursement of $200 is shown in an expenditure account. The account Ross James, Proprietor is unchanged because his investment has not been affected by the payment of rent. The reader may object to this because "rent" may be viewed as an item of "expense" which reduces the proprietor's interest in the business. The answer to this is that we are interested only in recording the sources and dispositions of cash;

expense is a technical concept which will be explained later. The payment of cash is here merely recorded as expenditure.

Mr. James now acquires fixtures for his store and issues a check for $2,000 to pay for them. However, there are various items in the lot of fixtures, and the credit to Cash in Bank of $2,000 would be accompanied by debit entries in separate accounts to record the cost of each class of equipment:

$$
\begin{array}{lr}
\text{Cash Register} & \$ \ \ 100.00 \\
\text{Counters} & 500.00 \\
\text{Soda Fountain} & 1,100.00 \\
\text{Wall Cases} & 300.00 \\
\end{array}
$$

The sum of these debits is $2,000, which indicates that the analysis is correct in a clerical sense (equal debits and credits). When the transaction has been entered in the accounts, the summary ledger will look like this:

Cash in Bank	1		Ross James, Proprietor 2		Rent	3
(1) 4,000	(2) 200		(1) 4,000	(2) 200		
	(3) 2,000					

Cash Register	4		Counters	5		Soda Fountain	6
(3) 100			(3) 500			(3) 1,100	

Wall Cases	7
(3) 300	

Each account of this summary ledger tells a story about a given item of accountability. The effects of all the transactions to date are summarized in the different accounts which show the specific effects of transactions, so that the change in each of the items of accountability is readily seen.

The aggregate effect of the entire set of transactions to date could be expressed in the form of a trial balance, showing the balances of all the accounts in the summary ledger (Figure 2–3). The trial balance lists the net effect of all the transactions entered in the accounts, and the equilibrium of debits and credits is tested in total.

FIGURE 2–3

JAMES PHARMACY
Summary Ledger Trial Balance, April 1—

Account No.		Debits	Credits
1	Cash in bank......................	$1,800	
2	Ross James, proprietor..............		$4,000
3	Rent.............................	200	
4	Cash register.....................	100	
5	Counters.........................	500	
6	Soda fountain.....................	1,100	
7	Wall cases........................	300	
	Total	$4,000	$4,000

The ruled lines used in the illustrative form have the same meanings as those used in balancing accounts.

The reader will observe that this trial balance might be used to make up a statement of cash receipts and disbursements. Merely arranging these figures so as to deduct the expenditure amounts from the investment amount will leave the balance of Cash in Bank.

Operating Transactions

Having carried the illustration to the point of some familiarity with the mechanics of double-entry procedure, we may now extend the process to cover transactions of the type that would recur in the regular operations of the store.

An initial shipment of merchandise is received, and a check for $1,342 is written to pay for the goods—transaction (4). This requires another account (Acct. No. 8 of the summary ledger), entitled Merchandise, which would be debited with $1,342. We might have set up separate accounts for different kinds of merchandise, but many small retail stores would find this impractical, if only because of the detail involved. Even though we shall later separate sales of merchandise by product lines or departments, we shall leave merchandise costs in one account, for present purposes.

Summary Accounting Devices

One of the ways to reduce the detail in accounting is to use mechanical or other devices to summarize information before it is recorded. The cash register is one such device; it is an adding machine attached to a cash drawer. When a sale is "rung up" and the drawer is opened to insert money or to make change, the machine will not only produce a receipt for the customer but it will also print the amount of the transaction on a paper tape inside the machine and add this amount in a totalizer. At the end of the day, the tape shows the number of customers, a list of the individual sales amounts, and the total sales. The last amount, plus the change fund that was in the drawer to start with, is the amount of cash that should be in the drawer. If all the sales are recorded (and there are ways of making this fairly certain), the machine gives a positive check as well as detailed information on cash sales transactions.

The machine may, if desired, be arranged so as to keep a separate total for each department or product, and it may also make a record of amounts paid out. The disbursements would, of course, be evidenced by receipted bills or other vouchers. Thus, the machine could do a large amount of the accounting work: it would keep a control over cash receipts and payments so that one would know how much cash should be in the drawer, and it would also give totals of the principal cash transactions. A daily check of the cash on hand with register figures and a consistent practice of making bank deposits daily would provide a reasonably good system of cash control. From the duplicate bank deposit slips, the tape records, and the receipts, bills, or vouchers, the transactions for the month could easily be summarized into the following tabulation: (transaction 6.)

Receipts from sales:		
Tobacco and candy	$ 495	
Soda fountain	601	
Drugs and sundries	648	
Prescriptions	514	$2,258
Disbursements for:		
Electric bill	$ 38	
Gas for heating	61	
Supplies	15	
Insurance	84	
Miscellaneous	24	
Merchandise	1,511	
Ross James personal	421	2,154
Net Increase in Cash on Hand		$ 104

To bring these details into a systematic record, this list of transactions will be entered in the summary ledger accounts, and those accounts would then appear as shown in Figure 2–4. It will be noted in the summary ledger that the disbursement for merchandise ($1,342) has been entered as transaction (4). The $50 change fund in the cash register (Account No. 9) was established by a withdrawal (5) from the bank. This is set up in a separate account because the money is in the form of spendable cash but restricted as to its use; it must be accounted for as a separate item.

FIGURE 2–4

Summary Ledger Accounts Showing Effects of Operating Disbursements

Cash in Bank	1		Ross James, Proprietor 2		Rent	3
(1) 4,000	(2) 200		(1) 4,000	(2) 200		
(6) 2,258	(3) 2,000					
	(4) 1,342					
	(5) 50					
	(6) 2,154					

Cash Register	4	Counters	5	Soda Fountain	6
(3) 100		(3) 500		(3) 1,100	

Wall Cases	7	Merchandise	8	Change Fund	9
(3) 300		(4) 1,342		(5) 50	
		(6) 1,511			

Electricity	10	Gas	11	Supplies	12
(6) 38		(6) 61		(6) 15	

Insurance	13	Miscellaneous	14	Ross James, Personal 15
(6) 84		(6) 24		(6) 421

Sales, Candy Tobacco 16		Sales, Soda Fountain 17		Sales, Drugs and Sundries 18	
	(6) 495		(6) 601		(6) 648

Sales, Prescriptions 19	
	(6) 514

The $421 debit to the account, Ross James, Personal, needs a bit of explanation. One might think that this withdrawal is merely a reduction of Mr. James's investment in the business, and that it ought to be debited to the Ross James, Proprietor account. However, the investment of $4,000 to start this business is a relatively permanent commitment—it is expected to cover the capital needs of the firm over an extended period. But the small monthly withdrawals are made in anticipation that the business ought to cover the relatively modest needs of the proprietor in the way of recurring personal costs. Thus, the $421 would include such things as Mr. James's house rent, his grocery bill, or day-to-day pocket money. It might even include the James's department store charges. These payments would be made from the funds of the business in anticipation that the successful operation of the firm would cover the ordinary living expenses of the proprietor who spends his working hours in the business. The difference in intent of the $4,000 investment and the $421 personal withdrawals is recognized by recording the latter in a separate account.

Financial Reports

From the information now in the summary ledger of the James Pharmacy we could prepare a report of the operations of the month

FIGURE 2–5

JAMES PHARMACY
Summary Ledger Trial Balance, April 30—

Account No.		*Debits*	*Credits*
1	Cash in bank...................	$ 512	
2	Ross James, proprietor............		$4,000
3	Rent..........................	200	
4	Cash register...................	100	
5	Counters......................	500	
6	Soda fountain..................	1,100	
7	Wall cases.....................	300	
8	Merchandise...................	2,853	
9	Change fund...................	50	
10	Electricity.....................	38	
11	Gas...........................	61	
12	Supplies.......................	15	
13	Insurance......................	84	
14	Miscellaneous..................	24	
15	Ross James, Personal............	421	
16	Sales, candy and tobacco..........		495
17	Sales, soda fountain..............		601
18	Sales, drugs and sundries..........		648
19	Sales, prescriptions..............		514
		$6,258	$6,258

as measured by cash receipts and payments. This might be done by taking a trial balance and then arranging the data from the trial balance in a proper form. Figure 2–5 shows the trial balance that would be drawn from the summary ledger after transaction 6 had been put into the accounts. A financial report made up from this trial balance would be a more meaningful arrangement of the data. It is shown in Figure 2–6. It should be noted that every amount that ap-

FIGURE 2–6

JAMES PHARMACY

Summary of Cash Transactions, Month Ended April 30, 19—

Receipts:

Ross James, proprietor, investment...........		$4,000
Sales:		
Candy and tobacco.......................	$ 495	
Soda fountain..........................	601	
Drugs and sundries......................	648	
Prescriptions...........................	514	2,258
Total Receipts.......................		$6,258

Disbursements:

Rent....................................	$ 200	
Cash register............................	100	
Counters................................	500	
Soda fountain...........................	1,100	
Wall cases..............................	300	
Merchandise............................	2,853	
Electricity..............................	38	
Gas....................................	61	
Supplies................................	15	
Insurance...............................	84	
Miscellaneous...........................	24	
Ross James, Personal.....................	421	
Total Disbursements...................		$5,696
Net Excess Receipts over Disbursements........		$ 562

Excess receipts over disbursements represented by:

Change fund in register.......... $ 50	
Cash in bank................... 512	
Total...................... $562	

pears in the summary ledger trial balance appears also in the financial report. The report shows the effect of all the cash transactions of the month, arranged in such a way as to summarize them without too much burdensome detail. Additional information, such as the number of transactions or the specific kinds of merchandise purchased, could be located from the supporting records in the files. In a small and simple business, such a financial report might serve to give interested parties a fair picture of what has happened during the month. Obviously, this report does not give as much information as would be desired in every case. There is no means of determining from the data here presented whether the operations have been profitable or not because there have been no attempts to trace costs into operations so as to establish net income. Yet the procedures established and illustrated in the chapter are useful to get "cash flow" data. The sales figures are entirely dependable measures of the cash sales; some of the expenditures are actually attributable to the April operations as expense. But the refinements needed to obtain a measure of income will be developed in the following chapter.

QUESTIONS

1. Why is it helpful to have accounts for various sources of cash re-receipts, or for different objects of expenditure? By reference to a family budget, illustrate a classification of automobile expenses for income tax reports. Indicate some kinds of internal tabulations of data about cash receipts and payments in a business firm, even when the firm does not extend or receive credit or defined payment arrangements. What advantage is there in keeping separate accounts for such tabulations?

2. The attempt to maintain detailed tabulations concerning receipts and payments involves a more extensive view of accounts—i.e., there are "status" accounts and "flow" accounts. Indicate the relations between these two kinds of accounts by a diagram to describe cash transactions in a business firm.

3. The fact that a transaction must involve at least two items of accountability requires double-entry procedure. Using a simple Cash on Hand account and other accounts to show sources of cash and objects of expenditure, show why double entry is mandatory for complete accounting.

4. Accounts which show *sources* of cash are opposite in "sign" from those which collect data about objects of expenditure. What effect do transactions evidenced by cash receipts have on the Cash on Hand account? Why? What effect does the making of a disbursement have on the cash account? On the account showing the object of expenditure? Why are these entries (a) opposite and (b) equal?

5. How does double entry reduce the chance for undetected error in a system of accounts? Show what would happen (a) if part of an entry were omitted, (b) if the digits in an account were transposed, or (c) if a decimal point was misplaced.

6. What kinds of errors are *not* likely to be detected by a double-entry trial balance? Illustrate. How *would* such an error be detected, if at all?

7. What is an item of accountability? Distinguish between three different classes of such items and indicate transactions that would produce an increase or a decrease in each kind of account.

8. What is a trial balance? How is it prepared and what does it show?

9. What has a cash register to do with accounting processes in a retail store? Does the resulting record have anything to do with control over the cash on hand? How is such control effected?

10. What does a summary ledger contain and why is it kept? What is the relation between a summary ledger and a trial balance?

11. This chapter presents a financial report called a summary of cash transactions. How does this report differ from a trial balance? Does this report explain or present all the transactions for the period? Why or why not?

12. Why does the excess of receipts over disbursements appear in two places in the summary of cash transactions? Does one figure establish the *correctness* of the other?

PROBLEMS

Adolph Insurance Agency

Having been a salesman for the Northern Light Life Insurance Company for a long time, Oscar Adolph decided in March of this year to establish an independent agency. He negotiated with several companies, and finally arranged agency contracts with Home Life of Canada, Acorn Fire and Casualty, Highway Indemnity, and Integrity Guarantors. The Home Life Company had been represented in the city and turned over 141 accounts of existing life and annuity contract holders. The other companies did not have any representatives and had not done business before in this area. Mr. Adolph was to act as a general agent for each of these companies, except for the settlement of claims; he was entitled to specified commissions for various services.

Late in March, Mr. Adolph opened a bank account for the Adolph Insurance Agency by depositing $500. He leased a small furnished office in the Mason Building for a year, paying $150 as the first month's rent with Check No. 1 on the business bank account. Check No. 2 was issued to cover the first month's telephone service, $12. To free his time for sales work, Mr. Adolph engaged Mrs. Agnes Augeberry to take care of the office, four hours per day, five days per week, rate $1.75 per hour.

During the first few days in April, the following checks were written.

No. 3: To H. H. Hockenberry State Treasurer, for license.............$15.00
No. 4: To J. K.Wagler for notary public seal........................ 20.00
No. 5: To R. B. Legalegle for costs and fees of notary appointment...... 34.50
No. 6: To Merchants and Traders Club, membership dues, April........ 15.00
No. 7: To Office Suppliers for stationery and supplies.................. 23.45
No. 8: To the *Daily Interrogator*, for advertising....................... 12.95
No. 9: To Marsden Department Store, March personal purchases........ 48.15

During the rest of the month the following transactions occurred:

Renewal premiums collected on Home Life contracts, $1,968.43, were deposited in the bank. A 5 percent collection commission was earned on this business. Advance premiums on new policies were $1,654.27, on which the agent's commission was $484.36. At the end of the month, Check No. 10 was used to make remittance to the Toronto office. The bank charged 2 percent exchange, and a $3 fee for writing the draft. These charges were subtracted from the remittance because the Home Company had agreed to absorb them.

Premiums on new property insurance of $275.80 were deposited in the bank. On this business, the agent's commission was 30 percent. The remainder was paid to the Acorn Company by Check No. 11. Auto insurance premiums deposited in the bank were $641.12. The net amount due the Highway Company after deducting 25 percent agent's commission was remitted by Check No. 12.

Integrity Guarantors sent Mr. Adolph a $50 check as a retainer in lieu of commissions. This check was cashed by Mr. Adolph to cover expenses as listed below. The new business written for this company was covered by merely forwarding the checks received from policy holders because Mr. Adolph had no authority to deposit them. The amounts totaled $307.50.

At the end of the month, Mr. Adolph paid Mrs. Augenberry $152.25 by Check No. 13. Check No. 14 was made payable to Mrs. Adolph to cover household expenses, $300. No. 15 covered the May telephone bill of $12, plus toll charges amounting to $14.75. From his personal notebook, Mr. Adolph found that he had spent $19.30 in taxi fares and $32.15 for lunches at the club, of which $18.40 were for his own lunches. He also noticed that he had written a check for $100 on his own personal account for his contribution to the Community Fund. He regarded this as a business expense, although he had made such a contribution annually for many years.

Required:

Use skeleton ledger accounts to record the transactions and make up from the accounts a report of cash receipts and disbursements. Note the kind of information that may be obtained from the accounts.

Electro-Radio Shop, Part II

Below are drawn up a set of skeleton summary ledger accounts which will reflect the sources of cash and the objects of expenditure for the transactions already entered in the records of the Electro-Radio Shop. Complete the transactions as already recorded in the Cash on Hand and Cash in Bank accounts, by making the appropriate entries in skeleton accounts listed:

Accounts

Proprietor's Investment	Rent Paid in Advance
Furniture & Fixtures	Radio Tubes and Supplies
Electrical Supplies	Repairs to Trade-in Merchandise
Auto Truck	Building Improvements
Sales, Radio Supplies	Sales, Small Parts
Sales of Appliances	Sales Taxes Collected
Deposits, Utility & Tele.	Advertising
Lamps and Appliances	Service Income

When these accounts are considered along with the cash data already recorded, you will be able to make a Statement of Receipts and Payments for the month.

Note the additional data that this kind of accounting provides as compared with that available from only the Cash on Hand and Cash in Bank accounts. Is this accounting system now entirely adequate? Indicate its deficiencies as you see them. We shall look at your answers when we have discussed Chapter 5 to see how well your list of deficiencies has been met.

Mack's Motorcar Maintenance, Part I

Martin Mack started the business known as Mack's Motorcar Maintenance on July 1 this year by opening a checking account at the California Bank, transferring $10,000 from his savings to that account. He had previously arranged to rent a building suitable for his purposes, and his first concern was to pay $600 rent for two months in advance. He also drew checks for electricity and gas deposit, $20; advance telephone exchange service for July, $10; $6,520 for tools and equipment; and $520 for a stock of accessories.

He made arrangements to handle Harbor Oil Company's gasoline and lubricants and made a payment of $1,750 for the initial stock of these products.

He decided to handle his cash receipts to minimize the risk of loss by making bank deposits at least once a day, keeping an even $50 in the cash drawer for change purposes. This, plus the practice of paying all bills by check would eliminate the need for a Cash on Hand account. He cashed a check for $50 to set up the change fund.

Below are listed a number of transactions that occurred during the rest of the month of July. These are in summary terms—that is, all transactions of the same class have been expressed in terms of their total, even though they would have been recorded individually.

```
Sales of gasoline and oil.........................................$1,769
Purchase of tires for stock.........................................  612
Purchases of supplies for cleaning, etc..............................  160
Payments for gasoline and oil purchases.............................1,506
Salary of helper for 4 weeks.........................................  394
Receipts from customers for repair and overhaul work.................  926
Purchase of parts used in repairing customer cars....................  337
Electric and gas bill................................................   23
Sales of accessories.................................................   66
Receipts from lubrication, washing, and minor services...............  113
Sales of tires.......................................................  214
Advertising—handbills and mailing....................................   65
Fire, theft, and liability insurance.................................  180
```

Required:

Set up the summary ledger for Mack's Motorcar Maintenance as it would appear at the end of July. Watch the equality of the double entries; check the trial balance of the ledger at the end of the month and prepare a statement of receipts and payments.

This problem is continued in Chapter 3.

Hi's Service Station

Hiram Malkus started an automobile service station on October 1 of this year. In anticipation of this he had negotiated to acquire the land and building of a predecessor business for $9,000 ($2,000 for the land and $7,000 for the building). Malkus had only $3,000 which he needed for working capital of the new firm, but his uncle loaned him the money to buy the property, with the express proviso that he was not to be involved in the business in any way. The building was transferred to Hiram Malkus who signed a personal note payable to his uncle for the $9,000.

Other transactions during the first week of operations were:

2. Malkus deposited $3,000 in the Local Bank, in the name of "Hi's Service."
3. Payment made to The Gas Electric Company to guarantee payment of bills, $75. These services were then connected.
4. Gas and oil were ordered from Poorfield Oil Company; $820 was paid by check on delivery.
5. Tires and accessories were purchased from Small Auto Supply Wholesalers; $600 was paid by check when these were received.
6. Cash sales of gas and oil $350, services income $65, and sales of accessories and tires $175.

7. Deposits of all cash receipts were made, except for $100 kept for change.
8. A used cash register was purchased for $100.
9. Malkus paid his personal house rent from the business checking account, $175.
10. On counting the cash in the cash register at the end of the week, it was discovered that there was $3.17 less in the drawer than the register totals indicated there should be.

Set up skeleton accounts for Cash in Bank and Cash on Hand (6 lines each) and twelve other accounts (3 lines each), and record the transactions. Prepare a statement of Cash Receipts and Payments from the accounts, and reconcile the net balance with the balances of the Cash accounts.

Ed's Cycle Mart, Part II

To help Ed avoid the anxious moments he had in the situations described in Chapter 1, problem 2, design a set of double entry accounts to fit the transactions of this firm. Use your imagination to expand the list of accounts to cover other classifications of receipts and payments that have not been identified in the earlier discussion. To test this set of accounts, enter in them (in double entry) the data presented in the Cash in Bank account set up earlier, make a trial balance and a statement of receipts and disbursements.

The M/R Cafeteria, Part I

Marks and Rowan established the M/R Cafeteria August 3, last year, each investing $25,000. Their two checks were deposited in the Shenandoah Mountain Bank to the credit of M/R Cafeteria, with either partner authorized to sign checks. During the next three months the following transactions occurred:

(1) A 10-year lease was signed by the partners covering the premises at Main and Broad Street where the cafeteria was to do business. Alterations to the building (new entrance, partitions, and additional electrical outlets) were installed. The contractors' bills amounted to $3,720 in total; this was paid by check. Rent paid, $1,600.

(2) New kitchen and serving equipment was installed by Mallory Restaurant Fixtures Company, for which $27,420 was paid in cash on delivery.

(3) Used office equipment (including an adding machine, typewriter, and cash register) were purchased at an auction sale. Marks used his personal check to pay for these items, since by that time the bank account was getting low. Since the firm needed dining room furni-

ture also before any sales could be made, Marks agreed to let this $2,400 stand as permanently invested capital.

(4)   The dining room equipment cost $12,240 and was paid for from the firm's bank account, and the firm opened for business.

(5)   Food purchases for the next three months were $13,239; electricity and gas bills were $482; payrolls, taxes, supplies, and miscellaneous costs were $14,270. These were paid regularly at the end of each month; only the totals concern us, so the monthly details are not given here.

(6)   Sales of meals for cash per cash register tapes total $28,034 for the quarter; these had been deposited daily as received, and only the totals for the quarter are given here. Cigarette sales totaled $423 for the quarter; various amounts had been taken from the vending machines and deposited in the bank at intervals during the quarter.

(7)   Marks withdrew $400 at the end of each month for living expenses, in lieu of salary; Rowan withdrew a total of $1,600 during the period for the same reason.

Required:

Record the foregoing transactions in skeleton ledger accounts, and without making a trial balance) prepare from the accounts a report of cash receipts and payments for the quarter. Show that this statement agrees with the Cash in Bank balance.

This problem is continued in Chapter 3.

TRANSACTIONS RELATED TO TIME PERIODS

Chapters 1 and 2 have presented the basic mechanics of accounting. We have seen how accounts are used to record cash receipts and payments, and how the entries made in those accounts may be summarized in a ledger and transcribed into a trial balance, and we have observed that the data in the trial balance may be arranged to produce a report of cash receipts and disbursements. This kind of accounting is simple and direct, and it does meet some of the need for business information. But cash transactions are related not only to the period in which they occur, but to other intervals of time that may benefit from them. We ought to classify receipts and payments not only as to their source or objects of expenditure, but also as to their relation to periods of time to which they are applicable. This is a basic step in understanding what an accountant means by revenue and expense.

Unrestricted Cash Receipts

Ordinary collections from customers via cash sales are complete settlements for goods or services delivered to them. Delivery and payment complete the transaction; there is no commitment by either the customer or the firm to do anything more about this sale. Even if the goods are later returned for exchange or refund, this is a separate event—a new arrangement outside the sale transaction itself. If a customer later complains about the quality or quantity of goods or service, and there is an adjustment of the price, this, too is a new event, not essentially implied in the sale. Even a guarantee which promises replacement, adjustment, or refund is conditional, not really a part of the sale itself. The cash sale transaction does not extend beyond delivery and payment, and the receipt of cash entails no restrictions. That is, the firm has no obligation to return, account for, or make any explanation to the customer as to what was done or may be done with this money. An unrestricted receipt that arises from the completion of a sale is revenue, the market price evaluation of the goods or service-output of the firm.

Restricted Cash Receipts

Of quite a different nature from sales receipts are investments in the business by a proprietor. The cash contributed to the firm by the proprietor is restricted, because the proprietor does not give up his money irrevocably. There are strings attached to the transaction in the way of implied promises and commitments between the proprietor and the business. It is expected that there will be an accounting for the funds advanced; even though the money is to be left in the business for use in whatever ways may be deemed expedient, the proprietor's investment is an accountability of the firm. If for any reason the business is terminated, the investment of the proprietor is expected to be returned, along with any increases or decreases in that amount that may arise from the operations of the firm. These understandings emphasize the separate existence of the firm as an entity in its own right, to be distinguished from its owners or other persons who may have dealings with it.

The fact that unrestricted and restricted cash receipts are fundamentally different makes it necessary to account for each of them in a different way. Receipts from cash sales are credited to revenue accounts, but the credit arising from the proprietor's capital contribution is carried to an "equity" account, to remove it from the current operating receipts category. Thus, we recognize two kinds of sources of cash receipts: current period revenues, and accountabilities to be carried over to the future. As will be seen later, there are other kinds of equities for which we shall need additional "future oriented" accounts.

Different Kinds of Cash Payments

Taking the proprietor's cash contribution out of current period receipts leaves the report of the James Pharmacy in an awkward condition. The cash is still accounted for by the cash account, but our omission of $4,000 from the operating or current period receipts leaves the effect of current operations as a decline of $3,438, revenues of $2,258 and disbursements of $5,696. Can it be that the firm "lost" this much during the month?

Careful observation will show that the gain or loss of a business is seldom measured correctly by its cash transactions. Some of the cash payments apply to the current month in full: the rental payment, for instance, covered the use of the store for the month of April. This is a recurring cost that is paid in the same month as the purchased service is used. But some of the other items are quite different.

The payments for store fixtures (cash register, counters, soda foundation, and wall cases) cover large "bundles" of service that will be useful for a long time. It is not logical to view these payments as being applicable only to the current month. The cost of such items should be spread over the period during which their service will be used. Similarly, the $2,853 merchandise cost is not all applicable to the month of April, for there are some of these goods still on the shelves. The cost of goods sold to customers during April is only part of the total purchases; the other part is available for sales in May or later. We could improve our reports a great deal if we were to divide costs between present and future usage, and thus reflect the flow of resources which the cash payment provided, in relation to their use in producing customer satisfactions and revenue.

Our James Pharmacy example contains several items of this kind; but before we attack this refinement of accounting, let us see how we can systematize the approach to deal with them.

Separation of Current from Future Items

A device that is often useful to classify amounts or to distribute parts of them to various subclassifications is a columnar analysis sheet, a distribution sheet, or simply a working paper or worksheet. We shall use a simple worksheet to make the classifications that we need for the James Pharmacy. A six-column page is used, arranged in three pairs of columns. The first pair of columns shows the debits and credits of the trial balance, the second shows the amounts applicable to the current month's operations, and the third shows the amounts deferred to the future. Such a worksheet appears in Figure 3–1. We have copied into the first pair of columns the trial balance from Figure 2–5, but it has been changed in one respect. In order to

FIGURE 3–1

JAMES PHARMACY   MONTHLY WORKSHEET   4/30/--

Summary Ledger Balances		Trial Balance		Current Month		Deferred Amount	
		debit	credit	debit	credit	debit	credit
1.	Cash in Bank	512					
2.	Ross James, Prop.		4,000				
3.	Rent	200					
4.	Cash Register	100					
5.	Counters	500					
6.	Soda Fountain	1,100					
7.	Wall Cases	300					
8.	Merchandise	2,853					
9.	Change Fund	50					
10.	Electricity	38					
11.	Gas	61					
12.	Supplies	15					
13.	Insurance	84					
14.	Miscellaneous	24					
15.	Sales, Candy and Tobacco		495				
16.	Sales, Soda Fountain		601				
17.	Sales, Drugs and Sundries		648				
18.	Sales, Prescriptions		514				
19.	Ross James, Personal	421					
	Totals	6,258	6,258				

be able to account for the proprietor's investment in detail, we have restated it to show his personal withdrawals as a separate (debit balance) account.

Now we shall examine each trial balance item and decide how much of the given debit or credit amount applies to the current period and how much should be deferred (see Figure 3–2). The first item, Cash in Bank, is clearly a future item; cash is by its nature future purchasing power, which is entirely available for future activities. Hence we carry this $512 into the deferred debit column, the left-hand column of the last pair. The account with Ross James, Proprietor, is a credit amount applicable to the future so it is carried entirely to the last column, deferred credits.

The debit item for rent applies to the current period and the entire amount is therefore carried to the debit column in the "current" category.

The next four items (the equipment items) raise a somewhat vexing problem as to how much of their cost should be deferred because we cannot be exactly sure of how long they will remain in service. However, we do know that it is wrong to charge their entire cost to the current month and it is also wrong to defer the entire amount. We therefore estimate the useful life of these items and prorate their cost on the basis of the amount of service used compared to the amount still available. Suppose we take it as fact (to make calculations simple) that these expenditures ought to be prorated over 8⅓ years or 100 months. Then we should carry 1 percent of the cost into April operations and leave 99 percent for application to future operations.

This analysis results in showing $1, $5, $11, and $3 in the debit column for the current period and carrying over the remainder of each of these trial balance debits to the debit columns in the deferred category, respectively, $99, $495, $1,089, and $297.

The merchandise cost of $2,853 gives us more trouble because we cannot make any simple assumption that will support a division of the cost between current and future periods. We can, however, count the items remaining unsold, and price each at its cost to determine the cost of the goods still on the shelves. This inventory (which we will assume comes out to $1,450) is the deferred portion of the merchandise cost, and the remainder, $1,403, is treated as the cost of goods sold, a current period cost.

It is likely that the electricity, gas, and supplies costs apply in full to the current month and that the amounts given measure current costs of operations. These debit items are carried into the current debit column.

The insurance premium is assumed to have covered a year in advance. Since one month has elapsed, 1/12th of the premium, $7, is considered as current, and 11/12ths, or $77, is applicable to the future. The $24 miscellaneous costs items and all of the sales figures are current; they are therefore carried over to the current columns as debit and credit items. The work sheet at this stage appears as shown in Figure 3–2. All of the current month items except the $421 withdrawal have now been separated from those to be deferred. Our debit-credit check, however, still serves us. The total debit amount in the Trial Balance is the same as the sum of all the debit items in the rest of the work sheet, except for the $421 we have not carried over ($6,258 = $1,768 + $4,069 + $421). The credit items also check ($6,258 = $2,258 + $4,000). But the reclassifications show that the operations of the month included *revenue* (credits) of $2,258 and *expense* (debits) of $1,768, a net effect of $490 (credit). This figure represents the current earnings of the business. Reduced by $421 drawings of Mr. James, there are still $69 of earnings retained in the business for future accountability to the proprietor. Therefore the $490 will be transferred by a balancing entry, debiting in the current and crediting in the deferred columns, thus showing the increase of the proprietor's interest via the earnings of the period. The $421 debit

FIGURE 3–2

JAMES PHARMACY   MONTHLY WORKSHEET   4/30/--

Summary Ledger Balances	Trial Balance		Current Month		Deferred Amount	
	debit	credit	debit	credit	debit	credit
1. Cash in Bank	512				512	
2. Ross James, Prop.		4,000				4,000
3. Rent	200		200			
4. Cash Register	100		1		99	
5. Counters	500		5		495	
6. Soda Fountain	1,100		11		1,089	
7. Wall Cases	300		3		297	
8. Merchandise	2,853		1,403		1,450	
9. Change Fund	50				50	
10. Electricity	38		38			
11. Gas	61		61			
12. Supplies	15		15			
13. Insurance	84		7		77	
14. Miscellaneous	24		24			
15. Sales, Candy and Tobacco		495		495		
16. Sales, Soda Fountain		601		601		
17. Sales, Drugs		648		648		
18. Sales, Prescriptions		514		514		
19. Ross James, Personal	421					
Totals	6,258	6,258	1,768	2,258	4,069	4,000

in the trial balance represents the proprietor's withdrawals in anticipation of profitable operations, a "distribution of earnings." These two items—earnings and earnings distribution—are both marked E in the work sheet as shown in Figure 3–3. They are thus associated with the proprietor's equity in the reports we shall prepare from this work sheet.

FIGURE 3–3

JAMES PHARMACY   MONTHLY WORKSHEET   4/30/--

Summary Ledger Balances	Trial Balance		Current Month		Deferred Amount	
	debit	credit	debit	credit	debit	credit
1. Cash in Bank	512				512	
2. Ross James, Prop.		4,000				4,000
3. Rent	200		200			
4. Cash Register	100		1		99	
5. Counters	500		5		495	
6. Soda Fountain	1,100		11		1,089	
7. Wall Cases	300		3		297	
8. Merchandise	2,853		1,403		1,450	
9. Change Fund	50				50	
10. Electricity	38		38			
11. Gas	61		61			
12. Supplies	15		15			
13. Insurance	84		7		77	
14. Miscellaneous	24		24			
15. Sales, Candy and Tobacco		495		495		
16. Sales, Soda Fountain		601		601		
17. Sales, Drugs and Sundries		648		648		
18. Sales, Prescriptions		514		514		
19. Ross James, Personal	421				421E	
Earnings Retained			490			490E
Totals	6,258	6,258	2,258	2,258	4,290	4,290

It will be noted that now both the current columns have equal totals and the deferred debit and credit columns are also in exact equilibrium. This is as it should be. We merely transferred the net credit of the current column to the deferred column by our last steps, and since the total amount of debits and credits were equal to start with, that equality is still evident in the completed work sheet. The equality of debits and credits again has served as a check against errors.

Financial Statements

The data shown in the work sheet may be presented in more formal style to convey information about the business to those who do not actually work with the records. The data in the Current columns are arranged to make up a statement of earnings (also called income statement, profit and loss statement, or operating statement); the data in the deferred columns of the work sheet are arranged to make up a position statement (also called a balance sheet). These statements are shown in Figures 3–4 and 3–5, respectively.

FIGURE 3–4

JAMES PHARMACY
Statement of Earnings
Month Ended April 30, 19—

Revenue:

Sales, candy and tobacco	$ 495	
Sales, soda fountain	601	
Sales, drugs and sundries	648	
Sales, prescriptions	514	
Total Revenue		$2,258

Expense:

Merchandise cost of goods sold	$1,403	
Rent	200	
Electricity	38	
Gas	61	
Supplies	15	
Insurance expired	7	
Miscellaneous	24	
Cost of using cash register	1	
Cost of using counters	5	
Cost of using soda fountain	11	
Cost of using wall cases	3	
Total Expenses		1,768
Operating margin		$ 490
Less: Proprietor's withdrawals		421
Earnings Retained in the Business		$ 69

FIGURE 3–5

JAMES PHARMACY
Statement of Position
April 30, 19—

ASSETS		EQUITIES	
Cash in bank	$ 512	Ross James, investment	$4,000
Change fund	50	Earnings retained in the business	69
Merchandise inventory	1,450		
Unexpired insurance	77		
Cash register	99		
Counters	495		
Soda fountain	1,089		
Wall cases	297		
Total Assets	$4,069	Total Equities	$4,069

The statement of earnings shows the results of operations during the period ended April 30. It lists the revenues, the expenses, and the resulting earnings of the firm; and it also reports the amount of income distributed to the proprietor. The net retained earnings represent another proprietor's equity, to be accounted for in future reports. The statement of position shows how the business stands at April 30 in terms of the costs that are still applicable to future operations (assets) and the obligations which are to be met sometime in the future (equities). Although they are arranged in a special way, these statements merely present the data shown on the work sheet to summarize the financial activities of the firm. The position statement balances for the same reason that the work sheet balanced; the net effect of *all* the transactions is carried forward into the future by way of the assets and obligations of the firm at the close of the period.

Terminology

The reader will note that we have added a number of new terms in our presentation of the financial reports. These terms arise from the fact that we have divided our data into current period and future period operations. Costs which we first recorded simply as expenditures have now been divided to those applicable to the current period (expenses) and those available for future operations (assets). Similarly, we have divided the sources of cash into those relating to current operations (revenues) and those having a long-term effect, representing obligations to be met, not merely contributions received. These future-oriented obligations we call equities. The following paragraphs will help further to clarify these distinctions.

We started our accounting records on a cash basis, but the accounts then used to record sources of cash and objects of expenditure gave us only a report concerning *cash* transactions. However, we have now learned that cash flows alone are only a part of what happens in a business, and that if we want to interpret events clearly, we must match the financial events in terms of a *period of time*. Cash receipts and payments are not adequate measures of business success or progress; some receipts are revenue but others entail obligations; costs must be assigned to the periods in which the services they represent are used. We employ technical terms to specify these new concepts.

Revenue is the amount of financial inflow arising from the delivery of products and service to customers during the current period. Equity is the amount of financial inflow that is *not* related to the current period operations but which involves obligations to be settled in some future period, as required by owner expectations and restrictions. Thus, the equity credit is carried forward via the statement of position until it has been settled or altered by repayment, renegotiation, or otherwise.

Correspondingly, we have two kinds of noncash debit items. Originally, we considered these debit items only as objects of expenditure, but we now separate them into two classes. The debits representing costs applicable to the current period we call *expense*. Expense is the cost of performing or delivering service to customers in return for revenue, and it must be reported separately from those resource costs such as inventory that are really available for future operations. Resources available for future operations are assets; this includes cash on hand and cash in bank. But all the things purchased for cash are also assets until they are put to use in operations. By counting the cost of the goods unsold, we separated the total cost of merchandise into its proper components: cost of goods sold was treated as expense; and the cost of goods unsold was listed as an asset, "merchandise inventory."

Summary

Our accounting concepts have changed now that we have recognized the need to separate current period items from future period items. This development is shown schematically in the diagram Figure 3–6.

FIGURE 3–6

Development of Account Classification

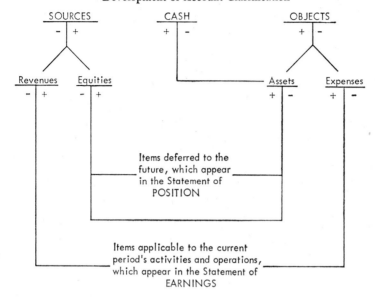

Another way in which those relations may be presented is in the flow chart shown in Figure 3–7.

The flow chart may be better understood if we note that the basic operation of any business firm is the conversion of assets (acquired from revenue or by investment) into expense (the costs of

FIGURE 3–7

Accounting Measurements and Classifications in Terms of Relationships of the Firms to Its Markets

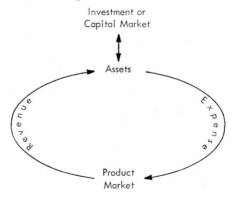

product made available to customers). Revenues (contributions from customers to compensate for product or service received) bring new assets into the firm. When revenues are equal to (or greater than) expenses, the cycle is self-sufficient and self-perpetuating.

The task of maintaining this operating cycle is the responsibility of management. Decisions of what costs to incur, what forms and kinds of products to create, how such items should be presented to the market, and what relations and results should be obtained in dealing with customers are management decisions. The results of operations of the business are reflections of management decisions, and the check upon managerial judgment is found largely in the revenue and expense flows of the firm. Thus the statement of earnings portrays an important phase of managerial responsibility. The debits and credits which make up this report show what has been done by the firm to satisfy market demands with appropriate and desirable products or services, at the minimum cost consistent with their acceptability.

Since in a price and profit economy, the price paid by the customer measures the desirability of the product to him, the revenue figure indicates the market's measure of the output value of the firm. On the other hand, the cost of providing that output tends to offset revenues and to reduce earnings. Earnings or "income" are the difference between revenue and expense. Unless there are earnings the firm will not grow, and it cannot continue to operate for very long.

The statement of earnings shows the results of product-oriented operations, but it also indicates how the aggregate net assets of the firm have been affected. The net credit represented by earnings (less distributions) is reflected in overall net asset increases. Thus there is a balancing effect in the position statement which makes the total assets equal the total equities. The additional net assets from retention of earnings—whether they are in the form of cash, inventory, or other assets—are balanced by the retained earnings credit carried into the statement of position.

There is likely to be a time lag in the operating cycle. The conversion of assets to expense is not immediate, and sales do not follow immediately. Some assets must be provided to permit the creation of expense before revenues are to be received. This provision of assets is made by investment. Investment transactions do not affect revenue or expense because as was explained earlier they involve restrictions as to future events and requirements. Thus, investment transactions result in the recognition of equities—obligations to repay or to account for the advances made.

Even though financing or investment transactions do not directly affect profits, the relation between the firm and the capital markets is important. Management has a responsibility to see that the restrictions arising from investments are complied with, and it must maintain the connections and working relationships that may be useful to the firm in financing its activities. The problems associated with maintaining proper relations with investors and suppliers are numerous and complex. Some of these problems will be discussed later, but some will be beyond the scope of this book. Nevertheless, accounts do show the net financial measures that must be dealt with.

The basic pattern of relationships among assets, equities, expense, and revenue applies to every enterprise—public or private—large or small—organized informally or with great legal formality—whether it was established or operated to produce a profit or not. Assets must come from somewhere; the flow of revenue must at least equal the expense of the enterprise. Unless someone is willing to cover enterprise expenses, the operations must obviously grind to a halt.

The accounting procedures we have now established are applicable to any institution, and they will provide reasonably adequate financial reports which follow, analyze, and present the data needed to reflect the flow of resources between the firm and its customers, as well as to indicate the status of the firm with respect to its future. The elementary and basic time separations thus far described are only some of the chronological problems of accounting. We shall examine more of these in Chapter 4.

QUESTIONS

1. This chapter has been concerned with matching cash receipts and cash payments with the operations of the period in a meaningful way. Why should we want to improve on the correct historical summary of cash receipts and payments?

2. "Revenues are unrestricted receipts." In what way are they different from restricted receipts? Give examples of each class. What general term is applied to all restricted receipts?

3. What are these restrictions that may apply to cash receipts? Give examples, not only for a business firm but for a hospital or a university.

4. Why is it necessary to distinguish expenditures applicable to current as opposed to future periods? When this distinction is made, what name is applied to the current period portion of an expenditure? What are those parts of disbursements that are applicable to future periods called?

5. What is a work sheet? What happens to the trial balance data in the completion of the simple work sheet as used in this assignment?

6. Why was the personal withdrawal account shown in the Trial Balance column of the work sheet instead of being combined with the rest of the proprietor's account?

7. The separation of disbursements into current and future period elements recognizes the expiration of costs. When we match unrestricted receipts and expired costs applicable to a given period, what name do we give the difference if the unrestricted receipts are greater than the expired costs? If the unrestricted receipts are less than the expired costs?

8. What effect does a loss have on the equity of the proprietor of the business? On other equities?

9. We started our discussion of accounting by recognizing two different kinds of accounts to reflect the flows of cash into and out of the business. How many kinds of accounts have we now recognized and what are they? In what kinds of accounts are the elements of income to be found? What are the kinds of accounts which will show the elements of financial position of the firm?

10. How can a firm's cash balance decrease even though the accounts show that the operations of the firm have been profitable during that period?

11. Does an increased cash balance necessarily mean that the company is profitable? How might a company whose results are unprofitable have an increasing cash balance?

12. It is possible to measure business profits by the excess of cash receipts over cash disbursements only under a specified set of conditions. What are these conditions? Why is such a situation seldom, if ever, observed in a typical firm?

13. What, in your own words, does a statement of position show? A statement of earnings? How, if at all, does the statement of cash receipts and payments relate to the other financial statements?

14. Ordinarily we think of cash receipts as favorable, and "expenses" as unfavorable. Are expenses undesirable? Why not?

15. Could a business have too much, as well as too little cash? What should happen if this is the case?

PROBLEMS

Problem 1

Art Baker's trial balance as taken after one month's operations was:

Cash in Bank.................$	700	
Rent......................	900	
Furniture & Fixtures.........	3,000	
Insurance..................	240	
Merchandise................	5,400	
Sales......................		$ 4,800
Baker, Capital..............		6,000
Baker, Personal.............	560	
Totals..............	$10,800	$10,800

Enter this trial balance in a work sheet form (six columns) changing account titles that are ambiguous.

Enter this trial balance in a work sheet form (six columns). Complete the work sheet, taking into consideration the following:

a) The rent payment was made at the beginning of the month, and it covers three months in advance.

b) Furniture and Fixtures have an estimated life of 100 months.

c) The insurance premium paid was for a year; it was paid when the business started.

d) An inventory of merchandise at the end of the month totaled $1,800.

From the figures in your work sheet, prepare a report of earnings and a statement of position.

Ed's Cycle Mart, Part III

Even after Ed Wiele had seen your analysis of cash receipts and payments, he was still concerned that perhaps he was losing money—i.e. not making a profit—from the operations of the firm. He tried to do this with a form 1040, but ran into troubles of interpretation. Use your accounting knowledge to help him, by using a work sheet and the following information to improve the information about his firm.

a) The cash register will remain serviceable for ten years.

b) Tools and equipment—in view of the misuse, loss and theft that will occur—are expected to last for only five years.

c) The insurance and rent payments apply to more than a single year.

M/R Cafeteria, Part II

After three months of operation, the trial balance of the M/R Cafeteria was as shown below; certain additional information is given in the footnotes to the trial balance.

Cash in Bank	2,686	
(1) Bldg. Improvements	3,720	
(2) Kitchen & Serving Eqt.	29,820	
(3) Office Equipment	12,240	
(4) Food Purchases	13,239	
Operating Costs	14,270	
Meals Sold		28,034
Cigarette Sales		423
(5) Rent	1,600	
Utilities	482	
Marks, Prop'r		27,400
Rowan, Prop'r		25,000
Marks, Personal	1,200	
Rowan, Personal	1,600	
	80,857	80,857

(1) 10 year lease
(2) 15 year use-life
(3) 6 year "
(4) Inventory $2,720
(5) 4 months

Enter these data in an appropriate six column work sheet, and analyze them in such a way as to prepare financial reports for the quarter. Profits or losses are shared equally between the two partners; use two lines on the work sheet to carry the partner's shares to the deferred columns.

Draw up a report of earnings and a position statement.

Mack's Motorcar Maintenance, Part II

The correct trial balance that should have been obtained from the first part of this problem is stated below. Giving effect to the information given, use the work-sheet to classify the account balances into current and deferred categories. Complete the work sheet and prepare a Statement of Earnings for the month of July, and a Statement of Position at the close of that month.

Additional information:
(1) The life of tools and equipment is assumed to be 100 months.
(2) Accessories on hand at the end of the month are $467 at cost prices.
(3) Inventory of gasoline and lubricants at July 31 is $1,589 cost.
(4) Cost of tires sold during July, $168.
(5) Supplies used during the month, $15.
(6) The insurance contract runs from July 1 through December 31 of this year.

MACK'S MOTORCAR MAINTENANCE

Summary Ledger Trial Balance

Cash in Bank	341	
Mack Investment		10,000
Rent Paid in Advance	600	
Electricity & Gas Deposit	20	
Telephone Charges, July	10	
Tools and Equipment	6,520	
Accessories on Hand	520	
Gasoline and Oil on Hand	3,256	
Change Fund	50	
Sales of Gasoline and Oil		1,769
Tires in Stock	612	
Supplies	160	
Helper's Salary	394	
Sales, Repairs & Overhauls		926
Parts Used R & O Work	337	
Electricity and Gas	23	
Sales of Accessories		66
Lube and Wash Sales		113
Sales of Tires		214
Unexpired Insurance	180	
Advertising Cost	65	
Totals	13,088	13,088

Pendleton Market

The retail store was started one month ago by three brothers. A trial balance taken from the summary ledger of the business at the end of the month showed the following data:

Trial Balance

Building and fixtures	$16,000
Cash in bank	4,116
Deposits, utility companies	45
Groceries purchased	43,537
Insurance premiums	132
J. J. Pendleton, investment	6,600
J. J. Pendleton, salary	430
Land	2,000
License fees	60
Meats purchased	19,112
M. B. Pendleton, investment	16,400
M. B. Pendleton, salary	500
Produce purchased	9,978
Refunds on groceries returned to wholesaler	74
R. L. Pendleton, investment	9,800
R. L. Pendleton, salary	450
Sales, groceries	37,412
Sales, meats	18,217
Sales, produce	9,392
Sales taxes	169
Supplies, miscellaneous services	1,228
Water, gas, and electricity	138

The following additional information is available at the end of the month:

(1) Inventory of groceries, at cost, $8,419; inventory of meats, at cost, $1,807; inventory of produce, at cost, $792.

(2) The insurance premium covers a 12-month period.

(3) Depreciation rate on building and fixtures, ½ percent per month.

(4) License fees cover six months in advance.

(5) Deposits, Utility Companies covers amount needed to guarantee payment of bills; it will be returnable only at termination of service.

(6) Supplies, miscellaneous services, sales taxes, and refunds apply to current month.

Required:

1. Prepare a work sheet, a statement of earnings, and a position statement.

2. Note the differences between the current period data as reported in the statement of earnings and the figures in the trial balance.

Chapter 4

CHRONOLOGICAL RECORDS AND PROCEDURES

We have established a structure of relationships between the firm and those with whom it does business, and we have a system of summary ledger accounts (grouped as assets, equities, revenues, expenses, and income distributions) in which to record the effects of business transactions. But these things alone do not meet all our needs for systematic accounting. We need some way to record transactions chronologically in some one place, so that the entire transaction can be seen as a unit.

The accounts in the summary ledger do report the overall transactions. But, since each transaction involves at least two accounts, only one part of a given transaction will appear in any one account. A debit to Cash will show that cash was increased by a transaction, but that is all. We are left in the dark as to what other account or accounts were affected by the transaction, unless we happen to remember it. When the number of transactions is large, memory is but a weak tool—indeed, one of the functions of accounting is to minimize dependence on memory. We can serve these needs by using a chronological record called a *journal*.

Journals

There are many different kinds of journal records. Some are of special design to fit the needs of a particular business; almost every business has some special features that make record-keeping an individual affair. Some journals are mechanical in nature, or are produced as offshoots from mechanical or electronic recording processes. The journal we use here is called the *general journal* because it is the simplest and most flexible type of journal. That is, it can be used to record any transaction completely showing debits and credits in a systematic but unspecialized form.

The form of the general journal is that of a book (which might be loose-leaf) in which is recorded the date of each transaction, the names of the accounts to be debited and credited, and the various amounts to be so entered. An explanation of each transaction would also be written to accompany the entries. For instance, the initial investment of Mr. James in the James Pharmacy would appear in general journal form as shown in Figure 4–1.

FIGURE 4–1

Page from a General Journal

James Pharmacy	General Journal		Debit	Credit	Page 1
Date			Debit	Credit	
Aug. 1	Cash in Bank Ross James, Proprietor To record the initial investment of Mr. James in the Pharmacy located at 10116 Fleet Street, Anywhere. The bank account is with the Third National Bank, Fleet and Regent Streets.		4 0 0 0 —	4 0 0 0 —	

The Journal may be used to preserve any desired information about the business or any of the transactions that occur. It may also be used as a formal bookkeeping device in which every transaction is entered to show its full effect, the individual debits and credits being later transferred to the summary ledger accounts by the process of posting. In such a case, the journal columns for reference will indicate the pages of the ledger to which the amounts were transferred. Perhaps the reader will remember similar reference columns in the formal account illustrated in Chapter 1. Modern accounting systems, however, use mechanical or electronic methods of data processing. There are many ways to add or subtract information from a given file or other collection of data which do not involve actual copying of data.

For our present purposes we shall use the journal form only as a means of writing out transactions to indicate the debits and credits involved, ignoring the methods of data processing that may be used. The other transactions we described for Mr. James in our earlier illustration would be written as follows:

(2)

Rent..	200	
Cash in Bank..		200

Check No. 1 issued to Mr. Harold Clubb for one month's rent on the store at 10116 Fleet Street.

(3)

Cash Register..	100	
Counters..	500	
Soda Fountain..	1,100	
Wall Cases..	300	
Cash in Bank..		2,000

Check No. 2 issued to Store Equipment Suppliers for fixtures, as per their Invoice No. 34478. See papers attached to this invoice for service, guarantee, and other similar data.

(4)

Merchandise..	1,342	
Cash in Bank..		1,342

Check No. 3 issued to Wholesale Drugs, Inc., for initial order of merchandise. See their Invoice No. 855568.

(5)

Change Fund..	50	
Cash in Bank..		50

Check No. 4 was used to withdraw $50 in change from the bank to be kept in the cash register. This amount will be left in the register at all times and will be added to the register total in order to check cash daily before making the bank deposit for the day.

(6)

Cash in Bank...	104	
Electricity..	38	
Gas...	61	
Supplies..	15	
Insurance...	84	
Merchandise..	1,511	
Miscellaneous..	24	
Ross James, Personal...	421	
Sales, Tobacco and Candy.............................		495
Sales, Soda Fountain.................................		601
Sales, Drugs and Sundries............................		648
Sales, Prescriptions.................................		514

To summarize transactions from cash register tapes. Invoices and receipts are filed with the register tapes.

The journal serves a useful function in providing a chronological record of transactions; it also shows the analysis that was made of a particular transaction before it was entered in the summary ledger.

"Adjusting" Entries

Now that we have a little more organized picture of the accounting system, it is worthwhile to consider what effect the work sheet procedures described in the preceding chapter should have upon the summary ledger accounts. We used the work sheet only to separate the current debits (expenses) from those applicable to future operations (assets); conversely, we separated current credits (revenues) from others involving future commitments (equities). In effect, however, this reclassified the data recorded in the summary ledger accounts. From this reclassification we prepared the financial reports; but the summary ledger was left in the same situation that it was before our work sheet operations. If it is worthwhile to separate current from future effects in the financial reports, it should be worth recording in more formal terms. The reclassifications we made in the work sheet may be entered in the ledger to show there the separation of current and future items. Referring back to the figures (Figure 3–1) taken from the summary ledger with which we began the work sheet, we may review them as follows:

The first item (Cash in Bank, debit balance of $512) is clearly labeled to mark it as an asset. Since this is correct and we know of no reason to reclassify it, we leave it unadjusted. The same is true of Ross James, Proprietor—credit balance, $4,000. This represents the initial investment of the owner in the business, the amount which he expects to leave invested so as to earn a return on it. It is properly stated as a credit item, and its label indicates its equity nature, so it is left unchanged. The rent item of $200 debit is the cost of using the premises during the current month; as such, it is an expense. If we keep in mind that this is indeed an expense and not a cost applicable to the future, we need make no adjustment. But if there were some doubt as to how the mere title "Rent" might be interpreted, we may transfer the rent amount to a more clearly labeled account. This would be accomplished by making entries in the journal:

```
Rent Expense...............................................200
     Rent.................................................        200
```

Putting these debit and credit items into the summary ledger would leave the "Rent" account with no balance and would show "Rent Expense" as $200, which is correct. Then, there would be no doubt as to how this amount should be reported in the financial statements. The reader will note that by merely changing the title of the ledger account, the effect would be the same; for that matter, we would have been more correct if we originally made the debit to a Rent Expense account rather than to a Rent account. As a matter of formal procedure, it is better to think of the change as a journal entry adjustment since we would then have a record of the change along with a full explanation.

Skipping the next four equipment items (we shall return to them later) we find the debit amount $2,853, labeled "Merchandise." We know, from having taken an inventory, that only $1,450 of merchandise cost is still available for future operations; the other $1,403 is the cost of the goods delivered to customers during the month. To reclassify and properly label these two elements, we make the following journal entries:

```
Merchandise Cost of Goods Sold..............................1,403
Merchandise Inventory.......................................1,450
    Merchandise..........................................          2,853
```

This change states the accounting elements properly and gets rid of the ambiguous title, "Merchandise."

A similar line of reasoning applies to the equipment items, except that we shall need some special terminology. It seems a bit awkward to have an account for "Cash Register Expense" and another for "Cash Register Asset," although that is exactly what we want to show. Further, the fact that the useful life of the equipment is not entirely certain makes us a little reluctant to use such definite labels as have been suggested. The amount of equipment cost absorbed in operations of the current period may be called depreciation (thus distinguishing the current period charge from the future-use carry-over), and the asset amount would be reduced by the following entries:

```
Depreciation of Cash Register.........................................1
    Cash Register.....................................................       1
```

This makes the expense element easy to recognize and shows the asset at its net remaining use-significance to the firm. We shall see a bit later how we may refine the accounting to separate estimates from recorded costs.

Corresponding entries would be made to record the depreciation of the other equipment items, and the result would be that there would be four depreciation accounts to appear among the expense items, and the asset accounts would be reduced to the amounts that should appear on the position statement.

The only other item that requires adjustment is the item of insurance, for which the entries would be:

```
Insurance Expired.................................................  7
Unexpired Insurance.............................................. 77
    Insurance...................................................        84
```

To separate expense and asset elements in the insurance payment and eliminate the ambiguous account, "Insurance."

The effect of these adjusting entries upon the summary ledger may be seen in the adjusted trial balance shown in Figure 4–2.

FIGURE 4–2

JAMES PHARMACY
Trial Balance
As Adjusted, April 30, 19—

Cash in bank........................	$ 512	
Ross James, Proprietor.................		$4,000
*Rent expense........................	200	
Cash register........................	99	
Counters............................	495	
Soda fountain........................	1,089	
Wall cases...........................	297	
*Depreciation of cash register...........	1	
*Depreciation of counters...............	5	
*Depreciation of soda fountain...........	11	
*Depreciation of wall cases..............	3	
*Merchandise cost of goods sold..........	1,403	
Merchandise inventory..................	1,450	
Change fund..........................	50	
*Electricity...........................	38	
*Gas................................	61	
*Supplies............................	15	
*Insurance expired.....................	7	
Unexpired insurance....................	77	
*Miscellaneous expense.................	24	
*Sales, candy and tobacco...............		$ 495
*Sales, soda fountain...................		601
*Sales, drugs and sundries...............		648
*Sales, prescriptions....................		514
*Ross James, personal..................	421	58
Totals........................	$6,258	$6,258

To facilitate comparison we have marked with an asterisk those items that appeared in the earnings statement. The items not so marked were shown in the position statement. As explained earlier the net sum of earnings retained in the business (the algebraic sum of the asterisked items) appears in the position statement as an addition to the equity of the proprietor.

This trial balance is exactly the same collection of data that appeared in the earnings and position statements earlier; the only difference is that we have here formalized the separation of current period from future period items.

Cumulation of Data in the Accounts

The reader has probably not noticed another significant difference between the accounts related to the statement of earnings and those related to the statement of position. Every account serves to accumulate information about some item of accountability: the Cash in Bank account shows the effect of all the transactions with the bank, and the sales revenue accounts builds up information about sales. But there is a difference between *status* accounts (asset and equity items) and *flow* accounts (revenues and expenses). Status accounts (cash, inventory, equipment, equities) typically are increased by some transactions, but decreased by others; but flow accounts build up in the same direction. That is, while cash balances go up and down over time, the amounts of revenue or expense will continue to grow as time passes. Unless we do something about it, each successive statement of earnings would add the revenue and expense flows of the current period to those that had occurred earlier so that the earnings statement would always show the entire accumulation of sales, depreciation or any other expense since the inception of the business. This is undesirable; typically, we want figures only for reasonably short periods, seldom longer than a year, and often for much shorter intervals.

Periodic Reports by Subtraction

The effects of continuous accumulation in revenue and expense accounts may be overcome by successive subtraction. By taking the flow account items in any given (adjusted) trial balance, we would get accumulated totals to date. But if we subtract from these accumulated totals the amounts obtained a month earlier, the difference would be the current month's results.

To take another example, suppose that an expense account for payroll at the end of January had a balance of $5,024. If the February 28 trial balance shows this balance to be $9,472, the difference, $4,448, is the amount of payroll expense accumulated in February. Thus the entire statement of earnings would show the cumulative (total to date) figures for successive months' sales and expenses. Then, by subtraction, we could establish the data for the current month. Such an arrangement and result is shown in Figure 4–3.

FIGURE 4–3

THE SERVICE SUPPLY CORPORATION
Monthly Cumulative and Current Month Earnings Data

Revenue and Expense Items	November 30 Cumulative	December 31 Cumulative	December Only
Revenue from sales.........................	$136,000	$150,000	$14,000
Cost of merchandise and supplies used.........	$ 72,200	$ 80,000	$ 7,800
Payroll costs...............................	42,200	46,900	4,700
Employer's payroll taxes....................	2,050	2,390	340
Gas, water, and electricity..................	1,010	1,100	90
Building rent expired........................	7,700	8,400	700
Depreciation of store fixtures................	367	400	33
Total Expense........................	$125,527	$139,190	$13,663
Operating net margin........................	$ 10,473	$ 10,810	$ 337
Provision for federal income tax..............	3,090	3,210	120
Retained Earnings..........................	$ 7,383	$ 7,600	$ 217

"Closing Books"

The process just illustrated would eventually become unmanageable. After a period of time, the accumulations would become quite large, and while it might be interesting to know the totals for each revenue and expense item over a number of years, this would soon be of no practical use. Seldom does a business manager want data about his business that accumulates for more than a year. Typically, we like to start each year fresh, beginning the count of operating flows anew. This requires that the accounts showing revenues and expenses be set back to zero.

To do this, we perform physically what we have been doing implicitly in every position statement: lump together the accumulated sales, expenses, and income distribution into a single amount of earnings retained in the business. This can be done for the Service Supply Corporation in Figure 4–3 by making the following entries:

Revenue from Sales.......................................	150,000	
Cost of Merchandise and Supplies Used..................		80,000
Payroll Costs......................................		46,900
Employer's Payroll Taxes.............................		2,390
Gas, Water, and Electricity...........................		1,100
Building Rent.......................................		8,400
Depreciation of Store Fixtures.........................		400
Provision for Federal Income Tax......................		3,210
Retained Earnings...................................		7,600

It will be noted that all the revenue and expense items in the trial balance are exactly offset and reduced to zero by this set of entries. The amount of earnings retained in the business will appear in the Retained Earnings account, just as it shows in the position statement (Figure 3–5). Sometimes the amount shown in the list above as "Retained Earnings" may be carried through a summary profit and loss or "income summary" account; this is only a bookkeeping device, since the net effect of the entire operation is to carry the overall amount to Retained Earnings.

The recording of such entries "closes" the flow accounts, and the process is therefore known as "closing the books." This term is, however, somewhat inaccurate, since the *status* accounts are not closed; status amounts are merely carried forward. Only the flow accounts are set back to zero. An easier way to accomplish this (in practical terms) is simply to remove the entire lot of flow account pages from the summary ledger without bothering to close them by the entries suggested above. This will leave the ledger out of balance by the amount of the net change in retained earnings; if that amount is added (as a debit or credit) to Retained Earnings, this imbalance will be corrected. Adding new pages for the next year flow accounts completes the changeover, carrying forward what should be carried forward and leaving the previous year's flow accounts to be filed until they are needed again.

Refinement of Position Statement Classification

Up to now, we have paid little attention to the arrangement of the assets and equities in the position statement. It may be well to note that all assets of a business are not alike in their liquidity. Inventories are not available for the payment of costs as cash is, and therefore inventories are listed below cash items in the position statement. Assets such as buildings and equipment are even less associated with current cash.

To follow through this notion of separating assets and arranging them in an order of liquidity, it should be noted that inventories normally "turn over" i.e., are exchanged for cash in a relatively short period. The cycle of business operations transfers cash to inventories and back to cash again when the purchased goods are sold. The circulating assets are thus quite different from long-term assets such as equipment, buildings, and the like. While the cost of buildings and equipment are recovered (through sales) a little at a time in each accounting period, some long-term costs have a quasi-permanent character. The land on which a building is located has no definable life period, and the services represented by land cost are practically inexhaustible for operating purposes. Thus land tends to be viewed as a permanent or very long-lived asset.

We should separate long-term assets such as land, buildings, equipment, and the like from the circulating, short-term, current assets such as cash, merchandise inventory, unexpired rent and insurance. But to emphasize the difference between current (circulating) assets and long-term (fixed) assets, we present the current assets in the order of their liquidity (with the assets nearest to cash listed first); long-term assets are arranged in a reverse order (with the more *permanent* assets listed first). Thus, a typical position statement will show assets arranged something like that shown in Figure 4–4.

FIGURE 4–4

MODEL COMPANY
Position Statement
June 30, 19—

ASSETS

Current Assets:

Cash on hand...........................	$ xxx	
Cash in bank...........................	xxxx	
Merchandise inventory..................	xxxx	
Supplies...............................	xx	
Unexpired rent.........................	xxx	
Total Current Assets................		$ xxxx

Long-Term Assets:

Land....................................		$ xxx	
Building............................$xxxxx			
Less: Accumulated depreciation..........	xxx	xx	
Equipment.............................$ xxxx			
Less: Accumulated depreciation..........	xx	xx	
Total Long-Term Assets.............			$ xxxx
Total Assets......................			$xxxxxx

Later when we have learned something more about credit and its effects upon accounting (Chapter 5) we shall make similar refinements to the equities side of the position statement. These will reflect the relative "currentness" of equities. But this need not be our concern at the moment.

Chronology of Bank Transactions

One of the ways to see how the handling of transactions between business firms may affect accounting records and their meaning is to consider the typical transactions with respect to cash in bank.

A business enterprise may receive cash from a number of sources. Examining these cash receipts may show them to consist of currency (coin and bills), bank checks, money orders issued by the post office or by other agencies, drafts payable on demand, or other negotiable claims to immediate payment. The definition of cash could be made narrow enough to exclude anything but actual bills and coins; but aside from retail stores, most companies handle very little currency.

Rather, it is common experience to receive payment in negotiable papers that may be used to obtain cash on demand. Thus, in practice, cash includes any claim to money payment that may be collected without demur or delay from a commercial bank. So long as these items remain in the custody of a firm, they represent cash on hand. However it is prudent to limit the holding of such items to as small an amount and for as short a period as possible. First, it is not safe to have large amounts of cash items on hand even with the protection of safes and strongboxes. Money may be lost or spent for unauthorized purposes if it is possible to obtain it easily without making a record of it. Second, the holding of cash items in a drawer or a cashbox merely delays the presentation of negotiable items. Further, the payment of bills or expenses out of cash on hand is not good practice because transactions may be overlooked or offset. In any but the smallest business, it is almost universal practice to bank cash receipts as soon as possible and make all payments by check.

Bank Deposits

Delivery of cash items to a bank for deposit is always recorded, not only in the ledger account of the depositor but in more detailed form on a business voucher (evidence of a transaction) called a deposit slip. A typical deposit slip is shown in Figure 4–5. The depositor will probably have some other details recorded than are shown on the deposit slip; all the bank requires for identification of a check is the number of the bank on which it is drawn. Many banks photograph all the checks that are cleared; therefore, the name of the depositor and the number of the drawee bank is sufficient to find all other desired information. Note the statement at the top of the deposit slip with respect to uncollected items. It is usually assumed that all items presented for payment will be honored by the drawee banks; few items are actually uncollectible. Therefore the depositor is justified in entering the deposit in his accounts with the entries:

```
Cash in Bank............................................1,942.16
      Cash on Hand......................................          1,942.16
```

The bank records the deposit when it is received by a credit to the depositor's account. This account is an equity item in the bank's accounting records, for it represents the amount that the bank must be ready to pay the depositor. Thus the depositor's account on the bank's ledger is reciprocal to the Cash in Bank account on the books of the depositor. Should the depositor mail the deposit to the bank (which is often done, especially if no currency is involved), there

FIGURE 4–5

A Deposit Slip

Deposited with AMERICAN NATIONAL BANK for the account of			
Bardsdale Farm Stores		No. 7-143-27	
185 River Road, Bardsdale, Iowa *October 12, 19–* Credit for checks and drafts is conditional; they may be charged back without notice if found uncollectible.			
CURRENCY	$ 1	327	45
CHECKS (please list separately)			
90-210/1411	$	17	71
14-410/630		75	84
Total Deposit	$ 1	942	16

will be a time lag of a day or two while the deposit is in transit. The entry of the deposit in the records of the bank will lag behind the entry in the depositor's records.

Payment by Check

A check is a written order prepared by the depositor, directing the bank to pay a certain sum of money on demand to some specified person or firm. It is used almost universally as a means of payment; when it has served its purpose as a check, it remains a permanent record of the transaction. Checks written are customarily regarded as disbursements at the time they are written; this is not quite precise because it takes some time for a check to "clear" the bank. During this period the bank still holds the amount for the depositor. The bank knows nothing about checks written until they are presented for payment, and this is an additional reason why the records of the bank will not always agree with those of the depositor. In order to have these two records agree, it is necessary to "adjust" for the outstanding checks.

Other Bank Charges and Credits

Banks make charges for incidental services, such as collecting out-of-town items, handling other special business for the depositor, or even for maintaining and servicing his deposit account. These service charges are often made only after a monthly review of the account, and the depositor is rarely able to keep a full record of the charges he incurs. Even if it is possible, few people keep a running record of bank charges. Thus, we have a third reason why the accounts on the bank and the depositor's ledger will not be in agreement. Sometimes banks receive funds for the depositor as a collection agent; this is still another reason for reconciling the accounts of the depositor and the bank.

Bank Reconciliation

In the process of handling numerous transactions between the bank and the depositor, it is quite possible that errors may occur; it is imperative that such errors should be found before they cause trouble. This is not so easy to do if the accounts are, as we have noted, not quite reciprocal. In order to check for errors, we compare the two accounting records, transaction by transaction. We make allowances for differences in timing, and make sure we are satisfied that both records are entirely consistent. In this process errors, misunderstandings, and unrecognized items may be specified and settled. We begin the reconciliation with the bank statement that is received from the bank. A typical bank statement is shown in Figure 4–6.

If at the end of the month (the date of the bank statement), the depositor's account with Cash in Bank shows a debit balance of

FIGURE 4–6

American National Bank
Monthly Bank Statement

Bardsdale Farm Stores
185 River Road, Bardsdale, Iowa

Account No. 7-143-27

Debits			Credits	Date	Balance
				1	7,414.59
140.56	26.78	43.17		2	7,204.58
721.98	442.50		1,942.16	4	7,984.26
			221.01	5	8,205.27
887.77	446.79	1,005.00	993.14	6	6,758.85
14.00	994.00		729.17	7	6,480.02
721.00	443.59			8	6,263.13
334.40		*37 Vouchers*		29	7,076.67
		Returned		30	6,742.27

$5,427.13, the difference between this and the $6,742.27 shown in the bank account requires some explanation, for certainly they cannot both be correct. Although the procedure of preparing a bank reconciliation may vary considerably, some specific steps are as follows:

1. *General Review.* Before the depositor actually compares the debits and the credits on the bank statement with his records, a general review should be made. The canceled checks, deposit slips, and other papers should be separated. Each of the canceled checks

FIGURE 4–7

should be examined to see that it is signed by the proper person, that the chain of endorsements on the back is reasonable, and that the items and amounts check with those on the bank statement. In the bank statement of the Bardsdale Farm Stores (Figure 4–6), suppose that the first item listed under the seventh of the month—a check for $14—appears as shown in Figure 4–7. This check was payable to Hamilton Mills, who transferred it to Homer Jones, who in turn negotiated it to International Sales Company, which company deposited the check in their account with the American National Bank. But since the check was written by another company, it should not have been charged to the Bardsdale Farm Stores account. This item represents an error on the part of the bank, and the bank should be so informed. This is also part of the reason for the difference between the bank statement and the Cash in Bank account of the depositor.

2. *Check Debit Items on the Statement.* Among the items shown as debits in the bank statement are *service charges;* these are evidenced by slips of paper called *debit memoranda,* and there might be several of these among the canceled checks which are sent with the statement. The service charges are items that should be shown on the books of the depositor as expense. Sometimes, the debit memoranda will include an uncollectible check that was deposited and is charged back to the depositor because of "insufficient funds," "no such account," or some similar reason. This is a claim against the person from whom the check was accepted and should be shown in the depositor's books as such. Thus, by examination of the debit memoranda, the need for adjustment entries appear; we shall shortly make some of these entries.

Next it must be determined what checks have been written and credited to the Cash in Bank account that did not reach the bank in time for payment within the month. The only way to establish this is to compare the checks returned with those issued and note the exceptions. Checks are usually numbered serially when issued; by placing the canceled checks in serial order, they may be compared with the issued checks as noted in the stubs of the checkbook or in the check register. First, however, we should establish the serial number of the last check written in the preceding month, and we should have a list of those checks outstanding when the last reconciliation was made at the end of the preceding month. The returned checks may then be compared with those that were issued and outstanding; the missing ones are those still not presented for payment. The Cash in Bank account has been credited for these, but the bank has no debits for them. This must be considered in the bank reconciliation.

In the process of comparing checks issued with those returned, it is essential to compare amounts carefully; sometimes a check will be written for the correct amount and then a transposed or otherwise different amount may be entered in the stub or other record of check issued. This will cause a difference between the depositor's record and that of the bank, and since it is an error on the depositor's books, it will have to be corrected by adjustment.

3. *Check Credit Items on the Statement.* Having compared the debit items in the statement with the credit items in his cash in bank record, the depositor will next review the bank statement credits

(debits to his own Cash in Bank account), which are his deposits. When checking the deposits shown on the bank statement with the depositor's record, two situations are common. A deposit may be entered (in the depositor's record) which the bank has not yet received; or the amount of a deposit as entered on the record may differ from that on the statement. In strict theory, cash not yet received by the bank is really in transit at the end of the month and an adjusting entry may be made to show this. Often however, the item is noted but not adjusted for, because the receipt of the deposit by the bank has already occurred and may be confirmed as an actual part of the bank balance. But if the deposit has not been received by the bank, investigation is indicated to determine the nature of this discrepancy.

The comparison of deposits may also reveal credits made in the bank's account that do not appear in the depositor's record. These may arise from special collections made by the bank for the depositor or the receipt of funds from foreign sources sent to the bank via foreign exchange houses. When such credits appear on the bank statement, they should also appear in the depositor's record, or an adjustment is necessary.

Bank Reconciliation Work Sheet

The reader has doubtlessly reached the conclusion that there should be some systematic way of putting the pieces of the bank reconciliation together. In an effort to explain why the balance figure on the bank statement differs from the balance figure in the Cash in Bank account, we have been describing various items that must be kept track of. To do this, we use a bank reconciliation work sheet (see Figure 4–7). It should be noted that the items mentioned in the reconciliation work sheet are listed in the order in which we have described them in the text; we have put in amounts to illustrate the effect of each item.

Adjustment Entries from Bank Reconciliation

When the bank reconciliation work sheet is completed, it shows the correct amount of cash in bank at the date of the bank statement. The work sheet is not complete until all the differences between the bank's record and the depositor's ledger account have been found— the adjusted balances must agree. When this *has* been done, however, the work sheet shows only why the two records do not agree; the items mentioned must be reviewed to see which require corrections or adjustments. In the present case, the bank should be notified at once of the error in charging the Bardsdale Fodder Sales Company check to the Bardsdale Farm Stores' account. The other differences in the bank columns of the work sheet are items that time alone will take care of. It may be well to check to see that the deposit in transit

FIGURE 4–8

Bank Reconciliation Work Sheet

Bank's Record

January 30, 19--
Depositor's Record

Dr.	Cr.	Items	Dr.	Cr.
	6,742 27	Balances, unadjusted	5,427 13	
	14 00	Bardsdale Fodder Sales Co. check charged in error. Add to bank amount.		
		Howard Howard's check returned for insufficient funds. Adjust books to reverse deposit.		130 25
		Bank Service charges, as per debit memorandum; show as expense.		7 40
1,868 69		Checks issued and outstanding at end of month (list attached).		
		Check No. 1668, written for $82.37 entered in check record for $28.73. This payment was debited to Merchandise Inventory account.		53 64
	374 26	Deposit in transit at end of month.		
		Error in entering deposit of Jan. 14. The $490 addition to Cash in Bank account should have been only $409.		81 00
		Collection of draft from Importers, Ltd., not shown in books.	107 00	
1,868 69	7,130 53	Totals	5,534 13	272 29
	5,261 84	Corrected Balance	5,261 84	

was actually received by the bank after a few days, but no other action need be taken with respect to the bank's part of the record. On the other hand, the items listed in the "book" columns require adjustments, to bring the depositors records to the proper state.

Howard Howard's check, which could not be collected, is not cash but a claim that we hope to collect; we call such a claim an *account receivable*. Thus the required entries are:

```
Accounts Receivable..........................................130.25
    Cash in Bank...........................................          130.25
```

The bank service charges are an additional expense that has not been recorded, and we charge this item by the entries:

<pre>
Miscellaneous Expense...7.40
    Cash in Bank...   7.40
</pre>

The error in writing Check No. 1668 had the effect of too small an amount entered as a debit in Merchandise Inventory account, as well as the too small credit to Cash in Bank. Therefore, we adjust by increasing both these items:

<pre>
Merchandise Inventory.......................................53.64
    Cash in Bank...   53.64
</pre>

Correction of the error in entering the deposit of January 14 depends upon the entries made at the time of the deposit. If the credit for that deposit had been to Cash on Hand account, the correction now would be:

<pre>
Cash on Hand...81.00
    Cash in Bank...   81.00
</pre>

Finally, the collection of the draft would have to be recorded; if this credit arose from a sale, the entries would be:

<pre>
Cash in Bank...107.00
    Sales Revenue...   107.00
</pre>

By the use of such entries as these, the account with Cash in Bank may be brought up to date and corrected for errors and omissions. This is a process that should be carried out monthly; errors disclosed by means of reconciliation of bank accounts must be corrected if the reports and measurements of business transactions are to be precise.

Summary

This chapter has presented some refinements of accounting method to supplement the system of the summary ledger accounts. We have recognized and solved the problem of accumulations in flow accounts, and we have set up a shorthand way of recording transactions as they are analyzed so that we need not search through the entire summary ledger to find the related parts of a transaction. We have applied accounting analysis to the reconciliation and correction of accounts with banks, and we have learned to use a simple bank reconciliation work sheet. We should now be ready to consider some further refinements in accounting procedure made necessary by the general credit-system of delayed payment under which most businesses operate.

QUESTIONS

1. What is a journal? What purpose does it serve in most accounting systems? What is the principal use we shall make of the journal entry form?

2. How is a transaction written in a journal?

3. What are "adjusting entries"? Why are they put into the summary ledger?

4. Why is cumulation of data a problem in interpreting revenue and expense data? What can we do to offset this tendency and get an earnings report for one month or one quarter?

5. What is the purpose of "closing entries"? Is there a way of avoiding such procedures? Would it be better to "close" the accounts monthly?

6. Why is it possible for the bank's account with a depositor to be different from that of the depositor's account with the bank even though *both* records are technically correct?

7. Why is it good practice to deposit all cash receipts promptly and to pay all bills by check? Give some examples of what would happen if we did not handle cash this way.

8. In making a reconciliation between a depositor's monthly bank statement and the account in the depositor's summary ledger for that bank deposit, are "outstanding" checks subtracted from the bank balance or *added* to the balance as shown in the depositor's books? Why?

9. If a check remains outstanding after several months, what should be done about it?

10. Should the bank be informed about all outstanding checks? Why or why not? Should the bank be informed about a check charged against the depositor's account in error? Why or why not?

11. Which items that appear in a bank reconciliation work sheet should be reflected in the depositor's accounting record by adjusting entries? Why is it important that these items be handled so?

12. In your own words, indicate what kinds of information an owner-manager of a business might gain from reading a full set of financial reports (cash receipts and disbursements report, earnings report, and position statement). What kinds of questions would arise in his mind after reading such a set of statements at the close of a given period? What might he do as a result?

13. Why is the order in which assets appear in the position statement important? What criterion is used to establish this order? What two terms are used to describe the most important *classes* of assets, and why is it necessary to distinguish between these two kinds of assets?

PROBLEMS

Browne's Auto Repair Shop

Martin Browne has two accounts with the Morris County Bank, one for his auto repair business and one for his personal affairs. At the end of January the statement for the auto repair business showed a balance of $3,976.70 while the bank account on the business ledger showed a net of $3,684.00.

A careful review of the details of the bank statement, the canceled checks, and other information revealed the following:

(1) A deposit was made to the bank account on January 31 by mail; this consisted of three customer checks amounting to $480 total.
(2) The bank statement showed a service charge of $6.50; this amount is correct, but $3 of it is applicable to the Browne personal checking account.
(3) Mrs. Browne had cashed a $50 check at the Mammoth Department Store, which was charged by the bank against the auto repair shop account.
(4) A personal check signed by Harold Patterson which had been returned marked "NSF." in December had been redeposited in January but not entered in the auto repair shop books. This check was collected and was credited to the shop account by the bank in the amount of $17.20 on January 14.
(5) Checks issued by the business but not reported as paid by the bank were:

No. 370..............	$ 44	No. 726..............	$30
No. 721..............	420	No. 731..............	82
No. 725..............	168	No. 733..............	68

Check No. 370 had been issued last August to a former employee who left town in October and had not been heard from since.

Required:

Prepare a bank reconciliation and indicate the adjustment entries that are required on the books of the auto repair shop. What, if any, of this information should be reported to the bank for correction of their records?

James Pharmacy

Trial Balance
May 31, 19—

Account	Debits	Credits
Cash in bank..............................	$ 432	
Ross James, investment.....................		$4,000
Rent expense.............................	400	
Cash register.............................	98	
Counters.................................	490	
Soda fountain............................	1,078	
Wall cases................................	294	
Depreciation, cash register...................	2	
Depreciation, counters......................	10	
Depreciation, soda fountain..................	22	
Depreciation, wall cases.....................	6	
Merchandise cost of goods sold...............	2,883	
Merchandise inventory......................	1,514	
Change fund..............................	50	
Electricity................................	83	
Gas......................................	96	
Supplies..................................	33	
Insurance expired..........................	14	
Unexpired insurance........................	70	
Miscellaneous expense.......................	52	
Sales, candy and tobacco....................		1,009
Sales, soda fountain........................		1,243
Sales, drug and sundries....................		1,172
Sales, prescriptions........................		989
Ross James, personal.......................	786	
	$8,413	$8,413

Required:

1. Use the listed data, and those given above, page 58 of the text, to prepare a set of reports for this business as at the end of May, 19—. The earnings statement should show columns for April, for May cumulative to date, and for May only. The statement of position should be appropriately classified and arranged, and it should compare the position at April 30 with that at May 31, by putting the data in adjacent columns.

2. What comments can you make about these reports and what they show about the operations of the business?

Brooks Lumber Company

The following trial balance was taken from the summary ledger of the Brooks Lumber Company, after a year's transactions had been recorded on a cash basis:

	Debits	Credits
Cash in bank..........................	$ 8,300	
Merchandise cost......................	249,400	
Insurance cost........................	4,200	
Payroll cost..........................	96,400	
Miscellaneous costs...................	54,800	
Sales................................		$307,700
Common stock........................		148,000
Land................................	5,000	
Building.............................	21,600	
Delivery equipment...................	16,000	
Total..........................	$455,700	$455,700

To interpret these figures, you have the following information:
(1)   Merchandise actually on hand end of year, $78,500, at cost.
(2)   The insurance item is a premium for three years, paid January 1.
(3)   The building is expected to be serviceable for 40 years.
(4)   Delivery Equipment is expected to be junked after 4 years.
(5)   Miscellaneous costs include electricity, repairs, advertising, supplies, postage, telephone, and so forth.
(6)   Common stock is the amount invested by Charles and Henry Brooks when the business was started January 1 this year.

Required:
1.   Transcribe the trial balance into a six-column work sheet.
2.   Carry over the debits and credits into appropriate current and deferred columns.
3.   Make up a position statement as at the end of the year.
4.   Make up a statement of earnings for the year.
5.   Write out in journal form, the entries needed to record the cost of goods sold, the depreciation of delivery equipment and building, and the insurance expiration at the end of this period.
6.   Indicate how one might cut off the cumulation of the flow accounts at the end of the year
     a) by formal entries to the accounts.
     b) by an informal procedure involving no accounting entries, except the net change in retained earnings.

Plum the Plumber

Mr. Plum is a plumbing contractor who keeps his business bank account under the name of Plum the Plumber. He pays all his bills by check, and deposits all receipts by mail to the bank on the day they are received. At September 30, his check book showed a balance of $4,107.10, when he received the following statement from the Metro Bank and Trust Company:

METRO BANK AND TRUST COMPANY
In Account with Plum the Plumber

Account 555–37356–2   For the Month of September

Balance, August 31......................................			$3,447.20
Deposits received			
9/1....................................	$528		
9/2....................................	720		
9/6....................................	470		
9/13...................................	450		
9/19...................................	375		
9/25...................................	750		
9/27...................................	480	3,773.00	$7,220.20
Checks paid			
No. 945–971 inclusive...............	$2,181.10		
973–977 "	614.70		
D.M. Wosmy check, NSF.... $160			
Protest fees.............. 7	167.00		
D.M. Service charges..................	6.40	2,969.20	
Balance September 30...			$4,251.00

Along with this statement was a credit memo indicating collection of a New York draft for $750 on H. M. Richfeller. Mr. Plum had remodeled Mr. Richfeller's summer home, and by instructions had sent a sight draft to Mr. Richfeller's office when the work was finished.

Mr. Plum's check record showed the following: Balance, August 31, $3,975.20. Deposits were entered for 9/1, $720; 9/5, $470; 9/12, $550; 9/18, $375; 9/26, $480 and 9/30, $840. The last check drawn in August was No. 944 for $322; this check had been paid and returned with the August statement. The checkbook balance at August 31 included the deposit mailed by Mr. Plum that evening for $528. Checks written during September totalled $3,303.10. No. 972 was for $42, and checks 978–982 inclusive totalled $465.30. The balance in Mr. Plum's check book stub after check No. 982 was $4,007.10, but the Metro Bank ledger account was $4,107.10.

Mr. Plum noticed that the account of Ben Benton showed a credit balance of $100 after 9/12 when a check had been received from him, but he was not aware of how this might have come about.

Required:

Prepare a reconciliation for Mr. Plum's bank account, with entries in Journal form for any unrecorded transactions, and indicate any other corrections needed.

Halloran Pharmacy

The accounts of the Halloran Pharmacy showed the following balances at the end of the first and second months of operations:

	Amounts at end of:	
	First Month	*Second Month*
National bank deposit account................	$ 925	$ 365
Rent expense.............................	200	400
Unexpired Insurance.......................	110	100
Sales, tobacco and candy....................	712	1,374
Electricity...............................	28	58
Supplies expense...........................	25	35
Sales, soda fountain........................	383	810
Gas for heating...........................	34	66
Merchandise inventory......................	1,523	2,018
Sales, drugs and sundries....................	854	1,685
Insurance expense.........................	10	20
Sales, prescriptions........................	482	1,070
Depreciation of equipment..................	20	40
Cash register.............................	198	196
Counters & showcases.....................	595	590
Soda fountain.............................	990	980
Wall cases................................	357	354
Merchandise cost, goods sold................	1,953	3,834
James Halloran, investment..................	5,000	5,000
James Halloran, personal....................	463	883

Required:

1. Arrange the second month data in the form of a trial balance, separating these items into debit and credit amounts.

2. Set up a columnar earnings report, showing last month's earnings, total earnings to date and the second month's earnings in a four-column form. The fourth column should show the *differences* between the first and the second month's results.

3. Use the asset data and the proprietor's accounts to make up a comparative position statement. The three columns in each side of this statement should show last month's balances, this month's balances and the increase or decrease for each asset and proprietor account.

4. Write a short summary of what these statements indicate about the transactions of the firm to date.

Chapter 5

EFFECTS OF THE CREDIT SYSTEM ON ACCOUNTING

In an earlier discussion, we established that cash disbursements could not properly measure expense because some disbursements applied to future periods and thus represented assets rather than expense. Similarly, we separated cash receipts into two groups: (1) revenue (applicable without restriction to current period operations) and (2) equities (receipts restricted by obligations to be settled or accounted for in the future).

Now we consider the effects of credit on the time dimension of transactions. We have already been concerned with credit in a limited way. Although we were ostensibly concerned with "cash," the Cash in Bank account represented merely a *claim* to cash which the bank was keeping for us. Further, when a customer's check proved uncollectible, we recognized that we had a claim for payment in the form of an account receivable. In this chapter, however, we are concerned with the proper timing of expense and revenue, and we shall see that the effect of credit makes any record of cash receipts and payments inadequate, especially for those situations in which the firm either receives or extends credit. If we wish to measure expense and revenue for a specified time period properly, we shall have to recognize the timing problem created by the system of delayed payments.

Credit Sales of Merchandise

The fact that transactions are not settled by immediate cash exchanges makes accounting even more of a necessity than it would otherwise be. We must have records to be sure that collections are actually made in the proper amounts and at the right time; otherwise we should have to rely on memory, and confusion would be inevitable. When goods are sold on credit, we use an account to record the amount that is due from the specified customer. However, it should be stressed that the sale has occurred, whether or not we have collected cash. The claim arising against the customer is enforceable by law if necessary, and there is no reason to defer the recognition of revenue. Therefore, a *charge* sale is recorded on the *seller's* books as follows:

Accounts Receivable...................................... 460
    Sales Revenue... 460

The receivable account is an asset—a resource available for future operations because it will produce cash. In practice, the firm will keep a separate record for each customer; but since all credit sales will be of the same nature, for convenience we shall here combine them into one account, assuming that individual records are kept in some other form.

The document that signals the sale event typically is a business paper called an *invoice*. The invoice states the names of the parties, indicates what has been shipped or delivered to the customer, the date and method of shipment, and the prices and terms of payment. Invoices are usually written at the time when goods or services are delivered, and they indicate the completion of the seller's part of the sale contract. A typical invoice is illustrated in Figure 5–1.

FIGURE 5–1

Invoice

MERRILL AND SONS
New York, Chicago, San Francisco

Invoice No. 8597
Date 3/11/—
Sold to HALLIBURTON AND EVANS   Purchase Order
        1669 Castleraugh Street   #B-446789
        Dublin, Arizona   Sales Order
        f.o.b. Tulsa, Oklahoma   #P1-B93847
Shipped via S.P. Freight, Collect; Weight 116 lbs.
        Terms: 30 Days from Date of Invoice

Ordered	Shipped	Description	Unit	Amount
5	5	41-X-7172 Motor housings	17.30	$ 86.50
10	10	41-Y-8779 Bearings	24.42	244.20
6	6	72-R-1449 Drive gears	21.55	129.30
				$460.00

The invoice as mailed or given to the purchaser is a notice that the contract has been fulfilled and that payment is therefore expected on the due date (often 30 days after the date of the invoice, though there may be other arrangements). The purchaser thus has information from which to record the cost of the merchandise. However, it is not logical to record a cost until the transaction is complete from the purchaser's viewpoint. This is when the goods are received. Typically, the purchasing firm has a receiving procedure which involves writing a memorandum called a *receiving ticket* to inform those who handle office work that the purchased goods have been received. The receiving ticket, matched with the invoice, is evidence to support the record of cost being incurred by entries on the *purchaser's* books:

```
Merchandise..............................................  460
    Accounts Payable.....................................          460
```

These entries recognize the cost of the items when they are received —the most logical time to make this record. The equity account, Accounts Payable, indicates the amount to be paid to the creditor on the due date.

It should be noted that by this system revenue is recognized by the seller, and the buyer charges his merchandise account with the cost, without any cash changing hands. Neither party waits for a cash transfer to record the sale-purchase transactions. Accrual accounting is based on the *economic* event of transferral of goods; the cash settlement is separate from the purchase transaction, and cash no longer has a direct bearing on the record of the sale or purchase transaction.

When cash actually does change hands, only the asset, Accounts Receivable, and the equity, Accounts Payable, are affected—costs and revenues remain as they were recorded; the receipt and payment of cash are now viewed only as asset or equity changes.

```
                        Seller's Books
Cash in Bank.............................................  460
    Accounts Receivable................................          460

                       Purchaser's Books
Accounts Payable........................................  460
    Cash in Bank........................................          460
```

Credit Sales of Services

Services as well as merchandise may be acquired on credit. Repairs, for example, are often handled on a delayed payment basis. The invoice gives details of materials used and work done, and states the amount and date when payment is expected. Usually the invoice is sent soon after the work is done, and no special attention is needed to record the transaction. Receipt of the invoice (and some check as to whether the service has been received) is sufficient reason to record the cost, and payment is made on the due date, as in the case of merchandise purchases.

Continuous Service

Some costs accrue on a continuous basis; in this class are the costs of service rendered by utility companies. Lines supplying gas, electricity, or water are connected to the customer's establishment, and the service is used as required. Typically, the invoices for such services are prepared from meter readings made monthly or bimonthly. Such invoices may be sent to the customer 10 or 15 days after the meter is read. Thus the cash paid to settle those invoices is a delayed recognition of cost. The meter may be read on the 20th of the month and the bill rendered as of the first of the following month, with payment deferred for still another 10 days. This means that service used in the first 20 days of September will be paid for near October 10; thus the cost is recorded in the wrong month. With bimonthly billing, the meter would be read only every *other* month, and the bills would appear on the first of November, January, and so on. Thus every other month would be charged with two months' consumption; the intervening months would show no service cost at all. Such procedures are wrong when they record costs in a period to which they do not apply, or when they omit costs that are really applicable to the period.

The way to avoid this effect in the cost records is for the customer to read the meters at the proper time to measure costs accurately. Instead of the 20th, meters should be read at the end of the month. The cost may be recorded before the invoices are received since the rates are known. Then at September 30, entries would record the cost incurred:

Electricity Cost.. 35
    Accounts Payable..   35

The bill received shortly thereafter might call for $23. When it is paid, it is charged to the Accounts Payable equity account, leaving a $12 credit balance. This $12 is the "unbilled electricity" at the end of September. By this procedure the cost is properly recorded, and the payments may lag without affecting current records. In this case, the difference in the cost charged to the current month is $12. It is possible that such differences may in fact be inconsequential and therefore ignored on "practical" grounds. But the point of theory is still valid.

Interest

Somewhat like utility services, but perhaps even less tangible, are interest charges. Sometimes the need for current cash requires a firm

FIGURE 5–2

PROMISSORY NOTE

Indianapolis, Indiana   August 10, 19--

Sixty___ days after date, we promise to pay

Fletcher Trust Company_____ or order $1,000.00

One thousand_____no/100 dollars,

together with interest at 6% per annum.

Wilshire Manufacturing Co.

_E. A. Eaton_____ Secretary _M. J. Johnson_____ President

to borrow. The receipt of current cash is evidenced by a promise to pay a larger sum or sums in the future. The basic paper underlying a borrowing transaction is a *promissory note*—an unconditional promise in writing to pay a determinable sum of money on demand, or at some future date. Figure 5–2 shows a simple note form. The interest to be paid on October 9, the maturity date, is $1,000 \times 0.06 \times 60/360$, which works out to $10; the maturity value is $1,010. Issuance of this note by signature and delivery and the concurrent receipt of $1,000 cash is recorded as follows:

Cash in Bank.. 1,000
　Notes Payable..   1,000

The interest, though determinable, is not recorded when the loan is negotiated; the cost of interest applies to the period of the loan, i.e.,

60 days after August 10. The $10 interest is not actually due and payable until October 9. Instead, it "accrues" or grows over the period in which it is earned. Therefore, if financial reports are to be prepared at the end of August, we shall take into account the interest accrued to that date: $1,000 \times 0.06 \times 21/360 = \$3.50$. The entries to record this are:

```
Interest Charges.........................................  3.50
     Accrued Interest Payable.............................          3.50
```

Because there is no invoice or other notice, we must compute and record interest periodically, or at least whenever financial reports are to be prepared.

Use of Accounts to Allocate Costs

In the early part of Chapter 3, we separated costs applicable to the current period from those deferred to future ones. This division may be made formally by the use of additional accounts to record expenses as separated from assets. For instance, the insurance cost as recorded was $84; we divided this into $7 current expense and $77 deferred (asset) cost. This division is usually accomplished in practice by making periodic entries like this:

```
Unexpired Insurance......................................  77
     Insurance.............................................          77
```

Such entries are made whenever it is desired to reflect the operating cost in reports. As a matter of practice, such items can be noted by a review of the items in the trial balance to see that the separation of current from deferred items has been made; alternatively, it is possible to set up a schedule listing all adjustments of this kind so they will be taken care of, as a matter of routine, at the end of each month or other reporting period.

Equipment Costs

One of the cost items separated into current and future amounts was the cost of equipment. While, logically, there is no difference between insurance premiums paid in advance and items of equipment, the accounting is usually different. Because equipment items are so long lived, it may be some years before their cost has been completely assigned. It is desirable, therefore, to maintain the original cost amount separate from the accumulated reductions arising from use in operating periods. This is done by using two accounts to show the asset amount. The first account shows the gross cost of the item, left undisturbed by the periodic write-offs to expense; the other account shows the accumulated effect of cost write-off, as each period's usage of the asset is recorded. Then, we may compare the original cost with the accumulated depreciation, and check the rate of write-off, or the indicated age of the asset. This shows both kinds of data concerning a given equipment item in the trial balance. Entries to record the cost assignment (depreciation) are:

```
Depreciation Expense, Soda Fountain.............................. 11
    Accumulated Depreciation, Soda Fountain....................        11
```

Note that depreciation *is* cost assignment, not provision for replacement, valuation, or appraisal. What we do is merely to amortize (spread out) the cost of the equipment over the period of use; we do not concern ourselves with what it is worth or whether it will be replaced. It is almost certain that it *was* worth at least what was paid for it and it is equally certain that (like all constructed items—buildings, machines, automobiles, furniture, and so forth) it will ultimately end up in the scrap heap. We may guess fairly well how soon that will be. However, we may decide *never* to replace it; it may be unnecessary or undesirable to do so. In any event, the replacement is not measurable or predictable as to cost or form, and we cannot report it in accounting until it occurs. Depreciation is cost assignment, nothing else. Accountants measure from costs or from bargained prices, not from values or undetermined future events.

The use of separate accounts for each equipment item results in (1) an unaltered record of the cost, (2) a current expense account, and (3) a cumulative record of the absorption or assignment of cost. The cost record, less the accumulated depreciation, is the asset amount that appears in the position statement; this net figure is the unamortized remainder of cost, which is applicable to future operations. Similar procedures apply to other depreciable assets.

More Complex Accruals—Payroll

Some costs accumulate over time in a specified pattern but are tied together in various ways. The typical cost item of this kind is payroll. The amounts paid to employees are not the actual amounts of their earnings for the period, nor do they reflect the employer's cost. Correct payroll expense can be recorded only by recognizing the obligations arising out of the employment contract; these are settled by cash payments at different times; such payments are only indirectly related to the rates of pay. An example will make this clear.

Practically every employer is subject to some taxes based upon payroll. Of these, the commonest are the Federal Insurance Contribution (FIC) and those amounts levied by the states and the federal government for unemployment compensation purposes. The FICA tax is based upon wages earned by any employee up to $7,800 per year; the total payroll thus established is taxed at 5.2 percent under current law. Unemployment compensation taxes vary in different states, and with the "experience rating" of the employer. The federal unemployment compensation tax may be as little as $\frac{5}{10}$ or $\frac{1}{2}$ percent, if the state tax is as much as 2.7 percent of a payroll including the earnings of employees up to $3,800 per year. But the state tax may (in California for instance) be as high as 3.5 percent. In such a case, the employer's total tax may be as much as 9.2 percent on the employee earnings up to $3,000 for any one employee in any one year. Earnings of more than $3,000 but less than $9,000 per employee are taxed (FIC) at 5.2 percent. Such tax provisions require records to determine the accumulated earnings to date for each employee so that the tax will not be paid on nontaxable payroll.

Taking the rates mentioned (the actual rate will depend on the particular situation, as indicated above) an employer may determine that his total employee earnings for a given quarter are $65,000. If this is late enough in the calendar year, some of these earnings may be excluded because the statutory total has been reached for some employees; we shall ignore this. The nominal earnings of the employee are the basic part of the employer's expense for the quarter and are recorded as follows:

Payroll Expense. 65,000
    Employee Earnings Payable.   65,000

This payroll might entail payroll taxes, 9.2 percent of $65,000, or $5,980; the tax obligation would be recorded:

Payroll Tax Expense. 5,980
    Payroll Tax Liabilities.   5,980

The fact that some of this would be payable to state and some to federal agencies might suggest the use of separate accounts for each; but we ignore this here for simplicity.

Now, assuming that the employees are paid the entire amount of their earnings, we consider the effect of taxes levied on the employee. He pays taxes of the same amount as the employer (5.2 percent) for FICA, based on the same $7,800 per year ceiling. But he also is assessed personal income taxes at rates determined by the amount of his earnings and his exemptions. The employer is required to withhold the amounts of these taxes and remit them to appropriate agencies. Thus the employee is paid something less than the amount of his earnings for at least two reasons. In some states and cities there are other taxes that are collected by withholding, and these all require the maintenance of records for each employee as well as reports to the agencies involved. We are not here concerned with such records, but the amount of those withheld taxes represents another kind of tax liability which arises when the employee is paid. If the entire employee earnings for the quarter are settled, the amount of FICA taxes will be the same as that computed for the employer (5.2 percent of $65,000 = $3,380) but the personal income taxes will have to be calculated separately for each employee. Suppose these add to a total of $11,700; the amount paid to the employees will then be $65,000 less $3,380 less $11,700, or $49,920. The settlement of the payroll would then be recorded:

Employee Earnings Payable	65,000	
Payroll Tax Liabilities		15,080
Cash in Bank		49,920

The withheld taxes payable are remitted to the appropriate agencies when required; but the time interval is quite short—not longer than the end of the quarter.

Sometimes all the withheld taxes are recorded in the same account as that used to record the employ*er*'s tax liability. This does no harm so long as there are detailed records to show how much should be paid to each agency and when. For financial reports of the enterprise, such details are seldom of much significance so long as the total obligations are shown at the proper amount.

One other complication must be noted here, however. It seldom happens that the amount of the employee earnings during a period is actually settled within that period, if only because it takes time to calculate and prepare the payroll checks. Generally, the accounting period and the pay period are not the same. While monthly salaries may be anticipated and payment made immediately at the close of the month, salaries payable weekly will hardly ever coincide with monthly report periods. Earnings that have to be calculated for each week to include payment for actual hours worked, including overtime premiums, sick pay, and such, cannot possibly be settled within the same accounting period in which the work was done and the payroll cost incurred.

When the payroll to be settled has been computed for a given pay period, the payroll settlement entry will be set up for the *pay period* rather than for the fiscal (accounting) period. Thus, in our example, there might have been 13 payments for different amounts than the $65,000 total for the quarter as indicated above; indeed, there is almost always some net amount of unpaid payroll at the close of any accounting period. The payment of payroll and related taxes is important to keep track of, but the payroll expense must include the total earnings and the relevant employer taxes accrued as outlined above. Cash payments do not properly measure payroll expense. There are other questions with respect to overtime premiums and other kinds of labor costs, but full consideration of payroll control is not essential at this point. We can, however, recognize here (1) why we cannot record transactions only in terms of cash receipts and payments, (2) why it is easier to measure costs by obligations or liabilities as they accrue, and (3) why it is desirable even in a small business to use systematic accounting methods to keep track of costs in terms of the liabilities that are incurred, instead of merely the payments that are made.

Summary

We have now transformed our cash record system into an *accrual* accounting system to record events *when they happen*, not when cash settlements are made. We have seen that cash may be received at various times from different sources; however, the delivery of goods or services is the revenue-determining event, not the cash received. We have learned that some costs are explicit—i.e., they are evidenced by invoices or other papers; but other events and costs are not signalled in this way. We may have to make entries even before invoices are received if costs are to be recorded properly. We have also seen that complex transactions such as payrolls make it essential to view and record such transactions on a full accrual basis. The accrual basis requires the recording of costs and revenues when they occur. Cash receipts are usually incidental to the recognition of revenue, and cash disbursements are merely the settlement of, or the reduction of liabilities recorded previously in equity accounts.

We are now ready to consider a reasonably realistic illustration of accounting on an accrual basis.

Illustration

The Martin Trading Company began business January 2 of the current year. Mr. J. M. Martin invested $20,000 cash to start the venture. During the ensuing 12 months, the following transactions occurred—presented in summary terms. That is, all similar transactions are combined with others of the same kind. If this had not been done, transactions starred (*) would be repeated, some of them many times in the course of the year.

CASH RECEIPTS

(1)	Proprietor's investment, as stated above.............	$ 20,000	
*(2)	Collections from customers for merchandise sold.......	140,000	$160,000

DISBURSEMENTS

*(3)	To other firms who supplied merchandise on credit.....	$ 96,400	
*(4)	To Realty Management Company for rent of building.....................................	8,400	
*(5)	To employees for payroll settlements (after deductions for taxes withheld, $6,800).........................	38,200	
*(6)	To government agencies for withheld and other payroll taxes.....................................	9,150	
(7)	To Flemington Equipment Company for store fixtures......................................	4,000	
*(8)	To utility companies for gas, water, electricity.......	950	157,100
	Cash on hand per books, December 31..........		$ 2,900

From this tabulation of cash transactions, it would seem that the business did not have a very good year; indeed, the cash balance as stated is quite small, even for a firm of this kind. However, the results of operations cannot be seen from the cash data alone; other transactions involving the recognition of revenue and assignment of costs must also be taken into account:

TRANSACTIONS NOT DIRECTLY AFFECTING CASH

*(9)	Sales of merchandise to customers on account.........	$150,000
*(10)	Merchandise and supplies received on order...........	100,000
*(11)	Payroll costs incurred (before tax deductions) to and including December 31......................	46,900
*(12)	Tax withholdings on payroll.......................	6,800
*(13)	Employer's payroll taxes..........................	4,390
*(14)	Total gas, water, and electricity consumed for the year..	1,100
(15)	Depreciation of store fixtures (10% per year)........	400

All these data may be arranged into entries as given below:

(1) and (2)

Cash on Hand and in Bank..........................	160,000	
J. M. Martin, Investment......................		20,000
Accounts Receivable..........................		140,000

(3) to (8)

Accounts Payable................................	96,400	
Building Rent Cost...............................	8,400	
Employee Earnings Payable.......................	38,200	
Payroll Tax Liabilities...........................	9,150	
Store Fixtures Cost..............................	4,000	
Accounts Payable................................	950	
Cash on Hand and in Bank......................		157,100

(9)

Accounts Receivable..............................	150,000	
Sales Revenue...................................		150,000

(10)

Merchandise and Supplies Inventory...................	100,000	
Accounts Payable..............................		100,000

(11)

Payroll Expense..................................	46,900	
Employee Earnings Payable......................		46,900

(12)

Employee Earnings Payable.........................	6,800	
Payroll Tax Liabilities..........................		6,800

(13)

Employer's Payroll Tax Expense......................	4,390	
Payroll Tax Liabilities..........................		4,390

(14)

Gas, Water, and Electricity Cost......................	1,100	
Accounts Payable..............................		1,100

(15)

Depreciation Expense, Store Fixtures....................	400	
Accumulated Depreciation, Store Fixtures...........		400

The reader will note that the merchandise and supplies cost is for all such items acquired. To separate the expense from the asset element in this $100,000, we take inventory and find $20,000 (cost) of goods on hand. This calls for the following entries:

(16)

Merchandise and Supplies Expense......................	80,000	
Merchandise and Supplies Inventory................		80,000

When the indicated debit and credit amounts are entered in the summary ledger accounts, the pages of the summary ledger will appear as shown in Figure 5–3. The accounts are then reviewed to separate those which cover the operations of the year (flow of revenues and expense) from those which reflect status at the end of the year. The revenue and expense items are shown on top of page 90.

FIGURE 5–3

MARTIN TRADING COMPANY
Summary Ledger Accounts
(At December 31, with all the Year's Transactions Entered)

Cash on Hand and in Bank				J. M. Martin, Investment			
(1) (2)	160,000	(3)–(8)	157,100			(1)	20,000

Accounts, Receivable				Accounts Payable			
(9)	150,000	(2)	140,000	(3)	96,400	(10)	100,000
				(8)	950	(14)	1,100

Building Rent Cost				Employee Earnings Payable			
(4)	8,400			(5)	38,200	(11)	46,900
				(12)	6,800		

Payroll Tax Liabilities				Store Fixtures Cost			
(6)	9,150	(12)	6,800	(7)	4,000		
		(13)	4,390				

Sales Revenue				Merchandise and Supplies Inventory			
		(9)	150,000	(10)	100,000	(16)	80,000

Payroll Expense				Employer's Payroll Tax Expense			
(11)	46,900			(13)	4,390		

Gas, Water, Electricity Cost				Depreciation Expense, Store Fixtures			
(14)	1,100			(15)	400		

Accumulated Depreciation, Store Fixtures				Merchandise and Supplies Expense			
		(15)	400	(16)	80,000		

Account	Debit Balances	Credit Balances
Building rent cost..........................	$ 8,400	
Employer's payroll taxes expense...........	4,390	
Sales revenue.............................		$150,000
Payroll expense...........................	46,900	
Gas, water, and electricity cost..............	1,100	
Depreciation Expense, store fixtures..........	400	
Merchandise and supplies expense............	80,000	
Total..............................	$141,190	$150,000

The accounts making up this part of the trial balance indicate an excess of revenue over expense of $8,810, which suggests a liability for federal income taxes.

Federal income taxation is an involved subject, and it cannot be dealt with in detail here. The amount of the tax does not depend upon accounting income but upon the legal or taxable income; some items are interpreted and reported differently for tax purposes than they would be for typical business reports. However, we may assume for the purposes of this illustration that the federal income tax liability arising from Mr. Martin's business is 22% of $8,810, or $1,938 for this year. The entry expressing this is:

(17)

Provision for Federal Income Tax.......................... 1938		
Income Tax Payable....................................		1938

The account debited represents a distribution of income which is subtracted in computing the net earnings retained in the business. Even though the income tax is not immediately due, the available income is reduced by the tax obligation. The credit should be carried to a special account for federal income tax payable, because this tax is different from other taxes in that it is determined by the income, even though technically defined. Taking into account the computation of income tax, the data covering the operations of the period may be summarized in a statement of earnings in Figure 5–4, page 91.

The items of accountability that appear in the report of earnings are only part of the accounts in the summary ledger. The other account balances are arranged in the form of a statement of position (sometimes called a balance sheet). Such a statement appears in Figure 5–5, page 91. It should be noted that this statement follows the classification of current and long term items suggested in Chapter 4; but here it is applied to the equities as well as to the assets. Here, as before, "current" does not refer to the period of time just closed; a current asset is one which is expected to be converted to cash within the next ensuing year at the latest. Similarly, a current debt or current liability

FIGURE 5–4

MARTIN TRADING COMPANY

Report of Earnings
Year Ending December 31, 19—

Revenue from sales..........................		$150,000
Expense:		
Merchandise and supplies expense............	$80,000	
Payroll expense...........................	46,900	
Employer's payroll tax expense...............	4,390	
Gas, water, and electricity cost..............	1,100	
Building rent cost.........................	8,400	
Depreciation expense, store fixtures..........	400	
Total Expense.......................		141,190
Operating net margin......................		$ 8,810
Provision for federal income tax.............		1,938
Retained Earnings.........................		$ 6,872

FIGURE 5–5

MARTIN TRADING COMPANY

(J. M. Martin, Proprietor)
Statement of Position
At December 31, 19—

ASSETS			EQUITIES		
Current Assets:			Current Debt:		
Cash on Hand and in			Accounts Payable........	$ 3,750	
Bank................	$ 2,900		Employe Earnings		
Accounts Receivable.....	10,000		Payable..............	1,900	
Merchandise and			Payroll Tax		
Supplies............	20,000	$32,900	Liabilities............	2,040	
Long Term Assets:			Income Tax Payable.....	1,938	$ 9,628
Store Fixtures..........	$ 4,000		Ownership Equity:		
			J. M. Martin, Invest-		
Less Accumulated			ment................	$20,000	
Depreciation........	400	$ 3,600	Earnings Retained.......	6,872	26,872
Total Assets......		$36,500	Total Equities.....		$36,500

is one that is to be paid within the ensuing year—presumably from the funds arising from the conversion of current assets. Long term debts are those which will not need to be paid until after one year.

Summary

This chapter has brought the effects of the credit system to bear on the operations of accounting. The discussion showed that we must go beyond the measurement of cash receipts and payments— even beyond the timing of collections and expenditures as between current and future periods. Cash settlements of transactions may be delayed by credit arrangements. This means that the proper reporting of revenue and expense for a period must be based on the economic events, not on cash receipts or payments. We have used the mechanics of accounting and the added accounts for assets and equities to hold over, or to take up, costs and other transactions when future cash payments or receipts are *arranged* for, rather than when cash changes hands. Only by doing this can we record and report the economic ebbs and flows which we call revenue and expense. The use of accounting to time the *economic* effects of transactions properly, apart from their purely cash-flow results, is important. By using proper timing to reflect sales costs and other data, we can obtain more detailed and precise measurements of revenue and expense and more realistic data about the economic position of an enterprise.

QUESTIONS

1. How important are credit transactions in the financial activities of individuals? Of business enterprises, generally? Name the ways in which you, personally, may be involved in credit transactions.

2. Does credit make accounting records more or less important than they would be otherwise? What kind of accounting records would be needed to record ordinary credit sales, payable within 30 days or at the end of the month (EOM)?

3. Why do we record revenue from a credit sale when we have actually received no cash? What is the evidence that a sale has occurred?

4. How does an individual who makes a credit purchase know the amount of his purchase? How does he record a purchase "on account"? What evidence does a business firm have that a purchase has been made? What procedures are necessary to make this a systematic process?

5. What happens in the accounts of the seller and the buyer when a remittance is made to settle for goods received earlier?

6. What kinds of service are typically acquired "on account"? What evidence is there of such acquisitions when there is no physical receipt of goods? Upon what basis are the costs of such services recorded—e.g., utility services, repairs and maintenance service by outside firms, interest, payroll?

7. What is reflected in the account, accumulated depreciation? What is the relation of this account to the periodic depreciation charge; to the cost of the asset to which it refers?

8. Ought a company maintain a separate account for each item of machinery, equipment, building, or other durable assets? Should there be a separate account to record the accumulated depreciation of each asset item?

9. Since the accumulated depreciation account has a credit balance, it could be confused with an equity. What is the basis for distinguishing between these two interpretations?

10. What features of payroll make the recording of payroll costs complex? Which of these are additional costs to the employer and which are not?

11. How many different accounts could be made use of in accounting for a payroll involving eight or more employees performing *different kinds* of work? When would each of these accounts be debited or credited, and what calculations would be required, assuming (1) that each employee has earned less than $3,000 during the current year to date, (2) that the employer is subject to maximum payroll taxes, and (3) that personal income tax withholdings apply to each employee at the rate of 18 percent?

12. What does accrual accounting involve that makes it more correct and informative than cash basis accounting as described in Chapter 2? Note that some of these differences appear outside Chapter 5 (i.e., some were discussed in Chapters 3 and 4).

PROBLEMS

Berkey Mercantile Company

The following data were taken from the summary ledger of the Berkey Mercantile Company, at June 30, this year. Prepare a report of earnings for the six month period and a position statement as at the close of the period.

Accounts payable..		$ 11,000
Accounts receivable.....................................	$ 20,000	
Accumulated plant depreciation..........................		9,000
Cash in bank...	6,000	
Common stock issued....................................		23,000
Current payroll costs (wages, salaries, and payroll taxes)......	24,000	
Depreciation of plant...................................	2,000	
Federal income tax charges..............................	5,000	
Insurance expense......................................	1,000	
Interest charges..	2,000	
Liability for income and other taxes.......................		3,000
Merchandise cost of goods sold...........................	36,000	
Mortgage loan payable..................................		14,000
Plant (land, buildings, equipment)........................	40,000	
Retained earnings......................................		4,500
Sales revenue..		80,000
Unsold goods on hand...................................	12,000	
Unexpired insurance premiums...........................	500	
Wages and salaries payable..............................		4,000
Totals...	148,500	148,500

Model Stores Company

Model Store Company began business on January 2, by issuing 3,600 shares of common stock for $36,000 cash. The cash was deposited in the Mutual Bank. Then the company acquired land at a cost of $8,000 and a building costing $12,000 for $5,000 cash and a $15,000 mortgage note which bears interest at 8% payable semi-annually. Life of the building is 20 years.

During the month, the company
(1)   Purchased merchandise costing $21,000 on 30 days credit terms.
(2)   Sold merchandise which cost $15,000 for $19,000. Of this $3,000 was for cash, and $16,000 "on account."
(3)   Insurance coverage was arranged for at an annual premium of $180; the premium is payable February 10.
(4)   Salaries paid, gross $1,500, less withheld income taxes $400, FIC withholdings 5.2%.
(5)   At the end of January, salaries earned for the month were figured at $3,000. Salaries are subject to employer's payroll taxes of 7.9%.
(6)   The taxes withheld from employes were paid on January 31.

Required:

Write entries in journal form to express the preceding transactions, and make other entries needed to prepare correct financial reports at the end of the month. Write up the financial reports in proper form.

Horton's Furniture Store

Mr. H. C. Horton started a retail business at the beginning of this year, by purchasing land ($10,000) building ($50,000) and equipment ($13,000). He had only $50,000 to invest; after arranging for a $30,000 mortgage at 8½% interest, he had only $7,000 in cash. He supplemented this with a loan from a cousin (giving him a note due in two years for a face amount of $8,000 with interest at 10%) and commenced business on January 2. During the year, the following transactions occurred:

Purchases of merchandise (on credit)		$154,516
Sales of merchandise (on credit; includes sales taxes)		202,130
Cash collections from customers		188,410
Cash payments:		
Settlement of invoices for merchandise	119,826	
Advance premium for 2 yr. insurance policy	474	
*Commissions paid to salesmen	5,852	
To Union Parcel Delivery Service	2,170	
*Office salaries and wages	7,160	
Property taxes	1,510	
Sales taxes	6,485	
To H. C. Horton for personal use	6,000	
		$178,477

*Includes payroll taxes to 8 percent and all withholdings.

At the end of the year, the following additional information was available:

(1) Merchandise inventory, end of year, $26,220.
(2) Additional property taxes accrued, $210.
(3) Depreciation of building, $1,000; of equipment, $2,600.
(4) Unpaid commissions, $220; unpaid office salaries, $112; unpaid delivery service charges, $46.
(5) Interest accrued on mortgage, $1,950.
(6) Interest accrued on note payable, $800.
(7) Estimated income tax liability, 22% of net income.

Required:

1. Prepare a skeleton account ledger with all transactions entered.
2. Prepare a Report of Earnings and Statement of Position in proper form.

Southern Company

There are 70 persons on the payroll of this company; all of them are subject to F.I.C. and unemployment taxes:

(1) The F.I.C. tax for employers is based on total earnings of workers, up to $7,800 per year. The current tax rate is 5.2 percent.
(2) A similar tax is levied on each employe's earnings up to $7,800 in any year. This is collected by deductions from earnings when wages or salaries are paid. The current rate is 5.2 percent.
(3) The employer is also subject to a payroll tax to cover unemployment compensation. This is nominally 2.7 percent of wages paid up to $3,000 per year, but the rate may be lowered by state Commissions, for those firms whose experience patterns justify this. The Southern Company is currently subject to a state tax rate of 1.8%.
(4) A related tax is imposed by the Federal Government; this may be regarded as $5/10$ or $1/2$ of one percent on wages paid up to $3,000 per year.

Various other payroll deductions were made in the processing of payroll settlements. Individual Federal Income Taxes must be withheld on all earnings in excess of exemptions claimed by the worker. The company has a contributory health insurance plan, for which premiums are deducted once in each month. There is a union check-off arrangement, by which the company is required to deduct union dues from earnings, and remit the amounts thus withheld to the union. Sometimes, employes purchase merchandise from the Southern Company, and pay for it by payroll deductions. There is also an Employes' Credit-Union, and there are deductions made for savings deposits or payments on loans.

During the two week period ended February 28, the 70 workers had earned a total of $14,500. When this payroll was settled on March 5, the payroll department had accumulated the following amounts for deductions:

Individual income tax withholdings required...........................	$1,802.00
Union dues payable......................................	140.00
Health Insurance Premiums, for February...............................	659.20
Current payments on employe accounts receivable......................	300.00
Authorized payments to the credit-union...............................	750.00

The withheld taxes are payable by immediate deposit to the government's account in the local Federal Reserve Bank. Other taxes are settled quarterly; the next settlement date is April 15.

Required:
1. Prepare entries for accruing salaries and wages at February 28.
2. Prepare entries to record settlement of the payroll, March 5, and transfers of money required at that date.

Steadman Wholesale Company

Balance Sheet
at October 31, 19—

ASSETS

Current Assets:			
Cash in Bank..............................		$ 14,400	
Accounts Receivable.......................		63,600	
Merchandise Inventory.....................		150,200	
Unexpired Insurance.......................		700	
Total Current Assets................			$228,900
Long Term Assets:			
Warehouse Equipment......................	$11,500		
Less Accumulated Depreciation.........	2,400	$ 9,100	
Delivery Trucks............................	$43,700		
Less Accumulated Depreciation.........	20,900	22,800	
Office Equipment..........................	$ 8,700		
Less Accumulated Depreciation.........	1,300	7,400	
Total Long Term Assets.............			$ 39,300
Total Assets......................			$268,200

EQUITIES

Current Debt:			
Accounts Payable.........................		$ 31,400	
Notes Payable, Current Portion.............		15,000	
Unpaid Payroll............................		17,100	
Payroll Tax Liabilities.....................		2,000	
Income Tax Liability......................		12,000	
Interest Payable..........................		600	
Total Current Debt................			$ 78,100
Long Term Debt: Equipment Notes Payable.....			30,000
Total Debt......................			$108,100
Stockholder Equity:			
Common Stock...........................		$100,000	
Retained Earnings.........................		60,100	
Total Stockholder Equity............			$160,100
Total Equities....................			$268,200

The October 31 position of the Steadman Wholesale Company appears above. During the month of November, the following transactions occurred:

1. Merchandise sales, $198,000, of which $50,000 were for cash.
2. Cost of merchandise sold, $144,000.
3. New delivery truck purchased for $3,000 cash.
4. Merchandise purchases, $90,200.
5. Additional common stock issued for $30,000 cash.
6. Cash collected from customers, $96,400.
7. Warehouse rent paid for November, $4,000.
8. Salaries and wages paid $34,600; this was net after FIC tax deductions, $1,530, and withheld income taxes of employes, $4,870.
9. Bills received for various expenses: (utilities, office supplies, truck maintenance, gas and oil), $8,200.
10. Depreciation of warehouse equipment, $330; of delivery trucks, $930, and of office equipment, $130.
11. Current portion of notes paid, with interest of $660, total $15,660.
12. Paid $99,700 to various creditors. (Accounts payable.)
13. Wages and salaries earned by employes during the month of November, $33,000; of this, $30,000 was subject to 8.3% employer's taxes.
14. Insurance expired for November, $350.
15. Taxes (withheld from employes) paid, $6,400.
16. Corporate income tax (figured on net operating margin less interest charges) at 22% on first $25,000 per year, 48% on amount over this.

Required:

A. Set up ledger accounts, and enter the October 31 balances.
B. Enter the November transactions, adding accounts as needed.
C. Prepare an earnings report and position statement in good form.

Apex Cleaners and Dyers, Inc.

Incorporated on January 2 of this year, this company raised its initial capital by issuing 30,000 shares of common stock for $150,000 cash.

On February 1, the company acquired a building suitable for its operations; the price was $30,000 for the land and $200,000 for the building. $20,000 cash was paid, and a mortgage of $210,000 was given in payment. The mortgage note called for interest at 8 percent per year, payable semiannually on February and August 1.

Operating equipment was installed in early February at a cost of $250,000; of this, $130,000 was paid in cash, the remaining $120,000 to be paid in six semiannual installments (August 1 and February 1) with interest at 7.2 percent per year (payable semiannually). After the installations had been completed, the firm opened for business on March 1.

Transactions for the period March 1 to June 30, inclusive, were as follows:

NoncashTransactions:

Sales and services billed to customers....................	$152,550
Merchandise and supplies purchased.....................	35,000
Merchandise and supplies used or sold...................	26,000
Employee gross earnings for the period..................	84,000
Employer's payroll taxes accrued for the period...........	6,972
Property and local taxes accrued........................	4,000
Insurance expired for the period.......................	500
Depreciation of building and equipment..................	8,600
Interest payable at close of business, June 30..............	10,750
Dividend declared June 30, payable July 15...............	1,000
Estimated corporation income tax to June 30, 22% of operating net margin, less interest charges	

Cash Transactions:

Receipts:

Collections from customers..........................	$124,000	
Bank loan, arranged May 1 (9 percent interest)..........	50,000	$174,000

Payments:

To trade creditors for merchandise and supplies..........			32,000
To reduce bank loan (June 30).......................	$ 40,000		
Interest thereon, through June 30....................	600		40,600
To employees for wages and salaries (net after taxes).......			66,774
Payroll and employee income taxes:			
5.2% employer's FICA tax.........................	$ 4,056		
2.7% employer's state unemployment compensation tax..	2,106		
0.5% employer's federal unemployment compensation tax...	390		
5.2% employee's FICA deduction....................	4,056		
Employee income taxes withheld....................	7,170		17,778
Commissions, power, repairs (miscellaneous services).......			10,250
Property, liability, and other insurance....................			1,200
Total Payments....................................			$168,602

Required:

Record all these transactions in skeleton ledger accounts and prepare financial reports for the period ended June 30.

Jamison Company

The following data are correct, but you are to use them to prepare a statement of income and a position statement at the end of the year.

Trial Balances at Beginning and End of the Year

	January 1	*December 31*
Cash on hand and in bank........................	$ 6,200	$ 5,700
Customer accounts receivable....................	21,000	27,000
Merchandise inventory...........................	28,000	32,000
Interest accrued receivable.......................	500	300
Prepaid general administration costs..............	2,000	3,000
Investments....................................	10,000	7,000
Building and equipment..........................	30,000	34,000
Total Debits....................	$97,700	$109,000

	January 1	December 31
Accrued payrolls and social security taxes........	2,200	2,100
Allowance for depreciation......................	9,000	10,200
Accounts payable for merchandise................	12,000	14,000
Property taxes payable........................	3,500	4,200
Mortgage payable............................	20,000	18,000
Common shares $100 par......................	28,000	33,000
Retained earnings............................	23,000	27,500
Total credits...........................	$97,700	$109,000

Statement of Cash Receipts and Disbursements

Receipts:		
Collections from customers....................		$159,000
Interest......................................		800
Investments sold.............................		4,000
Common shares issued........................		5,000
Total Receipts...........................		$168,800
Disbursements:		
To Merchandise creditors....................	$95,000	
On mortgage...............................	2,000	
Property taxes..............................	5,800	
General expenses............................	13,000	
Additions, building and equipment..............	4,000	
Dividends....................................	1,500	
Payrolls and fringe benefits....................	41,200	
Federal income taxes.........................	5,600	
Interest......................................	1,200	
Total Disbursements.....................		$169,300
Decrease in Cash over the Year................		$ 500

Wackbard Company

The position statement data for this firm at the beginning and the end of a fiscal year were as follows:

ASSETS	Beginning	End
Cash on hand and in bank................	$ 20,000	$ 10,500
Accounts receivable......................	36,000	50,000
Merchandise inventory...................	45,000	60,000
Unexpired insurance and rent.............	2,000	1,000
Land, buildings, and equipment...........	40,000	40,000
Total Assets......................	$143,000	$161,500
CREDITS		
Allowance for depreciation................	$ 16,000	$ 18,000
Accounts payable........................	30,000	40,000
Mortgage payable........................	20,000	17,000
Capital stock...........................	50,000	50,000
Retained earnings........................	26,500	35,000
Unpaid federal income taxes..............	500	1,500
Total Equities......................	$143,000	$161,500

The statement of earnings for this period showed sales revenues of $100,000; cost of goods sold, $50,000; and insurance and rent expense,

$3,000. There were various other operating expenses totaling $26,000, and interest charges of $1,500. The federal income tax *paid* was $9,000, and $1,000 in cash dividends were distributed to shareholders.

Required:

Assuming that all goods and services acquired during the year were acquired on credit, use the data given to derive a statement of cash receipts and disbursements.

Chapter 6

REFINEMENTS IN
MEASUREMENT OF REVENUE

Revenue is an important aspect of business operations. The determination of revenue is one of the most important tasks of the accountant. There are various factors that affect the timing and measurement of revenue; legal, economic, and technological factors make the problem somewhat complex in many situations. We are concerned in this chapter with the general question of when revenue actually comes into existence, so that it may be reported correctly and usefully.

Nature and Importance of Revenue

Revenue is the resource inflow that arises from the delivery of goods or services; it is measured by the contributions which customers agree to make, to compensate the firm for its product or service. This inflow may be measured by the amount of added assets (cash, receivables, or other resources) that arise from sales; but revenue is not the new assets. Rather, revenue is the source from which those assets arose—revenue is the stream of inflowing resources measured over a period of time.

Revenues are essential to the continued existence of the firm, for unless customers are willing to pay enough to cover the costs of producing the firm's services, the process of production cannot continue for very long. The function of the firm is to make its output available in the market. The production of that output may be financed initially in various ways, but the funds to cover the costs of operation must come ultimately from revenue.

Revenue is the basic measure of the volume of activity in a firm or in an industry. One firm is larger than another if the revenue stream is larger—if it does more "business" as measured by revenue. The growth of a business firm is often measured by the increase of its revenue. Revenue measures the "value added" by the firm's economic effort. It provides a market measure of the productivity of the firm.

Even more important, fluctuations in revenue amounts give an indication of the firm's operations relative to other companies or even general industrial activity. Changes in revenue over time may be mere seasonal fluctuations, or they may indicate cyclical patterns. They may also reveal growth rates which may be expected or which deviate from expectations. Watching the movement of revenue figures gives management a clue to the internal and external conditions that affect the firm's results. Many of management's decisions revolve around the actual and expected amounts of revenue because production and other plans are geared to meet customer preferences which gain expression through potential or actual revenue.

Finally, revenue is the market value of the gross output of the firm during a particular period. It is thus the starting point from which we can establish income or earnings from operations. The income figure (revenue less expense) shows the *net* productivity of the firm; it shows the excess of product value over the costs of producing and distributing that output. To establish the income of the firm, we must establish a dependable revenue figure. It should not be hard to see that revenue measurements are important and that they should be made carefully.

Recognition of Revenue

We have already seen that a basic question with regard to all transactions is that of proper timing. The timing of revenue transactions raises a number of issues related to legal as well as economic factors. Revenue arises from a transaction in which the customer receives some product or service for which he is expected to pay. The expectation of payment is justified because the agreement between buyer and seller is viewed as legally binding. The offer to sell (or the offer to buy) becomes an obligation to do so when it has been accepted by the other party; generally, the law will enforce the discharge of such obligations, with very few exceptions. The fact that agreements made in good faith are viewed as enforceable obligations is the basis for much of the confidence which underlies the entire system of business affairs.

It should be noted, however, that although the agreement may be valid and enforceable, it specifies only the intent of the parties. I may agree to sell a book for $5 and a customer may agree to pay $5 for it; this contract, however, is not the sale. The sale occurs when the subject of the contract actually changes hands. Then, the delivery of the goods or services discharges the seller from his obligation and gives him the right to receive payment. Thus, the typical signal for the recognition of revenue is the seller's delivery of the goods or services to the buyer.

In the great bulk of business situations, this is the reason why an invoice is the basis for recording sales and costs. The invoice relates the terms of the sales agreement to the items delivered; it is the seller's notice to the buyer that he has performed his part of the arrangement and that he expects payment according to the agreed terms. Of course there are a number of complications that may be involved, such as partial shipments, substitutions, and so forth; but the basic criterion for recognizing revenue is the delivery of goods or services. This procedure is followed even though the measurements may be only approximate. For instance, it may be quite difficult to establish just when professional services of an attorney or an engineer are delivered. However, even though the measurements may not be precise, or taken at a time when we would like them to be made, the underlying logic is that delivery of service is the basis for revenue recognition.

Variants of Sale Contracts: Cash with Order

One variation in the basic pattern of a sale is the case in which payment is made *before* the goods are delivered. If the customer pays cash with the order (as in the case of mail-order sales), he is merely making a tender of cash incidental to the contract. Since the sale itself is not complete because delivery has not been made, the proper record of the cash receipts would be credited to an equity account as follows:

Cash on Hand. 50
    Customer Deposits. 50

Then, when the goods or services have been delivered, the equity credit may be transferred to revenue. If a part of the goods paid for in advance are delivered and a cash refund is made for the remainder, settlement of this deposit equity would require the following entries:

Customer Deposits.. 43
    Sales Revenue..   43

and

Customer Deposits.. 7
    Cash in Bank..   7

The important aspect of deposits made with orders is that although new assets actually have been contributed by a customer, there is a restriction involved in the obligation to deliver goods and services or to refund cash. This restriction precludes the recognition of revenue because the receipt of cash is contingent upon the completion of the contract.

On Approval Sales

Sometimes goods are delivered to customers on a conditional basis, that is, with the privilege of return after examination and trial. After a specified interval, the customer is expected either to pay for or send back the goods. Goods not returned at the close of the trial period are considered sold, and the customer is expected to pay for them in the usual or specified terms. But such an arrangement is not a sale until the approval or trial period expires. The fact that the customer may avoid the transaction entirely during the trial period makes the whole contract executory and incomplete until its conditional nature disappears; there is no valid expectation of payment until the "on approval" condition is removed. Therefore, the proper treatment of an approval sale would be to record the transfer of merchandise not as a cost of goods sold but as a special kind of inventory:

Cost of Goods Shipped to Customers on Approval.................. 65
    Merchandise Inventory......................................   65

These entries merely transfer the *cost* of the goods from the regular Merchandise Inventory account to a special one to show that the goods have been sent out. But the fact of delivery is not sufficient in this case to support a sale because of the conditions in the contract. The entries given above would be reversed if the goods were returned before the approval period had expired:

Merchandise Inventory.. 65
    Cost of Goods Shipped to Customers on Approval..............   65

Costs incurred for transportation or to recondition the goods to make them resaleable are charged as ordinary expenses. Those services were given to the customer even though he did not pay for them. It should be noted that revenue is not a recovery of costs; it is merely a resource inflow arising from a completed sale. Expenses are costs of rendering the services from which revenue is expected to arise; there may be costs of rendering service (expenses) even when there is no revenue.

If the approval period expires or if the customer otherwise agrees to keep the goods and pay for them, the entries then indicated are:

Accounts Receivable..	100	
Cost of Goods Sold...	65	
Cost of Goods Shipped to Customers on Approval...........		65
Sales Revenue..		100

The later receipt of cash would be treated as any normal collection by credit to Accounts Receivable.

Of course, approval sales would have to be recorded on special invoices and some follow-up maintained to see that goods were either paid for or returned. But these procedures would not alter the accounting entries given above.

Consignments

In order to get wider distribution for their products, a firm (designated as the consignor) might send goods to various retail stores or other agents (designated as the consignees) for them to sell as agents for the consignor. The consignment agreement requires that the agents will display, demonstrate, and sell the goods; if they are sold, the agent will remit the proceeds of sale, less commissions and expenses incurred. When the goods are shipped to the agent there is delivery, but no sale, since there is no transfer of ownership. Hence on the consignor's books the shipment would be treated much like an "on approval" merchandise transfer:

Goods on Consignment......................................	80	
Merchandise Inventory..................................		80

The cost of the goods would thus be transferred to a special inventory account. If there were transportation charges incurred to ship these goods, this cost would be added to the inventory, as it would be an asset element deferrable to the period when the goods are sold by the agent. Thus, such charges would be recorded:

```
Goods on Consignment.......................................  12
    Cash in Bank...........................................       12
```

When the consignee sells the merchandise, he is entitled to reimbursement of certain specified expenses and his commission—say, 10 percent of the $150 selling price. He would remit the $128 net amount due the consignor ($150 less his commission of $15 and his own advertising and delivery costs of $7) with an appropriate report of the sale. The consignor would record the completion of the sale transaction by the following entries:

(1)

```
Cost of Consigned Goods Sold..............................  92
    Goods on Consignment..................................       92
        To transfer merchandise costs to expense.
```

(2)

```
Cash on Hand.............................................. 128
Consignee's Commission and Expense........................  22
    Consignment Sales Revenue.............................       150
        To record sales reported by consignee.
```

It should be noted that revenue is recognized only when the sale is *completed*. This means that delivery must be made to a customer who pays or promises to pay. Mere shipment of goods to a consignee is only a wider exposure of goods to customers as a part of the merchandising process. The expenses are recognized as soon as the consignor receives evidence of their incurrence—in this case the report of the consignee provides this. Consignment accounts are set up to reflect the kind of information that management would want concerning the operation. The amounts of consignment sales, cost of goods sold, and miscellaneous expenses are separated from other revenue and expense accounts so that these data are not merged with those from other classes of transactions.

Unsuccessful consignments will entail the return of the goods to the consignor. In such a case, the costs of shipment both ways would be expensed because there would be no justification for carrying such costs forward as assets. The services covered by these costs would have been rendered—i.e., the objective of display and demonstration at another location would have been achieved. The return of the goods means that those costs have expired, and this would be recognized by the following entries:

```
Merchandise Inventory.....................................  80
Expense of Unsuccessful Consignment.......................  29
    Goods on Consignment..................................       92
    Cash in Bank..........................................       17
```

The goods would be returned to inventory at their cost. Initial and return transportation and any other related costs (such as reconditioning the goods before attempted resale) would be treated as expense since such costs apply to the consignment, not to subsequent or other activities.

Earmarked or Special-Order Goods

Although revenue is as a general rule recognized only after delivery against a valid sales contract, there are some exceptions. Legally, the sale of *ascertained* (earmarked or specifically designated) goods is complete and title passes at the time of the contract. This gives the seller a right to collect even though delivery has not been made. Under some circumstances (when cancellation is unlikely) the contract to sell such items as antique furniture, works of art, or other highly individual items may be treated as a sale before delivery. However, such a situation exists only when nothing of material consequence still needs to be done by the seller. The crux of the matter is whether there is doubt as to the performance of the seller, or whether the transaction is only incidentally incomplete because, for example, the item is to be cleaned, polished, or refinished.

The legal rule arises from the fact that by setting aside or by making specified goods for his customer, the seller gives up the opportunity to sell that item to someone else. However, the accountant follows the legal pattern in measuring revenue only to the extent that it fits the criterion of completion. If delivery is really incidental to the sale, revenue may be recorded before delivery; but the surrounding conditions, rather than rigid following of legal rules, govern the actions and procedures in accounting for sales.

A "special-order" sale may raise similar questions; in addition, however, the special order often involves costs that would not otherwise have been incurred and which cannot otherwise be recovered. Usually, the contract will be drawn to specify the way in which payment is to be made so as to protect the supplier from loss. For example, a contract for an engineering survey may call for an initial retainer fee plus charges to be billed monthly and a final sum on delivery of the report. This automatically gives a better basis for spreading revenue over the period of the survey than would a lump-sum arrangement, payable on completion of the project. But here, too, the rule of reason is important; an extremely large retainer fee or final payment would evoke efforts on the part of the accountant to accrue the revenue on the basis of relative completion of the work rather than the cash payment received. This will be discussed shortly.

Cancellations

The general rule that a sales contract cannot be canceled capriciously applies to all sales. Technically, a buyer is bound to accept the goods purchased or compensate the seller for damages or loss. But this is often ignored in practice, especially when the goods are standardized and could readily be sold to someone else. Cancellations (agreements between buyer and seller to rescind the sales contract) are not infrequent; and the technical requirement of agreement is sometimes overlooked when amounts are small and customer satisfaction is important. It sometimes appears more a matter of etiquette than law to request permission to return goods or withdraw an order. Nevertheless, when costs have been incurred specially for the customer's benefit or loss suffered (because the item cannot be sold elsewhere or the costs incurred cannot be salvaged in some other way), the customer may be held to his bargain.

The typical situation of this kind is met by transferring costs to a special-order account in which they are accumulated until the work is complete. Then the costs would be considered assets until delivery, when revenue would be recognized. This is parallel to inventory accounting, in which the costs are treated as assets until the merchandise is delivered to the customer. Typical entries would be:

Special-Order Contract Costs	1,275	
Payroll		600
Materials		350
Other Operating Costs		325

(Repeated at intervals as amounts accrue over a period of time.)

On Completion

Costs of Goods Sold	2,648	
Special Order Contract Costs		2,648
Accounts Receivable	3,500	
Revenue—Special Order		3,500

(Total completed cost and sales price.)

The use of the special-order cost account makes it easy to establish the total cost to date at any time. When the work is finished, the delivery and the invoice mark the recognition of revenue and the expiration of the asset into expense. Both the revenue and the costs associated with this order would thus be reported in the earnings report for the period when delivery occurs.

Long-Term Construction Contracts

The situation and method just described would give little trouble if there were a number of special orders spaced through time, and individually of small amount. But some situations make special-order revenue a peculiarly difficult problem. A construction contract for a building, a battleship, or other large-scale project is a special order involving a large amount spread over a long period; often there are only a few such projects under way at a given time. In situations of this kind, merely postponing the recognition of expense (by carrying costs as assets) is an inadequate approach to the real problem.

A construction company, for example, agrees to build for a price of $15,900,000 a bridge that is to be completed in three years. Such a contract would almost certainly call for progress payments to the contractor along the way. Such payments are essential to finance the venture because few contractors would be able to raise the large amount of money or credit required. On a conventional basis there would be no revenue realized until the bridge was completed and turned over for use. Although the progress payments would meet the major part of the financing problem, they would not be a measure of revenue in most cases. Progress payments are typically set at a level sufficient only to finance costs—sometimes only *part* of the costs—incurred to date. To point up our example, suppose that at the end of the first year, the contractor has incurred costs of $4 million and has received progress payments totaling $3 million. Has he a loss of $1 million on this project? There must be a better answer than this!

One answer would be that gain or loss cannot be determined at all until the project is finished. There is some truth in this statement because it is always possible for many things to go wrong with a big construction job. However, assuming that the original cost estimate (still believed to be correct) was $15,000,000 and that there was (and is) an expectation of a $900,000 gain on the whole project, something can be done to make a less pessimistic report for the year just past.

It would be reasonable to assume that the expected gain ($900,-000) would be earned ratably as the work was done. The amount of work completed might well be measured by the cost incurred. This suggests that $4/15$ of the earnings have accrued. Thus, the fee of $900,000 might be spread over the construction period, $4/15$ or $240,000 being considered as earned to date. This would be expressed in following entries:

<pre>
Expected Collections from Construction Work.......... 240,000
    Income from Construction Project.................   240,000
</pre>

This serves to set up that part of the fee that has been earned (and will presumably be collected via progress payments) as an asset with a corresponding credit to income. The asset is not called an account receivable, for there is no *legal* claim for this amount; some companies call this item "unbilled charges." But the only contingency in this is time; the project will almost certainly be finished and the amount will be collected.

If the situation were to be reflected in the earnings report to show both the revenue and expense elements in this situation, the entry above would be replaced by:

<pre>
Expected Collections from Construction Work........ 4,240,000
    Revenue from Construction Project..............   4,240,000
</pre>

The Cash Received in Progress Payments account would have been credited when those amounts were received; this account would record a customer-deposit kind of receipt. However, such receipts are really reductions in the contingent claim that was set up as Expected Collections for Construction Work. Therefore, in the position statement these two items will be offset; in the present case, this leaves a net of $1,240,000 as an asset.

The expense side of the situation is the cost incurred *during this period* as accumulated in the Construction Work in Progress account. However, we do not want the process of accumulation to confuse the next period's data; we use a "contra" or offset account (akin to the Accumulated Depreciation discussed in Chapter 5) to show the absorption of cost into current period expense. This serves to retain the gross cost in the records, even though some of it has been "written off" into expense. The indicated entry is:

<pre>
Construction Project Expense....................... 4,000,000
    Construction Cost Absorbed....................   4,000,000
</pre>

Now, the revenue and the expense may be matched in the earnings statement to show the difference between $4,240,000 and $4,000,000 as the project income of $240,000. The statement of position would report the following:

ASSETS

Expected collections for construction work.......	$4,240,000	
Less: Cash received in progress payments......	3,000,000	$1,240,000
Construction work in progress (at cost).........	$4,000,000	
Less: Construction costs absorbed............	4,000,000	...

The next year's activities will serve to report additional revenue based on the then estimated proportionate completion, and the additional costs will be absorbed in expense. If all estimates are correct and the project reaches completion, the progress payments will cancel the expected collections and the costs absorbed in expense will offset the total cost of construction.

Should estimates of future costs be inaccurate, the revenues will be misstated unless corrections are made to past period figures through entries in the Retained Earnings account; these corrections would appear in the earnings report to change the balance carried forward as of the beginning of that year. These amounts should be adjusted for the associated income tax effects to avoid distortion.

Sales and the Accounting Unit

Revenue arises only when there has been a transaction with a customer; and a customer is logically someone *outside* of the selling company. Hence, interdepartmental transfers of goods or services are not viewed as sales, for they do not support a recognition of revenue or income. This general rule is based on the conception that revenue can arise only as the result of a valid contract or exchange. Since a business firm cannot contract with a part of itself, interdepartmental transfers can be recorded only as reclassifications of cost, not as revenue-producing transactions. For management purposes, however, it may be desirable to operate the accounting system *as if* the departments actually were separate firms. Anyway, this must be done in such a way as to separate interdivisional transfers from actual sales to outsiders; the transfers thus recorded in interdivisional sales, receivables, and payables accounts may be eliminated, and the inventory costs returned from an interdivisional to the enterprise basis when summary financial reports are prepared.

Summary

Generally, revenue is recognized by the delivery of product to the customer according to the terms of a clear agreement which yields an enforceable claim for payment.

Some complications affect the accounting for cash with order, on approval, consignments, or long-term service and construction contracts. The recognition of revenue in such cases must be made with due regard to the surrounding conditions, and the measurements are presented and accepted in the context in which they are made. The attempt to be exact in measuring revenue is not always successful.

However, it is possible to distinguish between a sale and something which is not a revenue-producing transaction. These distinctions are important and must be maintained.

There are other problems in determining the amount and the timing of revenue in specific situations which are dealt with in the following chapter.

QUESTIONS

1. Are there good reasons for having some clearly defined rules to determine *when* revenue comes into existence? What would happen if there were no such rules?

2. What difference does "correctness" of the amount of revenue make in the reports of a company? Is this merely a matter of establishing the amount of the income for the period?

3. Since the recognition of revenue is based on legal features of the sales contract, should the rules for recognition of revenue be specified in the laws under which business operates? What reason is there for leaving to accountants the decision of when and how to recognize revenue?

4. What is the basis for recognizing revenue in the great majority of cases? What evidence is there to indicate the completion of a sale?

5. When a customer pays in advance for merchandise, would it be correct to regard this as completing the sale, so long as an equity was set up for the amount of cost to be incurred in making delivery of the merchandise? If the transaction were recorded in this manner, could the customer cancel the order and require full refund if delivery had not yet been completed? If there is anything wrong with such accounting, how should an advance payment be recorded? What happens when delivery *is* made?

6. What is there about an on approval sale which precludes the recognition of revenue even though the goods have been shipped? What entries would you make to record (1) the on approval shipment, (2) the return of the goods by the customer, (3) the expiration of the approval period with no return of the goods from the customer?

7. What is a consignment? When is revenue realized by the consignor from a consignment? If a consignee makes a sale of consigned goods for $500 against which he has incurred expenses of $30 for service and delivery costs, what entry should be made on *his* records for this? On receiving the consignee's report of this sale, the consignor finds that he has recorded the cost of the consigned goods as $250. What entries should now be made on the consignor's books?

8. Record the return of this unsuccessful consignment: the goods had a selling price of $150, and the consignor had recorded their cost as $100 when they were consigned; advertising and shipping costs paid by the consignee, $22; costs of return transportation, $10; and probable resale value of these goods through regular channels is expected to be only $120 because they now are shopworn.

9. Schneider the tailor took an order to make a suit for Kaufer and received $40 from him as a deposit. The agreed price of the suit was $300. Kaufer became seriously ill before the suit was finished; and because his hospital expenses depleted his bank account, Kaufer refused delivery of the suit on the ground that he was unable to pay for it. Schneider had purchased materials to make the suit for $112 on account; he had used $10 of supplies from his inventory and incurred $15 cost for rent, light, heat, and power applicable to the transaction. There was depreciation on Schneider's tools of $5. Maurer agrees to buy the suit from Schneider for $200 cash if it can be altered to fit him. It costs Schneider an additional $15 to make the alterations, and Maurer accepts the finished suit and pays for it. Write entries for Schneider's books to show how much he earned from the making of this suit.

10. What conditions make it advisable to use "percentage completion" for recognizing revenue? Suppose a contractor agreed to build 30 miles of road for $900,000. The project included 20 miles of level, straight road and 10 miles of hills and curves. Level roadway was estimated to cost $20,000 a mile and hills and curves were estimated at $30,000 a mile when the bid was made.

    a) At the end of the first year, eight miles of straight, level road and five miles of hills and curves were completed at a cost of $310,000. On a percentage-completion-cost basis, what is the revenue on this project during this first year to the nearest hundred dollars?

    b) In the second year, the project was finished but the second year's costs were increased to 20 percent above the original estimates. Recalculate the revenue assignable to the first year and state the net income for each year on a percentage-completion-cost basis. (Ignore income taxes.)

    c) Suppose the contract had been obtained as two separate projects

—the price for the 20 miles of level, straight road being $25,000 per mile, and for the 10 miles of hills and curves, $40,000 per mile. If these projects are accounted for on a *physical* completion basis, what would be the income for each year? (Ignore income taxes.)

Which of the methods (2 or 3) appears to you to be the better? Why?

11. One division of a firm makes electric motors ranging from $\frac{1}{16}$ to $\frac{3}{4}$ horsepower with various voltages and ratings. Some of these motors are used by the household appliance division of the company in sewing machines, washers, dryers, refrigerators, dishwashers, and the like. The electric motor division treats the deliveries to the household appliance division as sales, billed at the same prices as to its other customers. An inventory in the household appliance division contains several thousand of these motors whose aggregate sales value is $65,000; these motors cost $38,000 to produce and the cost of transportation to the appliance division was $3,100. Comment and suggest the proper adjustment.

PROBLEMS

Western States Supply Company

The cash receipts of this company during the past year were:

Collections from regular customers.	$1,340,700
Advance deposits (includes $560 shipping costs).	35,670
Cash sales (includes $550 shipping charges).	26,200
Special order goods (includes $890 shipping cost).	13,460
Remittances on consignment sales.	33,750
Collections from fire loss settlements.	22,380
Remittances from customers, approval sales.	2,840
Customers' notes collected, with interest $230.	8,720
Sale of common stock.	13,500
Refunds from defective merchandise.	7,370
Total.	$1,504,590

The company delivers *all* its orders by way of freight, express, or parcel post; it prepays the delivery costs, charging them to the customer in the invoice for that shipment. The daily total of charges on those invoices is added to the customer accounts; the credits are to sales for the price of the goods, and to shipping expense for the delivery charges. Since the prepayments of delivery charges are carried to the shipping expense account, customer remittances will cover those costs with no expense to the company. Accounts receivable at the beginning of the year of $11,160 included $445 shipping charges; at the end of the year there were $2,814 of shipping charges included in the accounts receivable balance of $88,540. Shipping charges included in the collections from customers during the year amounted to $9,600.

There has been some trouble in collecting from certain charge customers, and the company has insisted on their remitting cash in advance for any orders placed. The amount received from these customers includes the shipping costs to be incurred. These orders are not always shipped immediately; at the end of the year orders amounting to $1,300 (including $50 shipping costs) were still not filled; other orders filled, ready for shipment but not yet shipped at the close of business December 31 were $3,310 with $110 of shipping costs not yet incurred by the company. At the beginning of the year there were no undelivered cash-in-advance orders.

Occasionally, the company receives orders for goods to be made according to customers' individual specification. Such orders were not accepted until June of this year, when the company adopted a policy of doing such work if cash was paid in advance for the full amount of the order, including shipping and delivery costs. The amount of such orders still remaining unfilled and undelivered at the end of the year was $6,730, which amount includes $120 for shipping and delivery costs.

The amount received from consignees, $33,750, represents the proceeds sent in by consignees, after they deducted commissions of $1,536 and expenses of sale, $4,204. It cost $375 to ship these goods to the consignee.

Collections from fire loss settlements have to do with the fire which destroyed a part of the company's plant in October. This amount includes:

(1) Sale of burned and water soaked merchandise to the Salvage Corporation, . . $16,220.

(2) Payment received from the Guardian Angel Insurance Company to cover losses on:

Merchandise.	$ 2,780
Equipment.	16,400
Building.	3,200
Total.	$22,380

Customers' notes collected include one note given by a customer in settlement of a past due account balance of last year; this note had been received before the close of that year, and at December 31 last year was carried at $4,126, which included $26 interest. The other note covered an October sale in the same way; its amount was $4,500. The difference between the $8,626 and the total collected ($8,720) is additional interest on the two notes. The $4,500 note included $60 shipping cost.

Collections from "on approval" shipments represents the full selling price of such shipments, plus the shipping costs of $112. There were also $4,316 of "on approval" shipments (shipping costs, $69) that have been accepted by the customers, payable 30 days after the date of acceptance. $1,300 of on approval shipments (shipping costs, $42) are being returned, but have not yet been received.

Refunds on merchandise returned is the amount remitted to the Western States Supply Company, because merchandise previously paid for turned out to be defective.

"Sale of stock" refers to the sale of 100 shares of the company's stock to its President, who wanted it for a present to his new grandson.

Required:
1. Compute the Western States Supply Company's sales revenue for the year. Use skeleton accounts to organize the analysis.
2. What amount of shipping cost was incurred during this year?

Oakmont Builders Supply Company

This company's market covered several states, and the line of merchandise was quite wide. Many of its customers were small contractors, local lumber yards, and small hardware stores.

At the end of the last fiscal period, the following information was collected concerning the company's activities related to the financial reports:

(1) Although the company prided itself on carrying a large inventory to meet its customers' needs, some items were occasionally out of stock. During the last month, this had occurred with several items. Orders for some $6,000 of merchandise (at Oakmont's regular selling prices) were on hand, but these had not been recorded because no goods had been shipped. Customers had paid in advance for some merchandise; $2,650 of such remittances had been entered as sales when the customer checks had been deposited. These customers had been told of the situation and advised that the goods would be shipped as soon as replenishments were received. The costs of these goods would probably be about $2,220, about $100 more than would normally be the case.

(2) Other orders had been filled by making substitutions; these had been billed at regular selling prices ($3,000 cost, plus 25 percent) and charged to Customer Accounts Receivable. The invoices were marked that these goods might be returned for full credit (including transportation costs) within 30 days if the goods were not entirely satisfactory. The company's experience with this policy had been that only about 20 percent of such shipments were returned, and that transportation costs ran about 5 percent of the selling value of the merchandise in such cases.

(3) Sometimes, customers who did not have established credit would order small amounts of merchandise to be sent "Parcel Post COD."

Such orders would be packed and delivered to the post office, and forms calling for the total charges (including delivery and collection charges) would be attached to the package. On delivery the postman collected the total amount and remitted this by money order payable to the shipper.

During the past period $11,000 of merchandise (selling price plus delivery and collection charges) had been handled in this way, charged to Open CODs account and credited to Sales. The postage and collection fees were paid by the shipping department along with the charges for other parcel post shipments, but it was established that $400 of such charges had been paid and debited to delivery expense.

At the close of the period, $9,960 cash had been received from the post offices, from COD shipments; this amount had been credited to the Open CODs account. $262 of such shipments had been refused by the addressees, and this amount had been credited to Open CODs and charged to Sales, but the $18 shipping and collection charges had been ignored. In addition, $12 due postage for return of these parcels had been paid and charged to office expense.

A check revealed that there were actually $778 of open CODs on which not enough time had elapsed to complete delivery or to have these goods or remittances returned. $38 of the postage and collection fees paid were for these shipments.

(4) One very good customer, the Minor Supply Company, had ordered a complete set of hardware for an entire residence, specially finished and plated. The regular price for this set would normally have been $1,500 (25 percent above Oakmont's cost); but the price was agreed on for this special order at $1,950 completed. After the Oakmont Company had expended $225 in labor and $50 in extra supplies on this order, the lot had been sent to the plating company, which had bargained for $75 for its work. Just after the plating company advised that the order was all ready for shipment, Minor telephoned to say that for reasons beyond their control they could not use the special hardware. It was agreed that the Oakmont Company would cancel the order but that Minor would cover the loss from this. It was estimated that these special items might sell in the normal channels for about $1,600.

(5) Oakmont had acquired 50 garage door openers as a special promotion item at a cost of $90 each. These were offered to Oakmont dealers on consignment, and the vendor sent all 50 of them as per Oakmont's instructions. No entries had been made for the purchase or these shipments.

Dealers were expected to make installations and remit the net proceeds from sales at $150 less installation costs and a 20 percent selling commission, when the openers were sold. $3,000 had been credited to the dealers' accounts for the remittances covering 30 openers sold. Five of the openers had been received by Oakmont from dealers who could not sell them; these returns had not been recorded, although $16 freight charges on them had been debited to delivery expense. Another 15 openers were still in the hands of dealers, unsold.

Required:

Write entries that should have been made to record the transactions described. Indicate any assumptions you make with respect to debatable items or interpretations.

Doppler Construction Company

This company constructed a dam across the Wahtahatchee River for the Western Tri-States Utility Corporation. The bid price on the entire project was $24,800,000; the cost estimate on which this bid was based was $23,400,000, including interest on financing required during the construction period, but not including general administrative overhead costs or profit.

At the end of the first year of work on this project, the Doppler Company's records showed the following data:

DOPPLER CONSTRUCTION COMPANY
Trial Balance
End of First Year, Wahtahatchee Dam Project

	Debits	Credits
Cash in bank	$ 369,540	
Construction in progress	9,120,000	
Inventories, supplies, and materials	987,080	
Other unexpired costs	183,740	
Investments	90,774	
Equipment and facilities	1,724,680	
Allowances for depreciation		$ 869,640
Accounts payable		754,379
Accrued wages, taxes, etc.		63,404
Accrued interest payable		9,400
Long-term notes payable		3,000,000
Common shares (10,000 shares, no par)		1,336,200
Retained earnings		708,217
General administrative overhead costs	201,795	
Dividends paid	70,000	
Cash received in progress payments		6,000,000
Investment income		6,369
Total	$12,747,609	$12,747,609

At this time (the end of the first year) Doppler engineers reestimated the total cost to be incurred on the project at $22,800,000 because certain efficiencies and economies had been achieved in arranging and conducting the work. They expected the project to be completed in another 18 months.

Required:

1. Make entries to recognize revenue and income taxes for the first year; and prepare financial reports. Tax rate, 48 per cent.

By the end of the second year, an additional $10,248,000 had been charged to the Construction in Progress account; the utility had remitted another $13,000,000 in progress payments; office and general administrative overhead costs incurred in the second year had been $187,314. Gradually rising wage rates and materials prices, however, had led the engineers to revise again their estimates of total cost for the project to $24,000,000. They expected that the job should be finished in another nine months.

Required:

2. *a)* Make entries to adjust the first year earnings (and taxes) in view of the revised estimates in the second year.

   b) Make entries similar to those in requirement 1, and the appropriate reports. Show prior year corrections as "retained earnings adjustments" in the statement of earnings.

At the end of seven months of the third year, the job had been completed and accepted. Construction costs of the last seven months totaled $4,612,000, including the removal of equipment, minor adjustments and refinishing, final delivery and acceptance. The utility company had paid $3,000,000 more in progress payments, and the remainder was in process of remittance. General and administrative overhead costs incurred by Doppler in the last seven months were $204,614.

Required:

3. Set up revenue and expense calculations for year 3 on the basis of the final figures—without revising years 1 and 2 as stated above in requirement 1 and 2.

4. Set up a final tabular statement, showing corrected revenue, expenses, and taxes for each of the three years as adjusted to the final results.

Chapter 7

REVENUE AND RECEIVABLES ADJUSTMENTS

The measurement of revenue involves not only issues of timing which we have discussed but also a number of other questions that arise partly out of credit and partly from other considerations. Risks of uncollectibility, return privileges, price concessions, out freight, discounts, and guarantees tend to complicate the problem of revenue measurement. These questions are dealt with in this chapter.

Credit Risks

Up to this point we have handled sales transactions as if we had no doubt of collecting the entire amounts billed. This is not far wrong, for the amounts agreed upon are almost always collected, if not exactly when due, then within some reasonably short time afterwards. Credit risks are usually accepted only after investigation and systematic collection methods generally insure that most sales are collected in full within the normal credit period. However, the reader may wonder what happens in those cases that for one reason or another do not "pay out." We need some way to take into account the limited but nevertheless expected shrinkage in revenue that will occur when some items turn out to be uncollectible.

One way to do this would be to assume that gross sales are an adequate measure of revenue. An uncollectible account would be considered a loss when collection is found impossible. But this is not a logical position, for revenue is based upon an expectation subject to risk. The risk in those expectations should be recognized in stating the revenue and the receivables. When a receivable turns out to be uncollectible, it should not be viewed as a loss but as part of an expected shrinkage. Thus, we can check the validity of those estimates. An uncollectible sale is not a loss anyway; a better way to describe the uncollectible sale would be to call it a gift of merchandise or service to the customer who did not pay for it. But the cost of the gift was shown when the sale was reported; it was a part of the expense in the cost of goods sold. The needed correction is, that what was nominally labeled a sale turns out not to be one. We want to reduce revenue for this expectation.

Thus it might appear that the recognition of an uncollectible account would require only a reversal of the sales transaction. A debit to Sales Revenue and a credit to Customer Accounts Receivable would reduce the revenue figure and remove the uncollectible receivable when the fact of uncollectibility was established. But this is only partially correct because the uncollectible receivable would be recognized only some time after the sale had been recorded. The revenue shown in one period might be reversed in a subsequent one; although the credit to Customer Accounts Receivable would be correctly entered when the bad credit risk was revealed, the Sales Revenue correction ought to be applied in the former period when the sale was recorded.

There are two ways to do this. The first is to make the debit side of the reversal entry in the Retained Earnings account, on the ground that the effects of earlier period sales revenue have already been closed into Retained Earnings. But a better way to handle uncollectible account write-offs is to anticipate them, estimating their amount in the period of sale so that the actual accounts found uncollectible may be absorbed by writing them off against the estimate.

Estimated Defaults

The credit risks of a company can be estimated with fair accuracy. One way to do this is to review the entire list of receivables on a given date, making judgments about individual accounts in terms of a percentage estimate of shrinkages on collection. The other method is to establish a percentage of sales (usually charge sales only) which may be taken as an aggregate basis for anticipating uncollectibles. A company with $240,000 sales in a given period, of which $25,000 remains uncollected, may estimate credit risks by

reviewing individual customer accounts receivable arriving at expected shrinkage of $1,000. Or, it might choose to estimate collec-
tion failures at ½ percent of sales, which would be $1,200. How-
ever the amount is measured, the record should show an anticipated
collection shrinkage against Accounts Receivable and an estimated
correction to Sales Revenue of the same amount. This is recorded:

Revenue Adjustment for Uncollectibles...................... 1,200
    Allowance for Uncollectible Receivables................   1,200

By these entries in the two contra accounts, both the revenue and
the receivables are reduced without disturbing the regularly recorded
amounts. Using related accounts to carry figures that should be
taken together (yet not completely merged) is not new for us. We
used such arrangements in connection with depreciation, and also
in connection with long-term construction costs. Estimates and
documented records are not the same thing, and they do not belong
in the same account. We may use *adjunct* (to be added) or *contra*
(to be offset) accounts to record such related but not strictly iden-
tical data. The Sales Revenue account would now be accompanied
by a contra revenue account, Revenue Adjustment for Uncollectibles. Similarly, Customer Accounts Receivable would be associated
with a contra asset account, Allowance for Uncollectible Receivables. These contra accounts would thus allow separate recording,
with the billed amounts in one account and the expected shrinkage
of revenue from non-collection in another.

Variations in Account Titles

It may be useful here to explain some variations in accounting
terminology. Account titles are merely labels to indicate the nature
of recorded data. It is possible to use a number of different words
to describe any given class of data. Some accountants use terms like
Loss on Bad Debts or Provision for Doubtful Accounts instead of
Revenue Adjustment for Uncollectibles. The author prefers to
use more precise terms. There is no loss, as such, in the write-off of
an uncollectible, nor is any provision being made; all we are doing is making an estimate of the error involved in recording revenue
at billed prices. Similarly, what we call Allowance for Uncollectible
Receivables may be labeled by some accountants a "Reserve for
Bad Debts." These terms are not used here because they do not
clearly state what they mean. Uncollectibles may be estimated
and, of course, they may be allowed for; but uncollectibility may

arise from various causes, and there is nothing particularly "bad" about it. There is nothing whatever "reserved" in any event; we merely try to measure the factors related to the revenue for the period.

The student may find practical terminology useful; we shall indicate departures from conventional terms when these exist, but we shall try to label things as nearly as possible in terms of what they are, rather than what they may be called.

Use of the Contra Accounts for Uncollectibles

To return to the main thread of discussion, we need to see how this procedure operates, once it has been set up. The Report of Earnings will show the revenue adjustment item deducted from sales revenue in the period when the sales are made. This allows the gross sales billed to remain to measure the volume of business, even though that figure is reduced by revenue adjustment for uncollectibles to establish the revenue amount. In the statement of position, the Customer Accounts Receivable will be reduced by the amount of Allowance for Uncollectible Receivables, thus showing the *net* expected future cash receipts as an asset item.

When a customer's balance is actually found to be uncollectible, the amount may be written off without disturbing the revenue of the later period or changing the net asset amount:

Allowance for Uncollectible Receivables.......................... 28
    Accounts Receivable....................................   28

The balance of Allowance for Uncollectible Receivables then should be the amount that is still expected to be uncollectible from the sales made to date. These uncollectibles will not affect future revenues or income because they are already allowed for in the current period reports.

Checking Anticipated Collection Defaults

Any estimate ought to be subject to some kind of verification to be reasonably sure that it is within certain limits of precision. One way of checking the correctness of the figures is to review the situation at a later date to see whether actual experience bears out the computation. Thus, at the end of a year, a review of accounts receivable might be used to check the Revenue Adjustment for Uncollectibles account as accumulated on a percentage of sales basis during the year. One of the tasks of the independent auditor is to make such a review. He will satisfy himself as to the adequacy of the estimate, with respect to the accounts still uncollected at the end of the year. It is possible that after such a review a correction or adjustment would be made, based on a calculation such as:

Aggregate monthly provisions at ½% of sales...........		$1,750
Less:		
Recognized doubtful accounts at 12/31................	$1,000	
Estimated additional shrinkages, 1% of other receivables....................................	500	1,500
Overestimated Uncollectibles....................		$ 250

This would be given effect through the entries:

Allowance for Uncollectible Receivables........................	250	
Revenue Adjustment for Uncollectibles....................		250

As a further check on the estimate, it would be possible when the accounts of a given year had all been either collected or written off, to compare the estimate with actual experience and make corrections. Suppose, for example, sales in a given year were $600,000; a provision of ¼ percent of sales (recorded monthly) accumulated to $1,500; at the end of the year an adjustment was made to add $150 to the allowance account; during this year $975 of customer accounts had been found uncollectible and written off. If collections of $540,000 had been made, the accounts at the end of the year would appear:

Year 1—Accounts Receivable		Year 1—Allowance for Uncollectible Receivables	
Sales 600,000	Collections 540,000	Write-offs 975	1,500
	Write-offs 975		150

and the balance sheet would show Year 1 Customer Accounts Receivable, $59,025, less the $675 Year 1—Allowance for Uncollectible Receivables, a net of $58,350. The revenue for the year would be $600,000, less $1,650 or $598,350.

The transactions of the following year would be recorded in separate accounts for year 2 (a special arrangement to make it possible for the first year's data to be followed up in detail). Toward the end of the second year, the first-year accounts might appear as follows:

Year 1, Accounts Receivable

(a)	600,000	(b)	540,000
		(d)	975
		√	59,025
	600,000		600,000
√	59,025	(f)	58,296
		(g)	729
	59,025		59,025

Year 1—Allowance for Uncollectible Receivables

(d)	975	(c)	1,500
√	675		150
	1,650		1,650
(g)	729	√	675

Now the whole story is before us, and the estimates of the preceding year may be verified. All of the receivables are either collected or uncollectible; there is no balance in the Year 1, Customer Accounts Receivable, but there is a $56 debit balance in Allowance for Uncollectible Receivables, Year 1. This implies an underestimate of uncollectibles in the year 1 sales, which might be corrected by the entries:

Retained Earnings. 56
    Allowance for Uncollectible Receivables, Year 1. 56

However, the typical situation does not often require such accuracy. Most accountants would be content to allow the relatively insignificant error to carry over into the second year without separating each year's accounting.

Bad Debts Recovery. To be really precise, the check we have just tried to make is inconclusive. There is still some chance that uncollectibility may not be finally established for some time. Even though an account is written off, it might still be collected. Should a customer voluntarily pay off an old balance we may have thought was uncollectible, the receipt of $30 on such an account would be only a further correction of the collection shrinkage. This might again suggest adjustment to Retained Earnings account, since the balance had been written off earlier. Usually it is simpler to allow such errors to "run over" as between years, and the collection would be credited to the allowance account because it was, after all, not a default—merely a long-postponed collection! Therefore, it is uncommon to find Customer Accounts Receivable and Allowance for Uncollectible Accounts segregated by years. The small carry-over errors are ignored.

Other Contra Accounts—Returned Goods

A customer may if the merchandise delivered to him is not satis-factory ask for permission to return it "for credit." Usually there must be some good reason, such as a difference in quality from that promised, or a variation in color or size; but some companies are quite liberal in permitting returns so long as the goods are salable and the privilege is not abused.

When goods have been returned by a customer, the basis for crediting his account is the issuance of a credit memorandum which is sent when the return shipment of goods has been received. This would be the basis for entries such as the following:

```
Merchandise Inventory.......................................  62
Revenue Adjustment—Returned Sales...........................  80
    Accounts Receivable.....................................        80
    Cost of Goods Sold......................................        62
```

The entries to Merchandise Inventory and Cost of Goods Sold re-verse the original sale at its cost price, thus increasing the asset and reducing expense for the amount of goods returned. The entries at sales price reduce accounts receivable, and the debit to the contra account, Revenue Adjustment—Returned Sales, reduces the revenue figure. This contra account is like the Revenue Adjustment for Uncollectibles account except that it is not an estimated item. The reason for using the contra account rather than merely reducing sales billed is the desire to maintain a statistical record of returned sales. Returned sales can be a problem in merchandising, as depart-ment store operations will show. So long as customers are willing to pay the higher prices necessary to compensate for the extra handling of goods that are returned, there is no harm done. But if merchandise returns involve extra costs of reconditioning or sale at low prices because of mussed, soiled, or "shopworn" appearance, the sales-return problem requires special attention. One way of knowing what the situation may be is to keep a separate account for sales returns instead of burying the sales reversal in the Sales Billed account.

Price Concessions

There are times when it may be wise to renegotiate a price rather than have merchandise returned or leave a customer dissatisfied. Thus an $80 charge to the customer might upon his complaint or request for adjustment because of minor defects be reduced to $65. This would be evidenced by a credit memorandum, as in the case of a return; but the record would be different because there would be no return of goods and no expense adjustment. The required entries would be:

```
Revenue Adjustment—Price Concessions.......................  15
    Accounts Receivable.......................................        15
```

Sometimes price concessions are called sales allowances, but this does not alter their real meaning. The use of a contra account gives a separate measure of this adjustment; subtracted in the earnings statement, this account serves to reduce the amount of sales billed to a more correct revenue figure, and to indicate the amount of such concessions.

Other Revenue Adjustments

We have defined expense as being the cost of goods or services delivered to the customer, a figure which may be compared with the net revenue (after adjustments by contra items) to show the results of basic operations of the firm. This definition leaves us with a need to maintain distinctions between sales adjustments and expense.

The cost of delivering goods to customers is expense if the firm does its own delivering; but when the seller ships goods by common carrier, he may price the goods to include or to exclude shipping costs. Thus if the price is quoted "FOB factory," the prepayment of shipping cost would be added to the customer's account, but this amount would not be revenue. Payment of such charges by the seller would be charged to Outward Transportation account as if it were expense. However, the entry recording the sale would credit the amount of shipping charges to Outward Transportation so that the net effect of the freight charge would be to increase Customer Accounts Receivable and to decrease Cash. Outward Transportation is a *clearing* account which should have no sizable balance in either direction under these operations.

Suppose, however, the price is quoted *delivered;* i.e., the quoted price includes delivery at destination. In such a case, the freight cost is absorbed by the seller and might appear on his books as an expense item. In some cases this would be awkward. If goods are sold and priced both on a factory and delivered basis, the amount of any given sale would be larger if the price "covers" the freight. But this is no increase in revenue, for the higher price merely reflects the method of paying the transportation company. If two companies followed different procedures one would show greater revenue, which would be exactly offset by the freight "expense." Since the seller delivers no added service for the freight charge that amount is best treated as an adjustment to the billed price.

Therefore, the outgoing freight charges are sometimes recorded as Revenue Adjustment for Out-freight rather than as expense. This way, the revenue figure shows the price paid for the goods at the factory; there would be no expense for outward transportation. This is really quite logical if one considers that the transportation is not a service furnished by the seller but an outside transaction merely arranged by the seller as a matter of convenience. Happily, the amounts in cases like this are seldom large and the distortion is not great even if the amount of out-freight is included in Revenue. But it is better theory to treat out-freight as a revenue adjustment rather than as expense, unless the deliveries are all made by the vendor himself.

Guarantees

Most mechanical devices and many other items are sold with an understanding that repairs or adjustments arising from defects will be taken care of (over some limited time period) without additional cost to the purchaser. The amount billed to the customer then includes not only compensation for the goods but also for the costs (not yet incurred) of replacing defective parts or making in-service adjustments. One of two things is indicated in such a case: either we should recognize an obligation to incur future costs or we ought to defer a part of the revenue to cover these costs when they do appear. It is usually easier to use an account, Revenue Adjustment for Service Guarantees to recognize the estimated amount of such warranty costs, or a percentage of the billed price, to be carried as a credit to Revenue Deferred to Cover Service Guarantees. This makes it possible for costs arising from repairs or replacements to be charged to the equity account instead of being absorbed as expenses in future periods against other sales. The figures in the equity account would compare the actual costs against the expectation. These figures would be helpful to decide questions about the company's service policy. It should be noted that the equity "Revenue Deferred to Cover Service Guarantees" is not a legal debt but rather a kind of restriction against those assets which arose from the sales figure as billed.

There are other cases of deferred revenue. Magazine subscriptions involve the receipt of cash with an obligation to provide service over the entire subscription period; the deferred revenue is taken up when earned, and the costs of rendering the service appear along with the proper amount of revenue to reflect income correctly. Coupons, tokens, and other means of collecting revenue in advance involve similar deferments in the accounts.

Discounts

Prices of merchandise or services are sometimes stated at list or suggested retail prices, subject to various discounts. Goods offered to a wholesaler may be quoted at the list price of $1,000 less 30 percent. This discount is allowed because the wholesaler performs certain services in the chain of distribution; if the goods are to be sold at retail for the list price, some amount must be allowed to cover the cost of the wholesaler's services. Hence the wholesaler is charged $700 for goods expected to retail at $1,000.

In turn, the retailer may be allowed a discount of 20 percent to cover his services in the distribution of the goods. Thus, the list price may serve as a convenient way to tie a series of prices together. Further, pricing at "list less 30 percent" enables actual prices to be varied to suit conditions without having to disturb catalog or published retail prices. Further, it tends to systematize and unify the system of prices. But it is nevertheless true that goods sold for $1,000 less 30 percent represent revenue only in the amount of $700; only the *net actual price* charged should be credited to Sales Revenue.

Cash Discount

The notion of a price concession for prompt payment is used as a collection device; it is called cash discount or purchase discount. The price on a given invoice may read $1,000, but somewhere on the form there may also appear a notation: "2 percent cash in 10 days, 30 days net," or 2%10/n30. This means that the price of $1,000 is for payment in 30 days; the buyer may, however, discount the invoice by remitting $980 ($1,000 less 2 percent) within 10 days from the date of the invoice.

The purpose of this is, of course, to promote faster collection. Buyers should be anxious to take advantage of this because 2%10/n30 is equivalent to interest at 2 percent for 20 days' anticipation of payment. This is equal to simple interest (really simple *discount* in the technical banking sense) at the rate of 3 percent per 30-day month, 36 percent per year.[1]

There are a number of ways to handle the cash discount situation. These may reflect the psychology of writing invoices or the desire to keep the accounting record in agreement with the stated amounts on the invoices. Some accountants would record sales revenue at the gross price but deduct the discounts taken by customers as an expense, Sales Discounts Taken. Other accountants would prefer to put this debit item along with other revenue adjustments as a correction similar to price concessions (as in the earlier section on that subject above). Still another way is to bill customers and record the sales revenue at the *net amounts,* then ignore sales discounts unless the customer fails to take them. Additional invoices would inform the customer of the lapse of the discount. Sales discounts *not* taken would then appear as added revenue in the financial reports. Here, we shall use a compromise method which shows sales discounts offered and sales discounts lapsed but keeps the Accounts Receivable at gross prices to agree with invoices.

Under this method of accounting, sales billed to customers would be summarized periodically by entries of the following form:

```
Accounts Receivable (gross price)........................  48,000
     Sales Discounts Available (discount)..................           960
     Sales Billed (net) ....................................        47,040
  To record sales as billed.
```

Customer payments within the discount period (amounting to $31,-360) are recorded by crediting customer accounts with $100\%_{98}$ of

---

[1] More accurately, the interest is approximately 3.06 percent per 30-day month on the net invoice price ($2/98 \times 30/20$). This, if compounded monthly, works out to 43.58 percent per year. Obviously, 2%10/n30 represents a very high rate of interest; it should certainly pay to borrow money so as to take cash discounts.

their remittances. The difference is taken up by a debit to Sales Discounts Available to Customers:

```
Cash on Hand.......................................  31,360
Sales Discounts Available.............................     640
    Accounts Receivable...............................          32,000
```

At any given time, the actual amount of Discounts Available to Customers should be the amount originally allowed when the sale was billed, less the sum of (*a*) those discounts applied or taken when remittances appeared, and (*b*) the discounts that lapsed (were made unavailable because the 10-day period expired). The amount of discounts lapsed may be found by examining the uncollected receivables; any uncollected item more than 10 days old contains a lapsed discount. At the end of a reporting period, the tabulation of lapsed discounts would be made and recorded by the following entries:

```
Sales Discounts Available...................................  216
    Sales Discounts Lapsed.................................          216
```

The revenue for the period would then be $47,040 + $216 or $47,-256. On the balance sheet, the situation would be presented:

```
Accounts receivable......................  $16,000
    Less: Sales discounts available............      104    $15,896
```

The computation might have been made, alternatively, by counting up at the end of the month the amount of discounts still *available* to customers on the remaining unpaid balances. Only those invoices issued in the last 10 days of the month would carry such discounts. The amount of these items would in this case be the $104 shown in the balance sheet; the entries for $216 would be made to adjust the Sales Discounts Available to Customers account for the otherwise unrecognized amount of lapsed sales discounts.

The superiority of this method of accounting as compared with the treatment of sales discount as an expense is worth noting. Sales discounts taken by customers are $640; the typical sales-discount-expense calculation would show sales revenue at $48,000, sales discounts taken would appear as a $640 expense; the effect would be a net of $47,360. But this is $104 greater than the figures resulting from the compromise method because of the $104 deduction from Customer Accounts Receivable for Sales Discounts Available to

Customers. The point is, that Customer Accounts Receivable represents expected cash collections. This is reduced by the availability of discounts, just as much as by price concessions or anticipated defaults.[2]

Installment Sales

Merchandise sales on installment terms create a problem for the accountant in measuring revenue for several reasons. First, such transactions are often viewed as merely conditional sales; indeed, in some situations the passage of legal title to the goods occurs only when the final payment is made. This view of an installment sale might be quite acceptable when the sale approximates a lease or rental arrangement because of the small amounts and short payment intervals—as for instance when a watch is sold for $35, with payments of $1 down and $1 per week. But installment sales can raise broader problems of measurement and timing that must be dealt with.

Proper accounting for installment sales is to treat them exactly as any other credit sale: take up the revenue (and the cost of goods sold) at the time of delivery, allow the appropriate amounts for collection default, guarantees, and so forth. This procedure may be a bit awkward because the revenue is recognized far in advance of any material amount of cash receipts. This may be of importance with respect to income taxes because the income tax would be payable before any substantial collections had been received. The argument for the position that revenue and expense of installment sales should be recognized only as cash is received, is stronger when uncollectible sales may cause repossession and resale of the goods. Thus, a $200 installment sale of a refrigerator that had cost $160 would be recorded:

Installment Accounts Receivable	200	
Deferred Cost of Installment Sales	160	
Deferred Revenue, Installment Sales		200
Inventory		160

Then, as cash collections are made, the following entries would appear:

---

[2] A further refinement is possible. It might be possible to estimate the proportion of the available discounts that will not be taken. That is, of the $104, perhaps $29 will lapse within the next 10 days. The $104 is thus too large, but the error is probably immaterial in most cases.

Cash (10 percent of total cash to be received).....................   20

    Installment Accounts Receivable...........................   20

Deferred Revenue, Installment Sales (10 percent of revenue).........   20

    Current Revenue, Installment Sales.....'.....................   20

Costs Applicable to Installment Income (10 percent of cost).........   16

    Deferred Cost of Installment...............................   16

Sometimes the deferred revenue and cost are lumped together and labeled Deferred Gross Profit on Installment Sales. When collections are received from customers in subsequent accounting periods, the Deferred Gross Profit account is debited and Realized Gross Profit is credited. This realized gross margin item is carried to the income statement of the year in which collection is made. If this procedure were applied to the data just presented, we could have the following results.

Instead of showing deferred revenue and deferred costs of installment sales, the first entries would show deferred gross profit of 20 percent of $200 ($40) which would be reduced as collections were made; each dollar collected would be assumed to justify the transfer of 20 cents from Deferred Gross Profit account to Realized Gross Profit account. If $155 of collections were made in the first year, $31 of profit would be realized. The remaining $9 deferred gross margin would be taken up as income when and if the balance of receivables ($45) was collected.

These procedures spread the income from installment sales over the collection period in proportion to customer payments received; thus they make income taxes less of a cash drain than might otherwise be the case. However, it may be necessary to separate receivables and deferred gross profit accounts by years, especially if the ratio of deferred costs to deferred revenues (or the deferred gross margin percentage) varies from year to year. Further, if the goods are repossessed, the related receivables and deferred-profit balances must be closed out. Then the repossessed goods must be resold for enough to cover the difference between these write-offs, or there will be a loss from the repossession.

Installment sales accounting may appear to be somewhat like the "percentage completion" basis of accounting that was discussed in an earlier chapter. There is some similarity; but construction-contract accounting accrues revenue on the basis of incurred *costs* (not cash revenue-receipts), whereas installment sales accounting defers revenue and certain applicable costs such as the cost of merchandise (but not sales commissions and salaries, delivery or advertising costs) to the period when customer payments are received in cash. In view of the tax effect, such procedures are also used in real estate or other long-term, deferred-payment contracts.

Summary

This chapter has presented some of the complications of revenue measurement; specifically, we have seen how the accountant deals with the problems raised by credit risks, returns, price concessions, and other revenue adjustments, such as guarantees, transportation, and cash or trade discounts. The special problem raised by installment sales calls for unusual procedures that diverge considerably from ordinary accounting methods. Accounting measurements are sometimes specially tailored to meet unusual or distorting conditions.

QUESTIONS

1. What are uncollectible accounts and why can these not be entirely avoided? Is an uncollectible account a loss? If so, why should a business firm allow such losses to occur?

2. What problems of measuring revenue arise from the acceptance of credit risk? Are these only a matter of determining the current amount of revenue, or is something else involved?

3. What is an allowance for uncollectibles? How is the amount established as related to a given point in time? Why are entries made to establish such an allowance? How is the allowance used?

4. At the beginning of a certain period, a company had $125,000 of uncollected receivables against which an allowance for uncollectibles of $8,200 (6.56 percent of the gross receivables) appeared. The company estimates that ½ of 1 percent of its credit sales eventually prove uncollectible. Is the situation described inconsistent? Explain.

5. During the year, the company in Question 4 had $1,250,000 of sales on account. What was its reported revenue? What effect would there be on this revenue figure if $5,200 of the initial accounts receivable were actually found to be uncollectible during the year? What effect would there be on the reported revenue if $8,000 of the current year's sales proved to be uncollectible during the year? If $2,000 more of these sales turned out to be uncollectible by February of the following year?

6. Suppose the review of accounts receivable (in another company) at

the end of the current year showed that of $537,000 uncollected accounts receivable on the books, $15,600 were entirely uncollectible, another $3,800 would probably produce a 50 percent pay out, and still another $4,200 would produce only 20 percent of their face amount. The allowance for uncollectibles had been credited with ¼ percent of the $8,400,000 sales billed ($21,000) for the current year, and the balance of the account was $16,300. (*a*) Would you make any adjustment to the allowance account? (*b*) If the balance of the allowance account had been $20,900, would your answer be the same?

7. What entries would you make for a return of merchandise billed to a customer at $100 which had cost $80 to acquire, if the merchandise were salable at regular prices? Would it make a difference if the goods had been damaged in transit because they had been carelessly packed when sent to the customer? Suppose that these goods would have to be sold at 25 percent less than the regular price.

8. Suppose that when the customer referred to in Question 7 reported the damage, the manager of the store offered to reduce the price to $90, which the customer then paid. How would the transactions be recorded and reported?

9. When goods are shipped with transportation costs prepaid by the seller, in what two ways may the shipment be billed? (i.e., at what price?) Set up entries for each treatment being careful to indicate the nature of the transportation cost.

10. How would you estimate the amount to be set up for guarantees on a product such as a vacuum cleaner guaranteed against defects for a year?

11. Explain why a company could *well* afford to borrow money, even at 12 percent per year, in order to take advantage of 3%/10, net 60-day terms of payment?

12. A home builder installs air-conditioning equipment on extended credit terms, three to five years. He accounts for such sales on an installment sales basis for tax purposes. Why would he want to do this? Illustrate, assuming the price of an installation to be $3,600 payable $100 per month for 36 months; this installation cost the builder $2,700, installed, in November last year; his fiscal period is a calendar year. (Ignore interest.)

13. Installment sales procedure (while used for tax purposes in many long-term transactions) is not generally considered to be an acceptable accounting procedure unless—because of the terms or conditions of sale—there is no reasonable basis for estimating the degree of collectibility. Why?

PROBLEMS

Scandinavian Company

Write entries in journal form for the following:

1. Merchandise sold to customers at regular gross prices, $75,000 terms 2% 10/n/30. The company maintains its accounts receivable at gross prices, but its sales are recorded at net prices.
2. Merchandise purchases, terms 3% 30, net 90: $80,000 less trade discount of 20, 15, and 5 percent. Payables are carried at net prices, and costs are recorded at net.
3. Goods shipped to customers, $45,000; shipments on consignment, $3,000. Both amounts are cost.
4. 40% of the accounts payable are settled within the discount period.
5. At the end of the quarter, $4,000 of the receivables were still subject to cash discounts. Discounts lapsed on accounts payable were $350.
6. Losses from uncollectible accounts are expected to be 1% of gross sales.
7. Jones and Wildman who owed $65 for merchandise were declared bankrupt two weeks before the end of the quarter. Creditors will not receive any part of their claims.
8. The last week of the quarter, $3,000 was received as advance payment for special merchandise to be ordered from another firm. This merchandise was expected to cost $1,800. It had not yet arrived at the end of the quarter.
9. Wages and Salaries earned for the quarter, $18,000. Wages and salaries settled during the period, $16,500 less 20% withheld personal income taxes, 5.2 percent FIC tax and state disability tax of 1%.
10. Employer payroll taxes for the quarter, 9.1% of earnings.
11. Payroll deductions paid in cash; but employer taxes are not payable until the 15th day after the close of the quarter.

Required:

Enter these transactions in skeleton ledger accounts, and show what balances remain at the close of the quarter. Are these reasonable?

Withington Pump Company

This company offers all of its customers a cash discount of 2% on any invoice that is paid within ten days of the billing date. During last year, the company's total billed sales were $2 million. Invoices were made out at gross prices, and accounts receivable were carried at gross prices.

The company's accounting procedure involved reviewing the accounts receivable at the end of each month and recognizing lapsed discounts for any account that had remained unpaid for more than 10 days. At the end of the year, the total of discounts taken by customers was $28,000;

the total of lapsed discounts was $9,000, but the end of year review of the accounts receivable also indicated that there was still $3,500 in discounts that could be taken by customers, if payment were made within 1 to 10 days.

Required:

1. Prepare entries to record the foregoing, using proper accounts to reflect the kinds of data mentioned, as adjuncts to the gross price receivables.

2. What comment do you have as to the transactions as described? How did this probably happen?

Occidental Sales Company

On the basis of statistical studies the company management had decided, that it would probably experience credit "losses" amounting to ½ of one percent of its sales on account. During last year, there were sales of $4,000,000 on account, of which $360,000 remained as receivable at the year end. The Allowance for Uncollectibles had been zero at the beginning of that year. Only $1,000 of uncollectibles had been discovered and written off during the year.

On reviewing the remaining receivables at the end of the year, the company credit manager listed $18,000 of accounts whose collectibility he stated to be 60%; another $6,000 of receivables were estimated as only 40% collectible and $4,000 were utterly worthless. The rest of the uncollected receivables ($337,000) were from the last month's sales. (The last month's sales were a little higher than average because of seasonal factors.)

In the following year, the company's sales rose to $5,000,000. The management still believed that its ½ of one percent estimate was sound and continued to provide for credit losses on this basis. Uncollectibles totalling $18,000 were written off during the second year, following bankruptcy or other evidence that collection could not be enforced. At the end of the second year, there was $500,000 remaining in uncollected accounts receivable. In this lot $23,000 was estimated to be only 60% collectible, $10,000 to be 40% collectible, and $9,000 worthless. The remaining $458,000 was from the last month's sales. But one of the lot of accounts written off during the early part of the year as worthless turned out not to be. This account for $1,300 was paid in full by the debtor, who had received an unexpected inheritance.

Required:

Using the above information write journal entries to reflect these situations in the company accounts. How would the accounts receivable appear on the position statement of the Occidental Sales Company at the end of the second year?

Richland Mercantile Company

The Richland Mercantile Company began business January 1 this year. At December 31, the records showed the following data concerning merchandise activities during the year. Calculate the net revenue of the firm for this year, the amount of cash collected from customers, and the cost of goods sold.

	Sales	Purchases
Gross amounts............................	$2,000,000	$1,500,000
Provision for uncollectibles................	10,000	——
Discounts allowed.........................	40,000	30,000
Discounts taken...........................	35,000	28,000
Discounts still available..................	400	1,700
Net uncollectibles written off..............	7,300	——
Open accounts at end of year..............	20,000	85,000
Expected uncollectibles, end of yr..........	3,000	——
Closing inventory at gross prices...........	——	40,000

How would the accounts receivable appear on the position statement at the year-end? Show in detail.

Bolton Wholesale Company

From the following trial balance, prepare a statement of earnings and a position statement at December 31 and for the period closed that date.

	Debits	Credits
Accounts receivable (net prices)...............	$ 25,230	
Accrued wages and salaries...................		$ 3,000
Allowance for depreciation, buildings and equipment...........................		8,000
Allowance for uncollectible accounts..........		1,230
Buildings and equipment.....................	35,000	
Common shares, $100 par each................		50,000
Cash on hand and in bank....................	8,000	
Dividends paid.............................	3,000	
Estimated income taxes payable..............		9,000
Federal income taxes........................	9,000	
Land......................................	10,000	
General administration costs.................	30,000	
Merchandise cost of goods sold...............	95,000	
Merchandise inventory.......................	35,000	
Miscellaneous debts........................		5,000
Mortgage payable, due 10 years hence..........		10,000
Sales revenue (net prices)....................		200,390
Sales discounts lapsed.......................		1,380
Sales returns...............................	4,000	
Sales price concessions......................	6,380	
Selling costs...............................	46,000	
Retained earnings (January 1)................		11,000
Revenue deduction, expected uncollectibles......	2,390	
Trade accounts payable......................		10,000
Total..................................	$309,000	$309,000

Comment on the method of accounting for sales.

Hopworth Wholesale Hardware

The data on page 140 were taken from the company records at the close of last year. However, the December figures need to be adjusted for $133 additional interest charges, and the federal income tax charges will have to be adjusted to reflect the proper amount at 22 percent of net operating margin less interest charges for the year. (The figure given for November 30 was correct.)

Required:
1. A three-column comparative earnings statement, showing (1) 11 months' total to date (2) results for December (3) year total earnings figures.
2. A comparative position statement for November 30 and December 31, showing the changes in the various asset and equity items.
3. A narrative report which highlights for managerial information, the salient observations and comments that these reports evoke.

HOPWORTH WHOLESALE HARDWARE

Summary Ledger Trial Balance
At November 30 and December 31

Account	November 30		December 31		Difference	
	Dr.	Cr.	Dr.	Cr.	Dr.	Cr.
Accounts payable		$ 5,657		$ 16,862		$11,205
Accrued payrolls payable		7,156		6,474	$ 682	
Allowance, depreciation of building		3,600		3,900		300
Allowance, depreciation of equipment		2,701		2,850		149
Allowance, uncollectibles		851		982		131
Building	$ 50,000		$ 51,400		1,400	
Cash in bank	6,124		3,924			2,200
Common shares outstanding		85,000		85,000		....
Customer accounts receivable	23,702		22,507			1,195
Dividends paid	4,000		5,000		1,000	
Equipment	14,080		14,460		380	
Federal income tax liability		2,800		2,800		....
General administration cost	29,817		32,941		3,124	
Interest charges	1,695		1,695		....	
Investments	24,300		35,400		11,100	
Investment income		945		1,462		517
Land	5,000		5,000		....	
Merchandise cost, goods sold	304,426		340,729		36,303	
Merchandise inventory	36,420		34,690			1,730
Mortgage on building		26,500		26,500		....
Provision for federal taxes	2,800		2,800		....	
Purchase discounts lost	52		174		122	
Retained earnings		20,959		20,959		....
Revenue deduction—out freight	753		859		106	
Revenue deduction—uncollectibles	951		1,403		452	
Revenue deduction price adjustment	1,252		1,397		145	
Sales billed		395,470		436,590		41,120
Sales discounts available		406		1,206		800
Sales discounts lapsed		1,235		1,497		262
Selling expenses	47,908		52,703		4,795	
Total	$553,280	$553,280	$607,082	$607,082	$59,609	$59,609

Chapter 8

REFINEMENTS IN THE MEASUREMENT OF EXPENSE

Enterprise productivity is reflected in revenue, the measurement of which has already been examined. But an even more important task of the accountant is to measure expense, which is the cost of producing those services for which customers are willing to pay. Expense is important, not only because it affects income but also because the efficiency of operations is reflected in the degree to which expense may be reduced without affecting the quality of products or services made available to customers. Managers are therefore interested in expense measurements as control tools.

Expense Comparisons

The measurement of expense may give management a useful basis for judging whether the operations were satisfactory, quite apart from any notions of income or cost recovery. One cannot study a set of expense figures without wondering whether all these costs were really necessary or whether this is indeed the best way to operate the firm. Although such questions cannot be answered directly by the expense data, a familiarity with expense data for a given operation over a period of time will tend to establish certain relationships that may be projected so as to set norms or standards. Expense control is an important aspect of management; it cannot exist, however, without expense measurement and interpretation.

How We Measure Expense

When we discussed revenue measurement, we found it necessary to consider all the factors and forces surrounding the sale. However, the costs that give rise to expense items are typically incurred before the sale occurs; we have to measure expense by *tracing* costs from the acquisition of goods or services through their subsequent conversion or combination, up to their delivery to customers. Expense is measured in money only by tracing the effects of disbursements back and forward over time. In some cases, we must anticipate the disbursement (as in the case of payroll for sales personnel) because the cost expires even before disbursement is made. In other cases, we may carry an expenditure in an asset account for a considerable period (inventories or property items) and parcel out the cost as the services or goods are put into the operating stream. The measurement of expense involves a careful tracing of costs so that we may assign them to the periods or the transactions in which the services are released and the costs expire.

Cost Transfers and Conversions

Costs present problems different from those associated with revenues, not only because they occur in different forms and at different times but also because a given cost item may be traceable to one of several time periods. Segregating revenues by time periods rarely involves more than a choice between two adjacent months or years. Revenues are hardly ever carried over long (10- or 20-year) periods, as the costs of long-lived assets must be. Further, revenues are recorded and brought to fruition by collection; seldom are there any extensions or transfers of revenue from one form to another. Costs, however, are carried through more or less long processes of conversion and transfer; they approach expiration via different channels.

Costs may enter the firm as tangible goods or materials, as personal or other kinds of service, as contractual rights (such as possession or use of a building or other property); they may represent mere advantages or privileges—as, for example, the costs of organization in the form of legal retainers, other fees and licenses, or such things as copyrights and patents. The enterprise does not sell the various acquisitions as such; they are made into the products that customers want. A manufacturing firm uses materials, services, and facilities to make a physical product, such as bread, clothing, or automobiles. But a retail store converts bulk packages to more convenient form, maintaining stocks, seeking out sources of supply, helping the customer to evaluate products, obtaining and transmitting information, and so on. Some kind of conversion and transfer of resources exists in every business, and the costs of acquired resources must be traced through the recombination and reclassification that occurs. This tracing of costs within the operating activities of the firm is important, not only because it serves to measure expense as such but also because it measures the costs of the various steps and processes that are carried on within the firm. The internal measurement and assignment of costs is an essential function which accounting is called upon to perform in order to facilitate management information and control.

Finally, the tracing of costs makes it possible to establish more clearly the ways in which resources have been employed. The control of resources requires that they be accounted for from the time they enter the business until they are gone; a good part of resource control is to establish whether or not those resources are used for the intended purposes, and that they are *all* accounted for. This is a management control function that may be assisted materially by accounting procedures. Part of this is exemplified by the difference between expense and loss.

Expense versus Loss

Most nonaccountants would not trouble themselves as to the difference between expense and loss; they are both "outgoes," and outgoes are bad. To the management-minded accountant, however, these two terms represent two very different ideas. Expense is the expected, normal, and necessary cost of providing goods and services for customers; it is typical, recurring, and usual. Loss, *per contra*, is an unexpected, abnormal, or unnecessary cost that carries no benefit to the projects or purposes of the firm (other than, perhaps, the lessons of experience). Both expense and loss are costs chargeable to past or current time periods because they cannot logically be carried forward as assets; but their meanings are quite different.

The impact of a loss is sometimes quite easy to see, as in the case of a casualty. A fire, flood, or other such event may cause the destruction of resources (inventory, plant); there is no doubt upon surveying the ruins that what was formerly considered postponable cost (asset) can no longer be viewed as available for future operations. The cost has expired. Since the expiration is an abnormal and unexpected one, not a provision of services for customers in even the broadest sense, it is a loss. It may be argued, of course, that such losses are avoidable because they can be shifted by the use of insurance; therefore, they arise from a lack of foresight and prudence. Perhaps the real cost of using the building or of carrying an inventory is understated when insurance is not carried, but the loss is still a loss when it occurs. Supposing the carrying amount of the building destroyed was $135,000 ($150,000 cost less accumulated depreciation of $15,000) but that the insurance coverage was limited to $100,000 by the terms of the policy, the following entries would be indicated:

Accumulated Depreciation, Building	15,000	
Claim against Insurance Company	100,000	
Loss from Casualty	35,000	
Building		150,000

Sometimes, the distinction between expense and loss is not so easy to make. It is not possible to trace every service so as to establish the amount received by each customer. Indeed, many services are rendered to customers who do not buy, and it is not possible to be sure that each purchaser actually does want and does receive all those services made available. It is common practice to *assume* that the customer actually does want and does pay for the services typically made available. For instance, the cost of delivery is not traced in a department store to each sale, for some packages are carried home by customers, even though the delivery service is available. In a successful business the assumption, that normal or typical costs which expired during a period are "expense," is generally a valid one. It really makes but little difference whether or not the customer accepts and uses all the services offered, so long as he (or she) is willing to pay for them in the price of the merchandise actually purchased. The important question is really whether the services in question are required to maintain customer relations and the volume of business desired. If so, there need be no concern about loss elements in the expense items.

Nevertheless, if the costs of services provided happen to exceed the revenue of the period, there is an obvious loss. Either the services that have been furnished were inefficiently rendered (at too high a cost) or they have been of a kind that could not be covered by the prices that customers were willing to pay. In any event, the result is undesirable, unexpected, and abnormal. Either the firm should convince its customers that the firm's service is worth higher prices, or the cost of services provided must be reduced—by greater efficiency or by curtailment. The failure of revenue to cover expense is perhaps only a reflection of inefficiency or ineffectiveness, but it is nevertheless undesirable, unexpected, and abnormal—a loss.

Write-downs and Write-offs

There are other cost expirations which must be classified as losses —at least in part. An example would be goods kept in stock over a considerable period. It is not uncommon for such goods to deteriorate or disappear; sometimes this is obvious, but again it may go unnoticed until a physical inventory reveals a shortage of stock on hand. It would perhaps be better to separate the normal from abnormal shortage from shrinkage or spoilage if possible. Normal shrinkage or spoilage is an expense, a cost of customer service. For instance, fruits and vegetables must be trimmed and culled for display; this means that fewer pounds are sold than were received, but this is part of the business of selling such goods. Some spoilage and shrinkage is expected; but when unusual circumstances arise or an unusually poor lot of goods is handled, the abnormal waste should be regarded as a loss. This means that management must have some typical standard of expected performance from which the accountant may separate the expense and loss elements.

Ordinarily, the shrinkage or spoilage is measured by checking a book inventory figure against the cost of the goods actually on hand. The fact that the goods on hand show a smaller cost than the book inventory (purchase costs less identified costs of goods sold) means that some goods have disappeared through waste or loss. The correction of the book inventory figure to recognize the shrinkage or spoilage would require entries such as the following:

Normal Merchandise Shrinkage Expense	752	
Excess Shrinkage—Loss	571	
Merchandise Inventory		1,323

To record normal shrinkage at 2 percent of the cost of goods sold and to write down inventory to cost of goods actually on hand.

Write-downs Resulting from Price Changes

The prices of goods and services do not remain constant. One of the difficult problems of accounting is to find a way to deal with price changes in the measurement of business events, and we shall later deal with this matter at some length. Right now, we shall have to accept as a working hypothesis the proposition that historical cost data are acceptable regardless of price changes, unless there are strong reasons for departing from this pattern. Should prices change, we will not ordinarily change the already recorded costs; the bargained price of a transaction as recorded in the first place is assumed to be an adequate measure for that transaction or the basis for tracing that item through the firm's operations.

Some accountants feel that when inventories are carried over from one period to another, they should be adjusted to market (replacement) prices if these are *lower* than cost. Assets are costs attributable to future periods, and such costs should not logically be larger than what would have to be paid to acquire similar goods through normal channels. In other words, the accountant would argue that there is such a thing as the cost of purchasing at the wrong time and that the costs of wrong timing belong to the period in which the error was made. The excess cost is a loss, not an asset. Therefore, if the book record of inventory shows a balance of $23,000, a cost tabulation of the goods actually on hand totaled $22,500, and the tabulation of the goods at replacement market prices showed $21,000, the accountant would make entries as follows:

Inventory Shrinkage Loss	500	
Loss, Inventory Price Declination	1,500	
Merchandise Inventory		2,000

Efficiency and Expense Measurement

The distinctions among assets, expenses, and losses have been carefully drawn; any cost which cannot be justified as a deferral to future operations is an expired cost, either expense or loss. Any expired cost that arises from unusual, unexpected, or abnormal conditions is a loss. The trouble is that we are not always able to state with assurance just how much of an expired cost is to be regarded as normal and how much of the expiration arises from abnormal circumstances. Managers are constantly on the alert to find ways to improve operations, either by providing more and better services or by reducing the cost of providing them; but we seldom have entirely clear notions as to what services are really essential or what they should cost. Thus we cannot always be certain whether a cost expiration is expense or loss; but when we are not able to decide otherwise, the expired costs are regarded as expenses. This sidesteps the question of separating loss from expense and leaves the expense figure subject to interpretation. An informed reader may apply his own judgment and evaluation to the figures.

Acquisition Cost Timing and Recognition

When we discussed revenues, we found it necessary to establish some acceptable signal to recognize the entrance of revenue. In the case of costs, we need a similar signal. Any one of the following events might be used to indicate the incurrence of cost: placing a purchase order, acceptance of the order by the seller, issuance of an invoice and transportation documents by the seller when goods are delivered to the carrier, receipt of such papers by the buyer, carrier's notice of arrival of the goods, delivery at the buyer's place of business, examination and review of the transaction preliminary to payment, or the disbursement to settle the invoice. Since we are concerned with recording cost on the buyer's records, the event used to signal cost incurrence must be something that will be brought to the buyer's attention in ordinary operations.

In some circumstances, the expenditure of funds is formally controlled by budget procedures that regard the placing of a purchase order as a commitment of resources; the cost is recognized at that point, even though the contract is not complete. This procedure is, however, limited to government or institutional practice. Few business firms employ such procedures, except to note, when such commitments are large in amount, that there is a contingent obligation to accept the goods if they are forthcoming at the offered price.

The legal liability on a purchase usually does not arise until delivery has been made to the carrier; thus, the receipt of the invoice and transportation papers is a notice of liability, for the goods are in transit for the buyer's benefit and risk. At this point, the goods are assets of the buyer and he is liable for payment. Thus cost should, technically, be recognized when the invoice is received. Yet this is not always done because there is still some doubt as to the completeness of the transaction. Even though the legal liability exists, the goods are not available to determine whether they are in fact what was ordered or whether they will be received in good condition free from offset or counterclaim against the seller. The recording of cost is typically deferred until the goods have been received and their quantity and condition noted, to be sure the transaction is complete. This is usually also the signal for authorization of payment according to the credit terms.

One might think from all this that it might be as well to wait until the check is written, and to recognize the cost at the time of disbursement. This, however, would not be a good plan, for there is considerable variation in credit terms; authorization for payment (i.e., indicating that the item is really a liability that ought to be paid when due) may be quite different, in point of time, from actual disbursement. Indeed, when credit terms are 30, 60, or 90 days after date of invoice, the goods might be received in less than 10 days and payment authorized at that time. But by the time disbursement actually is made, the goods in question might be converted to other forms or even sold and collected for, before they would be "acquired" by disbursement. Clearly, to wait for disbursement would distort the pattern too much. Thus, as a matter of good judgment, the signal for cost incurrence is the approval for payment when the goods have been received and checked and the papers have been reviewed to establish the completeness of the transaction.

Nonstorable Costs

The signal for recognizing the cost of personal and other nonstorable services is usually the rendering of the service. Even though payment is not made until the close of a pay period or a billing period, the costs are actually incurred when the service is received. This creates something of a problem, for the acquisition of services is not always explicit and manifest; sometimes services are acquired and put to use in a continuous stream. The only way to handle such a situation is to establish a procedure for periodic accumulation of costs by routine reports. For instance, labor costs may be reported daily or weekly, and the signal for recording payroll costs (including fringe labor costs such as overtime, vacation, and so on) would be the receipt of such reports. The reader will later encounter payroll procedures as a matter of system design, but it is well to recognize here that need for setting up a regular set of routines to recognize payroll costs. Other services (such as utility service, repairs, etc.) are recorded by reports, invoices or statements which notify of the incurrence of cost.

Some service items are acquired by advance payment; rent, insurance, and other continuing arrangements such as service contracts are costs when the liability for payment arises. Thus, an insurance contract may be negotiated by telephone with coverage beginning at once, even though the invoice will not be received for perhaps 30 days. The liability exists, however, and it would be correct to record the cost by the entries:

Unexpired Insurance.. 228
    Accounts Payable..   228

By this means, the insurance cost attributable to operations may be determined at any time, even though the payment is not yet due. When the premium is paid it will be charged to the Accounts Payable account as settlement of the liability. The cost is recognized by the receipt of the service and the obligation to pay, not by the disbursement. Thus, the typical signal for recognizing service costs, even in the case of nonstorable items, is the obligation to pay which arises when service is acquired. We may for practical reasons have to delay the record to be able to handle it efficiently, as in the case of payroll; but nevertheless it is the obligation to pay, not the payment, that initiates the cost record.

Initial Costs—Assets or Expenses?

The question of whether a cost is charged to an asset or an expense account is of importance only when we consider the effect of the transaction on the financial reports. Costs may be reclassified one or more times before the close of a fiscal period, and it is only at the close of a period for which reports are prepared that the classification is a critical matter. The really important question is not where the cost tracing begins but where it proceeds and where it ends, for the purposes of a given report. Indeed, one of the reasons for taking a trial balance is to make it easy to review the classifications, so as to uncover the need for adjustments and to transfer amounts to where they should be. A general rule, however, is to record costs initially in asset accounts unless it is fairly certain that the cost will expire before the next trial balance is taken. This makes it possible to review the trial balance in terms of verifying the assets, assuming that any other costs would have been appropriately considered as expired. However, even this does not preclude a brief review of expense charges to assure their propriety and correctness before reports are prepared.

The Amount of Acquisition Cost

Just as the measurement of revenue begins with a price quotation subject to adjustments and related calculations, the measurement of cost raises similar questions. We must put together those costs which apply to given items and separate those which do not belong together. The first question of this kind is the question of prices and discounts.

Trade Discounts

Acquisition cost cannot include any amount that will not ultimately have to be paid. The price of goods or services is the payment that must be made to acquire them, and this must not be clouded by roundabout methods of establishing the price. Some commodities are priced by reference to list or suggested prices with discounts allowed to wholesalers, jobbers, or retailers. Such discounts are not costs but means of computing the actual price. A television set with a list price of $500 may be sold by the manufacturer to a wholesaler or distributor at a trade discount of 50 percent; the retailer's price might be "list less 35 and 10 percent." This means in effect that the wholesaler's cost is $250 and the retailer's cost is $292.50 ($500 less 35 percent is $325; $325 less 10 percent is $292.50). Trade discounts are merely devices to permit the computation of a number of specific prices from one general list; they have nothing to do with cost, except to indicate how prices are figured. The consumer may pay something different from $500 for the set, for there may be a trade-in or other factors to consider. List prices are not real prices.

Cash Discounts

The general principle that cost is the amount necessary to settle the obligation arising from a transaction applies to cash discounts as well as to trade discounts. Cash discounts are often called purchase discounts and are thought to represent a kind of income earned by prompt payment. This is not an acceptable line of reasoning because income cannot arise from a purchase; purchase discounts are the cost reductions to be taken into account in arriving at the cash price of the goods. Therefore, the acquisition cost of merchandise billed at $2,000 less 17½ percent, terms 2 percent 10, net 30 days, is $1,617 ($2,000 less 17½ percent is $1,650; this, less 2 percent is $1,617). The most direct and simple accounting for this transaction would be:

Merchandise Inventory..................................... 1,617
    Accounts Payable..   1,617

The cost is thus shown as the amount of the obligation, the price to be paid for the goods. Since the discount was offered with the expectation (really a strong one) of prompt payment, there is no need to record the extra amount of the discount. However, the practice of writing invoices in terms of gross amount is very well rooted;

there may be an overpowering desire to record the invoice *gross* so as to tie the accounting record to the quotation on the invoice. This may be done by using an appropriate contra account for the discount such as:

```
Merchandise Inventory...................................  1,617
Purchase Discount Available.............................     33
      Accounts Payable...................................            1,650
```

The account, Purchase Discounts Available, is contra to the Accounts Payable account because it represents the amount to be deducted from accounts payable to establish the current amounts actually owed. It will be seen that in this case, such deduction would show the net liability as $1,617, which is correct. Now, as time passes, either of two things will happen when the 10-day period has elapsed. If the invoice is paid within the 10-day period, the entry for the disbursement would be:

```
Accounts Payable.......................................  1,650
      Purchase Discounts Available.......................              33
      Cash in Bank......................................           1,617
```

This would remove both the gross amount and the contra account item from the books, showing the equity as liquidated. Had the transaction been recorded in the simplest fashion with only the net price shown as a liability, a simple debit to Accounts Payable, credited to Cash in Bank would have accomplished the same result.

However, the item might be left unpaid after the 10-day discount period. In such a case, the amount of the liability has increased $33 through lapse of the discount. This might appear to be an expense or a cost of the merchandise (if it were still unsold), but such treatment is not really justified. The $33 is a penalty for late payment; there is no additional service potential added by this outlay, and it should really be considered a loss. This is further borne out by the fact that money to pay this invoice could have been borrowed at regular bank rates for a good deal less than the discount.

Therefore, the entries to be made at the end of the discount period should be:

```
Loss, Lapsed Purchase Discounts.........................  33
      Accounts Payable, or Purchase Discounts Available...........          33
```

The credit for the transaction would depend upon whether the purchase had been recorded at net or at gross amounts to begin with. In any event, the payment to be made (at the end of 30 days from the date of invoice) is $1,650.

Inward Transportation

Cost is the amount necessary to bring the purchased goods or services to the point at which they will be put to use. Hence, the cost must be increased by the actual amount of transportation charges. Such charges are sometimes included in the price when terms are stated FOB destination; however, unless the seller has priced the goods so as to be able to absorb the freight, there is likely to be a charge on the invoice to cover the freight. This charge means that the seller has, as a matter of convenience to the carrier and the buyer, prepaid the transportation costs. For example, an invoice may show the shipment of 130 coils at $7.20 each ($936), plus freight prepaid, $72. The total charges are thus $1,008. The invoice shows terms 3 percent 15, net 60, but this is applicable only to the cost of the goods, not the freight charges. Therefore, the cash discount is $28.08. The cash payment requested, then, is $979.92. Now, if the purchaser has a local trucker take these goods from the railroad platform to his warehouse or store, the $3.50 trucking cost would also represent an addition to the cost of the goods. Thus the whole set of data might be recorded by the following:

```
Merchandise Inventory...............................  983.42
     Accounts Payable..................................          979.92
     Cash in Bank.....................................            3.50
```

The total cost of the goods is net invoice cost ($936 less $28.08 or $907.92) plus the costs of transportation ($72 plus $3.50 or $75.50). This calculation follows the general notion that the cost of things is measured by the cash payment that would be required to settle the transactions at the time they occurred, to bring the goods or services to the point of use.

Complications with Destination Freight Payments

If the freight charges are not prepaid, they must usually be settled on delivery or within a very short period (24 or 48 hours) under transportation company rules. This means that the payment of freight or express charges at destination usually requires special handling by the consignee to make immediate payment possible. The worst complication is, however, that freight payment is separately recorded, even though it is part of the cost of the goods. The freight bill or other transportation voucher must be matched with the shipment to which it applies to charge the transportation costs where they belong. When there are only a few such transactions, this creates no great problem; but should there be many such shipments received, the matching process may be quite tedious. Imagine, for instance, the situation in a large department store with several thousand separate shipments being received each day, some with freight prepaid, some not; these shipments may involve several freight companies, an express company, and a number of trucking firms. In such situations, it may take much effort to match freight and drayage bills with the specific shipments to which they refer; the problem may be made worse if drayage charges, for instance, covered three or four shipments taken from the railroad platform by a trucker and delivered as one load with a flat charge for the lot. In such cases, it may be necessary to charge the transport costs to a separate account until they have been matched. The following entries would be made to transfer the costs:

Merchandise Cost of Goods Sold............................	137.33	
Merchandise Inventory....................................	64.79	
Unmatched Freight and Drayage Charges.............		202.12

In case the matching cannot be effected with any great degree of success even on a deferred basis, the company may carry all transportation charges into a single account (even those billed along with merchandise cost because they were prepaid by the vendors). The Unmatched Freight and Drayage Charges account would then be cleared by apportioning the total transportation charges between goods on hand and good sold by an entry like the one given immediately above. The amounts may be determined on an average experience such as a percentage of invoice cost, or on the basis of weight of each shipment to the total weight of all shipments. Such methods of assigning transportation charges are admittedly unscientific, but they may be more sensible than trying to trace costs which are by their nature and amount not worth much effort in clerical matching and assignment. This exception, however, does not alter the basic principle that both invoice charges and transportation costs follow the goods into the expense stream.

Cost Transfers and Expirations

As has been suggested in the discussion thus far, acquisition costs usually appear as assets, which are followed through the operations, and eventually written off into expense or treated as losses. But there is an intermediate stage which many costs go through; *during* a fiscal period costs may be considered as costs of operation, especially for managerial purposes. That is, quite apart from whether the cost incurred is to be viewed as an expense or not, costs can and do apply to current activities, as these are carried on from day to day. This is especially true in the case of manufacturing companies.

The product of a manufacturing firm is put together by changing the form and the content of materials by applying various labor, machine, and other services to the task of production. This in accounting language is treated as an "attachment" of costs to the product; the services applied are reclassified (in their cost counterparts) to make up the cost of product. Thus assets as well as current non-storable services are put together into the final product. The cost of product sold is treated as expense; but if the product is not sold it becomes a new kind of asset, finished goods. And, at the end of any fiscal period, there will be on hand some partially finished items, the cost of which is obviously to be treated as an asset, work in process.

Operating Charges

The process of cost attachment hinted at in the preceding paragraph is not a simple one; it is really quite difficult to trace cost items to specified lots of product unless highly technical methods are employed. Further, the managers' interests in costs lie in the way they are related to daily activities; the technical problem of allocating cost to manufactured product should not interfere with careful following of daily operations.

Many costs are incurred from day to day which are not clearly recognizable as assets nor definitely to be regarded as expense. In a business that does engineering, design, or promotional work, the distinctions between assets and expenses may be of little significance for daily operations. A research worker or engineer cannot always say for sure whether his current work will really result in a new design or an improved process, or whether it will produce merely "experience." This last item is not to be regarded lightly; often it is important to know that certain lines of investigation are not fruitful, or at least that some things have been tried, even though the results were negative. Yet the accountant would have no basis for reporting the costs of such unsuccessful investigations other than as losses. However, day-to-day activities are seldom much concerned with the ultimate classifications of costs as between accounting periods. Therefore, daily costs and sales are reported by the accountant so that managers may be informed of developments, even though revenue and the distinctions between expense and asset amounts cannot at the moment be clearly established.

Departmentalization of Operating Charges

Another reason for separation of operating charges as a concept apart from either assets or expense, is the pattern of managerial organization. Various executives who control different areas of operation incur costs by their decisions; the accounting system should show the costs incurred by the decisions of each of such executives. Some of these costs are expenses; some will be reclassified as assets (particularly those associated with manufacturing); some are perhaps losses arising from errors or misfortune; but all of them derive from, and are related to, executive decisions. Therefore, an accounting system will show classifications of operating charges for marketing, manufacturing, research and engineering, and general administration. In each of these groups there will be specific costs of various kinds such as are listed below:

OPERATING CHARGE CLASSIFICATIONS USED IN MARKETING, MANUFACTURING, AND OTHER DIVISIONS OF A BUSINESS

1. Payroll (includes salaries, wages, commissions).
2. Extra compensation (bonuses, premiums, payroll taxes, vacation pay, other fringe benefits).
3. Materials and supplies (also purchased parts and packing material).
4. Utility services (power and light, water, gas, and steam). (Telephone and telegraph usually separated.)
5. Travel and communication (includes telephone, telegraph).
6. Outside contracts (repairs, consulting services, work done by other firms such as printing, designing, etc.).
7. State and local taxes (other than payroll taxes in 2 above).
8. Memberships, public relations, and advertising.
9. Depreciation and amortization.
10. Various costs transferred from other divisions.

This pattern of classification can be used to set up an entirely adequate record of day-to-day costs. The same set of accounts might be used for each department within a given division, and a great deal of detailed information will be accumulated. Later, the reader will, sometime, want to learn how the accountant employs such a classification to make up reports for managerial purposes. Here, however, we are concerned only with tracing costs to measure expense.

Special Issues in Connection with Manufacturing Costs

The emphasis on a new term (operating charges) and the expansion in our conception of detailed operating accounts in a business are merely a more realistic way of looking at the costs of operating a business. In many respects, the idea of operating charges is much like the notion of expense. Both refer to costs applicable to operations during a period of time, and each is based on the tracing of expired costs into various operating accounts either as the costs are incurred (payroll, utilities, etc.) or as assets have been traced into expiration (inventory, prepayments, depreciation). But manufacturing costs raise a special issue. The operating costs traceable to manufacturing operations are not expense until they have been identified (and reclassified) with respect to the goods that have been

FIGURE 8–1

BLUE DIAMOND COMPANY
Manufacturing Summary
Period Ended April 30

Operating charges:

1.	Payroll	$33,470	
2.	Extra compensation	6,593	
3.	Materials and supplies	42,723	
4.	Utility services	1,247	
5.	Travel and communication	742	
6.	Outside contracts	274	
7.	State and local taxes	102	
8.	Memberships, etc.	15	
9.	Depreciation and amortization	977	
10.	Various other costs	35	
	Total Operating Charges		$86,178

Add decrease in work in process:

April 1		$ 6,659	
April 30		4,113	2,546
Cost of goods finished			$88,724

Less increase in finished goods Stock:

April 1		$12,978	
April 30		24,888	11,910
Cost of Goods Sold			$76,814

manufactured. Manufacturing costs are thought of as flowing from the stage of operating charges through work in process and finished goods into cost of goods sold. Only when goods are actually shipped to customers is there any expense connected with manufacturing. This makes it necessary to *compute* the cost of goods shipped to customers, using a schedule called the manufacturing summary. An example of this schedule is shown in Figure 8–1.

In this example the operating charges attributable to manufacturing are $86,178. These items would usually be accumulated in much greater detail so that the records would show the charges applicable to each department, section, or unit. This $86,178 is not expense, however, for we must take the change in inventories into account. Work in process declined over the period (more cost was embodied in finished goods than was incurred in operations), and the amount of inventory decline is added to show the cost of goods finished. But the *increase* in finished goods had the effect of "damming up" the costs because fewer goods were released for sales orders than were transferred to stock from the manufacturing operation. Thus the expense (cost of goods delivered to customers) is only $76,814.

In this case, it is easy to determine the cost of goods sold, because the amounts of inventories are given. In practice, however, work in process and finished goods inventory costs must be calculated. This involves something more than a mere counting of units of product.

Inventory Cost Determination

The costs given in the illustration may be used to show why the inventory figures cannot be easily derived from the operating charge total. Suppose there had been no work in process at either the beginning or the end of the month and that 14,363 units of finished goods had been added to stock, of which 13,260 were sold. $86,178 divided by 14,363 gives a unit cost of $6. But this unit cost would not be applicable to the goods that were sold unless the unit cost of the initial inventory was also $6. The goods were intermixed, and the costs ought to be combined too. This means that unless there were 2,163 units in the initial finished goods inventory (to give a unit cost of $6), the combined unit cost of all finished goods would be more or less than $6. Thus, inventories of work in process and finished goods will affect the calculation of unit costs (and of expense).

In addition to this, the company would probably have made several varieties of product; variations of size, color, or finish would make unit costs different. To illustrate, consider the galvanizing plant in which there is very little work in process. Even though the inventories did not affect the determination of expense very much, the processing of a 10-quart steel pail is certainly not the same kind of "unit" as the handling of a 30-gallon ash can. One product is 12 times the capacity of the other, with perhaps nine times the surface; but it may be covered with a coating half again as thick. To compute product costs (and determine expense) requires more than a mere division of total operating charges by units; we need a separate calculation to arrive at product costs. The complexities of cost

FIGURE 8–2

Costs of Manufacturing Operations, Factory Cost Applied to Product, and Asset and Expense Classifications in Ledger Accounts

Manufacturing Payroll	Manufacturing Materials, and Supplies
33,470	42,723

Manufacturing Extra Pay	Manufacturing Utility Services
6,593	1,247

Manufacturing Outside Contracts
742

Manufacturing State, Local Taxes
274

Manufacturing Travel, Communication	Factory Cost Applied to Product
102	(Contra Credit Account)　　　　86,178

Manufacturing Memberships	Work in Process Inventory
15	6,659　　　　　88,724 86,178

Manufacturing Depreciation and Amortization	Finished Goods Inventory
977	12,978　　　　　76,814 88,724

Manufacturing Miscellaneous	Cost of Goods Shipped to Customers
35	(Expense)　　76,814

(Total, 86,178)
Operating Charges

accounting need not now concern us; we can accept unit cost calculations as being beyond the scope of present discussion, so long as the results of technical computations are available and reasonable.

Factory Cost Applied to Product

To identify and trace product costs, we need a tabulation of the costs assignable to work in process by product batches. We might do this by transferring operating charges to the Work in Process account, crediting the operating charge accounts. This, however, would leave the operating charge accounts with zero balances. This is awkward because we want to compare operating charges week by week as they accumulate over the period. For management reports, we must find some way to keep both operating charges and classified product costs alive in the current record.

This problem of maintaining two cost classifications at the same time is similar to the situation that called for a separate contra account to record accumulated depreciation—the summarization of fixed asset cost applied to operations. We shall use an account, Factory Cost Applied to Product, to accumulate the credits arising from the transfer of costs to product classifications. Just as the credit from a depreciation entry is left in the Accumulated Depreciation account until the asset is disposed of, the credit in Factory Cost Applied to Product accumulates until the end of the year. At the end of the year, the operating charges and the Factory Cost Applied to Product accounts are reduced to zero by the closing process described earlier (Chapter 3).

The flow of costs in manufacturing may be a bit clearer if viewed schematically as presented in Figure 8–2, on the opposite page.

Treatment of Operating Charge Accounts in Financial Reports

The addition of the concept of operating charges to our other tools and methods does not much affect the form of the financial reports. The position statement will still show available resources (assets) against equities (obligations); the statement of earnings will still show the revenues and expenses used to arrive at income for the period. All we have done is to recognize the need for managerial information with respect to operating charges, and to trace costs through the manufacturing process to their final distination— expense in the form of cost of goods sold. But one minor complication does require attention—over- or under-absorbed costs.

Over- or Under-Absorbed Costs

In practice, the different kinds of products, and the need for specific kinds of cost data for managerial purposes, entails the assignment of cost to work-in-process accounts by the use of cost accounting methods. We do not here intend to go into the technical aspects of cost determination, but it should be noted that operating charges may accrue at a slightly different rate than that of the physical flow of product. Some costs are seasonal (heating, air-conditioning); others may be determined primarily by the passage of time (some salaries, rentals, or property taxes); others are erratic (repairs to equipment). Since the aim of cost accounting is to present typical or expected unit cost data, cost accounting assignments may be slightly different from the operating charges as incurred. Although these differences may be expected to average out over the year, there may be under- or over-absorbed balances from month to month. The method of dealing with these balances is to add the over-absorptions (or subtract the under-absorptions) from the total manufacturing charges in the manufacturing summary, so that only the amounts charged to work in process will affect the cost of goods produced in that statement. If the operating charges were, say, $400 more than the amounts charged to Work in Process, the $400 would be subtracted as a credit from the operating charge total and shown as a current asset in the position statement. On the other hand had the operating charges been only $86,000 total, the difference ($178) would have been added to operating charges (debited), and the corresponding credit would appear among current debt items as "over-absorbed" cost. Note that these are not material differences; had they been substantial the cost accountant would wish to check his data and correct it. At all events any such differences remaining at the end of a year would be carried to Cost of Goods Sold or otherwise treated as an expired cost or credit adjustment.

Summary and Conclusion

This chapter has served to sharpen the concept of expense by focusing attention on acquisition cost and its determination; we have traced a number of cost items through the operations of the firm to their final destination—expense. This tracing of costs into expense has brought out some distinctions between cost, expense and losses; we have seen the need for recognizing inventory losses from shrinkage and price declines, as well as other losses from casualties. In the determination of asset cost, we have given attention to the effects of discounts and of associated transportation costs in the determining of asset costs and expense. On the side of cost transfers, we have met a new kind of account—operating charges—especially adapted to manufacturing. The operating charge concept really applies to any day to day activity, whether it is regarded as expense or not, so long as the charges refer to some function of importance to management, e.g. research and development charges. While these may be regarded as expenses at the close of a period, they are regarded during the period as inputs to functional activities or other centers of managerial interest. Manufacturing costs are especially important in this connection, for the determination of inventories and the cost of goods sold depends upon cost accounting calculations which are related to, but not exactly the same as the costs of carrying on the manufacturing operation. We have added a new kind of schedule or subordinate accounting statement, the Manufacturing Summary; this statement reports the flow of costs through manufacturing operations to the expense item of cost of goods sold.

Our next concern is to complete the discussion of expense measurement, by considering certain aspects of long term asset amortization; these are important in financial reports, and are discussed in Chapter 9.

QUESTIONS

1. Distinguish between cost, expense, and loss. Why are these distinctions important?
2. Is inventory shrinkage an expense or a loss? What would determine your answer to this question in a particular case?
3. Why do most accountants think it is proper to " write down" inventories (or other assets) if market replacement prices fall below recorded costs? Is this inconsistent with the general definition of income?
4. What signals are ordinarily used to establish the incurrence of cost:
   a) For purchased materials or supplies?
   b) Personal services—payrolls?
   c) Fringe labor cost?
   d) Transfers, as from inventory to expense?
   e) Amortization, such as depreciation or deferred interest?
5. What difference does it make if the cost of insurance coverage is

not recorded until payment is made? Or whether the cost is initially recorded as unexpired insurance or as insurance expense?

6. Why are all acquisitions recorded net of all trade or cash discounts? What would be the cost of a machine with an invoice price of $5,000, less 30 percent trade discount, terms 2%/20 net 60; freight prepaid, $260; installation and testing cost, $530?

7. Are cash discounts (taken on merchandise purchased for resale) in any sense income? Why? What accounts ought to be used to record and report discounts on such merchandise?

8. In a department store there are numerous items of merchandise involving various kinds and amounts of inward transportation. What complications does this cause in determining the cost of the goods? How can this problem be resolved?

9. What is meant by operating charges, especially with reference to manufacturing operations? Is this conception related to financial measurements (i.e., expense, assets), or does the notion of operating charges have relevance only to managerial interests?

10. What are typical items in the category of operating charges? Are these likely to be similar in various departments and activities? Of what use is a standard classification (such as is used in the text) for a large business with more than a plant or sales office? Why would it be advantageous to have such details presented in reports to the manager for his *own* department operations only?

11. What problems arise in the determination of the costs of manufactured product:
    a) As to what is meant by a unit of product?
    b) With regard to variations in efficiency and changes in prices over the year, or seasonal fluctuations in such costs as heating or air conditioning?
    c) The fact that some costs change with the fluctuations in volume of operations, while others do not change?
    In view of these and other problems, is the cost of a unit of product really determinable from simply dividing the total costs of operating a factory by the number of units of product?

12. What is the function of the account with Factory Cost Applied to Product, especially with regard to the needs for weekly or monthly cost comparisons, as opposed to measuring expense, as "Factory Cost of Goods Sold"? The operating charges for a manufacturing operation during a given period were $220,000. The initial inventories were: materials and supplies, $45,000; work in process, $30,000, and finished goods, $50,000. The final inventories were: materials and supplies, $42,000; work in process, $38,000; and finished

goods, $47,000. How much were the Cost of Goods Finished and the Cost of Goods Shipped to Customers?

PROBLEMS
Richland Mercantile Company

Refer to this problem, end of Chapter 7, and compute the cost of goods sold.

Carlton Appliance Company

Costs incurred in the manufacturing division of this company for the first quarter of the current year were as follows:

Payroll for all employees and supervisors.....................	$ 89,000
Payroll taxes...	6,235
Materials and supplies withdrawn from stores.................	127,000
Electric power, gas, and water.............................	4,700
Rent, insurance, property taxes.............................	6,100
Depreciation of equipment.................................	7,200
Miscellaneous services....................................	3,565
Total Manufacturing Charges..........................	$243,800

The cost accounting department reported that the amounts of costs traceable to products worked on during this period were:

Direct Labor..	$ 60,600
Direct materials...	127,000
Other costs assigned at 90 percent of direct labor cost.	

The cost of goods completed and transferred to the warehouse during this period was $226,720.

The initial finished goods inventory was $35,400, but the final inventory had risen to $56,120.

Required:

Record the foregoing information in appropriate skeleton ledger accounts, to determine the Factory Cost of Goods Sold.

Axis Meter Company

Below are given certain accounts from the trial balance of the Axis Meter Company, at March 31, this year, and supplementary data related to the company's operations for the first quarter. Prepare, in good form, a manufacturing summary report for the quarter.

Materials inventory 1/1...................................... 18,200
Purchases of materials (terms 2% 10, net 30) at gross prices....... 56,000
Purchase discounts lapsed................................ 200
Freight charges on materials purchased....................... 100
Purchase discounts available, at 3/31........................ 320
Accounts payable for materials (gross price)...................   16,000
Payroll and payroll taxes (Manufacturing portion)............... 32,000
Manufacturing light and power costs.......................... 600
Taxes Payable on manufacturing property 1/1..................   700
Depreciation, factory building and equipment.................. 2,600
Misc. manufacturing supplies & services...................... 200
Work-in-process inventory 1/1............................. 9,700
Finished goods inventory 1/1.............................. 17,400
Factory cost applied to product.............................   89,500
Other accounts, net......................................   31,120

(1)   Inventories, March 31: Materials $17,700; Work in Process $10,200; Finished Goods $15,000.

(2)   Taxes payable on manufacturing property at 3/31, $2,100.

The Parts Manufacturing Company

This company is a wholly owned subsidiary of Mammoth Appliances Corporation. It is engaged in making parts for the parent company's products. Since it produces only for one customer on a captive basis, it has no selling staff nor any appreciable administration costs. All of the operating charges are manufacturing costs.

At the beginning of a six months' period, the Parts Manufacturing Company's trial balance showed the following items:

	Debits	Credits
Cash in bank....................................	$ 1,400	
Receivable from parent company...................	14,900	
Unexpired insurance............................	800	
Materials stores inventory.......................	30,300	
Work in process................................	15,700	
Finished goods.................................	53,800	
Plant and equipment............................	75,000	
Allowance for depreciation......................		$ 20,000
Accounts payable...............................		38,400
Accrued payrolls and taxes......................		7,800
Common shares.................................		120,000
Retained earnings..............................		5,700
Total.................................	$191,900	$191,900

During the next six months, the following transactions were summarized:

(1)   Materials purchased for stock, $42,300, on account.

(2)   Payrolls and payroll taxes cost incurred, $55,700.

(3)   Depreciation of plant and equipment, $2,500.

(4)   Electric power, gas, and water consumed (per meter readings), $1,800.

(5)   Insurance expired, $200.

(6) Cash paid for materials purchased, $44,000.
     Cash paid for payrolls and payroll taxes, $57,200.
     Cash paid for electricity, gas and water bills, $1,740.
     Cash paid for property taxes, $740.
(7) Materials withdrawn from stores for production, $42,000.
(8) Costs of manufacturing applied to products, $102,600.
(9) Cost of parts finished, $105,900.
(10) Cost of finished parts shipped to parent company, $109,400.
(11) Parts shipped to the parent company were billed at $120,340.
(12) The parent company made cash remittances of $110,000.

Required:

Record the transactions and prepare statements of earnings and position at the end of the six-month period. Show in a manufacturing summary report the details of manufacturing costs as they relate to the factory cost of goods shipped.

Mackensack Company

Costs incurred by the manufacturing division of this company for the first quarter of the current years were:

Gross earnings of all employees and supervisors	$38,000	
Payroll taxes, vacation pay and other fringe costs	9,500	
Materials purchased	62,000	
Electricity, gas, and water consumption	2,600	
Rent, insurance and property taxes	3,000	
Depreciation of building, machinery and equipment	3,500	
Miscellaneous repairs and other services	700	
New machinery purchased, end of the quarter	16,000	$135,300

At the beginning of the quarter there had been a material inventory of $10,000, and a finished goods inventory, $18,000. Costs traceable to products worked on during this quarter were; direct labor, $30,000, direct materials, $63,000, and other costs assigned on an average rate of 90% of direct labor cost. At the end of the quarter, the cost of work still in process was $22,000, and the manufacturing costs were under absorbed by $300. The cost of goods finished was $113,000, and the final inventory of finished goods was $28,000.

Required:

Use accounts to record the data applicable to manufacturing costs, and make up a manufacturing summary statement.

Stalwart Furniture Company

This company produces office furniture. In the Matsonburg plant only desks and chairs are produced, but the home office and the sales division are housed in the Matsonburg building.

Accounts to accumulate charges for four major divisions are kept in the Matsonburg location. They are: desk production, chair production, sales offices and general administrative offices. At the beginning of the year the operating charge accounts had no balances; but during the first quarter, the following transactions occurred, for which you are to write entries in journal form:

(1) Materials and supplies purchased $604,000; terms 2% 30, net 60.

(2) Payroll costs (employee gross earnings) desk production, $150,000; chair production, $400,000; sales department, $56,000, and general administration, $56,000. $110,000 of the desk department labor costs were direct labor; $325,000 of the chairs department labor costs were direct.

(3) Employer's payroll tax liability is 9.1%.

(4) Materials and supplies drawn from stores include: desk production, $201,000; chair production, $350,000; sales department, $11,000, and general administration, $4,000. Of these costs, $195,000 in desk production were direct, and $340,000 in chair production were direct.

(5) Space in the building is used as follows: desk production, 40%; chair production, 50%; sales department, 5%; general administration, 5%.

The following building ownership and maintenance costs were incurred: property taxes, $4,000; insurance expired, $1,750; repairs, painting and so forth, $800; depreciation of building $3,080; interest on mortgage, $2,470; utilities (water, gas, electricity) $1,400; oil (for heating) $2,200. None of these was paid for.

(6) Telephone charges $180; which were charged 75% to sales, 15% to general administration, 5% to desk production, and 5% to chair production were paid in cash.

(7) Travel expenses were $88,000 of which $6,000 is chargeable to general administration, the rest to the sales department. Paid in cash.

(8) Advertising, $25,250 payable in 60 days after close of quarter. Of this, some was for help wanted advertising: $80 for desk production; $140 for chair production; $30 for office help. The rest was for product advertising.

(9) A separate meter measures electric power consumption; readings of this meter indicate that power used cost $3,200. 30% of the power is used in desk production, 60% in chair production, 2% in sales department and 8% in general administration. (The President has his own personal elevator and air conditioner).

(10) Repairs and parts charges (all paid for) were for desk production, $860, for chair production, $2,200, sales department $149 and general administration, $240.

(11)   Depreciation of equipment for desk production $1,141; for chair production $2,041; sales department $115; and general administration, $360.

(12)   Factory costs are transferred to work in process as follows: all direct labor and direct materials costs are transferred to work in process as incurred. Other costs (indirect costs) are charged on the basis of rates per direct man hour: $1.20 for desk production and $1.35 per direct man hour for chair production. During this quarter, there were 58,000 direct man hours operated in desk production, and 100,000 direct man hours operated in chair production departments.

Required:

Post all the entries to a five column analysis sheet, one column for each department and a total column for checking purposes. Determine the over- or under-applied costs for the two manufacturing departments.

If the closing inventory of desks in process was $32,500, and the closing inventory of chairs in process was $97,520, what was the cost of desks finished and the cost of chairs finished during the quarter?

Chapter 9

LONG-TERM ASSETS AND THE MEASUREMENT OF INCOME

All assets are (as was pointed out in Chapters 3 and 4) in essence carryovers to the future period as resources available for future operations; most assets are deferred charges to future expense—cost incurred, but clearly not attributable to the operations of the period just closed. Some of the deferred costs are short-term in duration; usually merchandise and typical service costs for rent and insurance are carried over for only short periods of time. Other assets are of longer duration; and in addition to being classified separately in the position statement, they have characteristics somewhat different from those of inventories and prepayments. Long-term asset service potentials are, however, not clearly identifiable and traceable to specific physical units or services; the capacity of a machine or a building is not something that can be observed or connected with service flows, as can the costs of an inventory or an insurance contract. Thus, difficult and tedious problems are raised for the accountant by such long-term assets as (1) buildings, equipment, machinery, and other structures; (2) resources such as mines or wells which contain amounts of materials or usable facilities not easily determinable except by exploitation; and (3) intangible advantages such as going value and start-up costs, and outlays for organization or development.

Complications in Determining Cost: Installation

For long-term assets, acquisition cost may involve more than mere invoice price and transportation. A machine acquired FOB seller's plant for $2,650, terms 5 percent 10, net 90 days, with $274 freight prepaid would represent a net invoice cost of $2,791.50. To this would be added the cost of trucking the machine from the railroad to the buyer's plant; there would also be added to the cost of the machine, all those additional outlays which were necessary to install and make the machine ready for use. For example, the cost of making a concrete base for the new machine, the cost of special runways or scaffolds needed to complete the installation, the cost of labor to put together the parts of the machine or to get them into place for use, the cost of testing and adjusting the machine, including the salaries and expenses of engineers or other people needed to get the machine ready for use, would all be legitimate additions to the cost of the equipment. However, the cost of the new machine would not include the cost of removing or dismantling and disposing of old equipment replaced by the new machine, nor would it include costs not actually incurred, such as lost production during the changeover, or workers' paid vacations taken while the new machine was being installed. The principle is clear: cost includes the amount of actual outlay necessary for, and clearly related to, the acquisition of the new set of service potentials; it does not include anything else.

Application of the principle does, however, raise problems in practice. For instance, how does one handle the cost of breaking down and rebuilding the wall that had to be torn out to get the old machine out and the new one in? What does one do about parts salvaged from the old equipment because they will still be useful with the new machine, or how does one handle the loss arising from disposition of materials used with the old machine but which cannot be used with the new one? As may be imagined, there will be some differences of opinions in these cases. As a measure of the cost to be deferred, fair market value would presumably be used to state whatever is saved for future use.

Real Property

The basic notion in accounting with respect to land used for industrial or commercial purposes is that such land does not depreciate; its cost should not be spread over any time period because that period is indefinite, perhaps perpetual. Therefore, it may be an important matter whether a cost is charged to the land account or to the cost of the building; building costs are spread over time by depreciation charges, and land costs are not. A general rule is to charge permanently useful items to land cost; items that will last only for a limited period are charged to appropriate other accounts. Thus, the cost of options to purchase a land site, title search to establish ownership of the fee, legal charges for registry of deeds to land, the cost (if identifiable) of old buildings that must be torn down if the land is to be used (including the costs of tearing them down), and such assessments and costs as street, sewer, water, taxes, and other charges relatable to the property at the time of transfer and paid by the purchaser are all costs that should be charged against the land account. Any costs not so clearly related to the land acquisition and those that are attributable to only a limited period of usefulness— such as sidewalks, lawns, shrubbery, and the like—ought to be separated from the cost of the basic site. Such costs should be spread over the period of their use in the same way as building and equipment costs are charged to operations via depreciation entries.

Buildings, Machinery, and Equipment Costs

In trying to assign the costs associated with mechanical or constructed assets, one may easily observe that such costs are really conglomerate; every such asset is a collection of parts that may need to be replaced at different intervals. Such things as belts, gears, and wearing surfaces (bearings and the like) often must be replaced at relatively short intervals. But it is not always clear as to what relation exists between the parts and the whole. For instance, an automobile when purchased is equipped with tires that will certainly not last as long as the rest of the car. Of longer expectancy, but still not necessarily of the same durability as the basic frame and body of the car, are such things as batteries, generators, ignition parts. Of still longer tenure but still probably replaceable before the car is scrapped are engines, transmissions, radiators, and axles. When we say a car will last for seven years "on the average," it is quite difficult to be sure of what is meant.

On the other hand, there are costs of owning and operating an automobile that quite clearly are of currently expensable nature. Certainly fuel, lubrication, and minor adjustments would be considered as expense when they were incurred. Items such as license fees and insurance premiums would be prorated over the terms to which they apply. But an engine overhaul or the replacement of an automatic transmission would hardly be considered an expense of the month or even the year in which it was incurred. The complexities in this wide array of costs will call for certain expediencies in treating costs, simply because it is nearly impossible to be more than partially accurate in assigning them.

Criteria for Capitalization

Ordinary operating costs, maintenance, and repairs of a minor and recurring character are clearly chargeable to the period in which such costs arise. But to distinguish between this kind of cost and those which ought to be spread over longer periods, certain rules are typically invoked. One of these may be expressed by stating that any outlay of less than $100 in a small firm (or perhaps $5,000 in a very large company) ought to be expensed immediately, simply because it is relatively insignificant. An error in spreading a cost of this size may be of little or no consequence because there may be many of such outlays, spaced relatively evenly over the life of the asset to which they may be related. Another rule that might be established is that of some minimum service life. Certainly outlays for small tools or accessories that will not be useful for longer than a year might just as well be expensed without question; this may be extended to two or three years if the amounts involved are not too great. These two ideas may be combined in some situations, e.g., the rule might be to write off into immediate expense all costs which entail a single outlay of less than $500 *or* represent a potential service life of less than two years. With some such rules in force, the accounting for long-term assets is much reduced in detail and tedium.

Major Overhauls and Rearrangements

Even after rules are established by which capitalizations are distinguished from expense, some costs will require special attention. Re-roofing an entire building is likely to involve material amounts of money, and in many cases would be separately treated as a deferred cost to be spread over five years or so. The cost of making an extensive rearrangement of plant facilities or of rebuilding certain equipment to extend its useful life might be the basis for special charges spread over the several periods that presumably will benefit from these costs.

Generally, the criteria applied are (1) whether or not the expenditure extends the life of the asset, (2) makes it useful for some additional task, or (3) improves its efficiency over what that was originally; if so, the cost is attributable to future operations because of the added life or benefit. On the other hand, outlays which merely keep the machine or equipment in normal operating condition are current expenses. Those which serve to make good a deficiency in past maintenance are treated as expenses chargeable to the period in which such maintenance should have been done. Of course, this does not lessen the difficulty of deciding which period or periods should be charged with the cost. It is not always clear whether a machine is repaired or partially rebuilt; it is a moot question as to whether the cost should be charged to the last unit produced before the repair was needed, all the other units preceding that one (of which each contributed something to the need for repair or renovation), or to the units to be made in the future (which are possible only because the work was done to keep the machine running). Obviously, the outlays made to continue equipment in service are joint costs of all the results from operating the equipment over its entire life; there is no simple and direct way to assign such costs without some reservations.

Yet the very notion of "income for the year" demands that such costs be assigned in the most objective and consistent manner possible. Accountants thus will try to apply criteria that will at least apparently justify the cost assignments that have been made. This is seen also in the various ways in which depreciation charges may be calculated.

Some Refinements of Depreciation

Depreciation was defined in Chapter 2 as a spreading of the cost of a long-term asset over the period of its useful life. In earlier illustrations, we did not consider the costs of delivery, installation, and so forth; neither did we take into account the possible recovery that might be had from disposition of the asset when it had served its purpose for the firm. Although disposals often produce little net proceeds (the cost of dismantling and removal is likely to be as much as can be recovered from a worn-out piece of equipment), any net receipts or costs from disposition should be considered in determining depreciation. Thus, an asset which costs $3,600 delivered and installed and is expected to bring a net disposal value of $600 after five years of use would entail annual depreciation of $600. Initial cost of $3,600, less $600 scrap recovery, leaves a $3,000 depreciable amount; this divided by 5 gives $600 per year as the *straight-line* depreciation charge.

But there are other ways to assign the cost of such an asset. One might think of the asset as being really a capacity to render certain specified services—the number of ton-miles hauled in a motor truck, or the number of units of product to be turned out by a machine. When the output or service is likely to be distributed unequally over periods of time, it would appear worth considering whether the depreciation ought to be measured by physical usage. Thus, if the number of units of product expected over the five-year period were 4,000, 6,000, 5,000, 3,000, and 2,000 (not an unusual distribution), the depreciation would be figured by taking the total number of units (20,000) to establish a unit depreciation charge. The depreciable amount of $3,000, divided by the number of units expected output, gives a depreciation rate of $150 per thousand units. If the actual production were exactly as expected, the charges would be $600, $900, $750, $450, $300, a total of $3,000. But if the actual production were 3,000, 7,000, 6,000, 3,000, and 1,000, the spreading of the cost would be different. Of course, a difference in the total output from expectations would entail a change in the rate just as a change in the expected life in years would require this. If, after the first three years had turned up outputs of 2,000, 9,000, and 6,000, and the output for the remainder of the service life were 7,000 more units, the corrected rate would be $3,000/24,000 or $125 per 1,000 units. Indicated adjustments to the income of earlier years would add $50 to the income of the first year, $225 to that of the second, and $150 to that of the third year. But since the reports of earlier years would not be recalled for correction, the indicated adjustment would be:

Accumulated Depreciation	425	
Retained Earnings		275
Depreciation Charges (current year)		150

This entry is based on the assumption that the current year's depreciation had already been recorded at 6 × $150 or $900, which on the basis of revised expectations ought to be 6 × $125 or $750.

Production Hours Basis

If the machine in question were something of a general-purpose one (such as a lathe or a drill press), different amounts of machine time might be used for various products. Then it might be better to use a production *hours* basis of depreciation. Supposing the total expected use of the machine were 10,000 hours, the indicated depreciation rate would be 30 cents per machine hour ($3000 depreciable amount/10,000 hours). An actual production rate of 1,700 hours used in a given period would entail a depreciation charge of $510. Changes in expected usage would be adjusted as indicated above for the product units basis.

Declining Charge Bases

Both the product units and the production hours basis of depreciation might produce declining charges over the successive fiscal periods if the output or activity did in fact decline. However, there are depreciation methods which will produce declining charges over the term, even though they are time-based calculations. One of these is the "constant percentage of declining balance" approach. This method takes the position that while the percentage of depreciation remains constant, it should be applied to the steadily reducing principal amount to produce a smaller charge in each successive year. There is some justification for a declining charge in that the available or actually used services may be less valuable as the asset grows older —either because of the lessening of demand intensity in the product market or by increasing inefficiency and obsolescence of the productive factor. Many products and equipment tend to become inadequate or functionally less desirable over time, and thus there is merit in a declining charge for depreciation. In addition, increasing repairs and maintenance charges for older equipment might seem to justify a smaller depreciation charge in the later years. In any event, to achieve such a result as this, we could use a percentage rate that would cause the carrying amount of the asset to decline exponentially. The annual percentage would be determined:

$$r = 1 - \sqrt[n]{S/C} \qquad \text{which in this case would be} \qquad 1 - \sqrt[5]{600/3{,}600}$$

The residual or scrap amount is the terminal value of the series in which a flat percentage is applied to the reducing balance. The actual rate would be computed:

$$600/3600 = \tfrac{1}{6}, \text{ or } .1666$$
$$\log .1666 \text{ is } -1 + .22167, \text{ or } -.77833;$$
$$-.77833/5 = -.155666, \text{ or } (-1 + .844833)$$
$$\text{Antilog of } -1 + .844333 \text{ is } .699;$$
$$1 \text{ less } .699 = .301, \text{ the rate to be used.}$$

The annual depreciation charges would be:

Year 1: $3,600 × .301 =	$1,084 depreciation	$3,600 −	$1,084 =	$2,516
Year 2: 2,516 × .301 =	757 depreciation	2,516 −	757 =	1,759
Year 3: 1,759 × .301 =	529 depreciation	1,759 −	529 =	1,230
Year 4: 1,230 × .301 =	370 depreciation	1,230 −	370 =	860
Year 5: 860 × .301 =	259 depreciation	860 −	259 =	601
	$2,999 Final Balance (Recovery)			$ 600

Sum-of-Years'-Digits Method

The somewhat complex calculations of the "constant percentage declining balance" approach tends to evoke a practical approximation—the sum-of-years'-digits approach. This takes the sum of the years involved (in this case $1 + 2 + 3 + 4 + 5 = 15$) and uses the proportions of these numbers to their total (in declining order) to establish the depreciation percentage or amount. In this case the results would be a series, $\frac{5}{15}$, $\frac{4}{15}$, $\frac{3}{15}$, $\frac{2}{15}$, and $\frac{1}{15}$ applied to the depreciable amount of $3,000 to produce successive years' charges of $1,000, $800, $600, $400, $200. While this does not quite have the precise feature of a constant rate of depreciation, it is sufficiently close to fit what may appear to be the economic pattern of a declining usefulness for successive years' asset service. For long-life periods, the sum of year's digits may be calculated as $N(N + 1)/2$.

Double-Rate Declining Balance Approach

Another practical expedient in calculation, having its origin in liberalization of depreciation in the computation of income taxes, is the declining balance approximation obtained by using $1\frac{1}{2}$ times or twice the regular straight-line rate, applied to the declining balance, to compute the annual charges. The calculations are given below for the $1\frac{1}{2}$ and the double-rate approach so that the reader may compare these with other figures given. It will be noted that the tax provisions permit shifting to a straight-line basis on the remaining depreciable amount when this is to the taxpayer's advantage. The

DECLINING BALANCE DEPRECIATION CHARGES

	One and a Half Rate			Double Rate		
Year 1:	$3,000 × 30%	=	$ 900	$3,000 × 40%	=	$1,200
Year 2:	2,100 × 30%	=	630	1,800 × 40%	=	720
Year 3:	* 1,470/3	=	490	1,080 × 40%	=	432
Year 4:	980/2	=	490	* 648/2	=	324
Year 5:	490/1	=	490	324/1	=	324
Total			$3,000			$3,000

* Shift to straight line.

year in which this occurs is, for the double rate calculation determined for a useful life of n years,

$$n/2 + 1\frac{1}{2} \text{ if } n \text{ is odd; or } n/2 + 2, \text{ if } n \text{ is even.}$$

For the $1\frac{1}{2}$ rate pattern, the shift point is somewhat earlier, because there is less difference between the rates. At all events, the shift may be determined by successively comparing the accelerated rate depreciation charge with that which would write off the remaining depreciable amount over the net remaining life.

It should be borne in mind, however, that any pattern of depreciation charges will vary with the net disposal value and the useful life.

Compound Interest Methods

A few accountants advocate the use of compound interest methods of computing depreciation. Some justification for this exists, in that money invested in a long-term asset could have been used to produce income if invested otherwise. If the firm is really to use the asset effectively, the cost of using the asset ought to include an interest element to recognize the alternative productivity of investment. However, merely to charge interest on the asset balance in each year of use serves only to produce an interest income in that same year which offsets the expense.

Another way to approach this is to recognize that the interest elements are part of the amount which was capitalized when the asset was put into service. This approach requires compound interest calculations to arrive at depreciation charges. Compound interest arithmetic is discussed in Chapter 10 as part of financing transactions; the discussion of compound interest depreciation is deferred for this reason. Anyway, depreciation is usually regarded as a problem that is complex enough, without the use of compound interest. Unless compound interest methods really improve the results, they are not used.

Selection of a Depreciation Method

Obviously income taxation in a period of high tax rates would suggest the use of a method which takes as much depreciation into expense as early as possible. The declining charge methods would tend to do this, and among them the double-rate declining charge method would seem to be most accelerated. But this procedure is not available for any and every asset under extant tax provisions. Further, the method used for tax purposes need not be the same as that used in published reports. (We shall consider some complications in Chapter 13 arising from the use of different depreciation for tax and reporting purposes.)

There would seem to be a very real temptation for management to use the choice of depreciation method as a means of managing reported income, and there is no doubt that something of this kind does occur. The public accountant–auditor has some responsibility in this connection to see that this does not unduly affect the consistency and validity of reported earnings.

The really correct basis for choosing a depreciation method is that of approximating as closely as possible the release of service potentials into the operations of the firm. For example, it is not difficult to see that the service potentials in an office building would tend to be applied to the production of income most heavily in the early years, and less so when the building becomes older. This would suggest that some form of declining charge method would be preferable to straight-line computations. But in the case of a general-purpose machine tool whose functions are well established and whose likelihood of supersession or inadequacy is relatively low, a production hours or production units basis might be preferable. This is also likely to be the case with a blast furnace, especially with respect to the inner linings which burn out from usage much faster than the outer framework deteriorates. Thus, some cases suggest a "dissection" of the asset item to measure depreciation more logically; airplane engines are properly depreciated on a flying hours basis, while the airframe and outer structures are probably better amortized on the basis of time, since obsolescence is a fairly heavy factor in their retirement.

Further, the depreciation method should take some notice of repair and maintenance policy because of their impact on asset efficiency and use.

Adjustment and Correction of Depreciation

Depreciation charges are estimates, and there are times when such figures need to be revised or corrected. Sometimes this is not apparent until the asset is retired from service. An asset which cost $18,000 and has been depreciated for 9½ years at a 10 percent rate would have an accumulated depreciation balance of $17,100 and a net book amount of $900. If it is disposed of to realize a net $330 scrap value, $570 depreciation needs to be recorded to clear the accounts for this item. The $570 correction applies to the entire 9½ years, but it may be divided so as to correct the current half-year's depreciation.

Cash in Bank	330	
Depreciation Charges (current)	30	
Underdepreciation, Prior Years	540	
Accumulated Depreciation		900

The asset disposition could then be recorded,

```
Accumulated Depreciation............................. 18,000
     Machinery and Equipment..........................           18,000
```

"Underdepreciation, prior years" would appear in the statement of earnings along with other noncurrent items (after net income for the year); the current half-year expense charge would be $900 already recorded, plus the $30 addition. This amount is, alternatively, $\frac{1}{19}$ of ($18,000 − $330) which is also $930, the correct straight-line time depreciation for one half year.

This correction to current depreciation charges is so small as to be considered of little import, and the first entry above might have been:

```
Cash in Bank.............................................. 330
Underdepreciation Retired Assets............................. 570
     Accumulated Depreciation...............................           900
```

In this case, the minor error in current year income is ignored and the entire $570 adjustment is treated as a noncurrent item. Some accountants would label such adjustments "loss on asset retirement" (or "gain," for *over*depreciation); this is clearly a misuse of terms. Since depreciation is never more than an estimate, there is no real basis for reference to gains or losses in the final recovery.

Revisions

Depreciation computations may be revised before the asset in question reaches retirement. It is often easier to tell how well a piece of equipment is standing up after it has been in service for some time. A checkup on a given machine may indicate that although it was originally expected to remain in service for 12 years, its condition after 5 years of use indicates that it will still last for 10 years more. If its cost was $9,000, five years of accumulated depreciation has actually been recorded—total $3,750 ($\frac{5}{12}$ of $9,000). But the total expected life is now 15 years, and the accumulated depreciation should therefore be $\frac{5}{15}$ of $9,000, or only $3,000. Assuming that the machine had been purchased at the end of the third quarter of the year and that the revision is to be made as at the end of the third quarter of the current year, the indicated entries are:

```
Accumulated Depreciation.............................. 750
     Depreciation Charges (current).........................           112.50
     Overdepreciation, Prior Years..........................           637.50
```

The correction is divided over 20 quarters, of which three are within the current year; thus $\frac{3}{20}$ of the adjustment is a reduction of the depreciation already recorded for three quarters of this year; the rest is overdepreciation of prior years. The depreciation charge for the last quarter of the current year is, of course, $150 ($9,000/ (15 × 4). Total depreciation for the current year is made up of three quarters at the original rate, less the adjustment above, plus $150 for the last quarter. This is ($9,000 × ¾ × 8⅓ percent) — $112.50 + $150.00; or $750 − $112.50 + $150 = $600, which is correct, being ¹⁄₁₅ of $9,000.

Taxes and the Recalculation of Depreciation

As a general rule in the computation of income taxes, adjustments or corrections of prior years' income are not contemplated. Unless last year's tax return is amended, there is no way to adjust for errors in earlier years. In addition, there is a three-year limit on such action, which precludes complete adjustment in the great majority of cases. Therefore when any adjustment of expected use life is indicated, the required tax procedure is to adjust any and all differences by changing only the *future* depreciation charges. For the case just cited: an asset which cost $9,000 and had been in service for 4¼ years, depreciated at 8⅓ percent per year, would represent a net book amount of $5,812.50 ($9,000, less $750 × 4¼). If the expected remaining life at this date is 10¾ years, the tax deduction thenceforth will be $135.17 per quarter ($5,812.50/43) or $540.70 per year. This procedure carries the error of past depreciation charges into the future ones. The only justification for this is administrative expediency.

Trades

A company does not always continue to use each asset until the bitter end of its useful life. Machines are often exchanged for newer or larger ones. To make this situation concrete, suppose that a machine that has been used for eight years is traded in on a new one. The old machine had cost $9,000 and had been expected to last for 10 years; at the end of 8 years the accumulated depreciation applicable to this machine is $7,200 and its net "book value" is $1,800. Yet the firm is given a trade-in allowance of $2,500 (its current market value) on a new machine priced at $12,000; the difference is paid in cash. Entries to record the correction of accumulated depreciation would be:

Trade-in Allowance..	2,500	
Accumulated Depreciation..................................	7,200	
Machinery...		9,000
Overdepreciation of Prior Years......................		700

With this correction made, the new asset acquisition would be recorded,

Machinery..	12,000	
Trade-in Allowance.................................		2,500
Cash in Bank.......................................		9,500

This handling of the transaction assumes that the $12,000 price of the new machine is the actual cash price that would have to be paid without any trade-in. On this assumption, the cash equivalent of the old machine is indeed $2,500, and it is then clear that the depreciation charges for prior years' use of the old machine were too high by $700. Therefore, the record is corrected by the "overdepreciation" amount, which adjusts the retained earnings of prior years. As stated before, some accountants would treat all prior years' overdepreciation as a "gain" on disposition of the old machine. Certainly the adjustment is not a regular operating item, and it should not be considered as a current period credit (except that a part of the adjustment might be a correction of the current year depreciation).

Trade-in Allowances in Excess of Market Value

Sometimes the price of the new equipment is inflated so as to allow a certain generosity in trade-in allowances; in such a case, it is necessary to interpret the transaction carefully. Suppose that the trade-in allowance of $2,500 is clearly $1,000 more than the market value of the old machine; this means that the real price of the new machine is only $11,000. Then the combined entries would be:

Machinery...	11,000	
Accumulated Depreciation..............................	7,200	
Underdepreciation, Prior Years........................	300	
Machinery..		9,000
Cash in Bank.....................................		9,500

This situation sets up the new machine cost at a figure lower than the nominal $12,000 price because the trade-in clearly involves a $1,000 price concession. The correction to past years' depreciation recognizes that the net cost of using the old machine was greater than was originally estimated. It is handled like the overdepreciation item in the preceding example.

Tax Treatment of Asset Exchanges

The treatment given above is different from the method that is required for federal income tax purposes. Unless the implied sale of the old equipment is legally made an actual sale, the effect of the trade-in must be carried over into the cost of the new equipment. To conform to this pattern, it is necessary to set up the sale of the old equipment with correction of the past depreciation being considered (for tax purposes) a retirement gain or loss, and the deal will then be consummated with an actual cash receipt for the old machine. The new machine is recorded as if there had been no old machine at all, and a check is written for the full amount of the price of the new machine.

Unless the sale of the old equipment is actually made in this way, the tax treatment would be to carry forward the unrecovered difference in the old machine's cost (debit or credit) into the cost of the new machine. Thus, in *either* of the trade-in cases mentioned above, the tax basis of the new machine would (if the old machine were traded in and not sold) be $11,300, regardless of the actual price, since the new machine would be carried at the remaining net book amount of the old one ($1,800) plus the $9,500 cash actually paid in exchange.

Depletion

Quite similar to depreciation is that kind of amortization which is applied to so-called wasting assets: mines, timber tracts, oil or gas wells, and the like. Such assets contain or support basic materials that are drawn off for productive operations. The total cost of such assets may include prospecting, development, and carrying costs. While the general practice in accounting for long-term assets is to capitalize (defer) all related costs incurred prior to the attainment of normal levels of production, there are cases in which different parts of the cost are treated separately. For instance, stripping the overburden in anthracite coal mining is generally considered a cost of the coal that is later mined; some kinds of development costs are written off to expense on a time basis or some measure other than physical removal of the deposit; some costs related to prospecting and attempting to bring wells into production may be spread over the productive output of *successful* wells. Certainly it is easy to observe that some dry wells are inevitable, and the production from successful drilling may be the "best way" to account for unproductive activities. But there are situations in which losses must be absorbed as they occur. There are considerable variations in the methods used to account for development and research costs, although for a successful firm it might seem desirable to write off such costs as early as possible.

Depletion Allowances for Tax Purposes

Tax considerations raise the issue of percentage depletion, condemned by some and demanded by others. This is sometimes described as a clear subsidy, amounting for some oil and gas wells to 22 percent of gross revenues. A deduction *in lieu of* depletion is allowed on federal tax returns for firms engaged in specified activities. Some people view this as defensible compensation for discovery value. (There are various rates for different resources.) Such a provision in the tax law has, however, nothing to do with the depletion that is a part of earnings determination in published reports. Typically, depletion for accounting purposes is based on the total costs applicable to the wasting asset, spread over the expected yield in units of ore, lumber, oil, or other usable output. This unit charge is thus much like a production unit depreciation charge, which will vary with the volume of activity in different periods. Also like depreciation, depletion is necessarily an estimate, which may have to be corrected or adjusted when later events or other information may justify such action.

Leaseholds

Property may be rented by the firm over short or long time periods. The rights of the lessee and the lessor in such contracts do not always show in financial reports. So long as the lease is a pure rental arrangement covering a short period with no renewal provisions, the rental charge is probably an adequate measure of the expense— the cost of services used. Even minor complications as to improvements or alterations (which are paid for by the lessee, but which became the property of the lessor at the end of the term) do not entail more than a systematic amortization or depreciation charge to assign such cost against the periodic earnings.

Any advance payment on account of this is properly a cost to be assigned to the periods in which the property is used by the lessee.

If the contract covers a long period, this may raise not only an issue of long-term amortization but of the effects of interest on the contract. These complexities are reserved for discussion in Chapter 10. Here we wish merely to note that *advance payments* on leaseholds need to be systematically assigned to the periods in which the property is used. Such amounts are carried as assets during the term of the lease, at cost less accumulated amortization.

Investments

Business firms may invest in other enterprises; such investments are costs chargeable to the ultimate proceeds from the venture. These costs generally are held for periods of longer than a year and are considered to be long-term assets. But frequently there will be cash balances in excess of current needs, and such funds may earn something if put into short-term investments until they are again needed for operations. If these funds are put in the form of readily marketable securities (stocks or bonds listed and traded on an organized exchange), they may be considered to be current assets. Any dividends or interest on such securities will be considered income as they accrue; interest will be earned as it accumulates over time, and dividends become income when they are declared by the issuing company. Marketable securities carried as current assets may also produce income if they are sold at prices greater than their cost; but they are written down if market prices are below cost at reported dates, as in the case of inventories.

Long-term investments in shares of other companies may be accounted for in two ways. The first is to keep the investment at cost (unless there is reason to believe that there has been some *permanent* impairment of recovery) and to record income as in the case of marketable current issues when dividends are declared. However, especially when the investment is in the nature of a long-term affiliation, a somewhat different approach may be adopted.

Equity Increase or Decrease

A long-term investment in the shares of an affiliated company may be accounted for on an equity basis. The investment is recorded at cost, but the owning company's share of any reported income of the affiliate is added to the income of the parent by increasing the investment account:

```
Investment in Affiliated Company.............................. xx
    Income from Affiliated Company...........................         xx
```

Thus, the investment account will not remain at cost but will be increased by the owner's share of the increase in equity shown by the affiliated company's reports.

To carry this pattern through consistently, any *decrease* in the shareholder equity of the affiliate by way of losses or dividends will also be reflected in the books of the owner:

```
Losses of Affiliated Company................................. xx
    Investment in Affiliated Company........................         xx
```

or

```
Dividends Receivable........................................ xxx
    Investment in Affiliated Company........................         xxx
```

The reasons for this are clear if it is noted that any increase or reduction in the equity of the affiliate is thus reflected correspondingly on the investor's books. This changes the basis of income recognition, for an affiliated company might earn substantial income without declaring dividends, and the owner's income from the investment would not appear in his accounts unless the equity method of accounting were used. The equity method does recognize earnings from the investment before they are actually reduced to possession by dividends, but this is neither more nor less conservative than are the methods of accounting which measured that income.

Bonds, Notes, and Mortgages

Loans made to others, in any of the various forms that may occur, are investments. Interest income is recorded periodically on such investments as it accrues over time rather than waiting for actual payment on the due date. But interest may occur in two ways: as a specified rate of interest on the principal sum, or via discount. A loan of $1,000 might call for interest at 6 percent payable annually and repayment of $1,000 at the end of the term. This would mean that $60 would be paid at the end of each year. The accrual of interest at the end of a fiscal period (say, seven months after the loan was made) would take up income of $35, $7/_{12}$ of the annual amount. But the loan might have been arranged to call for only $940 to be advanced, and $1,000 to be paid at the end of a year. This is also a form of interest, and its accrual would be figured at the same amount for the same period of time. (The *rate of interest* would, of course, be a bit higher in the discount case because the principal advanced is less.)

Some loans may involve *both* interest and discount at the same time. A 10-year mortgage note may carry a stated principal amount of $20,000 and an interest rate of 6 percent per year; but because the market rates of interest are higher than 6 percent, the lender might require a discount of seven points on the loan—that is, he would advance only 93 percent of the $20,000 or $18,600, even though the rest of the contract was left unchanged. This would make the total cost of the loan $1,200 per year plus a $1,400 amount applicable to the entire period of the loan. The $1,400 may be amortized over the term to produce an annual cost of $140; this added to the specified interest makes a total of $1,340 per year. The company which makes the loan would record it as follows:

```
Loans Receivable.....................................  18,600
    Cash in Bank....................................            18,600
```

If the loan had been made 72 days before the end of the fiscal year, the interest accrual at the end of that year would be:

```
Interest Receivable (72/360 of $1,200)...................   240
Loans Receivable (72/360 of $140)......................    28
    Interest Income.....................................            268
```

A corporate bond is very much the same kind of thing; it is a promise to pay a principal sum at the end of the term plus interest at a specified rate. If the market situation calls for a lower rate than that specified in the bond, it would command a premium rather than a discount. When the market rate of interest is 6 percent, a $1,000 face value bond which pays $35 each 6 months and has 16 years still to run will command a market price of $1,102+. (Arithmetic of compound interest is discussed in Chapter 10.) This indicates that the interest stream of $35 payable each semiannum is *decreased* by the $102+ premium over the next 16 years. This may be put into account at the rate of $6.385 per year. Entries to accrue the income from this investment at the end of the fiscal year, 90 days after the purchase of the bond, but the day the bond interest is payable, would be:

```
Interest Receivable......................................  35.00
    Interest Income......................................            33.40
    Bond Investment......................................             1.60
```

Thus one quarter of year's premium is offset against the nominal interest for the current year. In future years, this will continue so that the carrying value of the bond will fall over the 16 years to the maturity amount of $1,000.

Determination of Cost in Noncash Transactions

Sometimes assets are acquired by issuing shares or exchanging other assets for those that are acquired. Since there is no actual cash exchanged or to be exchanged, the accountant must look to other sources for his index of cost. One way to do this is to ascertain (by independent appraisal, perhaps) the market value of the assets acquired, less any specified liabilities involved. Entries for such an acquisition might be:

Accounts Receivable..................................	52,000	
Merchandise Inventories..............................	79,000	
Unexpired Rent.......................................	400	
Allowance for Uncollectible Accounts................		1,300
Accounts Payable....................................		31,000
Common Shares......................................		99,100

In these entries there is a mixture of valuations. Accounts Receivable is the book amount of collections to be made from previous customers of the business from which the accounts are taken over; collectibility of these accounts is indicated by subtracting the allowance for uncollectibles, $1,300. Merchandise Inventories would probably be arrived at through the count of goods, priced at current replacement figures. The Unexpired Rent item is computed in accordance with the rental contract. Accounts Payable is the amount actually owed and payable to the creditors of the predecessor firm, and the credit to Common Shares is the net amount of investment equity; this credit is merely a balancing figure in the transaction, the net value of the considerations involved, in issuing, say, 1800 shares of stock.

This handling of the transaction would be satisfactory if the common shares were without par value and if market values of such shares could be ignored. If these were shares of $50 per value each, legal requirements would make it necessary to show the equity investment as $90,000; the additional $9,100 would appear as a separate item. Instead of describing this item as excess of investment over legal capital requirements (which it really is), accountants typically label it "Premium on Common Shares," "Paid-in Surplus," or "Additional Paid-in Capital."

Intangible Assets

Suppose that in the transaction just described, the actual market value of the common shares was $60 each. This gives another measure of the transaction, for the market value of the shares issued for the assets and equities acquired is $1,800 \times \$60$, or $\$108,000$. This suggests either (1) that there was a loss on the transaction (since the "net acquisition" was only $\$99,100$), or (2) that some other asset was included and not specifically recognized. The first proposition is not easy to accept; it seems a bit illogical to establish a *loss* on the basis of a mere acquisition, with no corresponding sale of the item or items purchased. Unless there is overpowering evidence of such a loss, accountants prefer to recognize the difference as attributable to those intangible advantages that the preexisting business may have had. There was an existing and operating organization, with a reputation and a following among customers and others. It is probable that the acquisition of those assets actually specified also brought along these intangible assets. At any rate, if there is a basis for considering the $\$8,900$ excess payment ($\$108,000$ less $\$99,100$) as deferrable to future operations, the entries would be set up as follows:

Goodwill.	8,900	
Accounts Receivable.	52,000	
Merchandise Inventories.	79,000	
Unexpired Rent.	400	
Accounts Payable.		31,000
Anticipated Collection Defaults.		1,300
Common Shares (stated value)		90,000
Additional Paid-in-Capital.		18,000

As a matter of conservatism, accountants usually try to write off the Goodwill, either by amortization or in a lump sum as soon as Retained Earnings account will absorb the charge. That is, in theory, based on the idea that the advantages thus acquired are either realized in the form of higher incomes, or they are merged in the future development of the firm. Whether or not this is so may be debatable.

There are other kinds of intangible assets. Special rights or privileges may be obtained from patents, copyrights, or franchises; these may be purchased from outside sources, or they may be developed within the firm as part of organized research and development, or even by casual suggestions or observations. If the ideas are purchased, the amounts paid to acquire them are clearly assets which ought to be charged to the periods in which their advantages reach fruition. Thus the cost of a patent or a copyright ought to be written off over no more than the legal term of protection; but it is often desirable to recognize that the period of economic life may be shorter than that of legal recognition.

When ideas or designs are developed within the firm, it is often difficult to establish the costs of such development. In any research or testing and innovation, there are partial failures which may really contribute to the ultimate success; but it may be hard to see which, if any, of the unsuccessful trials should have their costs added to the cost of the finally desirable result. To carry this idea to an extreme, consider the smoothly functioning organizational structure that is an attribute of a successful enterprise. Certainly this is an asset in the colloquial sense, but which costs really contribute to the building of such a structure? How are such costs to be separated from the ordinary costs of doing business? How should such a cost, if measured and recorded, be assigned to periodic revenue or to other operations? As long as the organization functions properly, one can hardly be sure that the cost has expired, even in part; on the other hand, if the effectiveness of organization disappears, it would seem difficult to charge this disappearance to the same period in which ineffectiveness is already fully and clearly shown. The answer to all such questions generally tends to be that intangible assets should not be recognized unless they are acquired by purchase from outsiders; often these costs are written off on an arbitrary basis and over relatively short periods of time.

Summary

The discussion of this chapter has been aimed at rounding out the measurements that apply to the determination of income by giving particular attention to the long-term assets. Starting from the more general notion of straight-line time depreciation, we discussed and compared production units production-hours and accelerated-early-charge procedures (constant percentage, sum of years' digits, one and a half, and double declining balance). The choice between these methods is a most difficult problem because of the many factors and the uncertainties which surround such estimates; the general approach is, however, to approximate, by way of judgmental decisions, a tracing of the economic services which are applied to the operations of the firm. Since these are estimates, they are subject to corrections, and their ultimate effect, when as asset is finally disposed of or traded for another one, should be adjusted for.

In reviewing the general aspects of accounting for investments, leaseholds, and intangible assets, we found somewhat similar approaches to amortization of all long-term costs. The problem of tracing such costs through acquisition and transfer to operating charges and expense of the various periods is one that makes accounting for income a challenge to judgment and estimation techniques.

But some of these techniques, particularly the effects of interest, are related to financing transactions, which are our next area of interest to be dealt with in Chapter 10.

QUESTIONS

1. Name three basic types of long-term assets and give examples of each kind. What difference is there between long-term assets and inventories or prepayments? How does this make measurements related to long-term assets more difficult and uncertain?

2. Cost of a long-term asset is sometimes more than the net invoice cost; what are the usual additional costs which may be added? What issues may arise in determining whether such costs are to be included?

3. What difference does it make whether or not the real estate improvements—shrubs, sidewalks, retaining walls, or driveways—are separated from land cost?

4. How does one distinguish in principle between costs that are chargeable to current expense from those which ought to be treated as assets? What limits are there to strict application of this principle, and what criteria are commonly employed to make this distinction? In the case of a household appliance dealer who operates a single delivery truck, how would you account for an $850 charge to overhaul a five-year-old delivery truck expected to last at least three more years? Would your answer be the same for a taxicab operator who has a fleet of six cars of varying age but driven 60,000 miles a year each?

5. The Boss Manufacturing Company recently spent $25,000 to refurbish one of its older buildings. The work consisted of general renovation—including new exterior doors, painting of wood and metal windows and trim, repairing roofs, replacing drinking fountains and plumbing fixtures, laying new carpets in offices, and tiling previously bare floors. The job was done by a single contractor on a flat-price bid: the entire $25,000 amount was charged to Accumulated Depreciation on the ground that these expenditures lengthened the expected service life of the building. Comment.

6. Distinguish between seven different methods of establishing periodic depreciation. What basis should be used for the following assets: (*a*) machinery used in producing staple products such as nails or wire, (*b*) an office building, (*c*) office furniture such as desks and tables, (*d*) an electric generating station of a public service company, (*e*) an electronic computer, and (*f*) a fleet of jet airplanes for passenger service?

7. When depreciation calculations are found in error, what in essence

is the approach used to make corrections? Assume a $10,000 asset to have been depreciated on a five-year life "sum-of-years'-digits" basis; it is discovered at the end of its third year of service that the expected remaining life is still four years. Make the calculations and write entries to correct the third years' depreciation charge and adjust other account balances. What computations would be required for tax purposes?

8. A machine which cost $8,000 has been depreciated on a straight-line time basis for 8 years of its expected 10-year life. It is traded-in on a new machine for a cash difference of $10,000. Write entries for the transaction, assuming that the firm cash price of the new machine is $11,600. Would the computations be any different for income tax purposes?

9. Assuming the *quoted* price on the new machine was $13,000 and the old machine could be sold for no more than $2,500. What change would you make in the entries (*a*) for proper accounting for the new machine, and (*b*) to meet tax rules, assuming the transaction was actually treated as a trade-in?

10. After spending $150,000 in exploration and geophysical surveys, a mining company acquires rights to exploit a given property for (1) a cash payment of $500,000 plus (2) a royalty of $20,000 per year for 15 years. (3) It is agreed that the property will be restored to its present appearance, all mine shafts permanently sealed, and all equipment removed, at the end of the 15th year. This is expected to cost about $700,000. (4) To operate the mine, it is necessary to spend $20,000 for roads and $60,000 for bridges. (5) Mining equipment and machinery will cost $1,500,000 to acquire and install. (6) Mine tunnels and shafts will cost a total of $900,000; these costs will be incurred $100,000 in the first year, $50,000 a year for 10 years, and $60,000, $70,000, $80,000, $90,000 and $100,000 in the last 5 years. The expected output of the mine is expected to be, in thousands of tons:

Year	Output	Year	Output	Year	Output
1.	6	6.	24	11.	16
2.	16	7.	22	12.	14
3.	18	8.	20	13.	12
4.	26	9.	18	14.	10
5.	24	10.	18	15.	6

Total: 250 thousand tons

Discuss the accounting problems related to these six numbered items of cost. How would you establish depletion (as opposed to depreciation) charges on this project?

11. There are basically two kinds of investment gains and losses—periodic income and capital appreciation. A company bought 35

percent of the common stock of a sales organization in Australia at a cost of $35,000. The stated purpose of this investment was to obtain sales representation in the growing Australian market; but this was of minor importance since only about 10 percent of the sales of the foreign company were products of the investor corporation. During the first year after acquisition, the foreign company reported income ("converted" to American dollars) of $20,000; in the second year a loss of $10,000, and in the third year a gain of $30,000 were reported. At the end of the third year, this stock was sold for $400,000. The quoted market values of those shares had been at the end of the first year $400,000; at the end of the second year, $300,-000. Dividends of $2,000 had been received in each of the three years. The sale at the end of the third year occurred because (1) the company's position in the foreign market was well enough established, (2) the company had need for $400,000 to finance a plant expansion, and interest cost for such funds would cost about 9 percent per year, and (3) the price of the shares was 38 times earnings, probably as high as could be expected for some time to come.

a) Prepare entries for this investment over the three-year period.

b) Would your answer be the same if the foreign company operated primarily in a South American or Middle Asiatic country?

12. What are intangible assets? Under what conditions are such assets subject to amortization or immediate write-off? Ought they ever to be carried at their cost for an indefinite period?

13. A $10,000 United States Treasury bond has attached coupons calling for $200 interest payments at six-month intervals. This bond is purchased at a price of $8,200 exactly nine years before its maturity date. When the bond has been held for six months, one of the interest coupons is cashed. Write the entries. Three months after this coupon is cashed, the fiscal year of the owner ends. Write entries to accrue the income on the U.S. Treasury bond.

PROBLEMS

Production Specialty Company

This company operates a custom machine shop and maintains a number of different kinds of metal working machines. One machine had an installed cost of $14,500 when it was set up; its estimated life at that date was seven years; the anticipated disposal value was expected to be $1,500 at the end of seven years, but it would cost $860 to remove it from service. The machine was used for three years without incident, but at the end of the third year the expected service life was reestimated as nine years (six years from that date).

When the machine was five years old, it was apparent that it would not be serviceable for more than another year, although the expected net recovery amount would still be $640 at that time. At the end of the sixth year it was disposed of, and the sales price was $1,000; leaving a net scrap recovery of $500.

Required:

Make all the entries that would be required to correct the depreciation charges on this machine at the end of the third, fourth, and sixth year.
1. On a straight-line time basis.
2. On a sum of years' digits basis.
3. On a double declining balance basis.

Hamilton Company

This company acquired a new lathe to replace one that had been in service for eight years. The old one had originally cost $7,500, and it had been depreciated over an expected life of 12 years.

It cost $600 to remove the old lathe, but $200 was received when it was sold for scrap. Additional work had to be done on the foundation before the new lathe could be installed; this cost $1,200. Other installation costs were $1,300, including $500 travel expense and fees for engineers to supervise the installation, $650 labor of regular factory employees, and $150 of estimated factory overhead (power, supplies, insurance, and property taxes during the installation period).

The invoice cost of the new lathe was $8,500, terms 2 percent 10, net 30, with freight charges added to the invoice (prepaid by the seller) amounting to $500.

Required:
1. Write out entries to record the transactions as stated.
2. Assuming that the company was allowed a trade-in of $1,500 on the old machine instead of selling it for scrap, write entries for the transactions, assuming that the trade-in represented a verifiable market value for the old machine.
3. What would be your answer if the old machine was traded in for an allowance of $2,000, other data remaining the same as in (2)?

Capalachian Corporation

At December 31, 19x, when the ledger was being brought to a point of preparing financial reports, this company had an investment account on its ledger with a balance of $650,000. The items represented by this account were:

(1)   500 shares of Viscoloid International Corporation, a stock listed on the Winnebago Stock Exchange. The cost of this investment seven years ago was $22,000. No dividends have been paid on these shares, even though the company had earnings averaging $2 per share each year. However, the corporation recently declared a dividend of $4.20 per share, payable January 10, 19xl to shares of record at December 20, 19x. The stock is currently quoted on the Winnebago Exchange at 56¼.

(2)   All of the outstanding stock of The Collingham Machine Company (2,000 shares). These shares were acquired ten years ago for $250,000. At the date of acquisition, The Collingham Machine Company had retained earnings of $20,000. During the ten years these shares have been held, The Collingham Machine Company has reported earnings of $160,000, of which $20,000 apply to 19x operations. Dividends have been paid amounting to $100,000, of which $10,000 were received by the Capalachian Corporation during 19x.

(3)   A mortgage note secured by pledge of the buildings in the Cactus Park shopping center, located near the Capalachian Corporation's plant. This note was acquired 3½ years ago, in consideration of $191,000 advanced to finance construction. However, the face amount of the note is $200,000, and the note calls for interest at 7% annually payable June 30 each year, and the note principal is due June 30, 16½ years hence. The only entry concerning this note during 19x was the collection of "interest" June 30, 19x.

(4)   Documents covering a patent which had been developed by employees of the Capalachian Corporation over a period of years prior to 19x. The costs attributable to this patent had amounted to $187,-000 at January 1, 19x, when the patent was finally granted. The Capalachian Corporation was offered $250,000 cash for this patent by the Consolidated Machine and Foundry Corporation on June 30, 19x, but the officers of Capalachian Corporation refused to sell, as they were sure it was worth much more. The patent has been used through the whole year 19x.

Required:
Write out entries which you would make to state properly the items listed, in the financial reports for 19x.

Maximus Manufacturing Company

The data given below are from the summary ledger of the Maximus Manufacturing Company at the end of the first quarter, this year. Some of the account balances have been labeled "beginning." This means they have not as yet been changed by the current period transactions. "End" means that all transactions affecting that item have been recorded. These data do not include the following:

(1) Manufacturing costs applied to product $12,600,000
(2) Cost of goods completed   12,900,000
(3) Closing inventory, finished goods   1,600,000
(4) Federal income taxes, at regular rates
        (22% of first $25,000, 48% on remainder)

Account Balances

Accounts payable......................................	$ 2,840,000
Accounts receivable...................................	3,900,000
Accrued payroll and payroll tax liabilities.................	790,000
Accumulated depreciation..............................	21,370,000
Allowance for uncollectibles...........................	10,000
Cash in bank...	1,012,000
Common stock..	15,400,000
Dividends declared....................................	1,200,000
Estimated liability, product guarantees....................	120,000
Finished goods (beginning)..............................	1,100,000
General administration costs............................	1,500,000
Interest accrued receivable.............................	8,000
Interest charges......................................	60,000
Investment income....................................	83,000
Lapsed sales discounts.................................	20,000
Loans payable to banks................................	730,000
Long-term investments.................................	1,210,000
Manufacturing costs...................................	12,710,000
Marketable securities..................................	239,000
Materials inventory (end)..............................	2,200,000
Materials inventory shrinkage...........................	40,000
Materials inventory price loss...........................	10,000
Organization costs....................................	60,000
Paid-in capital above legal requirements...................	1,814,000
Plant and equipment cost...............................	35,420,000
Retained earnings (beginning)...........................	?
Revenue adjustment for uncollectibles.....................	120,000
Sales billed..	22,000,000
Selling costs...	4,200,000
Underdepreciation, prior years..........................	22,000
Unexpired insurance, rent, etc..........................	20,000
Work in process (beginning)............................	2,100,000
Unpaid federal income taxes (beginning)..................	40,000

Required:

1. Prepare a report of earnings to show operating net margin and final balance of retained earnings, in good form.
2. Prepare a position statement as at the end of the quarter, properly classified.

Manning Manufacturing Company

This company began business January 2 of the current year. Transactions for the six months ended June 30 are given below. Record those transactions in summary ledger accounts and prepare a statement of earnings and a position statement as at the end of the period.

CASH TRANSACTIONS

Receipts:

Proceeds from issue of 20,000 shares of stock, stated value $10 per share..................		$220,000
Collections from customers..................		265,000
Bank loans................................		50,000
"Bad debts" collected (see below)........... .		200

Payments:

Purchase of land...........................	$ 40,000	
Purchase of building.......................	80,000	
Total.....................................	$120,000	
Less: 6 percent mortgage...................	90,000	$ 30,000
Purchase of equipment:		
Factory machinery.......................	$ 48,000	
Delivery equipment......................	9,000	
Office equipment........................	3,000	60,000
To trade creditors for materials and supplies....		*140,000
Repayment of bank loans....................	$ 40,000	
Interest thereon.........................	400	40,400
Payments to employees for personal services.....		126,480
Payments for taxes withheld from employees, $35,410 and employers' payroll taxes........		39,520
Miscellaneous services (power, repairs, etc., including $1,200 premium on property insurance for one year beginning January 2)...........		21,200
Payment for trade-in of equipment...........		3,100
Dividends paid to stockholders..............		16,000

* This $140,000 includes $430 of lapsed purchase discounts.

OTHER TRANSACTIONS

Sales at gross invoice prices (terms 2% 10, n/30)...............	$355,000
Sales discounts taken by customers, $4,800	
Sales discounts still available to customers at 6/30, $400	
Materials and supplies purchased (at net prices)...............	240,000
Materials and supplies drawn from stores for operations: factory, $160,000; selling, $4,000; office, $5,000..............	169,000

Employee earnings, with taxes applicable thereto:

	Nominal Gross Earnings	Employer Payroll Taxes
Factory....................	$120,000	$6,480
Selling....................	30,000	1,620
Office and general...........	18,000	970
Total.................	$168,000	$9,070

Insurance expired for six months is chargeable 60 percent to factory, 30 percent to selling, and 10 percent to general administration.

Depreciation on building is computed at 1½ percent for six months, chargeable to factory, 70 percent; selling, 20 percent; and general administration, 10 percent.

Depreciation of factory equipment is 10 percent per year; delivery equipment (selling) is depreciated at 20 percent per year, and office equipment (general administration) is depreciated at 8 percent per year.

Miscellaneous service costs (power, repairs, etc.) incurred: factory, $18,000; selling, $3,000; general administration, $1,000.

Interest on bank loans still unpaid at June 30, $300.

Mortgage interest at 6 percent per year is payable July 2, and January 2, next year.

Factory cost applied to work in process, $305,000.

Cost of goods completed, $258,000.

Cost of goods shipped to customers, $218,000.

Work in process inventory at June 30: cost, $47,000; market, $45,000.

Finished goods inventory at June 30: cost, $37,000; market, $39,000.

Estimated uncollectibles, $\frac{2}{10}$ percent of *gross* sales. Bad debts written off were $600, of which $200 was later recovered.

Estimated corporate income tax liability at June 30, $27,000.

On March 31, certain factory equipment that had cost $3,000 on January 2 was traded in for other more suitable machines. The price of the new machines was $6,000, against which an allowance of $2,900 for the old machines was made. $3,100 cash was paid to settle, as indicated above.

Chapter 10

FINANCING TRANSACTIONS

Up to this point in our discussion, we have emphasized what might be called *operating* transactions—those that are related primarily to the production of revenue and expense. We have paid relatively little attention to the way in which business operations are financed. The funds required to carry on an enterprise may be provided in a number of ways; this chapter is concerned with a detailed exposition of the financing devices and arrangements in common use.

Ubiquity of Financing Activities

The capital required to start and maintain operations is essential to the functioning of any business, for inventories and facilities must be available some time before customers can or will reimburse the firm for their use. Thus, the typical business buys its merchandise and services on credit and there are a number of payables outstanding at all times. These would include obligations for merchandise, utility services, payrolls, miscellaneous services, and taxes. Indeed, the usual procedure is to recognize costs by the incurrence or creation of obligations and to consider the cash payment as merely the settlement of these obligations. Thus, financing transactions (the receipt of goods or services in return for promises to pay in the future) often establish the cost that is traced into asset and expense categories. Similarly, the measurement of revenue is based on contracts that are settled by cash receipts at a later point in time; the business must meet its cash needs despite lagged collections from customers.

These observations about financing transactions indicate that the managers of a business have not only a problem of running the firm in such a way that it will produce earnings but also a problem of managing assets and equities (and the financing transactions related to them) in such a way as to be able to collect its receivables and pay its debts when they are due. This phase of management is an important area of concern because the way in which financing is done may have much to do with the success of the firm.

Collection of Receivables

Typically, the stream of cash collections from customers should be more than ample to cover the cash requirements for normal operations. Unless operations are unprofitable, the amounts collected from customers will be greater (over a period of time) than the corresponding payments required to cover operating expenses. This should especially be true if depreciation or other past cost amortizations are a part of the expense; the cash outlays for long-term assets provide operating service flows (expense) for long periods without requiring disbursements. Hence, the funds expected to arise from revenue will not have to be paid out to cover depreciation or amortization of long-term assets. Thus, even when there is a loss from operations, the cash effect of these operations may still (if the depreciation and amortization are together more than the loss) increase cash balances; depreciation and amortization do not require current disbursement.

For this reason, collections from customer receivables will tend to be somewhat more than the amounts needed to cover operating expenses. But this is true only when the level of operations (the volume of business being done) remains constant or declines. An increase in the volume of operations tends to require heavier cash outlays; although these payments are deferred by the effect of credit, the collections from customers on the expanded volume of sales may be deferred even more. Thus, an increase in the volume of business may actually tend to decrease the available cash because the lag in collections may be greater than can be made up by any rearrangement of expenditures.

This kind of fluctuation may be seasonal in nature; it is not unusual for the volume of business done by a firm to ebb and flow over the year. The lagging effects referred to in the preceding paragraph may then cause the cash balance to fluctuate as volume changes. At one time of the year when volume has just fallen, collections from customers may be larger than the demands for current expenditure; on the other hand, when the volume of business starts to expand, the demands for cash may be temporarily larger than customer collections will meet. The obvious answer to this kind of situation is to borrow funds for short periods of time to cover these fluctuations.

Bank Loans

When a company is in temporary need of cash to cover the effects of seasonal fluctuations in volume, the typical method of financing is via a short-term commercial bank loan. The company will arrange with the bank to receive an advance of cash in exchange for a promise to pay a larger amount on a future date—presumably after the increased volume of business will tend to be reflected in cash receipts higher than expenditure requirements. The loan would be recorded:

```
Cash in Bank.......................................... 14,775
Discount, Notes Payable...............................    225
    Notes Payable....................................          15,000
To record bank loan repayable in 90 days, discounted at 6
percent.
```

It should be noted that in this case the maturity value is reduced by a discount to establish the proceeds of the loan. Alternatively, the deal could have been arranged so as to figure 6 percent simple *interest* on the loan; this makes the maturity amount $15,225 and the proceeds of the loan $15,000. This would actually make the cost a bit less, relative to the amount of the loan; $225 is a smaller percentage of $15,000 than it is of $14,775. The way in which interest is computed is a matter of custom or negotiation. The fact to be noted is that the true interest is the amount by which the repayments exceed the advance and that this is compensation to the lender for the use of his funds. This is recognized as a cost (really a distribution of income) which applies to the term of the loan. The cost should be spread over the period of the loan, either by recognizing an interest liability or by adjusting the contra equity account. After 27 days, the adjustment would be:

```
Interest Charges......................................... 67.50
    Discount, Notes Payable (or Interest Payable)...........         67.50
```

At the end of the period of the loan, the entire $225 would have been charged off and would have appeared in the earnings statement as interest charges.

Other Ways to Meet Short-Term Needs for Cash

A company may raise cash to take care of current needs by speeding up the process of collection from customers. Customer receivables can be sold to an outsider who is willing (for a fee) to wait for collections.

The main trouble with this idea is that although the company knows its customers, the person who is asked to take over the uncollected receivables does not. The risks of collection are in fact a bit greater for the outsider than they would be for the company; the relation of purchaser and supplier is likely to be a continuing one, and the fact that the customer may wish to purchase from the company again has some bearing on the way in which he views his obligation to pay for goods. In any event, the outside agency usually is not willing to accept the receivables of a company at their face amount without some safeguard against the risks of uncollectibility.

Therefore, the *factor* (as the financing agency is called) will usually advance only a part of the amounts due from the customers; even then, the transfer of the claims against customers is made "with recourse." This last phrase means that the seller agrees to make good on any uncollectible items so that the factor will not lose because of the difficulty of collecting from some customers. Since (as was pointed out earlier) the uncollectible accounts are not identifiable, it is not possible to deal with the problem except by negotiation. The arrangement "with recourse" is the easiest way to avoid the heavy charges that would be needed to cover the risk of uncollectibility. Therefore, if a company discounts a block of customer receivables with a factoring agency, the record of the transaction would appear something as follows on the books of the company:

Cash in Bank	85,000	
Discount on Factored Receivables	5,000	
Receivables Transferred to Factor	100,000	
Contingent Liability to Factor		90,000
Customer Accounts Receivable		100,000

This transaction appears a bit complicated, but it may easily be understood by examining its parts. From an overall view, it appears that the factor has advanced $85,000 on the security of $100,000 of customer receivables, charging $5,000 "interest." The receivables transferred to the factor are, however, not sold outright; the factor expects to collect what he can from them, up to $90,000. The rest of the receivable amounts are still the property of the company. Therefore, although we reduce the regular Customer Accounts Receivable account by $100,000 (none of the factored accounts is an ordinary customer receivable any longer), we set up a separate contingent asset account for the items transferred. The reason for this treatment is that the status of those accounts is not clear until the factoring arrangement has been worked out over a period of time.

Similarly, although the factor is expected to collect from the customers, he has the right to collect from the company if the accounts prove difficult or impossible to collect during the factoring period. There is, therefore, a contingent liability to the factor which may be as much as $90,000. This contingent liability is directly associated with the contingent asset, Receivables Transferred to Factor, for the *company* still has the right to collect from its customers if the factor does not. These two contingent items are really offsets whose net amount is $10,000, the excess of receivables transferred to safeguard the factor from defaults. On the company position statement, these two items would appear:

Receivables transferred to factor......................	$100,000	
Less: Contingent liability to factor..................	90,000	
Net Amount Receivable from Customers...............		$10,000

The net amount receivable from customers would be treated as are other customer receivables, shown subject to the contra asset accounts for estimated uncollectibles and the like. The company's *ultimate* position with regard to the customer balance is unchanged. All that has happened is that the factor has made a loan on the security of customer receivables; even though the factor may be authorized to collect from customers, he looks to the company for ultimate settlement, and the company looks to its customers for payment if the factor does not collect.

Notes Receivable

Borrowing against customer balances may be more easily accomplished if the customer is willing to give a note to cover his indebtedness. A note is a written promise to pay a specified sum of money to the person who presents the note when it is due. The payee is designated as *bearer*, or as *the order of* some specified person. These qualities in the promise make it negotiable—it passes from one person to another as if it were money. The legal rules surrounding such instruments are more complex than we need to consider here; the important thing is that if a note is transferred from one person to another by endorsement, there is additional security behind the promise to pay. The holder of the instrument may call upon any of the endorsers to make good if the original promisor does not; the promise therefore becomes *two-name* or *multi-name* paper with an added guarantee of collectibility through endorsement.

Because of this, a company may ask a customer who has been slow in paying what he owes to settle his account with a note. The written promise to pay a specified sum on a certain date may be much more useful to the holder than an ordinary account receivable.

Because it is an unconditional written promise to pay a certain sum on a determinable future date, the note can be discounted at a bank. That is, the note may be used as security for a loan, which in turn will be settled by the promisor's paying the specified amount when the note matures. Suppose a customer who owes $1,480 gives the company a note for this amount, "with interest at 6 percent, payable in 90 days." The receipt of this note is entered:

Notes Receivable	1,480	
Customer Accounts Receivable		1,480

Interest accrues while the note is held. With interest at 6 percent per year, the value of the note will increase over its term by $1,480 \times 0.06 \times 90/360$, or $22.20, and the maturity value will be $1,502.20.

If the company prepares financial reports, say, 18 days later, the interest will have to be accrued for 18 days: $1,480.00 \times 0.06 \times 18/360$ is $4.44. The note would be increased to $1,484.44, and $4.44 interest income would appear in the report of earnings. But if the company needs cash, it may take the note to the bank for discounting at the end of 18 days. The bank views this as a loan of the *maturity* value of the note but charges discount at its own lending rate, say 10 percent. The proceeds of discounting would be computed by subtracting the discount ($1,502.20 \times 0.10 \times 72/360$, or $30.04) from the maturity value. The company would endorse the customer's note making it payable to *the order of* the bank, and the proceeds ($1,472.16) would be added to the company's deposit account in exchange for the note.

To record this transaction, proper accounting would require the $4.44 interest to be shown as earned before the date of discounting. The note is now security for the bank loan; but if the note is not paid at maturity, the discounter will be liable for the maturity amount of the note. The entries are:

Cash In Bank	1,472.16	
Contingent Liability on Bank Loan		1,472.16

and

Notes Transferred by Endorsement	1,484.44	
Interest Income		4.44
Notes Receivable		1,480.00

At this point, a position statement would show among the current assets:

Notes Transferred by Endorsement.................. $1,484.44
    Less: Contingent liability on bank loan............ 1,472.16 $12.28

This net amount of $12.28 is deferred interest cost; the bank retained $12.28 of the value of the note. Even though the contingent items offset each other at maturity, there has been a deferred net cost to the discounter.[1]

However, the $12.28 is really the net of *two* interest items. The note itself will earn $17.76 in growing from $1,484.44 to $1,520.20, and the contingent liability will increase from $1,472.16 to $1,520.20, producing an interest *charge* of $30.04. The two accruals might be prorated over the term as needed, but at maturity the net effect will be:

Notes Transferred by Endorsement........................ 17.76
    Interest Income.......................................   17.76

and

Interest Charges.. 30.04
    Contingent Liability on Bank Loan....................   30.04

Thus, both contingencies approach the maturity value at a net cost to the discounter of $12.28, the difference between $30.04 and $17.76.

When the note matures, however, the contingencies disappear. Whether or not the note is paid by the maker, removal of the contingencies will be accomplished by:

Contingent Liability on Bank Loan.................... 1,502.20
    Notes Transferred by Endorsement................   1,502.20

If the note is paid by the maker at maturity, no further entries are required. But if the note is *not* paid by the maker, the endorser company will have to pay the bank the maturity value of the note. The entries would be:

Claim, Defaulted Note............................. 1,502.20
    Cash in Bank..................................   1,502.20

This sets up the claim against the customer in a special classification which calls attention to its unusual character. If the customer pays

---

[1] Some accountants would argue that for practical reasons, the contingent liability might be reported by showing merely the face of the note ($1,480) as an offset to the original Note Receivable account, and to write off the net $7.84 ($1,480.00 less $1,472.16) as interest cost. However, if the note is not paid by the maker at maturity, the discounter will have to pay $1,502.20. If paid earlier for any reason, the bank would prorate its discount charge. The situation is not correctly accounted for by any procedure which ignores this.

the note sometime later, the collection will, of course, remove this account from the ledger; probably there will be some additional interest charged to the customer, which would be credited as interest income. If the note cannot be collected, the amount not collected will be written off just as for any other uncollectible receivable by charging it to the Allowance for Uncollectible Receivables.

Other Pledges

Loans are sometimes made against the security of inventories or investments pledged as collateral. That is, the borrower agrees to hold such assets subject to the claim of the lender; in some cases, the lender is given possession of the pledged property, but this is not necessarily the case. However, even if the pledged property may be in the possession of the lender it is still owned by the borrower; and there is no reason to offset the pledged property against the loan in the way discounted notes are handled. Unless the property actually passes from the control of the firm, the situation may be described adequately by a footnote, allowing the assets to be accounted for in the usual fashion. Of course, such assets are subject to some restrictions as to their use and as to the disposition of proceeds from sale, if such occurs.

Close Relations among Current Assets and Equities

Most of the transactions that affect current assets and current debts are very closely related. Purchase and sales of goods, payrolls, taxes, and current expenses are negotiated and settled in rapid succession, sometimes with a very short time interval between. These transactions are very numerous and often occur in small amounts which tends to make it difficult to separate them for financial management purposes. It is common practice to deal with the aggregation of current assets reduced by current debts as a single fund,—a separate collection of resources intended for specific purposes. The net sum of current assets and current debts is frequently referred to as *net working capital*, especially when dealing with the overall ebb and flow of financing transactions. If the whole group of current position items is viewed as a unit, short-term financing does not affect working capital since the assets added by short-term borrowing make for little, if any, *net* change in the fund. Similarly, repayments of short-term debt have no effect upon the aggregate net working capital. This concept tends to imply that short-term loans and advances are arranged without much formality as needed, and that long-term financing would be viewed as a separate matter. In the next chapter, we shall discuss this more fully from the viewpoint of reporting financing transactions in published statements.

Long-Term Financing

The simplest form of a long-term financing has already been described in terms of the investment of a proprietor in his business. This, however, is not a very fruitful way to raise long-term capital for a business of more than the smallest size. The resources of any one individual are quite limited. When the resources of the original proprietor and the accumulations from profits are not enough to finance desired expansion of the business, it may be possible to get an additional contributor to take a partnership share. This typically involves active participation in all phases of the business, not merely the advance of money or property for the use of the firm. Active participation in a business usually means delegation of management powers, and it entails some special arrangements for using and paying for partners' services, as well as compensation for furnishing capital; and there will have to be some way to divide profits. The amount of a partner's investment will be credited to his capital or investment account just as in the case of a sole proprietor, but the division of income may involve more complex arrangements.

Distributing Partnership Income

It may be agreed that A is to be credited with $1,000 per month for his personal services to the firm, while B is to receive only $400 per month because of his lesser experience and the fact that he spends only half time in the firm. It may also be agreed that each partner is to receive an interest credit at the rate of 10 percent per year on his capital equity and that remaining profits (or losses) shall be shared equally. Suppose that A has a capital equity of $12,000 and B has one of $20,000, and that the net income (before income taxes or partner's distributions) is $19,000 for the year.

The flow accounts for the year would not be carried in this case to a retained earnings account, for this is not a corporate enterprise. The account in which partnership earnings are summarized is called Undivided Profits. When this credit balance of $19,000 has been carried into the Undivided Profits account, the following entries distribute the gain for the year:

Undivided Profits......................................	16,800	
A, Personal..		12,000
B, Personal..		4,800

To credit the partners with agreed share of income for services rendered to the firm.

Undivided Profits......................................	3,200	
A, Personal..		1,200
B, Personal..		2,000

To credit the partners with agreed share of profit as compensation for capital invested.

These two distributions would leave the Undivided Profits account with a $1,000 debit balance. This debit balance would be disposed of as a "loss" to be shared equally:

A, Personal...	500	
B, Personal...	500	
Undivided Profits......................................		1,000

Thus, the $19,000 net income before taxes would finally be distributed $12,700 to A and $6,300 to B.

Of course, partners may agree to divide profits and losses in any way they choose. There are legal rules as to what shall be done in the absence of such an agreement, but these need not concern us here.

Perhaps it should be pointed out that withdrawals of cash by the partners to cover personal expenses are perforce treated as debits to their personal accounts (as was done in Chapters 2 and 3 for the sole proprietor). The debits thus built up are expected to be covered by the distribution of income; if not, they are treated as net reductions of investment at the close of the year. Also, it should be mentioned that partnerships as such are not subject to federal income taxes; each partner's share of income is taxed as if he were a sole proprietor, at the rates which apply to his own situation. Therefore, the income tax charges and the corresponding liabilities are omitted from partnership records.

Corporate Share Equity

The ownership of a corporation so far as accounting statements are concerned is made up of two parts: invested capital and retained earnings. When a corporation is formed and shares are issued for the initial capital contributions, the amount invested would logically be credited to the account with common stock or other shares. This is true only in some cases, however. Many shares of stock are given *par* or *stated* values when the corporation is organized. These values supposedly earmark the amount of investment contribution made for each share. Thus, if 500 shares of stock have a par value of $50 each, the legal capital contribution that should be made for them is $25,-000. Actually, the appraisal of the market enters even new issues of shares, and the amounts that investors are willing to contribute for a share in the company may be more or less than the par figure. Since it is illegal to issue par-value shares at a discount in many states, the par value is set low enough so that there may be some amount of "premium" (excess over par value) contributed for the shares. Thus, the issuance of 500 shares of $50 par value each might bring $280,000 in cash investment, and the excess of $30,000 might be credited to an account labeled Premium on Common Stock. The investment of the stockholders would thus appear in two accounts.

A similar situation exists in the case of no-par shares if they have been given a stated value, except that the excess over the stated value is typically labeled Additional Paid-In Capital. The stated value differs from par value principally in that the par value is printed on the stock certificate, whereas the stated value is not mentioned on the certificate. Indeed, it is possible that the directors may determine the stated value of shares after the corporation has been formed, although there are some legal restrictions on this. We are not here concerned with legal technicalities, except in the way the law affects the accounting process. Hence, for our purposes, the difference between par, no-par, and stated-value shares is merely the way in which the initial investment contributions are recorded.

Classes of Shares

A corporation may issue different kinds of shares, each with different rights and privileges. Preferred stock typically has a preference as to the payment of dividends, which means that no dividends may be paid on the common shares until the preferred shares have received their specified distributions. For instance, a preferred stock may be entitled to dividends of $6 per share per year before any dividends may be declared on the common shares. Thus, if there are 4,000 preferred shares and 5,000 common shares and the first quarter's earnings are $7,000, the preferred dividend requirement is $6,000 (4,000 × $1.50) and the dividend that can be paid to the common shares is $1,000, or 20 cents per share. The laws regulating dividends are somewhat complex, but typically dividends are limited to the earnings or profits of the company; even though retained earnings of one period may be applied to dividends in a later one, distributions cannot be more than the earnings of the company.[2] If the earnings were only $5,000 in this case, the preferred share requirement would more than exhaust the available earnings equity; thus, the preferred shareholders might be paid $1.25 per share, but no more dividends could legally be paid, and common shareholders would receive nothing.

Cumulative Preferred Stock

Although the preferred stock has a priority over common shares in the receipt of dividends, this could be interpreted as referring to each year or specific distribution. That is, in the case just mentioned, the unpaid 25 cents per preferred share might "lapse" if the preferred shares were not cumulative. However, most preferred stocks are made cumulative by agreement, and dividends in arrears do not lapse. But dividend arrearages are not legal debts of the company until there is a legal declaration of those dividends payable on a specified date.

Participation

At common law, shares of a corporation are alike, and each share has precisely the same rights as the others, unless they have been made different by the charter or bylaws of the company. Hence, participation of shares is inherent. That is, each share has the right to a prorata part of the entire dividend distribution, unless other stipulations are made. The preference as to dividends with regard to preferred stock is such a stipulation. But the granting of preference in the receipt of dividends would seem to indicate a limitation as well. That is, the very granting of preference would imply that preferred shares have no further rights to dividends after their specified rate of dividend has been paid. Some preferred shares are therefore desig-

---

[2] Right here, perhaps, is the place to stress the fact that dividends are not "paid out of" retained earnings but are merely charged against that equity. Dividends are paid from cash or other property; the debit carried to Retained, or Current, Earnings is merely the reduction in the shareholder's equity occasioned by the transfer of shareholder equity to the form of current debt, Dividends Payable, which is then settled by a cash payment.

nated as participating, which means that they have rights to dividend distributions even after their preferred rate has been paid. This may be defined as an equal amount per share, preferred and common alike; or it may be applied equally in total amount to each *class* of stock, then divided among the shares in each class. But participation may be limited, so as to apply only after the common stock has received dividends equal to the preferred. For instance, a corporation with 10,000 shares of $50 par value 6 percent preferred stock and 15,000 shares of common stock may wish to distribute dividends in the amount of $60,000, the earnings of the year. If the preferred shares participate equally with the common shares (class for class), they would first receive their preferred rate, $30,000; the remaining $30,000 would be distributed to the common stockholders at a rate of $2 per share.

Participation on a share-for-share basis would yield a different result. If the total distribution were to be $100,000, the basic preferred dividend would leave $70,000 for participation. This in most cases would be applied first to give the common shareholders $3 per share (an amount equal to that received by each share of the preferred stock) or a total of $45,000; the remaining $25,000 would be distributed (share for share) to preferred and common shares at $1 per share. The preferred and common shares would, on this basis, receive $4 per share each. The participation feature is not too common in extant financial practice for fairly obvious reasons.

Earnings Retention

From an operating viewpoint, there is no compelling reason for the distribution of income to shareholders. Actually, the funds that might be distributed are useful for the expansion or the financial rearrangement of the firm. But stockholders look upon dividends as a tangible embodiment of income, and stocks which pay no dividends are not always viewed as entirely desirable. However, the pressure of personal income tax in recent years has put some emphasis upon the desirability of *not* receiving dividends in cash. The gradual growth and expansion of the firm would tend to be reflected in higher market values for the shares, and the stockholder might thus convert what would otherwise be ordinary dividend income to a capital gain; for those individuals who have substantial other income, the tax cost would be lowered considerably. The great majority of large companies tend to pay out only a part of their earnings in cash, leaving perhaps as much as 50 or 60 percent of the earnings in the business for growth.

Stock Dividends

In the effort to work out something of a compromise as between one shareholder's desire for dividends and another's wish to reduce income taxes by avoiding cash dividends, some companies have attempted to meet both desires by the use of stock dividends or dividends payable in shares. Instead of paying a cash dividend of, say, $4 per share on a stock with a market value of $60, the company may issue an additional share of stock for each 15 now held. This looks like a dividend of 6⅔ percent on the market value of the share, but the issuance of the additional shares takes nothing out of the business. All that happens is that there are $\frac{1}{15}$ more shares outstanding than before, each of which is worth slightly less than before the dividend, so far as underlying values are concerned. Whatever the value of the stock equity was before the stock dividend, it is not increased by merely cutting it up into smaller pieces. The shareholder may convert his share dividend into cash by selling it; thus, he may appear to make the distribution a cash dividend. But this really means that he is disposing of a part of his interest in the business. If the market happens to be rising, he may fail to see the real effect of his action.

On the books of the company, there must be some shift in the share-equity accounts, if only to show the change in the number of outstanding shares. Usually this is done by reducing Retained Earnings by the total par, stated, or market value of the dividend shares and crediting this amount to the common stock account. In the given case, entries to record a 1,000-share dividend at market price would be:

```
Retained Earnings...................................................60,000
    Common Shares.................................................60,000
```

This entry serves to show the change in number of shares, and it calls attention to the decision that $60,000 of earnings are to be retained permanently. Of course, the retention of earnings was actually accomplished by the decision to avoid a cash dividend. The increase in number of shares really serves only to reduce the amount of shareholder equity per share, which is offset by the increased number of shares. Generally, legal accounting rules demand that retained earnings be reduced when such shares are issued; this is probably intended to serve as a brake on stock dividend transactions.

Other Earnings Retentions

Sometimes, the decision to retain earnings may be indicated by setting up special equity accounts. These special accounts should be labeled "appropriations" of earnings. These labels may refer to "maintenance of working capital," "financing extensions of plant," "absorption of anticipated losses," or the like. No great harm is done by setting up such special equity accounts so long as their use has no effect on the calculation of income. Unless this is carefully watched, however, such transfers could be misused to transfer income from one year to another, by setting up the special equity by charges to one year's earnings, then carrying back that equity credit to inflate the earnings of subsequent years; or, the special equity might be debited with costs otherwise chargeable to income. This would be misleading, to say the least.

These appropriations of retained earnings are sometimes referred to as "reserves," which is really quite confusing, especially to those not acquainted with financial jargon. Actually, to most people, a reserve means something set aside against a future need; this implies the segregation of cash or other property for such purposes. A *real* segregation of *property* is in accounting language a fund, not a reserve. It is therefore desirable to avoid the term reserve in these circumstances. "Appropriation" is not an ordinary word, and it carries less misleading implications. However, it is not widely used in financial reporting.

Restrictive Agreements

Sometimes, there are specified contractual arrangements to make sure that earnings are retained in the business. Creditors (especially mortgagees or bondholders) sometimes require that the company pay *no* dividends unless the annual earnings shall be above some level (say 10 percent of the outstanding mortgage or bonds). To achieve this, retained earnings may be transferred into an equity account of the appropriation variety; under some conditions, this may be called—by those who ought to know better—a "Reserve for Sinking Fund." The term arises from the fact that the company may have been required to set aside actual cash or securities for the purpose of retiring its debts systematically. Such a segregation of assets is a fund, and it may be called a sinking fund because it is intended to cover the outstanding debts. But the appropriation of retained earnings has nothing to do with the debt retirement; it is merely a way to show the effect of compliance with contractual arrangements. Earnings thus appropriated insure that some of the shareholders' interest stays in the company and that the continued operation of the company (on which the value of the creditors' claims really depends) will to that extent protect the creditors against loss.

Debt-Financing Instruments for Long-Term Loans

All companies raise some of their funds from the issue of shares; but there are reasons why it may be advantageous to use long-term debt financing. Debts may be of various kinds, but all debt contracts represent advances by creditors which are expected to be repaid along with interest as compensation for the use of the funds advanced. The reasons for preferring debt financing are worth considering.

For one thing, debt financing cost—or interest—is an acceptable deduction in the computation of corporate income taxes, whereas dividends are not. Since the current corporate income tax is 48 percent for corporate taxable income in excess of $25,000, the result is to reduce the apparent cost of debt financing to 52 percent of its quoted rate. That is, a company that borrows money agreeing to pay 5 percent interest on the loan annually, incurs a net cost of only 2.6 percent after taxes. Of course, this is only true when there are earnings sufficient to cover the interest deduction; but carry-forward and carry-back provisions make this only a minor limitation. The effect of income taxation (treating interest as a deduction) is to make debt more attractive as a method of financing than it otherwise would be.

Variations in Debt Patterns

There are many ways in which borrowing arrangements can be made in terms of the time period, the spacing of interest payments, the repayment of principal, the kind of security involved, and various other factors. Some long-term financing differs from short-term debt only in terms of the period of time over which the arrangement runs. Even bank loans may run longer than a year; three-and five-year loans are not uncommon, and the lines of demarcation between one kind or class of arrangement and others are not easy to draw. But all debt arrangements have some elements in common.

Ordinary Mortgage Loan

To illustrate the simplest type of long-term financing, consider the mortgage loan. A company builds a plant building which costs $50,000, and the amount required to pay the construction contractor is borrowed from a real estate financing firm, interest at 6% payable annually, but the principal to be retired in blocks of $10,000 each five years. On this basis, the company will pay off its debt in 25 years, and interest on the unpaid balance will be paid annually. During the first five years, the interest payment at the end of each year will be $3,000; the $10,000 principal payment made at the end of the fifth year will reduce interest payments during the ensuing five-year period to $2,400; in the third five-year term, the interest will be $1,800; the fourth term will require annual interest of $1,200 and the interest charge for each of the last five years will be $600. These items would be accounted for in exactly the way they have been described, except that if the fiscal year of the company does not coincide with the contract year on the loan, there will be accruals of unpaid interest at the ends of the years to take account of the different dates involved. This is not of special importance when the amounts of interest are the same in adjacent years; but when changes occur because of principal repayments, the accrual affects the interest cost of a given fiscal year. Suppose the loan contract year is April 1 to March 31 and the company's fiscal period is the calendar year. At the end of the fifth calendar year, the unpaid principal would be $50,000, of which $10,000 would have to be retired on the following March 31. In the balance sheet at the end of the fifth year, this $10,000 would properly be shown as a current liability, and the other $40,000 as a long-term debt. There would be $2,250 of interest accrued payable ($9/12$ of a year at $3,000). At the end of the sixth year, the interest payable would be only $1,800 ($9/12 \times $2,400$) and no part of the principal would be current. Interest charges for this sixth year would be $2,550 ($750 [1st quarter] + $1,800 [rest of year]). Note that the interest charges would be quite different from the cash payments. Interest paid in the sixth year is $3,000 on March 31 when a $10,000 repayment of principal was also made.

Amortized Mortgages

The company might easily find these arrangements awkward, for each five years it must raise $10,000 for repayment of principal, and the interest charges are a greater burden in the earlier years than in the later ones. It is possible to set up this loan so that it could be handled with equal annual payments, to combine principal and interest, and still work off the debt in 25 years. To see how this is done, we shall have to use compound interest calculations.

Compound Interest Factors

Any sum that earns interest at the rate i over one interest period will accumulate to $(1 + i)$ times the initial amount. If nothing is paid on the debt or the interest, the interest is added to the principal and the same accumulation process operates for the second interest period; at the end of the second period, the initial amount has accumulated to $(1 + i)$ times the amount carried over from the first period. In terms of the initial principal, the accumulated amount at the end of the second period is $P(1 + i)(1 + i)$ or $P(1 + i)^2$. The accumulation by compound interest may thus be expressed by the general pattern, $P(1 + i)^n$. That is, a given principal, invested at i percent per period, is multiplied by the *conversion* factor $(1 + i)$ as many times (n) as there are interest periods in the investment term.

Similarly, any sum due a number of periods in the future may be reduced to its "present worth" at i percent per year by *dividing* by the conversion factor. $10,000 due one year hence at 6 percent per year now represents $10,000/1.06, because if this sum is invested now at 6 percent, it will accumulate in one year to ($10,000/1.06)(1.06), which is $10,000. Discounting and accumulation by compound interest are precisely reciprocal operations, and there is no bias in the arithmetic. A sum may be discounted for any given number of periods and reaccumulated without changing the original amount. This is not true of simple interest; the simple interest accumulation factor is $(1 + ni)$ under simple interest because the interest is not added to the principal at the end of an interest period. The simple discount factor is $(1 - nd)$ which is not reciprocal to the accumulation factor; the bias involved in discounting and reaccumulation makes simple interest unsatisfactory for periods longer than a year.

The pattern of successive division used in compound discount may be symbolized by negative sign exponents of the conversion factor. Thus, the discount factor over six periods is $(1 + i)^{-6}$ which is the same as $1/(1 + i)^6$, which is $1/(1 + i)$ multiplied by itself six times. This involves quite a bit of arithmetic, but tables of the compound interest factors reduce the computations. $10,000 due five years hence with interest at 6 percent per year is $10,000[1/(1.06)^5]$. The conversion factor $(1.06)^{-5}$ is given in a table as 0.747258. Thus, the present worth of $10,000 due five years hence at 6 percent per year is $7,472.58. Using the technique and the tables, we can establish the present worth of all the principal repayments on the mortgage under discussion:

Payment due 5 years hence	$10,000 $(1.06)^{-5}$..........	$ 7,472.58
Payment due 10 years hence	$10,000 $(1.06)^{-10}$..........	5,583.95
Payment due 15 years hence	$10,000 $(1.06)^{-15}$..........	4,172.65
Payment due 20 years hence	$10,000 $(1.06)^{-20}$..........	3,118.05
Payment due 25 years hence	$10,000 $(1.06)^{-25}$..........	2,329.99
Present Worth of Principal Repayments..............		$22,677.22

The present worth of the future interest payments is obviously $27,-322.78, the difference between the $50,000 present worth of the principal now and the $22,677.22 present worth of the discounted repayments of principal. To see how the present equivalents of the interest payments may be established directly by compound interest methods, we shall make use of the notion of annuities.

Annuities

An annuity is a series of uniform payments (each called a "rent") payable at the end of successive (equal) interest periods for a given term. Many contractual arrangements involve annuities, such as rentals under a lease, insurance premiums, repayments of principal, and payments of interest on a given principal. The earmarks of an annuity should be emphasized: the payments must be equal in amount, they must be spaced to coincide with the interest conversion period, and the first (and succeeding) rents must be due at the *end* of each interest conversion period. If we have a table of discounting or present worth factors $(1 + i)^{-n}$, we could make from it another table of annuities discounted to present worth by adding the successive items in order to form a cumulative table:

At 6%	*Present Worth of $1* *Discounted for n Periods*	*Cumulation, Present* *Worth of a Series of* *$1 Rents Over n Periods*
$(1.06)^{-1}$	0.943396	0.943396
$(1.06)^{-2}$	0.889996	1.833393
$(1.06)^{-3}$	0.839619	2.673012
$(1.06)^{-4}$	0.792094	3.465106
$(1.06)^{-5}$	0.747258	4.212364
etc.	etc.	etc.

There is a mathematical formula for the present worth of an annuity,[3]

$$C_{\overline{n}|} \text{ at } i = \frac{1 - \left(\dfrac{1}{(1 + i)^n}\right)}{i}$$

but there is no need for it if tables for this factor are available. In the case of our mortgage loan, the "interest" payments for the first five years are $3,000 per year. These, according to the table given immediately above, are now worth $3,000 (4.212364), or $12,637.09. The "interest" payments for the ensuing five years are $2,400 each; these, at the beginning of the sixth year, are worth $10,109.67. To bring this back to the present time (five years before the beginning of the sixth year), we must discount $10,109.67 using the factor 0.747258. ($10,109.67 × 0.747258 = $7,554.53). The computations we have just made may be diagrammed:

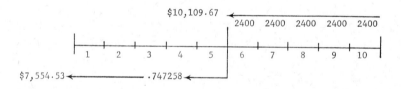

Similarly, the third (five-year) group of "interest" payments are $1,800 each annually. These, discounted to the beginning of the 10th year, are $7,582.26; this amount brought 10 years forward to present worth by the use of the discount factor 0.558395 yields $4,233.90. The fourth block of "interest" payments is $1,200 per year; discounted to the beginning of the 15th year they amount to $5,054.84, and discounted as a sum for 15 years to the present, this is $2,109.21. The last five interest payments are $600 each; the annuity of these five payments is worth $2,527.42 at the end

---

[3] We use $C_{\overline{n}|}$, instead of the more common symbol, $A_{\overline{n}|}$; $C_{\overline{n}|}$ means the commuted value of an annuity. A suggests "amount," which is ambiguous.

of the 20th year; this sum discounted to the present is $788.06. The present worth sum of all these annuities is $27,322.79.

The sum of the present worths of principal repayments computed earlier is $22,677.22. These two present worth figures combined give $50,000.01, the initial amount of the obligation. This is more than a mere curiosity that the present worths of the future principal and "interest" payments should precisely equal the initial amount of the obligation. This equality of present worths to initial amount exists because the interest is computed at 6 percent per year on the future payments; we have been placing quotation marks around the word "interest" (payments) for a good reason. The company must pay those future sums which discounted at the stated interest rate of 6 percent per year will equal the obligation. It really makes no difference whether the payments are labeled "interest" or principal, so long as their discounted values equal the initial obligation.

Transformation of Debt

This "equality of present worth" notion can be applied to rearrange future payments in a number of ways without changing the interest rate. For example, we may now convert or transform the obligation into a series of equal annual payments that will discharge the debt over 25 years, combining "interest" and "principal" in a single series of rents. The present worth of annuities for many rates and terms may be found in published tables. If we look for the 25-year item in a 6 percent "present worth of an annuity" table, we will find the entry, 12.783356. This means that an annuity of 25 one-dollar rents is equal at 6 percent to a present worth of $12.78+: our annuity (of ? dollars) discounts to a present worth of $50,000. Therefore, division of $50,000 by 12.783356 will give the annual rent required to amortize $50,000 and interest over 25 years. This is found to be $3,911.34.

Sinking Funds

Occasionally, the lender prefers not to arrange payments to suit the convenience of the borrower but would rather have the entire principal settled in a lump sum. Suppose in this case that the loan had been arranged so that "interest" on the $50,000 would be paid annually, but the principal would be settled at the end of the 25 years in a single amount. Since the annual "interest" payments are equal to the interest of 6 percent on the $50,000 principal, the amount of the obligation remains at $50,000 until the end of the 25-year term. How might the borrower arrange to get the advantage of annual repayments without seeking out another lender?

The answer to this is the accumulation of a sinking fund, which is a calculated and formal way of paying off a debt by annual installments, through the device of investing to "save up" the principal payment by regular annual deposits. Here we may use tables that give the *accumulated or terminal amount* of an annuity (at the *end* of the term). Assuming that we could find some investment opportunity that would yield 6 percent compounded annually, the figure in the "sum of an annuity" table for 25 periods at 6 percent is 54.864512. This indicates the annual deposit to be $50,000/54.864512 or $911.34. It should be noted that the difference between this annual payment and the one set up as an annuity repaying both interest and principal is the $3,000 annual "interest" ($911.34 = $3,911.34 = 3,000.00).

Sinking funds are not in common use, for the lender usually is willing to adjust the terms of his loan. But in the case of a bond issue, where the lenders are numerous and such negotiations are not feasible, the sinking fund may be a useful device.

Corporate Bonds

When a corporation attempts to borrow a large sum, say, several million dollars, it may be impossible to find a single lender who could or would advance such a sum. Investors typically seek some degree of diversification to reduce risk and would be unwilling to stake such a large amount in one venture, even if they had such sums to invest. The corporate bond issue is an answer to this problem. On the basis of a contract with an intermediary, such as an investment banking firm or syndicate, the corporation issues, not one note or promise to pay, but a large number of small ones, typically in multiples of $1,000. These "bonds" are documents which set forth the general terms of the overall contract, and they usually have attached to them a number of coupons to be used in collecting the semiannual "interest" payments as these become due. The "interest" rate shown on these coupons is the coupon rate, and the amount of principal to be repaid at the maturity of the loan—say 20 years hence—is the face amount of the bond. Securities such as this are bought and sold in the organized exchanges, and the individual investor may acquire as many bonds of a given kind as he may desire; he may sell them through the exchange at any time at the price then current.

The fact that bonds have market prices which change over time is a complication. The rate of return on a bond investment is often not the same as the coupon rate because the price of the bond is not "par," the same as its face value. When a bond sells for more than its par value, the rate of return is actually less than the coupons call for; when the bond sells for less than its par value, the rate of return is greater than the coupon rate. To illustrate, a $1,000 face value bond, maturing in 20 years, with $30 interest coupons dated at semiannual intervals, would sell at par if the current market yield on such securities of like risk were 3 percent each six months, or 6 percent compounded semiannually. If the market appraisal of this bond were a bit different and investors expected a slightly higher rate of interest, say, $3\frac{1}{2}$ percent semiannually, the bond would have to sell at a discount. The actual price would be established by computing the present worth of the obligations at the $3\frac{1}{2}$ percent (market) rate of interest. The indicated calculations are:

(1) Present worth of $1,000 to be received 20 years hence,

$$\$1,000(1.0350)^{-40} = \$252.57$$

(2) Present worth of 40 interest coupons of $30 each,

$$\$30(C_{\overline{40|}} \text{ at } 3\frac{1}{2}\%), \$30(21.355072) = \$640.65$$

The sum of these two items, $893.22, is the price at which the future receipts will yield $3\frac{1}{2}$ percent each six months.

Shortcut Computation of Bond Prices

It is possible to compute bond prices with only a "present worth of one dollar" (F^{-n}) table available. Any bond whose coupon rate is equal to the market rate will sell at "par"—that is, the annuity of interest payments will exactly offset the effect of discounting the repayment of principal. Thus, the present worth of interest coupons may be computed by subtracting the discounted principal from par. In a $3\frac{1}{2}$ percent market, a 20-year bond with $35 coupons will sell for $1,000. If from an F^{-n} table we can establish the $3\frac{1}{2}$ percent present worth of $1 for 40 periods as 0.252572, the present worth of the principal repayment is $252.57 and the present worth of the series of 40 payments of $35 each is therefore $747.43. A bond with \$30 coupons would be different from one that sells at par only because of the different semiannual "interest"; that is, a \$30 "interest" annuity would be worth $6/7$ as much as that for a bond with \$35 coupons. The interest annuity on the 3 percent bond would thus be $6/7$ of \$747.43 or \$640.65; and its price would be \$252.57 + \$640.65 or \$893.22, exactly as if the annuity table had been used.

Coupon Rate Higher than Market Rate

A bond may be attractive enough to cause investors to be willing to accept a lower rate of interest than that specified in the bond coupons. If investors were willing to accept $2\frac{3}{4}$ percent each six months for a bond with \$30 semiannual coupons, the price would be computed as follows:

(1) $\$1,000(1.0275)^{-40}$ $\$1,000(0.337852) = \$\ 337.85$
(2) $\$30\ (C_{\overline{40}|}\ \text{at}\ 2\frac{3}{4}\%) = \$30(24.078101)$
                  $= \$722.34$

or,

$$\frac{12}{11} \times \$662.15(1,000.00 - 337.85) = \underline{\ \ \ 722.34}$$

Sum, price to yield $2\frac{3}{4}$ percent semiannually   \$1,060.19

Issue of Bonds by the Corporation

The corporation would record the issue of bonds at par for cash by crediting the Bonds Payable equity account with the par value of the entire issue and debiting Cash in Bank. The payment of interest would be recorded by the usual procedure; accrual entries would time the interest charge to fit the fiscal reporting period of the company. But sometimes even the *original* issue of bonds occurs at a price above or below par. Bonds issued at a premium (a price higher than par) will entail the use of a separate account, Premium on Bonds Payable. Suppose there were 5,000 bonds of the kind just referred to, issued at a price of $106\frac{1}{8}$; the corporation would receive \$5,306,250 for the issue. The indicated entries are:

Cash in Bank..................................... 5,306,250		
Bonds Payable.............................	5,000,000
Premium on Bonds Payable....................	306,250

In this case, the true interest rate is about 2.7 percent semiannually, less than the coupon rate of 3 percent. Therefore, although the corporation will pay the dollar amounts called for by the coupons on the bonds, its interest charges are less because of the premium in the issue price. Hence, when the first interest coupons are due, the company will pay $150,000 in "interest," but its actual interest charge should be 2.7 percent of the issue price ($5,306,250) or $143,268.75. The difference between the cash paid and the correct interest cost, $6,731.25, would be treated as amortization of the premium. Since the obligation at maturity is only $5,000,000, the premium is reduced by the excess of cash paid over interest cost as a "repayment of principal." The entries are:

Interest Charges.	143,268.75	
Premium on Bonds Payable.	6,731.25	
Cash in Bank.		150,000

The carrying value of the liability is thus reduced to $5,299,518.75; the second interest coupon would entail an amortization of premium arrived at by computing the true interest cost, 2.7 percent of $5,299,518.75 = $143,087.01, and subtracting this from the "interest" payment of $150,000. The amortization is $6,912.99. This process will eventually reduce the premium amount to zero at maturity of the loan and will show the correct interest charge in the reports of the corporation. That is, the rate negotiated upon issuance of the bonds will be applied over their life to state the interest cost. As a practical matter, this procedure may be simplified by merely amortizing the premium on a straight-line basis, $\frac{1}{40}$ of $306,250 each six months. The semiannual amortization would thus be a uniform $7,656.25 over the entire 20-year period.

Bonds Issued at a Discount

Should the bond market be less favorably disposed toward a given issue, it may sell initially at a discount because investors demand a higher rate than the coupon rate for the loan. Thus, if the market rate for the bond described earlier were 3½ percent semiannually, the price would be $893.22, or, in terms of the typical market quotation, 89⅜, to yield slightly less than 3½ percent each six months. The market price establishes the amount of the discount on the issue; 10⅝ percent of $5,000,000 would be $531,250. Entries for the original issue would be:

Cash in Bank.	4,468,750	
Discount, Bonds Payable.	531,250	
Bonds Payable.		5,000,000

The same pattern of amortization would be applied as was used to handle a bond premium, except that the write-off of discount would make the interest charges higher than the "interest" payments because the discount on the loan is a form of interest. Thus, the first semiannual interest payment and straight-line discount amortization would be recorded by the entries:

Interest Charges	163,281.25	
Discount on Bonds Payable		13,281.25
Cash in Bank		150,000.00

The credits to Discount on Bonds Payable in each period will write off the extra interest over the 20-year term, and the obligation will increase to the face value of the bonds at maturity. The computations of a "yield-rate" amortization would be like those discussed above except for the rate of interest.

Retirement of Bonds before Maturity

For various reasons, a company may decide to pay off its bonds before they mature. In such a case, a prorata part of the then remaining discount or premium must be treated as an element in the retirement transaction. This is actually a correction of interest charges in prior years, but, like over- or underdepreciation, is often reported as a single adjustment in the year of retirement.

Summary

Financing transactions constitute a broad field of interest, and this field covers a good many transactions, of which the major ones have been discussed in this chapter. The greatest single source of finance in any business arises from normal and recurring deliveries of goods and services to customers and the collections which follow. This kind of financing covers the regular and ordinary cash needs, but sometimes seasonal or other conditions will cause unusual demands for cash. Some of these can be reduced by the management of working capital to keep inventories and receivables and current payables from advancing beyond the levels of adequacy. When the volume of business suddenly increases, the need for short-term loans will become apparent, however, because collections from the higher sales will lag, while ordinary payments cannot be postponed for very long. Bank loans, factoring, and other short term loans are typical sources of short-term funds. These involve simple interest or discount calculations, as well as contingent liabilities that must be recorded.

Long-term sources of capital include additional investment by the proprietor or by partners; incorporation opens the way to greater sources of capital by the issuance of shares to a wider group of investors. But all of these raise certain issues of income distribution, and for a corporation there may be different kinds of stock and dividends. There are also "dividends" in the form of shares of stock. Earnings retention is a major method of corporate expansion, and nearly all companies retain a substantial part of their earnings even when contractual arrangements with creditors do not require this. The growth of the stockholders' investment is advantageous to creditors as well as to the company.

Because of tax effects as well as for other reasons, debt is increasingly favored as a source of external long-term financing. But debt may take various forms, all of which are related in some way to the general compound interest model. Mortgage loans were the example to work out the notions of present worth and the future worth of specific sums of money due on different dates; but the amortized mortgage brought the annuity concept to our attention. The commuted and terminal values of annuities were applied to corporate bonds and sinking funds. The accounting for bond investments and bonds payable served to introduce straight line and effective rate amortizations of premiums and discounts related to bonds.

There are other issues of long-term financing that are of interest to accountants. Some of these are currently receiving attention, even though they are not actually part of what is regarded as conventional accounting. These are not included in this chapter for this reason. But for those who may be interested in further applications of the compound interest model to leases and depreciation, these are discussed in an appendix to this chapter.

Our next concern will be the following of the overall effects of financing transactions, to summarize the broad flow of resources in and out of the firm. This will involve the preparation of a new kind of report from those we have thus far recognized—the Statement of Funds.

QUESTIONS

1. What are financing transactions and how are they different from operating transactions? Why are financing transactions important for the success of the firm?

2. What is the *primary* source of funds for a business enterprise? How is it possible for a company which is incurring losses to have increasing cash balances?

3. The balancing of cash receipts and cash payments is easy when the volume of business remains constant. But reductions in volume can produce excessive cash balances, and vice versa. How is this?

4. When cash requirements ebb and flow seasonally, there is a real use for seasonal loans. The primary function of commercial banks is to meet the short-term needs for cash which many businesses encounter. Write entries for a typical short-term bank loan covered by a note for $1,000 payable in 60 days, discounted at 6 percent. Supposing the loan was negotiated November 16, what entries would be needed to state current interest charges correctly at the close of the calendar year?

5. The Opportunity Company has $50,000 of good accounts receivable which are due on the average 58 days hence. The company needs $30,000 now to handle an advantageous purchase of merchandise, terms on which are COD. The Civil Credit Corporation advances $30,000 against $40,000 of Opportunity Company's accounts receivable for 50 days for a finance cost of $500. Write entries for this transaction.

6. After negotiating the transaction in Question 5, the Opportunity Company finds itself in need of more ready cash. An important customer, Schulder, owes the firm $3,000 and has given a 7 percent 90-day note for this amount. The note is due in 54 days when the Opportunity Company discounts it at the Merchants' Bank, whose discount rate is 9 percent.
    a) What will the note be worth when it comes due?
    b) How much will the company get from discounting Schulder's note at the bank?
    c) Write entries for the discounting transaction showing the contingent liability.
    d) If Opportunity Company's fiscal year ends 26 days after the note is discounted, write necessary entries to state the current interest charges correctly in the financial reports.
    e) If Schulder does not pay the note at maturity, what entries for Opportunity Company?

7. What is meant by net working capital and why is this concept useful—especially since most short-term financial transactions do not materially affect its amount?

8. Alter and Jung form a partnership to operate a retail store. Alter contributes merchandise at an agreed valuation of $15,000, and a store building and fixtures at a value of $40,000. Jung contributes $20,000 cash. It is agreed that interest shall be credited to each part-

ner annually at 10 percent of his average capital investment and that Jung shall receive a salary of $1,000 per month, to be withdrawn in cash at his discretion, but not before it has accrued. Remaining profits and losses are shared equally. During the first year, operating profits before interest or salary were $10,500. Jung had drawn his salary for the first eight months, but the last four months' salary have not been drawn.

a) Write entries to record the activities of the firm for the first year. (Record the profit by charging the gross amount to Cash in Bank and assume all monthly transactions to occur on the last day of the month.)

b) Draw up the personal accounts and show the entries and balances at the end of the year.

9. a) What is the difference between preferred and common shares of a corporation?

b) Is a cumulative preferred stock really a better investment than a noncumulative preferred stock? Why?

c) Give an example to indicate what may be meant by participating preferred stock.

10. a) Why would one stockholder really prefer not to receive dividends from a company in which he had invested, while another stockholder would like to receive dividends amounting to the total earnings every year?

b) Could this situation be obtained by the use of "dividends" in shares of stock? How is such a stock dividend recorded by the company? What effect does the stock dividend have on the financial position of the company that issues it?

c) What are "appropriations" of retained earnings? How could these affect the shareholder's interests?

11. a) Casa Grande Company acquires a new plant, financing part of this by a mortgage loan of $100,000, with interest at 6 percent; principal payments $20,000 per year starting at the end of the sixth year. What is the discounted amount of this mortgage at its inception? What is the interest charge for the first year?

b) If the Casa Grande Company had negotiated this loan on an annual payment amortized mortgage at the same interest rate, what would be the annual payment to cover interest and principal?

c) Suppose the contract were set up to call for a lump-sum repayment of principal *and* interest at the end of 10 years (no payments of interest until maturity), how much would be required to pay off the debt? What amount could be invested annually to accumulate this amount supposing the sinking fund would earn 10 percent per year?

12. Ventura Island Development Corporation arranges to issue $10,000,-

000 in 20-year 10% bonds (semiannual coupons) at a time when the applicable corporate bond yield rate is 9 percent.

a)   Write entries to record the issue of these bonds.

b)   Record the *first* semiannual interest charges using the straight-line method of amortization.

c)   Record the *second* semiannual interest charges using the yield rate amortization.

13. *a)*   After these Ventura Island bonds were outstanding for 18 years, the company purchased $100,000 face value of them at a market price of 101. Write entries to record the retirement of these bonds.

   b)   Suppose an investor (not the issuer) had purchased $10,000 of these bonds at 101. How much interest income would he record at the end of the first six months?

PROBLEMS

Palomar Machine Company

Just when the peak business of the year had gotten under way, this company had an opportunity to purchase certain equipment at the very advantageous price of $13,000 if payment could be made immediately. The use of this equipment would improve substantially both the quality and the output volume of the company's product, and the management was quite anxious to take advantage of this opportunity. Costs of installation would be about $2,000 and would also have to be paid immediately because it consisted largely of construction labor and materials on which no extended terms could be obtained. Thus, the company needed $15,000 extra cash to handle this proposition.

Although there would be ample amounts of funds available from customers within a month or two, the current cash balances of the company were barely enough to meet current payrolls and suppliers invoices for regular manufacturing materials and parts. It was clear that if the new equipment was to be purchased, additional financing would have to be arranged.

The company's current accounts receivable totaled $75,000, against which there was an Estimated Defaults account of $1,400. There were two customer notes receivable on hand: the first, a $6,000 90-day 7 percent note that had already been held for 16 days; and the second, a non-interest-bearing note for $10,800, due in 72 days.

The Financial Credit Corporation would advance $15,000 for 90 days on the security of $20,000 of accounts receivable, with recourse. The charge for this advance would be $300, payable at the end of the term.

The Cosmopolitan Bank discounts notes of the sort held by this company at a rate of 8 percent per year.

Required:

1. Give the entries that would be required to record the advance of funds from the Financial Credit Corporation.

2. Give the entries that would be required to record the discounting of the notes receivable.

3. Assuming that the fiscal period of the borrowing company ended 23 days after (1) or (2) occurred, set up the "adjusting" entries to show the proper interest charges for the fiscal period.

4. Show the entries required to retire the Financial Credit Corporation advance.

5. Suppose that the $6,000 note was paid when due but the $10,800 note was not paid until 15 days after its due date (interest at 6 percent added). Give the entries required for these transactions.

Pamela Products, Inc.

An issue of $10,000,000 face amount of 20-year, 4 percent bonds with "interest" coupons dated May 1 and November 1 of each year was sold on November 1 last year to yield 5 percent compounded semiannually to maturity.

The following interest factors are available:

Present Worth of $1

1%	1½%	2%	2½%	3%	N
0.9053	0.8617	0.8203	0.7812	0.7441	10
0.8195	0.7425	0.6730	0.6103	0.5537	20
0.6717	0.5513	0.4529	0.3724	0.3066	40

Present Worth of $1 Per Period

1%	1½%	2%	2½%	3%	N
9.4713	9.2222	8.9826	8.7521	8.5302	10
18.0456	17.1686	16.3514	15.5892	14.8775	20
32.8347	29.9158	27.3555	25.1028	23.1148	40

Required:

1. How much was received as proceeds of the issue?

2. Present entries to accrue interest at December 31, last year on the books of the issuing company—
   a) On a straight-line basis.
   b) On an effective-rate basis.

3. Present entries to record interest coupon payment, May 1 this year—
   a)   On a straight-line basis.
   b)   On an effective-rate basis.
4. Present entries to record interest coupon payment, November 1 this
   year—
   a)   On a straight-line basis.
   b)   On an effective-rate basis.

Panamalian Development Bonds

This bond issue carries coupons that call for 4 percent interest, payable
semiannually. An investor considers the purchase of a $1,000 bond of this
issue, 27 years before maturity, just after the interest coupon had been
cashed on an interest payment date. The quotation was 94⅜ (percent of
par).

Required:
1. If the market rate for similar investment is 4½ percent compounded
   semiannually, by how much is this bond over- or underpriced?
2. Assume that the bond described above is purchased at the proper
   price to yield 4½ percent compounded semiannually. Give entries to
   record the purchase of the bond and to record the interest accrual
   and collection of the coupon due six months after the purchase date.
3. Assume that this bond is held until 7½ years before its maturity. On
   that date when the market rate is 4 percent, compounded semiannually, an interest coupon is cashed. What is the "book" value of
   the bond investment immediately after this coupon is collected? What
   amount of "true" interest was included in the collection of the coupon as recorded by accounting?
4. Six months after (3)—seven years before maturity of the bond, the
   current market rate for corporate bonds of this kind is 3½ percent,
   compounded semiannually. A prospective buyer offers $1,025 for the
   bond (flat, without the matured coupon). Should we sell?
5. Supposing we do sell the bond, after negotiation, to yield 3 percent
   compounded semiannually; make entries to record the sale and to
   show the gain on disposition.

Interest Tables (F^{-n})

Periods	1½%	1¾%	2%	2¼%
7	0.985222	0.885644	0.870560	0.855769
15	0.799852	0.770876	0.743015	0.716226
27	0.668985	0.626995	0.585862	0.548391
30	0.639762	0.594248	0.552071	0.512980
54	0.447542	0.391869	0.343234	0.300722

Periods	3%	3½%	4%	4½%
7............0.813092		0.785991	0.759918	0.734828
15............0.641862		0.596891	0.555266	0.516720
27............0.450189		0.395012	0.346817	0.304691
30............0.411987		0.356278	0.308319	0.267000
54............0.202670		0.156035	0.120282	0.092837

Windermere Public Service Company

A \$5,000,000 bond issue with coupon rate of 5% compounded semi-annually (2½% each six months) was sold to yield 4½% over its 20 year term. Write entries to record the issue, and to record the interest accrual at the end of the year, 3 months after the issue date. Use the straight line method of amortization.

After this bond has been outstanding for ten years, an investor acquired one \$5,000 face value bond of the issue mentioned above, to yield 5½%. Write entries to record his investment, and to take up the interest income when the coupon due six months after the acquisition is cashed. Use the effective rate method of amortization.

Present Worth of $1

2¼%	2½%	2¾%	4½%	5%	5½%	N
0.8005	0.7812	0.7624	0.6439	0.6139	0.5854	10
0.6408	0.6103	0.5813	0.4146	0.3769	0.3427	20
0.5130	0.4767	0.4431	0.2670	0.2314	0.2006	30
0.4106	0.3724	0.3379	0.1719	0.1420	0.1175	40
0.3287	0.2909	0.2576	0.1107	0.0872	0.0688	50

Present Worth of $1 per Period

2¼%	2½%	2¾%	4½%	5%	5½%	N
8.8862	8.7521	8.6401	7.1927	7.7217	7.5376	10
15.9637	15.5892	15.2273	13.0079	12.4622	11.9503	20
21.6453	20.9303	20.2493	16.2889	15.3725	14.5337	30
26.1935	25.1028	24.0781	18.4016	17.1591	16.0461	40
29.8344	28.3623	26.9972	19.7620	18.2556	16.9315	50

Alepachecot Industries

An issue of \$20,000,000 face amount of 20 year bonds, with 6 percent "interest" coupons dated April 1 and October 1 was delivered to an underwriting syndicate by the Alepachecot Industries Corporation on December 1 this year. The bonds were to be purchased by the syndicate at a price to yield 7 percent compounded semiannually from that date to maturity. The following interest factors are available:

Present Worth of $1

2%	3%	3½%	6%	7%	N
0.8203	0.7441	0.7089	0.5584	0.5083	10
0.6730	0.5537	0.5026	0.3118	0.2584	20
0.5521	0.4120	0.3563	0.1741	0.1314	30
0.4529	0.3066	0.2526	0.0972	0.0668	40

Present Worth, $1 per Period

2%	3%	3½%	6%	7%	N
8.9826	8.5302	8.3166	7.3601	7.0236	10
16.3514	14.8775	14.2124	11.4699	10.5940	20
22.3965	19.6004	18.3920	13.7648	12.4090	30
27.3555	23.1148	21.3551	15.0463	13.3317	40

Required:

1. Show how much was received by Alepachecot from the bond issue.
2. Give entries to accrue interest at December 31, this year on the books of Alepachecot.
   (*a*) On a straight-line basis
   (*b*) Using the effective rate
3. Give entries to record interest payment, April 1, next year.
   (*a*) On a straight-line basis
   (*b*) Using the effective rate
4. Give entries to record interest payment October 1, next year.
   (*a*) On a straight-line basis
   (*b*) Using the effective rate

Andalusian Company

A $4,000,000 issue of 6% bonds was sold by the Andalusian Company to yield 5% on a semi-annual coupon basis. This issue matured in blocks of $1,000,000 (face amounts) at the end of the 11th, 12th, 13th and 14th years after issue. Compute the proceeds from the issue, and show how the discount or premium should be amortized.

Write out the entries required if all aspects of the transaction are carried out as expected at the end of the thirteenth and during the fourteenth year.

1.025^{-n}	n	$C_{\overline{n}}$ at .025
.9518143962	2	1.9274241523
.5808646690	22	16.7654132404
.5528753542	24	17.8849858326
.5262347214	26	18.9506111434
.5008777836	28	19.9648886553

Patrician Products Corporation

A $10 million par issue of 8% (semi-annual coupon) bonds, originally sold to yield 8½% compounded semi-annually, has been outstanding for 14 years of its twenty year term. The current market yield rate for bonds of this risk class has fallen to approximately 6¼% compounded semi-annually. Just after the 28th set of coupons had been paid, it was suggested that it might be advantageous to refund this issue; it was callable at 104. After a short negotiation, a syndicate offered to take over a new $10 million 10-year, 6¼ percent issue at a price to yield 6 percent compounded semiannually.

Required:

1. Supposing that this offer was accepted by the Patrician officers, write out the entries to pay off the old bondholders from the proceeds from the new one.

2. Draw up a statement to indicate whether or not this was a desirable move for the company. Compare the outlays and costs.

Interest Tables of F⁻ⁿ

n	3.000	3.125	3.250	4.000	4.250
10	0.744094	0.735124	0.726272	0.675564	0.659537
12	0.701380	0.691246	0.681270	0.624597	0.606858
14	0.661118	0.649986	0.639056	0.577475	0.558387
20	0.553676	0.540407	0.527471	0.456387	0.434989
24	0.491934	0.477821	0.464129	0.390121	0.368277
28	0.437077	0.422483	0.408393	0.333477	0.311796
40	0.306557	0.292039	0.278226	0.208289	0.189215

n	6.000	6.250	6.500	8.000	8.500
10	0.558395	0.545394	0.532726	0.463193	0.442285
12	0.496969	0.483117	0.469683	0.397114	0.375702
14	0.442301	0.427952	0.414100	0.340461	0.319142
20	0.311805	0.297455	0.283797	0.214548	0.195616
24	0.246979	0.233402	0.220602	0.157699	0.141152
28	0.195630	0.183143	0.171479	0.115914	0.101851
40	0.097222	0.088479	0.080541	0.046031	0.038266

APPENDIX TO CHAPTER 10

Special Applications of Compound Interest to Accounting

There are at least two areas in which long-term financing contracts may suggest the use of compound interest for better perspective. While the ordinary rent payment for space in an office or apartment building is a simple compensation for services received, the leasing of an entire plant, or of large amounts of equipment over a long term with option to purchase at the end for a nominal sum really transfers many elements of ownership to the lessee. The lease merely provides security for a virtual credit sale. The fact that a leased asset provides the same benefit as full ownership—without that asset appearing on the position statement of the company using it—has become a matter of some concern to accountants in recent years. The situation is clearer if we consider a typical set of conditions.

A manufacturing company wishes to build a new $1 million plant, and a financial institution (say, an insurance company) has funds to invest. The company may merely borrow the money to build the plant from the insurance company, paying the going rate of interest as it applies to whatever repayment plan may be chosen. In such case, the manufacturing company's position statement will carry the plant, land, and building as a $1,000,000 asset, and the loan payable to the insurance company will show as a long-term debt of the same amount. The interest charges and depreciation of the plant will appear as costs in the earnings statement of the manufacturer, and the interest will be income to the insurance company, on whose books there will be a loan investment account of $1,000,000.

But the manufacturer may just as well arrange with the insurance company to lease the building—built on designated land and to the user's specifications. This could hardly be a perpetual lease, nor would it run for very many years at the same rental. Indeed, it may be desirable to make special arrangements in the form of options granted to the lessee permitting it to extend the lease, or to purchase the building and land at the end of the lease term. There may be other covenants, such as for the maintenance costs, real property taxes, renovations, and the like; such complications need not concern us, here. The point is that the manufacturer will have exactly the same facilities as if the building had been built with borrowed money, but the debt and the asset would *not appear* in the position statement. This would distort "rate of return on investment" calculations.

This distortion could be reduced by capitalizing the lease on the records of the lessee. Suppose the contract calls for payments of $93,000 at the beginning of each year for 20 years, with an option to purchase the property outright at the end of the term for $140,-000. Whatever may have been the lessor's basis for setting these terms, the lessee will view them with reference to his cost of capital. This will be, most properly, that rate of return which he might expect to earn from alternative employment of the funds required; but it may also be measured by the current and prospective cost of acquiring funds from outside sources—by borrowing or through added investment by common shareholders. Taking the cost of capital as one element in the situation, the lease contract is a deferred payment contract to pay $93,000 annually over the 20-year term. The option to purchase the building at the end of the term is not an obligation, and it is avoidable; therefore, we ignore it. At an 8 percent cost of capital, the 20 rent payments have a present worth of:

a) $93,000 payable at the beginning of the first year..............$ 93,000
b) $93,000 at the end of each of 19 years at 8%; this is $93,000
    (9.6036).. 893,134
    Total... $986,134

This sum is the cost of the entire contract, and it may be recorded:

Leasehold.. 986,134
    Long-Term Lease Rents Payable..................   986,134

This entry adds a long-term asset and a long-term debt to the position statement of the lessee. The asset is the right to use the property over 20 years; its cost will be amortized by whatever procedure most nearly reflects the consumption of services—straight line, production hours or units, or one of the decreasing-charge procedures. The debt will be paid off in the same fashion as would an amortized loan, and the interest recorded in the same way. Entries for this in the first year will be:

Beginning of the Year

Long-Term Lease Rents Payable........................ 93,000
    Cash in Bank.......................................   93,000

End of Year

Interest Charges....................................... 71,451
Long-Term Lease Rents Payable........................ 21,549
    Current Liability, Lease Rent......................   93,000

The interest charge is 8 percent of the balance of the debt, after the first payment was made: $986,134 less $93,000 is $893,134; 8 percent of $893,134 is $71,451. That part of the $93,000 payment which is not recorded as interest is a reduction of the principal, just as in any amortized loan.

It may be argued that this interest factor is not interest actually paid or accrued but merely the lessee's "cost of capital"; since this does not represent a bargained transaction, it is not properly measured. But it would be certainly incorrect to record the contract undiscounted as 20 times $93,000 or $1,860,000. Any deferred obligation is made less by the fact of deferral; and the amount of discount is measured by what those funds might earn (or save) during the deferment. Further, the building could have been built by the company for $1,000,000 in any event. Thus, the amount of $983,134 and the interest rate of 8 percent are justified by surrounding evidence.

There is another side to the question of interest, however. If the debt is discounted and used as the basis for interest charges, ought not the asset be considered and the depreciation figured by using interest factors? This brings into view another approach to depreciation or amortization charges—that they, too, may reflect interest over the long period of investment.

Compound Interest Depreciation. In order to illustrate the use of compound interest in depreciation calculations, it will be better for comparative purposes to work with the illustration used in Chapter 9: an asset costing $3,600 with an expected disposal value of $600, after five years' service. Using 8 percent as the cost of capital, depreciation is established as follows:

The Annuity Method. Every compound interest calculation considers the time-value of money, for amounts received or paid at different points in time are not comparable unless discounted or accumulated to express them at the same date. Thus the services to be received from this asset are $3,600 less $600 to be recovered five years hence. This is $3,600 − $600 $(1.08)^{-5}$, which is $3,600 − $600 (.6805) or $3,191.70. This, in turn, is the present worth of a five year commuted annuity of $x per year. Dividing the annuity factor 3.9925 into the $3,191.70 gives $799.38—the annual rent equivalent (over a five year term) to the present worth of the services to be received. This $799.98 is the annual charge for depreciation under the "annuity" method, which treats the asset as a compound interest investment yielding 8% per year but which will be reduced to the $600 disposal value at the end of the term. This is seen in the accompanying amortization table (Table 10–1).

The depreciation charge of $799.38 in each year serves to write off the asset, but this amount includes interest income on investment. The entries for the first year are conventionally regarded as being:

Current Year Depreciation............................ 799.38
　　Accumulated Depreciation.......................... 511.38
　　Income from Investment............................ 288.00

This allows for the fact that the sum of 5 charges of $799.38 is $3,996.90 as shown in the table; the net cost of the asset is actually written off by the net amount in the last column. It is usually argued that this is correct rather than to consider the "imputed" interest

TABLE 10–1

Compound Interest Depreciation

(asset cost $3,600; disposal value $600 after five years' use; interest at 8 percent)

Year	(1) Investment, Beginning of Year	(2) 8% Interest on Beginning Amount	(3) Gross Service Flow	(4) Net Service Flow (3–2)
1	$3,600.00	$288.00	$ 799.38	$ 511.38
2	3,088.62	247.09	799.38	552.29
3	2,536.33	202.91	799.38	596.47
4	1,939.86	155.19	799.38	644.19
5	1,295.66	103.65	799.38	695.73
6	599.93			
Total		$996.84	$3,996.90	$3,000.06

as added to the net depreciation amount. This results in an increasing series of depreciation charges running from $511.38 in the first year to $695.73 in the last. If the interest were really to be considered part of the cost of using the asset (and not offset against the depreciation annuity) the credit for interest would be to the account in which interest cost is accumulated. We shall consider such a treatment later; but "annuity depreciation" as recorded by those who espouse it produces a series of increasing charges, net of interest income.

The Sinking Fund Method.   Another variant of the compound interest approach to depreciation produces results similar to those of the annuity method. It views the depreciation charge as a contribution to a mythical fund with which to replace the asset at the disposal date. The terminal value of an annuity of five periods at 8 percent is 5.866601; dividing this factor into the $3,000 net replacement cost produces an annual charge of $511.38. But to this is added the interest earned on the deposits in the fund; the second year charge is $511.38 + 8% of $511.38 or $552.29; the third year charge would be $511.38 + 8% ($511.38 + $552.29) or $596.47. These are the same amounts as in the "net charge" column of the amortization table just described. The logic of this approach may be more acceptable if one is able to think of the depreciation charge as money collected from customers to replace the asset when it is worn out. This is sometimes argued for a public utility where the rate of return is more or less assured. But most accountants insist that depreciation is amortization of cost, not a provision for replacement; the rate of return is not predictable for industrial or commercial ventures, and in any case, the increasing charge pattern of compound interest depreciation is not in keeping with typical experience. Few if any assets yield their service so that the earliest years are the least, and the final year the most, productive. Further, this increasing charge pattern is accentuated by higher rates of interest or longer life. A $1,000 asset with a five year life, using a 20 percent interest rate would be written off by $134.38 in the first year, but the fifth year would have to absorb $278.65. A similar asset used over a twenty year life at 20 percent would have $5.36 written off in the first, and $171.14 in the last year. Such charges do not mirror any reasonable pattern of service flow from typical assets.

The advantage sometimes claimed for compound interest depreciation is that it shows a level rate of return on investment in the declining asset balance over the entire term. This is admittedly correct, and it is not so with conventional straight-line depreciation. To illustrate, suppose the revenue is $799.38 annually and $600 is charged as straight-line depreciation; the dollar *amount* of income will be $199.38 in each year, but the *rate* of return will be 5.535 percent (199.38/3,600.00) in the first year, and it will increase in each year up to the last, in which it will be 16.616 percent (199.38/1,200.00). The result of using compound interest depreciation would be to report as income the "interest" in column 2 of the table for each year. This is in every year 8 percent of the investment for that year, as might be expected. If depreciation is established as the remainder when 8 percent of investment is deducted from gross receipts, it is obvious that deducting such depreciation from the gross receipts will product an 8 percent return on investment. If $d = R - 0.08\,I$, it adds little to say that $R - d = 0.08\,I$.

However, it has still been argued that the compound-interest method of depreciation nevertheless is time-adjusted, and that it is the *only* method of depreciation that considers the time value of money. This is not really correct. The fact is that any pattern of depreciation may be made time-adjusted. To illustrate this, suppose we assume that expected services to be had from this asset (in terms of units of output or machine hours) were stated for the individual years:

Year 1, 5,000; year 2, 12,000; year 3, 8,000; year 4, 6,000; year 5, 2,000. If these unit services are discounted just as if they were monetary amounts, they would be 5,000(0.9259); 12,000(0.8573); 8,000(0.7938); 6,000(0.7350); 2,000(0.6806). Their sum would be

TABLE 10–2
Time-Adjusted Production Units Depreciation Amortization Table

Year	Investment Beginning of Year	8% Capital Cost	Total	Depreciation Charge*	Balance Forward	
1.........	$3600.00	$288.00	$3888.00	$ 590.02	$3297.98	
2.........	3297.98	263.84	3561.82	1416.48	2145.34	
3.........	2145.34	171.63	2316.97	944.32	1372.65	
4.........	1372.65	109.81	1482.46	708.24	774.22	
5.........	·774.22	61.94	836.16	236.08	600.08	*Disposal*
Total..		$895.22		$3895.14		

* Includes interest.

4,629.5 + 10,287.6 + 6,350.4 + 4,410.0 + 1,361.2 = 27,038.7. Dividing the total discounted services into the present worth capital cost of $3,191.64, we get a unit charge of $0.11804. This unit charge multiplied by the actually expected units of service in each of the years, produces depreciation charges of $590.02; $1,416.48; $944.32; $708.24; and $236.08. Table 10–2 shows how these charges work out over the five year period.

The calculations are similar to those in Table 10–1 with the important difference that the interest charges are included in (not subtracted from) the depreciation figures. The total of the depreciation charges is more than the asset cost; in fact, the total $895.22 interest added to the asset account is absorbed in the depreciation charges. This was accomplished by discounting the service flows to compute the unit charge for asset use. The depreciation charge for each year absorbs interest in proportion to the use made of the asset in that year, not the amount charged to the asset as interest on investment. But further, this interest is treated as a cost of using those services, not as merely an offset to the gross depreciation charge. Thus, this approach would appear to be more nearly logical as a time-adjusted depreciation pattern. If the 8% really represents the cost of capital, these 8% capital cost items should be credited to interest charges in each year. The increased gross cost of the asset from year to year represents the accumulated amount of the asset, as interest growth is added from year to year; but the depreciation charges amortize the entire accumulation over the asset's useful life.

This method of depreciation appears to be more logical than other time-adjusted procedures, but unfortunately it has not been given much attention by accountants. Perhaps this is partly justified, because it is not really necessary to use time adjusted depreciation methods on each asset, properly to reflect interest on investment. In the case of a leased asset, the interest charge associated with the lease liability reflects the cost of capital to some extent, even if not exactly in accord with the asset balances over the years. If it is really desirable (as it may be for internal administration) to show the cost of capital invested in assets of various divisons, there is no objection to making an interest charge against any internal operation, crediting this to a nondivisional "interest income" account. Thus, there will be no actual net cost or income to the whole enterprise from such calculations; the interest charges and credits offset each other and have no net significance in the measurement of overall results.

Accounting Practice as to Leases

To return to the main theme of leases, it may be noted that, in general, there are few companies that are enthusiastic about the capitalization of leases. Understandably, the capitalization of short-term leases does not affect income very much; and the capitalization of frequently renewable or cancelable leases has not much to recommend it, unless the amounts involved are really material. Yet, if a company pays advance rentals for 5 or 10 years in a lump sum of substantial amount, the amount should certainly be capitalized to avoid the distortion of financial position that would otherwise result. When deferred (annual) payment leases are capitalized by the *lessee* company, the financial obligation typically is handled as an amortized loan in the fashion described several pages above. The capitalized leasehold is generally depreciated just as other assets would be, using a conventional method as described in Chapter 9, or one of those outlined immediately above.

A *lessor* company, however, may be merely a financing agency (a bank or insurance company) or it may be the producer and servicer of the equipment—a machinery manufacturer, for instance. In the first case, the lessor (financing) company will probably treat the lease as an amortized loan, setting up a receivable for the present worth of the future payments to be received. The interest rate would be the market rate for such loans; the earliest rent payments would be regarded as nearly all "interest income," but successive payments would involve less interest and more retirement of principal. This would tend to accelerate the recognition of income from the transaction in contrast to the level annual cash receipts. Except for tax reasons, few financing institutions would prefer to defer income via the annual receipts basis—i.e., a constant proportion of each rent payment being considered as income.

The lessor company that is also the producer of the leased item might also view the lease transaction as a financing arrangement. In such case, the rent payments may be capitalized as a loan receivable whose present worth would probably be somewhat greater than the cost of the equipment. If so, this would produce an operating margin (a "manufacturing gain") from the sale. This manufacturing gain could at once be reported as income; but there would also be an interest income from the loan receivable by using the "financing" approach to accounting for the rental payments.

On the other hand, the transaction could be treated as an "operating" lease, i.e., as actually "renting" the asset. In such an event, the leased equipment would remain on the books of the lessor at cost, which would be depreciated in some conventional pattern. The income from such an interpretation of the transaction would consist only of the annual rent receipts, less the depreciation, and other expenses.

It is also possible for a lease transaction to be considered an "installment" sale, in which the profit margin would be spread over the term as a percentage of each cash receipt (see Chapter 7). This produces still other results in financial reports. In view of the quite different presentations that may be obtained by different approaches and their use for income tax determination as well as the measurement of income, it is easy to see that accountants do not agree on a single procedure that should be used in all cases. The fact that business transactions are often interpretable in different ways is not merely that accountants prefer such arrangements; sometimes it is not easy to establish whether a lease is a sale, with incidental financing arranged by the seller, a loan set up to provide security for the lender, or a rental contract with some security for the parties as to the duration of the period of asset use. Until these distinctions can be set apart by completely objective criteria, there will be some difference of interpretation, in which the accountant must exercise discretion and judgment.

Summary

In this appendix, several applications of the compound interest model have been made. We started with the question of whether long-term leases not subject to cancellation ought to be shown as assets on the books of the lessee; the difference between a purchase of an asset financed by a long-term loan, and a lease which runs for a similar period, is not really great. Further, the use of leased assets tends to reduce the investment factor in the denominator of the rate of return computation, and thus overstates the investment result when lease financing is used. However, the compound interest model applied to the lease liability produces higher interest amounts in earlier periods than a level annual rent payment would; this can affect the determination of income.

A second issue was the use of compound interest depreciation methods. The annuity and sinking fund computations were seen to produce increasing cost patterns for depreciation charges, which are not acceptable for most industrial and commercial applications, although there is some justification for them in the case of public utilities.

It was demonstrated that the claimed advantage of being "time adjusted" was not limited to the annuity and sinking-fund methods. It was also shown that compound interest calculations could be applied to different configurations of usage, such as the production hours or units approaches.

Lastly we considered the effects of lease financing on lessors, and particularly the way in which a manufacturing profit could be established when a producer of special equipment leased it, instead of making an outright sale with conventional financing.

This set of issues makes up the most striking case we have yet seen of the fact that business transactions are not so sharply defined as to justify only one method of accounting. Actually, in some cases, there is a real need to establish the criteria to be applied when deciding how a transaction should be reported.

QUESTIONS

1. Braun and Schuchter Engineering Corporation leased an office building for $50,000 per month over a ten year period. The lease was renewable at $40,000 per month for another ten years after the initial term. Alternatively, the corporation could purchase the building for $200,000 at the end of the ten year term. How would this lease transaction appear in the first ten earnings statements of Braun and Schuchter if the lease was not capitalized? In the position statements during the term of the lease? What entries would be made if the corporation exercised its option to acquire the building at the end of the term? If the lease were capitalized, what differences would result?

2. Should depreciation of capitalized leased assets be recorded by the lessee? What method of depreciation ought to be used?

3. What are the arguments in favor of recording depreciation on any asset (leased or purchased outright) on a compound interest basis? What are the arguments against using compound interest depreciation? Can these arguments against compound interest be overcome by the way in which the compound interest figures are used? Explain.

PROBLEMS

Evendale Country Club

At the request of its younger members, the club has decided to acquire a number of indoor amusement devices whose installed cost will be $45,000.

This equipment will operate with only minor repair and adjustment costs, but it will need to be generally overhauled and renovated at the end of the third year of service (cost, $5,000); at the end of the sixth year (cost, $8,000); and at the end of the tenth year (cost, $12,000). The equipment will last a total of 15 years, at the end of which time it will be removed at a net salvage recovery of $1,200.

Since the club is financed only by the contributions of its members, and since it owes more than $100,000 on a mortgage loan to build its building, there is a feeling that the indoor recreation should cover all its costs, including interest at the rate being paid on the mortgage, 5% annually.

Compute a level annual charge to be made to the indoor recreation activity, so as to cover interest and depreciation on a 5% basis over the life of this equipment.

Interest Tables
at 5%

F^{-n}	C_n	n
.95238	.95238	1
.90703	1.85941	2
.86384	2.72325	3
.82270	3.54595	4
.78353	4.32948	5
.74622	5.07569	6
.71068	5.78637	7
.67684	6.46321	8
.64461	7.10782	9
.61391	7.72173	10
.48102	10.37966	15

At the end of the third year, the overhaul is found to cost $6,000, instead of the $5,000 expected. A reassessment of the future outlook suggests that the six year renewal will cost $9,000, and the ten year one will cost $14,000. Although interest has been properly figured at 5% for the first three years, it appears that a more realistic view would be to use a 6% rate for this fourth and later years. In any event, the scrap value at the end of the use life of the equipment will be zero, in view of rising labor costs.

Interest Tables
at 6%

F^{-n}	C_n	n
.94340	.94340	1
.89000	1.83339	2
.83962	2.67301	3
.79209	3.46510	4
.74726	4.21236	5
.70496	4.91732	6
.66506	5.58238	7
.62741	6.20979	8
.59190	6.80169	9
.55839	7.36009	10
.41727	9.71225	15

Recalculate and adjust for the changed pattern, in terms of accounting entries for the first three years.

De Coverley Equipment Company

This company has recently acquired a new annealing plant, at a cost of $150,000. In order to finance this equipment, it executed a purchase-money mortgage for this amount at an annual interest rate of 10%. Assuming that this rate represents the company's cost of capital for such equipment, work out depreciation schedules (amortization tables) for a ten year life at 10 percent per year. Assume services to be delivered by the plant will be

a)   at an equal rate each year.
b)   in accordance with the following schedule:

Year	Tons	Year	Tons
1.......	40	6.......	100
2.......	90	7.......	90
3.......	180	8.......	60
4.......	160	9.......	30
5.......	140	10.......	10

The disposal value will be zero at the end of the term.

$$(1.10)^{-1} = .9091 \qquad (1.10)^{-6} = .5645$$
$$(1.10)^{-2} = .8265 \qquad (1.10)^{-7} = .5132$$
$$(1.10)^{-3} = .7513 \qquad (1.10)^{-8} = .4665$$
$$(1.10)^{-4} = .6830 \qquad (1.10)^{-9} = .4241$$
$$(1.10)^{-5} = .6209 \qquad (1.10)^{-10} = .3855$$
$$C_{\overline{10}|} \text{ at 10 percent} = 6.1446$$

Suppose this equipment had been leased over a nine year period at a capital cost of 10% per annum, what would be the annual rental charge, assuming there was no renewal, but an option to purchase for $1,000 at the end of the ninth year?

Write entries to amortize the liability on the lease, and to depreciate the asset over the ten years.

Helton Realty Corporation

This company was formed to acquire a tract of seashore property, and to build a resort hotel in Montresor. The land had been acquired on a thirty-one year lease which called for annual rentals (in advance) of $100,000 per year. The lease was renewable at $150,000 per year for another 31 years. The hotel building took a year to complete; its total cost was $6,000,000, including the first land rent payment and interest during construction on the $6,000,000 bond issue used to finance the building. This bond issue was to be paid off 30 years after the completion of the building, and was sold at par, with interest coupons calling for 5% per year, payable annually. The original shareholder investment ($50,000) had been used entirely for organization costs and legal fees.

When it was completed, the building was leased to "Montresor Helton, Incorporated" for thirty years, at a rental of 40% of the gross revenues, but not less than $400,000 per year, payable each December 31. It was expected that the hotel would have gross revenues of at least $1,800,000 per year under normal circumstances, and the management of the Realty Corporation considered that this, like other similar investments, should return 10% to cover the cost of capital and investment risk.

At the end of the first year, the hotel had gross revenue of $1,600,000. But toward the end of that year, however, the surrounding territory had begun to develop; the management of Helton Realty Corporation believed that these developments warranted an expectation of $1,800,000 revenue from hotel operations in the next year, and $2,000,000 per year in subsequent years.

1. Present a balance sheet for the Helton Realty Corporation as at the *beginning* of hotel operations; (a) in conventional form with leases disclosed by footnotes only, (b) showing leases capitalized within the financial report.

2. At the end of the first year of hotel operations, one of your clients has been approached to buy an interest in the Helton Realty Corporation. He asks you for advice in this situation. Prepare:

    a) A balance sheet in conventional form.

    b) A balance sheet following capitalized lease accounting.

    c) A discounted "cash flow" computation of the value of the investment at 10%.

    d) A "statement of present worths" to give effect to complete revaluation of the Helton Realty Corporation. (Statement of position, using values as discounted at 10%).

	At 10%
An ordinary annuity of 28 payments	9.307
An ordinary annuity of 29 payments	9.370
An ordinary annuity of 30 payments	9.427

	At 5%	At 10%
$1 discounted 30 periods	.23138	.05371
$1 discounted 29 periods	.24295	.06304
$1 discounted 28 periods	.25509	.06934

Chapter 11

THE STATEMENT OF FUNDS

Now that we have reviewed the processes of accounting in sufficient detail to have some idea as to the determination of earnings and financial position, we need to recognize an important gap in the reporting scheme. Despite the fact that accounting provides a record of every transaction that can be measured in money, the reporting forms pay little attention to the amounts, timing, and effects of *financing* transactions. The only things that appear in a statement of earnings are those which affect revenue, expense, or income distributions. And, although the position statement does show the net effect of all transactions upon financial position, it does not show in specific terms how that position was attained. The only item of financial position that is explained by the earnings statement is the amount of the retained earnings; all the asset and equity items other than retained earnings are presented without an explanation of how those amounts came to be.

This is not too surprising in view of the emphasis we have placed upon *economic flows* of resources and commitments. We have not paid much attention to reports that deal with cash receipts and payments—financing transactions. The best way to explain the need for the statement of funds is to review the overall pattern of accounting reports to see what financial information is not presented in position and earnings statements.

Operating versus Cash Transactions

Ever since the beginning our approach has been moving away from the cash flow as a basis for measurement of business events.

245

In our preoccupation with determination of income, we have stressed the need for accrual analysis to reflect properly the flow of economic resources, and we have emphasized that the timing, and to some degree the amounts, of economic service flows are not measured by receipts and payments. This is still true; there can be no doubt whatever that the real content of the transactions of business is modification and transfer of services, goods, rights, and duties; these must be measured when they occur and in terms of what they *involve*, which is only incidentally a matter of cash transfers. We have repeatedly stressed that cash payments typically represent only the settlement of previously existing equities. The creation of those equities was the basis for recognizing cost; and the tracing of costs into various operating charge, expense, or asset classifications was done quite independently of cash transactions— which might either precede, or follow, the cost incurrence.

But in Chapter 10 we recognized the importance of financial transactions and the need for recording and reporting such transactions adequately. For several reasons, this problem is even a bit more important than it seemed there.

Basis for Fund Reports

Accounting statements should, supposedly, present all the important financial information about a firm that can readily be put into concise and direct form. This is certainly achieved in the statement of position and the reported earnings. But these reports omit certain essential data that are needed to see clearly what has happened during the period.

Some transactions are not mentioned specifically in the position or earnings statements at all. Their effects are there, to be sure, but their nature and amount is visible only in asset or equity changes. For example, the acquisition of new plant or equipment would not be reported as a transaction item; of course, the asset amount on the balance sheet would change, but the transaction would have to be inferred from the change in the asset. This could be dealt with by setting up a schedule to show the details of entries in the plant or equipment accounts. But this is not common practice.

Even when the details of asset acquisitions are shown by separate schedules, the full effect of the transaction does not show. Where did the funds come from to finance such expenditures? The same or similar questions could be asked about changes in investment, long-term debt, corporate shares, or other items. Unless the financing aspects of such transactions involve gain or loss (and many of them do not), such transactions do not affect the earnings statement, and they are revealed only partially by tracing balance sheet changes. Sometimes additions and retirements (of unknown amounts) offset each other to further complicate this situation.

Some of these overlooked transactions *do* involve gains or losses and thus get some attention in the report of earnings. The retirement of old plant might result in an adjustment for over- or underdepreciation in prior years, or there might be capital gains or losses from the sale of investments; there may be unamortized discount applicable to bonds retired or interest charges on funds borrowed or lent. But the gain or loss aspect—the earnings effect—is only part of the financing or retirement transaction. The other parts—the amounts borrowed or lent, received from the issuance of shares, the sale of old plant, and so on—do not appear explicitly in the ordinary financial statements.

Lastly (perhaps most important) there is no easy way to see how the operations (sales, expenses, gains, and losses) have affected the position of the firm. Although every transaction may be recorded fully and accurately, it is possible to be confused about the effect of earnings on financial position. Two confusions stand out in this respect. One is the idea that earnings provide money with which the firm may pay for new assets or retire debt or pay dividends. The reader is, of course, aware that this is *not* so; we long since divorced the measurement of income from cash receipts and payments. But many people who think they understand accounting have the idea that "profits provide funds"! Actually, some revenues do not bring in money in the same period as the sale; and many expenses do not involve payments in the same period. Some costs (like payroll) lag a little; others (like materials, supplies and miscellaneous services) may lag a month or two; but still others, like depreciation, are amortizations of cash outlays made years ago. Thus income does not represent funds because neither expense nor revenue is timed concurrently with cash events. Perhaps the greatest confusion in this respect is that, somehow, depreciation is a source of funds. Of course, this is nonsense; for if it were true, there could never be any shortage of cash for any purpose, as long as we could make another or a larger depreciation entry!

Problems of this kind make it essential that some kind of report be used to show financial ebbs and flows in such a way that readers may understand the nature and amount of such transactions as are not clearly reported by the conventional position and earnings statements.

Resource Flows

To approach the fund statement logically we need to go back to some basic concepts. We saw in Chapter 2 that accounting quantifies resource flows by using money measures (adjusted for proper timing) of transactions. The diagram presented at that time, however, showed only one cycle of input and output—the

FIGURE 11–1

Financial Cycles in a Firm

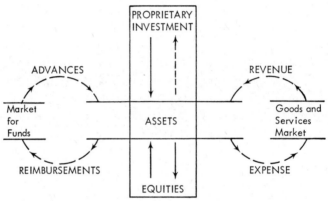

revenue-expense pattern. Assets and equities were then pictured as more or less incidental or static items, taking up the slack and absorbing the differences in timing as resources were put through the operating cycle.

That diagram may now be expanded to emphasize the financing flows in the firm, and a more realistic pattern can be seen in Figure 11–1.

In this diagram, the position of the *revenue and expense* cycle is placed parallel to that of the *financing* cycle which represents short- and long-term credit. Proprietary investment is shown as a separate and different item because of its residual equity and indefinite term features (note the *dotted* line pointing upwards in the diagram). However, the financing cycle is similar to the revenue-expense cycle in that advances are matched with reimbursements in much the same fashion as are revenues and expenses. At the close of any given period of time there may be assets in the firm arising from financing as well as from revenues and expense; equities may arise because of the timing of reimbursements after the close of the period, just as deferred revenue is set up to recognize the liability to deliver service in a future period.

Internal Cycles

Business resources circulate, not only in terms of the cycles shown in the diagram but also within the firm. Assets may be converted to other assets; receivables are collected; materials and other costs are accumulated into work in process and finished goods inventories; plant and equipment is converted through current operations to other forms, on the way to ultimate expense recognition. Thus there are asset conversions within the firm itself.

In addition, there may be transactions to replace one equity with another. Short-term bank loans may be converted to mortgages, or old bond issues replaced by new ones. Bonds may be converted into preferred shares, or either of these to common shares. Stock splits, rights, warrants, and dividends in shares may occur, all of which may change the existing pattern of equities.

Collection of Flow Data

The reader will recall that in order to present earnings statement data in detail, we established a set of cumulative or flow accounts so that the retained earnings balance could remain unchanged throughout the period. Those transactions which would affect the current earnings were set up in these flow accounts for the current period; at the close of the period these flow accounts were set back to zero, their balances transferred into Retained Earnings by closing entries.

We could, if we chose, do this same thing not only with Retained Earnings but also with every balance sheet item; thus we could collect the details of transactions that changed the amounts of plant, bonds payable, or any other asset or equity; and we could make up another financial report from these data that would explain every balance sheet item. This would be cumbersome because of the large number of accounts involved, however; some other method of accumulating the flow data must be devised.

Relevance of Detail

One of the reasons why such series of flow accounts are not set up for every balance sheet item is that some of the internal cycles of financing are quite detailed without being especially informative. For instance, there would be many payments to creditors or employees for merchandise or services; these details are not really of much interest since their aggregate amounts are fairly well portrayed in the earnings statement as merchandise and payroll costs. Although the timing and amounts would be slightly different as between expense and disbursements, the difference is not usually large enough to be of great consequence. Similarly, for overall reporting, the collections from customers do not represent a drastically different figure from the net revenue. Most transactions that involve only current asset and current debt accounts are of this nature: they are fairly well reflected in the earnings statement, and they represent large numbers of routine transactions which if reported would not add much to the information already conveyed in the earnings report. To emphasize this, consider the pattern of materials transactions in a manufacturing firm: goods are received and recorded as inventory, credited to current payables; settlement for these purchases reduces the payables and cash in bank; issues from stores are charged as manufacturing costs, credited to inventory; assignment of costs to product calls for Work in Process debits, credited to Manufacturing Cost Applied; when products are finished, there will be transfer from Work in Process to Finished Goods; finally, the costs of goods sold are credited to Finished Goods account. Only the last transaction is reported in the earnings statement; the others, which are summarized by the last transaction, represent details useful to management, but they are not significant overall enterprise changes. For these reasons, we choose to establish the funds statement to report changes in net working capital, leaving the intraworking capital transactions *out* of the report.

Changes in Net Working Capital

There is, however, another reason to emphasize net working capital changes in the fund statement. A while back, we pointed out that the relation between income and cash was remote and that depreciation could not provide funds. However, the income transactions *do* affect net working capital. Nearly every item in the income statement has a direct effect upon net working capital. Revenues are recorded by increases in Customer Accounts Receivable; expenses are mostly reductions of inventories and prepayments or they are accompanied by direct cash disbursements or the incurrence of current debt. In any case, the earnings report reflects much of the net working capital change.

This is even true for depreciation; although it is absurd to suggest that depreciation provides cash, it is absolutely true that depreciation provides services from long-term assets to be used for current purposes. Depreciation of plant buildings and machinery is part of Work in Process, Finished Goods, and Cost of Goods Sold; depreciation of office equipment is recorded as a current operating charge (Selling, General Administration Cost), later transferred to expense. The reports merely omit the transfer from fixed asset to current status.

An Analytical Methodology

Since we have decided not to use detailed flow accounts in the collection of financing data, we must get the essential information

FIGURE 11–2

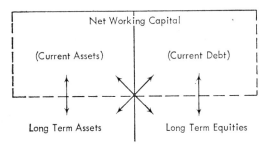

from some other source. We have decided to emphasize net working capital rather than cash flows because we wish to omit tedious intra-working capital details. Thus, we must locate and identify net working capital changes within the nonworking capital accounts.

This, however, is exactly as it should be. Net working capital can change only when there is some accompanying change in long-term assets or long-term equities. Figure 11–2 may help to make this more clear.

Each arrow indicates the debit-credit effect of a transaction that changes the net working capital. If we could locate these transactions we could get the data to explain the financing flows over the fiscal period.

Methodology.   Since the transactions of the year are recorded in the usual ways, we make no change in procedure. But, at the end of the year, we may go back and pick up, by analysis of the long-term asset and equity accounts, those transactions which did affect net working capital. For example, we may have in the Plant and Equipment account the following data:

Plant and Equipment

Jan. 1	450,000		
May 31	15,000	Apr. 30	10,000
June 30	50,000		

Tracing back these data to the original evidences (journal or vouchers) we find that the item of May 31 was the purchase of a new machine to replace the one scrapped on April 30. The $50,000 item on June 30 is a building addition, financed by $10,000 cash and a four-year installment loan for the balance. The scrapping of the old machine involved only a debit to the Allowance for Depreciation, since it had been fully depreciated. Thus, there are two financing transactions here, the first a current debt (working capital) acquisition, the second affecting long-term debt as well as net working capital.

Analytical Work Accounts

In preparing a fund statement we want to make an analysis of each long-term asset or equity account. In order to do this and have some check on the completeness of our analysis, we use skeleton accounts of a special kind shown in Figure 11–3.

The net debit or credit *change* in the account over the period is written in as shown. Then, as the analysis proceeds, we can tell

FIGURE 11–3

Plant and Equipment

55,000	

when we have located all of the data we want. If we use an account like this for each noncurrent item in the balance sheet, we know what changes are to be traced. We may also set up a skeleton account for net working capital changes, in which we will record the data that will be shown in the fund statement. The procedure is best demonstrated by the use of an illustration.

Illustrative Analysis of Net Working Capital Changes

In Figure 11–4 appears the conventional position statement and earnings report for the Illustrative Company and certain supplementary and explanatory data.

To prepare the statement of funds, we shall set up special skeleton work accounts of the sort described for each of the noncurrent assets and equities, plus another for "Net Working Capital Changes." The accounts appear on page 258; for the moment we will discuss the entries to be made in those accounts and show them as we go along in journal form. Then their effect may be seen in the work accounts when we need to deal with the aggregated data. Since the details to be recorded in these skeleton work accounts are most numerous with respect to Net Working Capital Changes and Retained Earnings, those two skeleton work accounts are drawn to larger scale.

We shall take the earnings statement as a starting point, for, as we have already noted, perhaps the most important of the effects upon net working capital is that shown by revenues and expenses. The first issue to be met is just which of the figures in the statement of earnings should be used to show the effect of regular customer operations in the fund statement. The most satisfactory answer to this is to use the operating net margin, $885,000. This has the disadvantage of forcing us to report interest and dividend income in the fund statement as a separate item, even though it appears in the income statement. However, the gain on the sale of plant could not be reported in the fund statement as such (the proceeds from the sale and the effect on working capital are *not* $31,000 as reported in the income statement); since we must adjust this latter item, it is just as well to start the fund statement with the net operating margin figure. The entry required to put this into our work sheet is:

(1)

Changes in Net Working Capital...................	885,000	
Retained Earnings................................		885,000

FIGURE 11–4

ILLUSTRATIVE COMPANY

Comparative Position Statement
As at December 31

Working Capital	19x0	19x1	Increase
Current Assets:			
Cash and cash items..................	$ 917,000	$ 500,000	$417,000*
Receivables (net)....................	1,077,000	1,092,000	15,000
Inventories.........................	1,240,000	1,512,000	272,000
Total Current Assets............	$3,234,000	$3,104,000	$130,000*
Current Debt:			
Accounts payable....................	$ 234,000	$ 306,000	$ 72,000
Dividends payable...................	45,000	40,500	4,500*
Accrued wages, etc..................	101,000	112,000	11,000
Estimated income taxes..............	150,000	225,000	75,000
Total Current Debt..............	$ 530,000	$ 683,500	$153,000
Net Working Capital...........	$2,704,000	$2,420,500	$283,500*
Investments.........................	100,000	505,500	405,000
Plant and equipment.................	3,491,000	3,023,000	468,000*
Accumulated depreciation..............	1,260,000*	1,105,000*	155,000*
Goodwill and organization costs..........	516,000	280,000	236,000*
Total Working Capital and Other Assets................	$5,551,000	$5,124,000	$427,000*
Long-Term Equities:			
Preferred shares.....................	$1,000,000	$ 700,000	$300,000*
Common shares......................	2,750,000	3,013,000	263,000
Retained earnings..............	1,801,000	1,411,000	390,000*
Total Long-Term Equities...............	$5,551,000	$5,124,000	$427,000*

* Deduction.

ILLUSTRATIVE COMPANY

Earnings Statement (Condensed)
Year Ended December 31, 19x1

Revenue...............................		$6,105,000	
Expense...............................		5,220,000	
Operating net margin......................		$ 885,000	
Add interest and dividend income...........	$33,000		
Gain, sale of plant......................	31,000	64,000	$ 949,000
Deduct, loss, sale of securities..............			86,000
Income subject to federal taxes.............			$ 863,000
Federal income taxes.....................			442,000
Balance for stockholders...............			$ 421,000
Dividends, preferred shares...............		$ 65,000	
Dividends, common shares.................		256,000	321,000
Transfer to retained earnings...........			$ 100,000
Add retained earnings, beginning of year......			1,801,000
Total..........................			$1,901,000
Deduct:			
Write-off of goodwill...................		$ 212,000	
Dividend in common shares..............		275,000	
Common shares retired..................		3,000	490,000
Balance of Retained Earnings, End of Year....			$1,411,000

FIGURE 11–4 (*Continued*)

Other Information

The gain on sale of plant arose from disposition of land, buildings, and equipment no longer required for operations because the product involved had been discontinued. Proceeds from the sale were $119,000 cash and $400,000 in 5 percent mortgage notes of the purchasing company. These mortgage notes were charged to the Investments account. Allowance for depreciation on the building and equipment sold was $280,000 at the date of sale.

Loss on sale of securities arose from the retirement of $300,000 of preferred stock by delivering to the former preferred shareholders various investment securities having a cost of $386,000.

Goodwill written off was that associated with the product discontinued and was charged directly to Retained Earnings account. This write-off was entirely separate from the amortization of organization costs amounting to $24,000 charged to operating expense. Operating expense also included $125,000 of depreciation for the year.

The secretary of this company retired during the year. The company purchased the common stock owned by the former secretary for $15,000 cash.

There were additions to plant and equipment during the year amounting to $300,000, and investments were made in various affiliated companies which amounted to $391,500.

Interest and dividend income is added to the work sheet by the following:

(2)

Changes in Net Working Capital........................	33,000	
Interest and Dividend Income......................		33,000

The entry that was made to record the sale of plant and equipment can be reconstructed from the data given. The charges are to Cash, $119,000; mortgage notes charged to Investments, $400,000; Allowance for Depreciation, $280,000. The credits are: Gain from the Sale of Plant, $31,000; and Plant and Equipment, for the difference between the charges and the gain, $768,000. This entry is put into the skeleton accounts:

(3)

Changes in Net Working Capital........................	119,000	
Investments...	400,000	
Accumulated Depreciation............................	280,000	
Retained Earnings................................		31,000
Plant and Equipment.............................		768,000

The transaction resulting in the "loss on sale of securities" was recorded:

(4)

Preferred Shares.....................................	300,000	
Loss on Sale of Securities...........................	86,000	
Investments......................................		386,000

This entry is put into the skeleton accounts to complete the record, even though it did not affect net working capital (see entry 7).

The charge for federal income taxes produced a reduction in net working capital, even though the taxes were not paid in full; the credit to a current debt account reduces net working capital just as definitely as does a cash payment. Thus, the working capital effect of income taxes is properly shown by the entry:

(5)

Retained Earnings....................................	442,000	
Changes in Net Working Capital...................		442,000

Similarly, the dividends declared are brought into the solution:

(6)

Retained Earnings....................................	321,000	
Changes in Net Working Capital...................		321,000

The goodwill written off was merely charged to Retained Earnings; the entry made for this write-off was:

(7)

Retained Earnings....................................	212,000	
Goodwill and Organization Costs..................		212,000

Entry 7, as well as entry 4 dealing with preferred stock retirement, does not show any effect on net working capital, and none of these figures will appear in the funds statement. These entries are made here only to fill in all the gaps in the accounts so we can be sure that all pertinent data are considered.

The write-off of organization costs of $24,000 does not appear explicitly in the earnings statement because this charge was combined with operating expenses. This increased expenses and reduced net operating margin, even though it did *not* affect working capital. Thus, our use of $885,000 in entry 1 as the effect of net operating margin on the net working capital was too small by $24,000. This is adjusted by making the following entry:

(8)

Changes in Net Working Capital......................	24,000	
Goodwill and Organization Costs..................		24,000

What has been said about the write-off of organization costs is equally true of the depreciation charge. We have used the net operating income of $885,000 to portray the effect of regular operations on net working capital. However, the depreciation—however real it is from any viewpoint—did *not* reduce the net working capital. Thus we make allowance for this by the entry:

(9)

Changes in Net Working Capital......................	125,000	
Accumulated Depreciation.......................		125,000

It should be noted that the two entries just presented for organization costs and for depreciation are, like the rest of the entries being made here, exact counterparts of the transactions as originally recorded. Even though it is true that there were charges made to operating accounts rather than to net working capital, we have treated the operating accounts as if they were working capital items by using the net operating margin figure to represent all revenue and expense accounts. Further, it should be noted that depreciation would in a manufacturing firm be carried into inventory and cost of goods sold; the charge to inventory is a charge to a current asset account. Unless the depreciation and similar amortizations charged to expense are handled in the manner shown here, it is necessary to restate the entire income statement so as to exclude those items which did not affect net working capital. This would mean that in the presentation of expense the depreciation and amortization charges would be excluded, which is arithmetically the same as has been done here.

The retirement of common shares is reflected by the entry:

(10)

Common Shares...................................	12,000	
Retained Earnings................................	3,000	
Changes in Net Working Capital.................		15,000

The amount paid for the shares was $15,000, but only the excess over the legal or stated amount was charged to retained earnings. This is as it should be for the legal equity was retired. However, net working capital was reduced by the cash payment of $15,000.

Common shares issued as dividends increased the amount of common shares outstanding and capitalized part of the retained earnings. This entry did not affect net working capital but is put into the work sheet to maintain the completeness of the data:

(11)

Retained Earnings................................	275,000	
Common Shares..............................		275,000

Additions to the Plant and Equipment and to the Investments during the year are reflected as follows:

(12)

Plant and Equipment..............................	300,000	
Changes in Net Working Capital.................		300,000

(13)

Investments......................................	391,500	
Changes in Net Working Capital.................		391,500

All the entries presented above (nos. 1–13) would appear in the skeleton accounts as shown below. The items have been keyed by number to the entries, and those in the Changes in Net Working Capital and in the Retained Earnings accounts are labeled in detail. The reader may see for himself the difference in these two accounts, which reflects the difference between the statement of income and retained earnings and the fund statement.

Changes in Net Working Capital

			$283,500		
Net operating margin	(1)	885,000	Federal income taxes	(5)	442,000
Interest and dividends	(2)	33,000	Dividends declared	(6)	321,000
Plant and equipment sale	(3)	119,000	Common shares retired	(11)	15,000
Organization costs	(8)	24,000	New plant and equipment	(12)	300,000
Depreciation	(9)	125,000	New investments	(13)	391,500

Investments

$405,500			
(3)	400,000	(4)	386,000
(13)	391,500		

Plant and Equipment

		$468,000	
(12)	300,000	(3)	768,000

Allowance for Depreciation

$155,000			
(3)	280,000	(9)	125,000

Goodwill and Organization Costs

		$236,000	
		(7)	212,000
		(8)	24,000

Preferred Shares

$300,000			
(4)	300,000		

Common Shares

		$263,000	
(11)	12,000	(10)	275,000

Retained Earnings

$390,000					
Loss, sale of securities	(4)	86,000	Net operating margin	(1)	885,000
Federal income taxes	(5)	442,000	Interest and dividends	(2)	23,000
Dividends	(6)	321,000	Gain on sale of plant	(3)	31,000
Write-off goodwill	(7)	212,000			
Dividends in common shares	(10)	275,000			
Retirement of common stock	(11)	3,000			

The changes in the net working capital and those in the long-term asset and equity items are recorded as equal debits and credits in the skeleton accounts. The individual debit changes are: $405,500 + $155,000 + $300,000 + $390,000, a total of $1,250,500. Credit items are $283,500 + $468,000 + $236,000 + $263,000, a total of $1,250,500. The transactions that have been entered in the body of the accounts exactly match the changes over the year. Thus, we are reasonably sure that no essential items have been overlooked. The fund statement therefore may be made up from the Changes in Net Working Capital account. The formal statement is shown in Figure 11–5.

FIGURE 11–5

ILLUSTRATIVE COMPANY

Statement of Funds

Year Ended December 31, 19x1

(Statement of Changes in Net Working Capital)

Net working capital was increased by:		
Regular operations, through—		
Operating net margin......................		$ 885,000
Amortization of organization costs..................		24,000
Depreciation charges.................		125,000
Interest and dividend income...........		33,000
Proceeds, sale of retired plant and		
equipment........................		119,000
Gross increase in net working capital..................		$1,186,000
Net working capital was decreased by:		
Federal income taxes............................	$442,000	
Dividends declared.............................	321,000	
Common shares retired............................	15,000	
New plant and equipment..........................	300,000	
New investments in affiliated companies................	391,500	
Total Decreases in Net Working Capital.............		1,469,500
Net Decrease in Net Working Capital for the Year.....		$ 283,500

It should be noted that the statement presented here has been subtitled "statement of changes in net working capital," and that it does in fact end with the decrease in net working capital as shown in the comparative balance sheet. There is in this case no need to present a detailed schedule of net working capital items because the comparative balance sheet is drawn to show those data directly.

Summary

The fund statement is a useful device to supplement the statement of income in presenting narratively the financial operations of the period. Financing transactions of importance are put into proper perspective to explain the change in net working capital more fully than could be done by the income statement alone.

The statement of funds is much like a derived statement of cash receipts and disbursements. The method of preparing it is an extension of conventional "cumulation account" technique which is easily applied in skeleton accounts on a simple work sheet. After this process is understood, it would be easy to pick out those transactions which belong in the fund statement by mere inspection of the noncurrent asset and equity accounts.

Some question may be raised about certain transactions that have been excluded from the statement of funds. In this illustrative case the retirement of the preferred shares does not appear in the report because there was no effect upon net working capital from that transaction. One could argue that this is an important financial transaction, even though it had no effect upon net working capital; perhaps one might feel that it really ought to be included in the report. The question can be answered best in terms of the judgment of the accountant. There are transactions of importance that are not forced into the mold of formal reporting by mere rules and definitions. There is no harm in admitting that what is done in accounting reports is partly a matter of judgment. Certainly no report can do everything, nor is it always true that everything must be done according to rule. The professional position of the accountant does not rest on procedures and processes but on the use to be made of them. The usefulness of the statement of funds must be its justification.

QUESTIONS

1. One notion about the statement of funds is that it summarizes the cash transactions of the firm; another is that it explains what has happened to profits. Is either of these statements entirely true? What is the purpose of the statement of funds?

2. The statement of funds really encompasses all the transactions of the firm during the fiscal period; even the data reported in the statement of earnings are included, at least in summary terms. Is this statement correct? What kinds of transactions are specifically excluded from the statement, and why?

3. Why is the statement of funds typically set up so as to use the net change in net working capital as the balancing or concluding figure? Could this balancing figure be some other amount, say the change in the amount of cash and receivables (combined)?

4. Why is depreciation added back to the income figure in the statement of funds? Does this not indicate that depreciation is only a "book entry" which has no real effect? What other kinds of items should be treated in the same way as depreciation? Why are such items added back if they are really required to compute income?

5. With full disclosure by the use of footnotes or other explanations, any reader of a properly set up comparative position statement and earnings report can prepare a statement of funds without access to company records. Explain how this can be done, using skeleton accounts to arrange and classify the data.

6. In preparation of a statement of funds by the use of skeleton accounts, why are there no skeleton accounts for cash, receivables, inventory, and current debt items? If we are trying to explain the changes in net working capital, how can we refuse to look at the changes *within* the net working capital accounts?

7. Where in the statement of funds would a transaction such as writing off Goodwill against Additional Paid-In Capital (Paid-In Surplus) appear? This entry would necessarily have to show in the skeleton accounts (why?); should it not then have to be reported in the statement of funds?

8. The state of Mantaria deeded to the Rural Electric Power Co-operative a plot of land encompassing a water fall to be used for hydroelectric power production. The land was valued at $2,000,000, and the transaction was recorded as a credit to Capital Contributions in Aid of Construction, a long-term equity account. In the statement of funds for the cooperative at the end of the first year, would this grant appear? Why?

9. Castle Inn Foods, Incorporated, located a canning plant in the city of Matsonville because the city gave the company a building and land which had been forfeited for nonpayment of taxes. The city had bought the property at a tax sale for $23,000. The gift was conditional upon the company's providing employment at current pay rates for at least 300 people over a five-year period, after which title to the property would be transferred. Castle Inn Foods remodeled the building at a cost of $15,000 and installed new equipment in order to carry on regular processing operations on a year-round basis. At the end of the first year, the remodeled plant was appraised by the American Appraisal Company at net reproduction cost of $49,875, of which the land represented one seventh. The building was expected to last another 19 years.

   a) Is the building an asset of the Castle Inn Company? If it is, what is its cost? If not, how would one compare the cost of operating this plant with that of other plants?

b) How, if at all, would the plant assets (land, building [reno-
vated], and equipment) appear in the statement of funds?
Where would the depreciation charges appear in the statement
of funds?

10. Does a stock dividend appear in a report of earnings? In a statement of funds? Is it *explicitly* reported in the position statement?
If your answers to these questions are negative, how would such a
transaction be reported?

11. The practice of adding back depreciation and other long-term
amortizations to net income in order to show the effect of profit-
oriented operations upon net working capital has aided, if not pre-
cipitated, the notion of "cash flow" used by financial analysts as a
measure of company activity. This notion has even been described
as "cash earnings" by people who ought to know better. Typically,
this figure is established by adding back only depreciation and depletion. Why is it misleading to describe such a figure as "cash flow"
or "cash earnings"? If the figure so calculated was merely labeled
"net earnings before depreciation and depletion," would it still be
misleading?

12. Institutions such as hospitals are sometimes described as "nonprofit"
organizations. Would such an enterprise have no need for a report
of earnings? At the recent annual meeting, the directors of the Community Hospital learned that the enterprise had earned a profit of
$20,000 in maintaining operations which had grossed $2,000,000 in
fees, board and room, and pharmacy sales. One member of the
board suggested that a check for $20,000 should be sent to the
Charity Crusade because the hospital was not intended to "make
money" for anybody. But the bank deposit account was only $3,000
and the weekly payroll of approximately $22,000 was due in five
days. Another member of the board suggested that the only way
to meet the payroll was to borrow; the bank of which he was president would lend the money by discounting a $22,200 note signed
by the hospital officers for 60 days at 6 percent yer pear. A third
member of the board objected that this was tantamount to borrowing money to give it away, which he believed not to be the function
of a Community Hospital. The accountant presented a statement
of funds to assist in clearing up matters. What items do you think
were in the statement of funds that helped the directors to understand the situation? Does this suggest that a report of earnings ought
not be prepared for a "nonprofit" organization?

PROBLEMS

Morton Products Company

Comparative balance sheets and the report of earnings for the past year appear below. Recast these data to make up a statement of funds.

Comparative Balance Sheets (000 omitted)

	Last Year	This Year	Change
Cash and bank deposits..................	$ 250	$ 100	$ 150
Accounts receivable....................	1,750	1,900	150
Inventory............................	4,000	5,350	1,350
Prepayments.........................	30	40	10
Total current assets.............	$ 6,030	$ 7,390	$1,360
Accounts payable.....................	1,450	1,150	300
Current bank loans....................	700	500	200
Taxes, interest & payrolls payable........	110	170	60
Total current debt..............	$ 2,260	$ 1,820	$ 440
Net working capital.................	$ 3,770	$ 5,570	$1,800
Other assets:			
Plant and equipment (net).............	$ 6,900	$ 9,000	$2,100
Investments in other companies........	950	2,400	1,450
Total net working capital and			
other assets.................	$11,620	$16,970	$5,350
Financed by:			
Bonds payable, due 1984..............	$ 3,500	$ 5,200	$1,700
Common shares $100 par..............	7,000	9,800	2,800
Retained earnings....................	1,120	1,970	850
Total Financing.................	$11,620	$16,970	$5,350

Statement of Earnings (000 omitted)

Sales revenue...........................		$9,260
Costs other than depreciation..............	$7,060	
Depreciation..........................	430	7,490
Operating margin.................		1,770
Interest charges........................	$ 200	
Income and other taxes..................	320	
Dividends............................	400	
Total distributions................		920
Increased Retained Earnings..............		$ 850

The Walton Company

Comparative Trial Balances

	This Year	Last Year	Increase (Decrease)
Cash in bank.............	$ 5,000	$ 20,000	$(15,000)
Receivables (net).........	25,000	30,000	(5,000)
Inventories..............	50,000	40,000	10,000
Plant....................	120,000	100,000	20,000
Allowance for depreciation............	42,000	45,000	(3,000)
	$158,000	$145,000	13,000
Current debt.............	$ 60,000	$ 80,000	$(20,000)
Mortgage payable.........	28,000	10,000	18,000
Common shares...........	52,000	40,000	12,000
Retained earnings........	18,000	15,000	3,000
	$158,000	$145,000	$ 13,000

Statement of Income and Retained Earnings
(Condensed)

Operating net margin..........................		$23,000
Overdepreciation in prior years..................		1,000
Total.................................		$24,000
Less:		
Taxes on income.................	12,000	
Dividends......................	9,000	21,000
Net Increase in Retained Earnings...............		$ 3,000

(1) Overdepreciation refers to assets which had cost $12,000 and against which an allowance for depreciation of $11,000 had been accumulated, which were sold for $2,000.

(2) Current year depreciation changed against operating income, $8,000.

Required:

Prepare a Statement of Funds for the Walton Company, using the skeleton account analysis.

Moray Company

Comparative Trial Balances

	December 31		Increase
	1954	*1953*	*(Decrease)*
Cash.........................	$ 38,000	$ 41,000	$ (3,000)
Accounts receivable............	65,000	35,000	30,000
Inventories....................	175,000	100,000	75,000
Prepaid expenses..............	7,000	4,000	3,000
Investments...................		60,000	(60,000)
Land.........................	70,000	40,000	30,000
Buildings.....................	160,000	80,000	80,000
Machinery and equipment.......	180,000	120,000	60,000
	$695,000	$480,000	$215,000
Allowance for uncollectibles.....	$ 2,000	$ 1,000	$ 1,000
Accumulated depreciation......	55,000	35,000	20,000
Accounts payable..............	48,000	34,000	14,000
Notes payable (due in 1958).....	40,000	——	40,000
Common stock................	400,000	300,000	100,000
Retained earnings.............	150,000	110,000	40,000
	$695,000	$480,000	$215,000

Income Statement
For Year Ending December 31, 1954

Sales (net)...		$200,000
Less:		
Operating expenses*......................	$107,000	
Gain on sale of investments................	3,000	
Loss on sale of machinery†................	1,000	
Income taxes............................	35,000	140,000
Net profit to stockholders................................		$ 60,000
Dividends...		20,000
Increase in Retained Earnings............................		$ 40,000

* Includes $25,000 of depreciation.
† Cost $8,000, cash proceeds of sale $2,000.

Required:

Using the above information prepare a Funds Statement.

Maree Company

From the following, prepare a Funds Statement.

Balance Sheet Data

	January 1	December 31	Increase (Decrease)
Current assets........................	$ 600,000	$ 750,000	$150,000
Investments..........................	800,000	600,000	(200,000)
Plant...............................	1,100,000	1,450,000	350,000
Goodwill............................	500,000	200,000	(300,000)
Total Debits.....................	$3,000,000	$3,000,000	0
Current debt........................	$ 300,000	400,000	$100,000
Accumulated depreciation..............	470,000	500,000	30,000
Mortgages...........................	200,000	300,000	100,000
Common shares.......................	1,200,000	1,500,000	300,000
Retained earnings.....................	830,000	300,000	(530,000)
Total Credits....................	$3,000,000	$3,000,000	0

Analysis of Retained Earnings

Balance, January 1...	$830,000	
Add net operating margin (after $60,000 depreciation)......	20,000	
Gain on sale of investments...........................	14,000	
Total...		$864,000
Deduct:		
Loss on sale of plant (original cost $100,000)..............	$ 16,000	
Income taxes..	10,000	
Goodwill write-down................................	300,000	
Cash dividends..	3,000	
Interest charges......................................	5,000	
Stock dividend.......................................	230,000	564,000
Balance, December 31...................................		$300,000

Anderson Manufacturing Company

From the following post-closing trial balance comparison and the supplementary information, prepare a Statement of Funds for the year.

Debits	January 1	December 31	Increase	Decrease
Cash and bank deposits.............	$ 8,000	$ 10,400	$ 2,400	
Accounts receivable...............	62,000	68,000	6,000	
Notes receivable.................	8,500	7,500		$ 1,000
Inventories......................	214,000	233,500	19,500	
Unexpired insurance..............	650	425		225
Land...........................	25,000	40,000	15,000	
Buildings.......................	140,000	250,000	110,000	
Machinery......................	230,000	417,650	187,650	
Patents........................	20,000	18,000		2,000
Discount on bonds...............		9,500	9,500	
Investment securities.............	16,000			16,000
Organization costs...............	2,000	1,000		1,000
Goodwill.......................	30,000	32,000	2,000	
Total Debits................	$756,150	$1,087,975	$352,050	$ 20,225

Credits			Decrease	Increase
Accounts payable................	$ 77,000	$ 88,000		$ 11,000
Notes payable...................	90,000	80,000	$ 10,000	
Accrued federal tax payable.......	17,000	18,000		1,000
Estimated uncollectibles...........	1,200	1,300		100
Accumulated depreciation.........	147,000	169,000		22,000
Bonds payable...................		200,000		200,000
Common stock..................	200,000	400,000		200,000
Retained earnings................	223,950	131,675	92,275	
Total Credits...............	$756,150	$1,087,975	$102,975	$434,100

(1) The reported net income was $42,725 after interest but before income taxes.

(2) $500 of discount on bonds was amortized into income for the year.

(3) Organization costs of $1,000 were absorbed in current income.

(4) $2,000 of patent cost was charged against operations for the year.

(5) A loss of $100 from the sale of securities was charged to current operations.

(6) Current provisions for depreciation were $28,000.

(7) Common stock of legal value of $100,000 was issued for cash at 98 percent of legal value; the discount was charged to Goodwill.

(8) Machinery that had cost $15,000 and against which depreciation allowances of $4,000 had been set up, was sold for $5,000; the capital loss was absorbed in retained earnings.

(9) An appraisal of land made during the year increased that account $15,000; the credit for this was carried to retained earnings.

(10) Federal income tax accrued for the year, $23,000.

(11) Major overhauls and machinery rehabilitation costs were charged to the Allowance for Depreciation account, $2,000.

(12) The bonds payable were issued at 95 on January 1.

(13) Cash dividends of $21,000 were paid December 19.

Mallee Metals and Materials Corp.

From the following data, prepare a Statement of Funds.

Comparative Balance Sheet

	Last Year	This Year	Change
Assets			
Cash on hand and in banks...............	$ 152,928	$ 221,314	$ 68,386
Notes receivable........................	41,368	85,618	44,250
Accounts receivable (less allowance)......	249,628	378,920	129,292
Due from affiliated companies...........	116,283	146,962	30,679
Inventories............................	896,763	950,319	53,556
Prepayments...........................	29,615	47,837	18,222
Total current assets................	1,486,585	1,830,970	344,385
Investments, affiliated companies.........	643,828	668,828	25,000
Outside investments................	227,396	208,316	19,080*
Land, building, and equipment...........	2,392,875	3,380,317	987,442
Accumulated depreciation.............	465,928*	562,928*	97,000*
Total Assets....................	$4,284,756	$5,525,503	$1,240,747
Equities			
Accounts payable......................	215,962	127,824	88,138*
Notes payable.........................	230,000	170,000	60,000*
Dividends payable.....................	68,048	79,138	11,090
Accrued interest, taxes, etc..............	87,368	96,218	8,850
Total current debt...................	601,378	473,180	128,198*
Ten year 6% bonds payable.............		500,000	500,000
Less unamortized discount..............		36,000*	36,000*
Net Long-Term Debt.............		464,000	464,000
Share equities:			
Preferred stock......................	174,200	236,500	62,300
Common stock.......................	2,600,000	3,000,000	400,000
Capital surplus......................		479,326	479,326
Employee's pensions reserve...........	2,619	3,500	881
Dredging reserve.....................	6,927	7,317	390
Contingency reserve..................	120,615	122,876	2,261
Retained earnings, unappropriated.......	779,017	738,805	40,212*
Total share equities..............	3,683,378	4,588,324	904,946
Total All Equities.....................	$4,284,756	$5,525,503	$1,240,747

* Deduction

The following additional data are to be used with the trial balances on the first page, to prepare a Statement of Funds.

(1) The Net Income for the year, as carried to Retained Earnings, was $754,467.

(2) At the beginning of the year, $500,000 of 10 year 6% bonds were issued at 92.

(3) Outside Investments included stock in Ballarat Brewing Company; this had cost $55,000. This company failed during the year, and the stock was sold for $5,000. The loss was charged to Reserve for Contingencies. Certain other investments carried in this account at $10,000 were found worthless, but the loss was absorbed

in current income. Other changes in this account may be attributed to sales of securities at their book value of $15,000, and the acquisition of other new securities.

(4) The plant and works of the company were appraised at the beginning of this year. Recording this appraisal resulted in a write-up of $496,452, the credit for which was carried to Capital Surplus. Extensive additions and improvements were made from the proceeds of the bond issue.

(5) Depreciation was computed on the appraised plant amounts, and amounted to $132,717 for the year. $17,126 of this, however, was depreciation on appreciation, and was credited back to income by charging capital surplus.

(6) A storehouse had to be torn down and removed to make way for new building. The cost of the storehouse ($30,000) had been entirely written off in depreciation charges, and the salvage proceeds were exactly equal to the costs of removal.

(7) Actual expenditures for renewals and replacements amounted to $5,717; these were charged directly to the Allowance for Depreciation.

(8) In addition to the loss on the Ballarat Brewing Stock charged to the Reserve for Contingencies, there was also debited to that account a prior year Federal Tax assessment amounting to $47,739. As a result of these unusual charges, the directors voted to transfer $100,000 of Retained Earnings to the Reserve for Contingencies. A charge of $1,200 was made against the Employees Pension Reserve, and $4,560 was charged against the Dredging Reserve.

(9) On July 1, a dividend of common shares was voted, which increased the amount of common stock outstanding to $3,000,000.

(10) Cash dividend transactions were:

Preferred	Common	Date Declared	Date Payable
$3,048	$65,000	Dec. 31, last year	January 15
3,325	65,000	March 31	April 15
3,500	65,000	June 30	July 15
3,717	75,000	Sept. 30	October 15
4,138	75,000	Dec. 31	January 15 next year.

Hector and Bramble Company

Comparative Position Statement (in thousands)

Assets

	1968	1969
Current Assets		
Cash...	$ 34,939	$ 38,612
Government securities held to cover income taxes.......	63,683	67,379
Other Marketable Securities (at cost, approx. market).....	250,439	310,588
Accounts receivable (less reserves)...................	85,074	108,889
Inventories (lower of cost—partly lifo—or market)......	218,087	240,939
Total Current Assets........................	$ 652,222	$ 766,407
Property, Plant & Equipment, at cost		
Land...	$ 19,684	$ 21,480
Timberlands, less depletion.........................	18,738	17,888
Buildings and equipment...........................	659,892	705,964
Total......................................	$ 698,314	$ 745,332
Less accumulated depreciation..................	251,206	281,962
Net Property, Plant & Equipment....................	$ 447,107	$ 463,370
Other Assets		
Sundry investments, loans and receivables.............	$ 19,066	$ 22,860
Goodwill, patents, licenses...........................	25,620	25,620
Prepaid expenses and deferred charges................	13,865	14,457
Total other assets...............................	$ 58,551	$ 62,937
Total Assets..............................	$1,157,880	$1,292,713

Liabilities

	1968	1969
Current Liabilities		
Debt due within one year...........................	$ 13,853	$ 18,045
Accounts payable and accruals.......................	114,574	126,261
Federal taxes on income............................	63,683	67,379
Other taxes......................................	32,620	33,553
Total Current Liabilities.....................	$ 224,730	$ 245,238
Long-Term Debt		
Debentures, 3⅞% due 1972–1986...................	$ 60,075	$ 60,075
Notes, 3¼% due 1971–77..........................	23,760	20,790
Debt of foreign subsidiaries due 1970–1989.............	23,645	26,005
Total Long-Term Debt.......................	$ 107,480	$ 106,870
Reserves		
Self-insured risks.................................	$ 3,923	$ 4,006
Foreign exchange fluctuations.......................	1,900	1,900
Deferred income taxes.............................	36,446	42,318
Total Reserves.............................	$ 42,269	$ 48,224
Capital and Retained Earnings		
Preferred shares ($50 par)...........................	$ 2,250	$ 2,250
Common shares ($1 par)............................	42,066	43,629
Additional paid-in capital..........................	81,654	113,428
Earnings retained in the business....................	657,431	733,074
Total capital and retained earnings..............	$ 783,401	$ 892,381
Total Liabilities and Capital........................	$1,157,880	$1,292,713

Statement of Earnings (in thousands)

Year Ended June 30, 1968 and 1969

	1968	*1969*
Income:		
Net Sales.......................................	$1,654,462	$1,913,722
Interest and Other Income...........................	13,300	15,206
Total Income..............................	$1,667,762	$1,928,928

Costs and Expenses:

Cost of Products Sold.	$1,005,250	$1,190,061
Marketing, General and Administration.	416,301	467,602
Interest Expense.	5,339	5,841
Other Charges.	817	1,502
Federal and Foreign Income Taxes.	124,290	133,110
Total Costs and Expenses.	$1,551,997	$1,798,116
Net Earnings.	$ 115,765	$ 130,811

Distribution of Net Earnings:

Common Dividends.	$ 65,142	$ 71,904
Preferred Dividends.	180	180
Dividends of Subsidiary Prior to Acq'n.	—	1,644
Retained in the Business.	50,443	57,083
Total Distributions of Income.	$ 115,765	$ 130,811

(1) Accumulated earnings retained in the business were increased $18,560 by the addition of the prior year retained earnings of the acquired company; the pooling also increased the Common Shares stated value by $1,650 and the Additional Paid-in Capital by $40,139.

(2) Depreciation for 1969 was $31,020 on a straight-line basis. A tax reduction of $6,807 resulting from the use of accelerated depreciation and guideline lives for tax purposes has been offset by additional provision for taxes on income. The reserve for deferred income taxes as shown in the balance sheet reflects the cumulative tax reductions to date, and it will be held for possible use in future years when depreciation charges for tax purposes may be lower than the straight-line charges made on the books.

(3) The investment credit under the revenue act of 1969 has been included in net earnings. The amount of credit which was included in the reserve for deferred income taxes at June 30, 1968 has also been credited to current earnings. These amounts were considered not material.

(4) During the year, options were granted for 37,650 shares of common stock at $77⅛ and 54,000 shares at $79.25; options for 30,250 shares were exercised at the average of $35.07 a share, and options for 2,090 shares were cancelled. At June 30, 1969, 208,555 shares were issuable under outstanding options. There were 167,170 shares available for granting options at June 30, 1968, and 77,610 at June 30, 1969.

(5) A total of 117,000 shares of common stock were purchased for option and other purposes during 1969.

Required:

Prepare a Statement of Funds, in which the effects of pooling of interest are shown.

Chapter 12

BUSINESS COMBINATIONS

Underlying all business activity there is a desire for growth. Not only is the size of a business a source of satisfaction to those who own and manage it, but there are economic and technological advantages associated with larger firms. Up to this point, the only ways we have considered open to a business enterprise to expand its operations are (1) retention of earnings, (2) increasing proprietorship by additional investment, and (3) going into debt by issuing bonds, mortgages, or long-term notes. Still another kind of expansion is possible—the merging of two or more businesses to form a larger enterprise. For smaller businesses this involves negotiation of partnership arrangements that are of interest only to the immediate owner-managers of the firms; but in the case of corporations, the number of interested parties makes the problem a bit more complex. There are a number of accounting issues that arise from such amalgamations that are especially interesting in the case of corporations. This chapter is concerned with those issues.

Combinations

There are various forms in which combination of business enterprises may occur. It may be effected by the purchase of one company's assets (along with, or without concomitant liabilities) by another company. It may also arise from the two companies exchanging shares; or one company's assets may be exchanged for shares of the other company; afterwards the shares are distributed to its stockholders in dissolution. A combination typically does, however, result in a single successor company; it does not matter which

272

company remains in existence, but the intercompany ownership of shares is not continued. Thus a combination differs from a consolidation, which covers the case in which shares of one company are held by another company to control the operations of the first. This latter situation—though it may appear similar—involves different accounting treatment and is therefore discussed later.

Purchase of Assets

The simplest way to effect a combination is for one company to purchase the assets of the other one. This serves to amalgamate the basic means of operation. If, in addition, the know-how or management skill available in the acquired company can be kept in active service, so much the better. But payment for the assets will leave the acquired company in a position to liquidate, pay off its debts, and return the remaining resources to its shareholders; after this, the legal shell may be disposed of by canceling the corporate charter. But such a transaction raises some problems. It is likely that the assets will be sold for something more than their book amounts; there will be an attendant income tax liability for the selling corporation. Also, when the proceeds are returned to the shareholders in winding up, there is likely to be an additional tax liability for those shareholders if the amounts received are greater than cost to the shareholder. Further, for such a plan to succeed, the existing management must be at least agreeable to the proposition; if they oppose it, much confusion may result. Lastly, the purchase of assets requires the transfer of large amounts of cash; both between the companies and between the acquired company and its shareholders and creditors. Not many mergers are worked out this way between large companies.

Purchase of Shares

One way to reduce the difficulties associated with the purchase of assets is to acquire the shares instead. This reduces the amount of cash required by taking over the debts of the old company; and it avoids the corporate tax because the acquired corporation does not sell its assets. Exchange of shares also avoids the task of enlisting the cooperation of the management of the acquired company; this may be important if the older management is not deemed necessary to the success of the future operations. To see how this might work out, suppose that the Dominant Company has a position statement of a given date, as follows:

DOMINANT COMPANY
Condensed Statement of Position
Immediately before Merger

ASSETS		EQUITIES	
Cash in bank...............	$100,000	Current debt...............	$120,000
Receivables (net)...........	80,000	Long-term debt.............	200,000
Inventories................	300,000	Common stock (30,000 shares,	
Plant and equipment.........	600,000	$10 par)................	300,000
Accumulated depreciation.....	100,000*	Retained earnings...........	360,000
Total Assets..........	$980,000	Total Equities.........	$980,000

Dominant Company's management is interested in acquiring the business of Subordinate Company, which on this date has the following position statement:

SUBORDINATE COMPANY
Condensed Position Statement
Immediately before Merger

ASSETS		EQUITIES	
Cash in bank...............	$ 60,000	Current debt...............	$200,000
Receivables (net)...........	100,000	Common shares (30,000 no	
Inventories................	200,000	par)....................	300,000
Plant and equipment.........	700,000	Retained earnings...........	360,000
Accumulated depreciation.....	200,000*		
Total Assets..........	$860,000	Total Equities.........	$860,000

Suppose that Dominant Company were to offer to buy Subordinate shares at $22 each. This may be sufficiently attractive for all the shareholders to accept it, and Dominant Company would record the agreements to transfer Subordinate shares by the entry:

Investment in Subordinate Company...................	660,000	
Accounts Payable, Subordinate Shares..............		660,000

Presumably, it would have arranged to raise extra funds needed to pay for these shares; suppose it had issued long-term notes to get these funds:

Cash in Bank.......................................	700,000	
Long-Term Notes..............................		700,000

When payment has been made for the shares and the certificates have been received, Dominant Corporation becomes the sole owner of the share equity of Subordinate Company. It will set up its own management and turn over the assets and debts to Dominant Company in exchange for the Subordinate shares. Then, since the Subordinate Company will have no assets, no shareholders, and no debts, it will be dissolved. Dominant Company would have taken over the Subordinate assets and equities by the entries:

Cash in Bank...	60,000	
Receivables (net)....................................	100,000	
Inventories..	200,000	
Plant and Equipment.................................	700,000	
Accumulated Depreciation.........................		200,000
Current Debt.....................................		200,000
Investment, Subordinate Company..................		660,000

Dominant Company may call attention to the combination by changing its corporate name to Dominant *Corporation*, and its new position statement after the acquisition of Subordinate Company would be:

DOMINANT CORPORATION

Statement of Position
Immediately after Merger

ASSETS		EQUITIES	
Cash in bank..............	$ 200,000	Current debt..............	$ 320,000
Receivables (net)..........	180,000	Long-term debt............	900,000
Inventories................	500,000	Common stock (30,000	
Plant and equipment........	1,300,000	shares).................	300,000
Accumulated depreciation....	300,000*	Retained earnings.........	360,000
Total Assets..........	$1,880,000	Total Equities.........	$1,880,000

Evaluation

Acquisition of Subordinate Company by purchase of shares required less cash than an outright purchase of assets would have done. By purchasing shares, it was possible to avoid the taxable gain otherwise to be shown on the Subordinate's books, even though the old shareholders would be taxed on the liquidation of their investment. The transaction could have been consummated partly in the open market, and despite the objections of a hostile Subordinate management; once an acquisition move is well under way, objections to it may be weakened and overcome.

On the other hand, acquisition of the shares left the assets at their book amounts; even if they were actually more valuable at replacement costs, this transaction as described would not permit such recognition; any necessary payment to cover such enhanced values would be recorded as goodwill—and goodwill is not amortizable for tax purposes! Worse, the purchase of shares required a sizable amount of cash. To raise this, Dominant Corporation had to float a loan of substantial amount, leaving its financial position somewhat distorted. The shareholder equities now represent only about a third of the assets, and the corporation is top-heavy with debt. Yet the former shareholders of Subordinate are left holding $660,000 cash which they will want to reinvest. This suggests that it might be desirable to find some way to exchange rather than purchase shares.

It might be a little troublesome to work out a deal whereby Subordinate shareholders could exchange their shares for shares of Dominant; this would raise bargaining issues, for seldom are two stocks exactly comparable so as to exchange share for share. Working out a ratio of exchange could be a fairly complicated process if one considers future as well as past earning power, current values as well as book amounts of assets, and other factors that may be important in a particular case. But it can be done. In the present case, the position statements suggest that if the assets and debts have been properly stated, the two companies could be combined on a share for share basis. Supposing that this were acceptable to both groups of shareholders, the entries to effect the combination would appear on Dominant's books:

Cash in Bank	60,000	
Receivables (net)	100,000	
Inventories	200,000	
Plant and Equipment	700,000	
Accumulated Depreciation		200,000
Current Debt		200,000
Common Shares 30,000 shares ($10 par)		300,000
Additional Paid-In Capital		360,000

It will be noted that the transaction is treated as an investment of additional assets and assumption of debt, with an added shareholder investment on the books of Dominant. Thus, the required legal capital is $300,000 greater (30,000 shares at $10 par), and the rest of the added equity is treated as additional paid-in-capital—contributed capital in excess of legal requirements. The exchange of shares has frozen the retained earnings equity that did exist in Subordinate Company, turning it into invested capital. However, the debt situation which arose in the purchase arrangement has been avoided, and the overall arrangement may be otherwise entirely equitable. So long as the relative position of the two shareholder groups are acceptable to them, it may not be necessary to restate the book figures, even though it may be that actual replacement values are higher than the book figures, and that some intangible assets have not been recognized. Indeed it may be undesirable to restate assets and intangibles if the combination is to be considered a tax-free transfer for the Subordinate shareholders; since they have merely exchanged *shares*, no new basis for income tax is recognized.

Further, under existing state corporation laws, it is possible to handle the combination as a statutory merger in which even the retained earnings balances need not be disturbed. By adding this idea to the exchange of shares, we evolve the notion of a "pooling of interests" which has become a common treatment for combinations of this kind.

Pooling of Interests and Revaluations

As the pooling of interest notion developed from the simple exchange of shares without revaluations, it became the practice to treat such combinations (where this is not precluded by law or convention) as statutory mergers, in which nothing is changed except the names of the companies on the stock certificates. In the present case, this could be true; all that has changed is that those who held Subordinate Company stock now hold Dominant Company stock in the same amounts. Since there has been no change in the former business activities, no break in the continuity of management (even the top managers of the Subordinate Corporation could be merged into the new organization) and no shift of material amount in the holdings of shares, the new organization is for all intents a mere summation of the two old ones, including the retained earnings balances. Under the pooling concept, this case would show no additional paid-in capital but $720,000 retained earnings.

But the combinations are worked out in some situations in which there are revaluations and shifts in ownership, and where the companies are not related in activity nor of the same approximate size. In such cases, there are different views among accountants as to whether the pooling concept is really acceptable. To see what may be involved in such a case, let us consider some other possibilities.

Suppose the two groups of shareholders agree on the following adjustments and corrections to be made to their companies' status:

(1)   Subordinate's inventories are stated at a figure which is lower than replacement cost by $30,000; these should be revised upward.

(2)   Plant and equipment of Dominant is to be written down to ⅔ of cost to reflect a more conservative depreciation policy in line with that of Subordinate Company.

(3)   Receivables of Subordinate are presumed to be subject to

greater shrinkage than has been provided for; they should be reduced by $2,000.

(4)   Legal and other fees and costs amounting to $20,000 will be paid for and absorbed by Subordinate Corporation.

(5)   Dominant Company is to recognize a liability for officers' retirement pensions in the amount of $115,000.

Indicated adjustments to the position accounts of Subordinate would be:

Inventories..	30,000	
Cash in Bank..		20,000
Receivables...		2,000
Retained Earnings...................................		8,000

Similarly, there would be need to record the following on the books of Dominant Company:

Retained Earnings....................................	215,000	
Accumulated Depreciation............................		100,000
Pension Liability....................................		115,000

These adjustments will leave the retained earnings of Subordinate at $368,000 and those of Dominant at $145,000. The combined shareholders' equities are then $668,000 and $445,000—roughly a ratio of 3 to 2. This might be the basis for exchanging each share of Subordinate Corporation for one and a half shares of Dominant Company. After the exchange, the position statement of the combined companies (now under the name of Dominant *Corporation*) would be:

DOMINANT CORPORATION
Position Statement (Condensed)
After Combination

ASSETS		EQUITIES	
Cash in bank..............	$ 140,000	Current debt..............	$ 320,000
Receivables...............	178,000	Long-term debt (and	
		pensions)..............	315,000
Inventories................	530,000	Common stock (60,000	
Plant and equipment........	1,300,000	shares $10 par).........	600,000
Accumulated depreciation....	400,000*	Additional paid-in capital....	368,000
		Retained earnings........	145,000
Total Assets........	$1,748,000	Total Equities.......	$1,748,000

When shareholders bargain for position in a combination, it becomes clear that there are cases when the orderly progression of accounting, matching costs and revenues with periodic operations, needs some adjustment. Whenever a business changes hands in whole or in part, there is an opportunity (if not an obligation) to re-examine the prospects of the firm and to restate the asset amounts, because the venture represents a "fresh start" for the continuing company. We shall have occasion to discuss the issues of price changes a bit later; but certainly in the case of setting up a new or a reconstituted enterprise there is ample reason to adjust the accounts substantially so as to establish a new basis for measuring future results. In the present case, with such extensive revaluation, it is hardly possible to justify this combination's being treated as a pooling of interests. Thus, we have applied the *purchase* interpretation; the company therefore has only the retained earnings that was left after revaluations for the acquiring company. The subordinate company retained earnings appear as additional paid-in capital.

Other Issues in Pooling

Since the assumption made by the pooling of interests approach is that the two companies are merely "added together" without change in any basic sense, it is only a small step to report the earnings of both companies for the whole year in the next annual report, regardless of the date of combination. And these combined earnings would be compared with similarly combined earnings for the preceding year. The reader might easily be impressed with the great change in "his" company. On the other hand, if the combination is treated as a purchase, only the earnings after the date of combination ought to appear in the next annual report, and the next year earnings would be compared with only the acquiring company's prior year figures.

A more important issue may arise when assets of the acquired company, carried at historical cost via pooling, may later be disposed of. The gain from such a sale will, of course, be reported as an extraordinary item, net of income tax; but there will still be an increase in income. Under purchase accounting, the restatement of assets at fair current values in the combination would eliminate the chance of such earnings. Such gains would have been recognized by the acquired company before the combination and would not affect later reports.

There is also the question of whether the assets of the *acquiring* company ought not be restated in current prices or at least adjusted to current price levels. But tax considerations enter into this, as well as for the acquired company.

Still another issue is raised when combinations are effected by issuance of securities convertible into common stock. The use of convertible debt or preferred shares may add leverage to the financial structure to increase earnings per share when total earnings are slightly or not at all increased. The potential dilution of common stock equities if those securities are converted may be substantial. Thus it has been required that the calculation of earnings per share must be made so as to show this dilution effect. The denominator of the calculation of diluted earnings per share would include the total number of shares represented by not only the common stock outstanding, but all convertible issues, warrants, or options to acquire common stock that might ultimately become common shares. While this problem is not peculiar to the pooling issue, a number of situations have arisen in which mergers have been effected so as to influence earnings per share by the use of convertible preferred stocks or bonds, warrants or other potentially residual securities. These procedures result in a calculation of earnings per share at artificially high levels, in view of the possibility of conversion's increasing the number of common shares.

Present Status of Rules concerning Combinations

The question of pooling versus purchase has raised much discussion among accountants, and only recently the Accounting Principles Board of the American Institute of Certified Public Accountants has tried to clarify the situation through its official *Opinions*. The most recent pronouncement restricts the use of the pooling doctrine to those exchanges in which the combination is effected by mere exchange of shares between companies, without change in the assets or the overall financing of the companies. Thus, there can be no pooling in the case of cash purchase of shares, nor where additional financing or shifts in the plan of capitalization and debt are part of the deal. The participating companies must be autonomous and independent before the merger, and there are restrictions on reporting the sale of assets during two years following the pooling, as well as other requirements. All combinations that do not meet the specific requirements for pooling *must* be accounted for as purchases, and considerable disclosure requirements have been set for any combination—either pooling or purchase.

The impact of pooling on accounting for combinations will doubtless be reduced by this action; but a great many combinations already established through pooling procedures will be unaffected by the latest opinion.

Consolidations

A consolidation differs from purchase or pooling; the formalities of transfer and amalgamation are not fulfilled. A company may acquire a subsidiary merely by purchasing a controlling interest in the stock. The advantage of this, and of creating subsidiary corporations *de novo*, is that the individual companies may be operated as a family of related but independent units. They have their own managers, their own financial reports; each can deal with its problems without involving the others because they are separate corporations.

Yet, a controlling company can adjust the policies and procedures of the subsidiaries for the benefit of its own interests, and it is often necessary to view the entire group of affiliated companies as if they were a single enterprise. Even though there is no formal and permanent combination, we may want to put together the reports of all the companies on a consolidated basis, to give a single, unitary picture of the activities of the group. The process of making up such reports from data supplied by the individual member companies is called consolidation of those reports.

The first fact to notice is that we need some criterion as to when the process of consolidation is justified. Certainly, when all the shares of a company are owned by a parent corporation, the subsidiary company is in effect merely a separate department that should obviously be considered a member of a group. But corporations sometimes own only portions of the shares, of which some may be voting and some nonvoting shares; how much control of a subsidiary company is had in such a case? The minimum rule followed by most accountants is that the parent company must own more than 50 percent of the voting shares of a subsidiary company to warrant consolidation; actually, the percentage is usually much higher than this when consolidations are made. The truth is, of course, that control of a corporation may be had even with substantially less than 51 percent of the voting shares. The general apathy of shareholders and the pattern of following the judgment of others may give a relative minority group effective control of operations; in the practical situation, even as little as a fourth of the outstanding voting shares may actually control the situation. There are other ways in which control may be exercised than by mere voting rights, and there are arguments for considering other criteria for consolidation. However, accountants do not ordinarily include in a consolidated report a subsidiary that represents less than legal control, more than half of the voting stock being owned by the parent.

General Pattern of Procedures in Consolidation

Once it has been decided what companies are to be included in the affiliated group for which the consolidated reports are prepared, the procedure for consolidation is to take adjusted trial balances for the individual companies at some specified date and add them together as a first approximation to the consolidated reports. Then, since there is a certain amount of duplication and double counting in the data thus combined, appropriate changes are made to remove the items that have been duplicated. The changes required to remove duplication of data are made in the form of elimination entries which look very much like adjusting entries used in the case of a single company work sheet when financial reports are being prepared. But it should be stressed that the combined trial balance does not exist in any accounting ledger or record. The sum of the trial balances of the individual companies is an artificial thing in that there is actually no set of ledger accounts in which those amounts appear; we have added together a number of sets of data to get a larger set from which broader conclusions may be drawn; we do not have a trial balance in more than a theoretical sense.

Eliminations

Elimination is the process of removing the double counting of some items when trial balances or reports of affiliated companies are combined. The logic underlying this general approach may be a bit clearer if we consider the nature of the double counting that eliminations are intended to remove. The first of these is the situation that underlies the whole process of consolidation and justifies it: the ownership of subsidiary company shares by the parent company.

When the subsidiary company was organized, it set up the usual accounts for outstanding shares, with perhaps some additional paid-in capital. Then, as it operated independently—before the parent company acquired control—the subsidiary company grew by various means, including the retention of earnings. Thus, when it became a subsidiary company, there was a certain interest in the form of retained earnings which the parent company bought. Thus, when the parent corporation purchased all of the outstanding stock of the subsidiary, for say, $220,000, the debit to the parent company's investment account represented exactly the reciprocal of the total share equity of the subsidiary at that date. The credit balances on the subsidiary company ledger—Common Shares, $100,000; Additional Paid-In Capital, $30,000; and Retained Earnings, $90,000— are the same thing as represented in the investment account of the parent. Moreover, these two representations are actually irrelevant for reporting the operations of the group. The only actual shareholders are those of the parent company, and both the investment account of the parent and the share equity accounts of the subsidiary company are eliminated.

Minority Interest

The foregoing has assumed that the parent company owned all the outstanding shares of the subsidiary. This is obviously not always the case, for some shareholders prefer not to sell out when the parent buys control of the subsidiary; or for other reasons, the parent does not acquire all of the voting shares. Suppose the parent had acquired only 80 percent of the shares of the subsidiary, paying $176,000 for them. Its investment account would then be reciprocal to 80 percent of the total share equity of the subsidiary, $80,000 of Common Shares, $24,000 of Additional Paid-In Capital, and $72,000 of the Retained Earnings accounts, total $176,000. In preparing a consolidated report, these reciprocal elements would be eliminated because they are irrelevant for the group report. The remainder of the subsidiary share equity, however ($20,000 of Common Shares, $6,000 of Additional Paid-In Capital, and $18,000 of Retained Earnings) would not be eliminated, for these shareholder equities actually exist and are part of the financial structure of the family group. Such share equities are called "minority interests." They may exist in any one or more of the affiliated companies, with respect to any kind of shares. There may be large minority interests in preferred shares if these are nonvoting. There may also be minority interests in bonded indebtedness of the subsidiary company.

Retained Earnings in Consolidated Reports

Typically, equities in retained earnings exist only for common shares; many companies do not have preferred shares at all, and many preferred shares do not participate with common shares in the distributions of dividends. Thus, most minority interests in retained earnings apply to common shareholders. But there is one important aspect of retained earnings that must be stressed here. Equities in retained earnings acquired by purchase are eliminated in the consolidation; that is, it is not possible to increase the *parent* company's gross equity in accumulated profits by the *purchase* of shares. The minority equity is not subject to this restriction; minority interests in the retained earnings of the subsidiary (the company in which those shares actually exist) appear on the consolidated balance sheet of the group, even though through condensation they may not be visible in detail. The share equity section of the consolidated balance sheet will thus contain the share equity items of the parent company as they appear on the books of that company; to this will be added a "minority interest" which, if detailed, will report the amounts of Common Shares, Additional Paid-In Capital, and Retained Earnings applicable to minority shareholders as shown by the books of the company in which they own shares.

Effect of Consolidation on the Measurement of Income

The process of eliminating the parent company investment against the outstanding shares and retained earnings of the subsidiary company thus acquired has the effect of limiting the showing of earnings from the subsidiary company in the combined reports. The only profits or earnings retentions that can appear in a consolidated report are those that have been earned after the date of acquisition; these are divided between majority (parent company) and minority equities as their interests appear. For example, suppose that the subsidiary company in our previous paragraph operated for a year and showed as a result a net earnings figure of $30,000. Eighty percent of this figure would be added to the retained earnings equity for majority (parent company) stockholders, 20 percent would be added to minority interest. Thus the majority shareholder would have a share in subsidiary earnings which arose *after* the date of consolidation, but none of the earnings of the subsidiary prior to the acquisition. The minority shareholder would claim a proportion of the total retained earnings of their company undiminished by any elimination.

Acquisition at More or Less than Book Value

The situations thus far described have implied that the investment of the parent was made at the same amount per share as was shown on the books and reports of the subsidiary. This, unfortunately, is not always so. Prices in the market are not the same as share equities in accounting reports. If the parent company had acquired its 80 percent share of the subsidiary by payment of $180,000 instead of the $176,000 book value, there is a question as to how to interpret the extra $4,000. It cannot be eliminated, for it is not the reciprocal of the underlying equities; the amounts simply do not balance out. Therefore, the $4,000 must appear as a special item, somewhere in the final consolidated reports.

The $4,000 cost of investment that is in excess of the underlying equities really arises from the use of a different valuation than has been used in the accounting records. Market prices of shares of stock are based upon expectations, not on the current situation as established by past events; these expectations may be colored by special-interest interpretations or by bargaining of the parties. Some accountants would carry the $4,000 debit excess as a form of intangible assets, "Goodwill from Consolidation." Other accountants would deduct the $4,000 from the equity of the majority shareholders on the ground that it is the cost of acquiring control of the subsidiary, whose only value must be seen in future profitable operations. Practical considerations obviously favor the second view.

By a similar line of reasoning, a subsidiary control acquired at *less* than book value results in a "Additional Paid-In Capital from Consolidation." The credit excess arising from acquisition of $176,000 of underlying equity for a cash consideration of $170,000 is not a gain but an adjustment to reflect a market valuation of the shares. Therefore, it is treated as an adjustment of capital structure, affecting the majority shareholder interest in much the same way as would a retirement of some of the shares at less than their recorded equity per share.

Intercompany Receivables and Payables

The purpose of consolidation is to achieve a group pattern of action, and it is obvious that advances of cash or property on credit will occur as between affiliated companies. Whatever the real assets are, they appear in the trial balance of the company that holds them; intercompany receivables and payables are mere double counting of the advance. To put the matter another way, if two members of a family, A and B, arrange that A should loan B $100, the actuality of the immediate transaction between them cannot change the fact that the *family* has neither borrowed nor lent. The interfamily transaction exists only as between the members, not for the group as a whole. Therefore, amounts due from other companies in a consolidation shown as receivables in some trial balances and payables in others are eliminated. Properly, this kind of elimination would also be required in the case of pooling or purchase, for the same reasons.

Intercompany Sales and Purchases

The intercompany receivables and payables just mentioned arise sometimes from sales of goods or services as between companies. Just as loans arranged between two brothers do not affect the indebtedness of the family, sales between two members of the family are not sales but intrafamily transfers. Therefore, the amounts that appear as sales in some trial balances, which are also treated as purchased merchandise or service costs in some others, must be offset and eliminated. This would also be the case for rental arrangements, management fees, and other intercompany transactions. Transactions that are offset by reciprocal counterparts elsewhere in the group data are not transactions for the group. This is true, even when some of the companies are not wholly owned. It may appear that a sale made by a parent to a partly owned subsidiary is an actually complete sale so far as the minority shareholders are concerned, and that therefore only the proportionate percentage of the transaction should be eliminated. But this is incorrect; on the books of the subsidiary, the minority shareholders will see their own position reflected as the transaction is recorded, therefore no concern need be paid to their "interest" in the purchase or sale, beyond seeing that the minority share of any gain or loss is added to or subtracted from their equity. Since the minority interest is established by the records of the company in which the minority exists, the process of consolidation can ignore the minority interest in all those transactions which are eliminated to avoid overstating the operations of the group as a whole. Again, this kind of elimination must also be made in pooling or purchase combinations, if there are such intercompany transactions.

Intercompany Income Distributions

The elimination of intercompany sales and acquisition costs, including management fees, rentals, and the like, will eliminate intercompany income and expense. But such things as interest charges, dividends, and the like require special attention.

Interest income and interest charges should be eliminated when they arise between companies in the group, as should the accompanying items of interest receivable and payable. However, it should be recognized that when there are minority interests in bonds payable, the interest charges applicable to those minority interests are real items to the consolidation because they are distributions of income to outside interests. Elimination applies only to those aspects of income distribution as are transactions between the affiliated companies.

This last is especially true of dividends declared. The income recorded by a parent company arising from its share of dividends declared or paid by a subsidiary is not group income, even if the dividends are actually paid. All that has happened is a transfer of cash when the payment occurs; for the income, whatever it is, appears in the operating accounts of the subsidiary. The amount of this income cannot be counted again, even in part, as a dividend income or a distribution as between companies. Therefore, the intercompany dividend charges and dividend incomes are eliminated. Again it should be noted that the amount of dividends declared or paid for the benefit of minority interests are real and will still appear in the consolidated reports. Thus, if a subsidiary declares a $10,000 dividend of which 20 percent is applicable to a minority interest in that company, the elimination would be only $8,000. This would of course be to some extent taken care of in the fact that the parent company would take up only 80 percent of the dividend, and the elimination would thus be seen in its proper light. However, the point needs to be stressed that the eliminations apply to intercompany items exclusive of minority interests in income; the latter hold equities in the group, even though they may not have the status of majority or controlling shareholders. But in a combination via purchase or pooling, it may be more a matter of 100 percent elimination, because the acquired company is fully owned.

Cost Adjustments

The corrections to be made to the combined trial balances of affiliated companies in the preparation of consolidated statements have thus far been straightforward removal of double counting, aimed at items that were specific in amount, even though in some cases they were proportionate parts of larger items. There are some things, however, that require certain changes in the recorded *amounts* of transactions when consolidated reports are to be prepared. These are something more than mere eliminations of double counting. They are better described as adjustments to restate intercompany costs at proper amounts. These have somewhat intricate effects which we shall consider at some length. However, it should be stressed that although we use the term adjustments to refer to these items, they do not appear on *any* actual accounting records, and they are not adjusting entries to reflect otherwise incompletely recorded transactions. What we are here concerned with is a difference in the conception of cost as between the viewpoint of the individual company and that of the group of companies as an enterprise unit.

Inventories

The basis of quantifying all inventories (in fact to state any and all assets) is cost. This is the outlay required to bring the item in question under the control of the management and to make it usefully available for operations. Thus the cost of inventories includes the invoice cost plus transportation and make-ready. This gives no particular trouble for the individual company, but when affiliated companies sell their products to each other, it becomes another matter.

Suppose a company manufactures a product which costs $4,000 and sells this item to an affiliated company for $5,000. This is, let us say, the typical and normal price for such an item, and there is no question of the propriety of the transaction. The purchasing company takes up this item in its inventory at the $5,000 "cost" to it, which, so far as the company as an individual is concerned, is the outlay necessary to acquire it. But from the viewpoint of the group, the cost of the inventory is overstated. This may be clearer if the case is put into the family analogy. If B sells goods that cost $4,000 to his brother C for $5,000, what did the goods cost the *family?* The answer is that the interfamily transfer did not increase the cost of the goods, even though it may have increased their value. Hence, the inventory remaining unsold must be written back to the intercompany cost level.

Had these goods been sold to outsiders, there would be no problem, even though the "cost of goods sold" would be inflated on the books of one company to support the earnings reported to the shareholders by the selling company, another member of the group. Whatever earnings there were in the final sale, a markup between companies would only effect the division of earnings between the company that made the product and the company that finally sold it. But if the goods remain unsold in an inventory of one of the affiliated companies, there is no profit in any intercompany "sale." Therefore, such inventories, carried at selling price of the producer in the inventory of an affiliate, must be written down to cost, the appropriate figure for the carrying amount of assets.

This write-down to cost of inventories sold to affiliates is complicated a bit when there are minority interests in the selling company. On the books of that company there are earnings recorded that add to the equity of minority stockholders. From the viewpoint of the minority interest, these earnings are legally and equitably realized. If the inventories are reduced to cost, either the minority interest must be reduced prorata or the minority portion of the earnings recorded by the sale to the affiliate must be charged against the other (majority) share equities. The earnings realized by the minority interest ought not be taken from their equity, and it ought not to be charged against majority equities. The answer is to view the minority share of the intercompany profit as a cost of transferring the goods from one company to another. Therefore, the write-down is limited to the majority share of the intercompany "gain"; the inventory is thus increased by the share of earnings accruing to the minority interest in the selling company.

Exactly equivalent reasoning applies to plant and equipment items that are transferred from one affiliate to another. This is, however, a bit more complicated because the "intercompany cost adjustment" affects depreciation charges on long-term assets, and thus must be taken into account over a considerable period of years. We need not here do more than notice that this exists. The technical aspects of such adjustments are beyond the scope of our present interests.

Other Problems in Consolidations

There are a number of other issues that arise when accountants prepare consolidated statements for affiliated groups of companies. There may be various classes and types of shares in the individual companies that have different rights to dividends and different asset preferences. Some companies may have special appropriations of subsidiary retained earnings which must be shown in the consolidated reports, even though their amounts may have to be "eliminated" from total Retained Earnings as reciprocals of investment amounts. Various types of bonded or other indebtedness may exist, and there may be premiums or discounts under amortization besides receivables, payables, and interest distributions. There may be various kinds of complicated ownership arrangements, as when a parent company owns control in an intermediate company that has subsidiaries in its own right; actually, two or more companies may each

FIGURE 12–1

PARENT COMPANY AND SUBSIDIARY COMPANY, CONSOLIDATED

At the end of the last year, the summary ledger trial balances of these two companies were as shown below:

Debit Balances	Parent	Subsidiary	Combined
Cash in bank............................	$ 40,000	$ 20,000	$ 60,000
Accounts receivable (net).................	110,000	240,000	350,000
Inventories (at cost).....................	120,000	90,000	210,000
Dividends receivable.....................	4,000		4,000
Prepayments............................	10,000	10,000	20,000
Plant and equipment cost.................	200,000	300,000	500,000
Investment, Subsidiary Co. (3,200 shares, at cost).................................	432,000		432,000
Cost of goods sold.......................	400,000	200,000	600,000
Selling and administration costs..............	230,000	150,000	380,000
Interest charges.........................		2,000	2,000
Federal income taxes.....................	90,000	70,000	160,000
Dividends declared......................	40,000	20,000	60,000
Total............................	$1,676,000	$1,102,000	$2,778,000
Credit Balances			
Accounts payable........................	$ 129,000	$ 47,000	$ 176,000
Dividends payable.......................		5,000	5,000
Accumulated depreciation.................	80,000	130,000	210,000
Common shares, $100 par each..............	600,000	400,000	1,000,000
Retained earnings.......................	40,000	20,000	60,000
Sales revenue...........................	800,000	500,000	1,300,000
Income from Subsidiary Co.................	27,000		27,000
Total............................	$1,676,000	$1,102,000	$2,778,000

Note 1: The Parent Company's investment in the subsidiary company was acquired several years ago when the subsidiary company had a balance in its Retained Earnings account of $150,000 credit.

Note 2: Selling and administrative costs of the Subsidiary Company include a $10,000 management fee paid to the Parent Company.

Note 3: The Subsidiary Company had borrowed (and repaid) certain amounts from the Parent Company during the year, for which interest of $1,000 charged by the parent company was paid.

Note 4: Subsidiary Company sales include $100,000 of goods at regular sales prices "sold" to the Parent Company during the year. $20,000 of this, still unsettled, appears among the receivables and payables.

Note 5: $10,000 of the intercompany sales remain unsold in the closing inventory of the Parent Company at "cost."

own portions of each others' shares in a circular pattern of mutual ownership. Financial reports that are prepared at different dates may have to be consolidated, with consequent problems of interpreting interim operating results. Finally, shares of the affiliated companies may be acquired at different times so that there are "layers" of investment to be analyzed and eliminated; there may be various kinds of adjustments of capital structure, shares exchanged for others, "stock dividends," and the like. And, of course, there is always the possibility of one or more companies in the affiliated group disposing of the controlling interest in subsidiary companies. Consolidated reports bring the accountant a full share of complexities. We need not concern ourselves with all these matters here and now; what we do need to recognize are those major aspects of consolidation that have been described in detail. Perhaps the entire matter will be a bit more clear if we work through a typical (though perhaps simple) illustrative case (Figure 12–1).

The first step in preparing the consolidated reports is to list the amounts in the combined trial balance in the first pair of columns of the multicolumn work sheet (Figure 12–2). Alternatively, one might use T-accounts, one for each accountable item, as shown on each line of the work sheet. Then we may arrange to remove the double-counted items; the "elimination entries" in the work sheet (or in the T-accounts) are here presented in journal form, even though they are *not* entries in any set of records and will not appear in any journal.

The first elimination has to do with the investment account on the books of the parent company, reciprocal to the common shares and retained earnings of the subsidiary company:

(a)

Common Shares, Subsidiary Company....................	320,000	
Retained Earnings, Subsidiary Company.................	120,000	
Investment in Subsidiary..........................		432,000
Additional Paid-In Capital from Consolidation........		8,000

This removes from the combined trial balance 80 percent of the common shares and 80 percent of the retained earnings at the date of acquisition of the subsidiary. The excess of book equity acquired over the cost of the investment is carried as Additional Paid-In Capital since there is no clearly indicated asset overvaluation at the date of acquiring the subsidiary investment.

The $10,000 management fee was not a cost or an income to the

Consolidating Worksheet

FIGURE 12-2

PARENT COMPANY AND SUBSIDIARY COMPANY

At 12/31/--

Account Titles	Combined Trial Balances		Eliminations		Consolidated Earnings		Consolidated Position	
	Dr.	Cr.	Dr.	Cr.	Dr.	Cr.	Dr.	Cr.
Cash in Bank	60,000							
Accounts Rec'ble	350,000							
Inventories	210,000							
Dividends Rec'ble	4,000							
Prepayments	20,000							
Plant Cost	500,000							
Investment Sub. Co.	432,000							
Cost of Goods Sold	600,000							
Selling & G.A. Costs	380,000							
Interest Charges	2,000							
Federal Inc. Taxes	160,000							
Dividends Declared	60,000							
Accounts Payable		176,000						
Dividends Payable		5,000						
All'ce for Dpr.		210,000						
Common Shares		1,000,000						
Retained Earnings		60,000						
Sales Revenue		1,300,000						
Income from Sub. Co.		27,000						
Additional								
Paid-in Capital								
Minority Interest								
Majority Interest								
Total	2,778,000	2,778,000						

group, even though it was an actual charge for actual services between the companies. Since it was an entirely intragroup transaction, it is eliminated as follows:

(*b*)

Income from Subsidiary Company........................	10,000	
Selling and General Administration Costs..............		10,000

Similarly, the charge for interest, credited to Income from Subsidiary Company is not a transaction which established income for the group, even though its effect was quite correctly shown on the individual company books. The elimination is:

(*c*)

Income from Subsidiary Company........................	1,000	
Interest Charges.....................................		1,000

The "sales" between the companies are from the viewpoint of the group mere interdepartmental transfers of goods, and the receivables and payables are intrafamily items, not assets or equities in the group picture. They are eliminated:

(*d*)

Accounts Payable.....................................	20,000	
Sales Revenue.......................................	100,000	
Accounts Receivable.............................		20,000
Cost of Goods Sold.............................		100,000

The reduction of cost of goods sold is, of course, not quite correct, for there was an intercompany write-up of the inventory, and this must be allowed for in correcting the expense of the group. But it is easier to make this elimination as if the goods were all disposed of and show the inventory correction as a separate item:

(*e*)

Cost of Goods Sold....................................	2,400	
Inventories..		2,400

This correction of inventory is computed by (1) recognizing that the amount of unsold goods is $10,000 at selling price between the companies, (2) obtaining the profit percentage on the "sale" from the data in the subsidiary company's records, (3) allowing for minority interest in the profit as recorded between the companies, and (4) eliminating the majority share of profit from the book cost, to reduce the inventories to intercompany cost basis. Thus, the amount of the inventory cost adjustment is $10,000 \times 30$ percent (the net margin percentage of the subsidiary company)[1] $\times 80$ percent (the

---

[1] $\dfrac{500,000 - (200,000 + 150,000)}{500,000} = 30$ percent.

parent company share of the subsidiary profits), and the amount of the adjustment is $2,400.

We have taken care of all the items mentioned in the notes, but there are still some double-counted items in the data. Dividends receivable and payable appear on the trial balances; these are mere intercompany items, and of the subsidiary dividends declared during the year, only 20 percent are real dividends, the other 80 percent were already shown as "Income from Subsidiary Company." Since the subsidiary income will actually appear in the consolidated reports as a part of the earnings statement data, there is no need to show these items in the reports as well. The necessary eliminations are:

(f)

Dividends Payable..	4,000	
Income from Subsidiary....................................	16,000	
Dividends Receivable................................		4,000
Dividends Declared..................................		16,000

When all the foregoing eliminations have been placed in the appropriate columns of the consolidating work sheet and the net amounts are carried over to the final columns, the work sheet will appear as shown in Figure 12–3. (Similar data would appear in T-accounts if those had been used.) The amount of consolidated earnings retained for the period is $122,600, divided between minority ($11,600) and majority ($111,000) shareholder equities. The computation of the minority interest is based on the data of the subsidiary company:

Sales revenue............................		$500,000
Cost of goods sold.......................	$200,000	
Selling and administration costs...........	150,000	350,000
Operating Net Margin....................		$150,000
Distributions, interest....................	$ 2,000	
Federal income taxes.....................	70,000	
Dividends declared......................	20,000	92,000
Current Earnings Retention..............		$ 58,000

Of this, the minority shareholders are entitled to 20 percent, $11,600. It will be noted that all of the elimination data applicable to the determination of consolidated net earnings retained affect the majority interest only. This is as it should be; the parent company shareholders are the ones who benefit from the consolidated operations, and it is their interest in the subsidiary company that we are trying to measure without double counting.

Consolidating Worksheet

FIGURE 12-3

PARENT COMPANY AND SUBSIDIARY COMPANY

At 12/31/--

Account Titles	Combined Trial Balances Dr.	Combined Trial Balances Cr.	Eliminations Dr.	Eliminations Cr.	Consolidated Earnings Dr.	Consolidated Earnings Cr.	Consolidated Position Dr.	Consolidated Position Cr.
Cash in Bank	60,000						60,000	
Accounts Rec'ble	350,000			(d) 20,000			330,000	
Inventories	210,000			(e) 2,400			207,600	
Dividends Rec'ble	4,000			(f) 4,000				
Prepayments	20,000						20,000	
Plant Cost	500,000						500,000	
Investment Sub. Co.	432,000			(a)432,000				
Cost of Goods Sold	600,000		(e) 2,400	(d)100,000	502,400			
Selling & G.A. Costs	380,000			(b) 10,000	370,000			
Interest Charges	2,000			(c) 1,000	1,000			
Federal Inc. Taxes	160,000				160,000			
Dividends Declared	60,000			(f) 16,000	44,000			
Accounts Payable		176,000	(d) 20,000					156,000
Dividends Payable		5,000	(f) 4,000					1,000
All'ce for Dpr.		210,000						210,000
Common Shares		1,000,000	(a)320,000					680,000
Retained Earnings		60,000	(a)120,000				60,000	
Sales Revenue		1,300,000	(d)100,000			1,200,000		
Income from Sub. Co.		27,000	(b) 10,000					
			(c) 1,000					
			(f) 16,000					
Additional								
Paid-in Capital				(a) 8,000				8,000
Minority Interest					11,600			11,600
Majority Interest					111,000			111,000
Total	2,778,000	2,778,000	593,400	593,400	1,200,000	1,200,000	1,177,600	1,177,600

Retained Earnings in the Consolidated Position Statement

The work sheet shows the retained earnings of the affiliated companies as a $60,000 debit balance, before the current period results are transferred to these accounts. This debit balance may be a bit confusing, unless we see the reasons for its existence.

The retained earnings amounts in the individual trial balances were $40,000 for the parent company and $20,000 for the subsidiary company. The elimination of reciprocal balances at the date of acquisition removed 80 percent of the $150,000 subsidiary retained earnings at that date. Since the subsidiary Retained Earnings account declined from $150,000 to $20,000 after the date of acquisition, there were either losses or dividends in excess of earnings amounting to $130,000 during that period. Thus, the retained earnings equity of the parent company shareholders really declined (so far as the group is concerned) by 80 percent of this $130,000. Then, the retained earnings equity on a consolidated basis for the parent company shareholders at the beginning of this year was $40,000 (the amount shown on the Parent Company's ledger in the original trial balance) less $104,000 subsidiary declines since acquisition, or a net debit balance of $64,000. The minority interest (which is not affected by intercompany factors) was 20 percent of the book amount in the subsidiary trial balance, $4,000 credit. The net sum of these amounts is the $60,000 debit balance shown in the final columns of the work sheet. Another way to see this is to allocate the retained earnings equities at the beginning of the year:

Allocation of Retained Earnings 1/1/—

Equity per Books Company	Total Amount	Subsidiary Co. Minority Interest 20%	Parent Company Shareholders
Subsidiary Company...............	$ 20,000	$4,000	$ 16,000
Parent Company..................	40,000		40,000
Total.......................	$ 60,000	$4,000	$ 56,000
Less eliminated equity at date of acquisition.....................	$120,000 Dr.		$120,000 Dr.
Net Balances.....................	$ 60,000 Dr.	$4,000 Cr.	$ 64,000 Dr.

Now, if we add to these equities the allocation of earnings retained during the current period, we will have the final equities for the consolidated position at the close of the year:

Changes in Retained Earnings Year Ended 12/31/—

	Subsidiary Co. 20% Minority	Parent Company Shareholders
Balances, beginning of year..................	$ 4,000 Cr.	$ 64,000 Dr.
Current earnings retention...................	1,600 Cr.	111,000 Cr.
Total, December 31, 19—..............	$15,600 Cr.	$ 47,000 Cr.

A check on this calculation may be had by allocating the book equities as they would appear on the individual company position statements at the end of the year:

Allocation of Book—Equities in Retained Earnings At December 31, 19—

Company	Total Amount	Subsidiary Co. 20% Minority	Parent Company Shareholders
Subsidiary.......................	$ 78,000	$15,000	$ 62,400
Parent.........................	107,000	. . .	107,000
Gross book equities..............	$185,000	$15,600	$169,400
Eliminations:			
Acquisition...................	$120,000		
Inventory write-down...........	2,400 Dr.		
Total Eliminations..........	$122,400 Dr.		$122,400 Dr.
Net Equities....................	$ 62,600 Cr.	$15,600 Cr.	$ 47,000 Cr.

These equities are thus the correct ones to appear in the consolidated position statement. The consolidated reports are shown in Figure 12–4. The statement reporting changes in retained earnings to reconcile with the position statement amounts was already presented (Changes in Retained Earnings) above.

Comments on the Consolidated Statements

The most important thing to note about consolidated statements is that they are not the reports of any company as such; nor are they based upon one single set of records maintained for the purpose of reporting the activities of the group of companies. The consolidated statements are fictitious in the sense that they report the results and position of an accounting entity that really has no legal existence. The results as portrayed in the consolidated statements are those that *would* have been reported if the group of companies had legally been combined into one unit. From an economic viewpoint, however, the consolidated reports show more nearly what is needed than could any single set of reports for one company, or even for each individual company in the group. When it is recognized that consolidations often show as a unit the activities of as many as a hundred

FIGURE 12–4

PARENT COMPANY AND SUBSIDIARY COMPANIES

Consolidated Position Statement

At December 31, 19—

Current Assets:

Cash in bank	$ 60,000	
Accounts receivable (net)	330,000	
Inventories (at cost)	207,600	
Prepayments	20,000	$617,600

Current Debt:

Accounts payable	$156,000	
Dividends payable	1,000	157,000
Net working capital		$460,600
Plant and equipment cost	$500,000	
Less: Allowances for depreciation	210,000	290,000
Total Net Working Capital and Plant Assets....		$750,600

Share Equities:

Parent Company, 6,000 shares, par value $100 each		$600,000
Retained earnings in Consolidated Companies (Parent Company, $107,000)		47,000
Capital surplus from consolidation		8,000
Total Share Equities, Parent Company Shares		$655,000
Subsidiary Company, 20 percent minority interest:		
800 shares, $100 par value each	$ 80,000	
Retained earnings	15,600	$ 95,600
Total Share Equities, all Companies		$750,600

PARENT COMPANY AND SUBSIDIARY COMPANIES

Consolidated Statement of Earnings

Year Ended 12/31—

Sales Revenue		$1,200,000
Cost of goods sold	$502,400	
Selling and administration costs	370,000	
Total Expense		872,400
Operating net margin		$ 327,600
Income distributions:		
Federal income taxes	$160,000	
Interest charges	1,000	
Dividends declared	44,000	205,000
Earnings retained during the period		$ 122,600
Applicable to minority shareholders		11,600
Earnings Retained for Majority Shares		$ 111,000

or more affiliated companies, the task of reading the individual reports is seen as impossible, and the value of the consolidated reports is clear.

However, adding together the data for a number of companies can give impressions that are not entirely dependable. For instance, the amount of cash (or any other item in a consolidated report) is not a single amount that may be used without restriction; the makeup of the cash, inventory or any other item is a combination of amounts in the hands of various companies. Some of these companies may not be as subject to majority decisions as might seem. Cases in equity may be brought to enjoin the transfer of funds or other assets if this appears unduly to jeopardize minority interests.

The share equities are stated in a consolidated position statement as they would work out with complete transferability of assets among companies; but it should be noted that in our example, the equity in retained earnings on a consolidated basis for the Parent Company shares is much smaller on the consolidated basis than it would be on a legal company basis. This is because the subsidiary has had losses since acquisition. However, this could easily be the other way around, i.e., Consolidated retained earnings could include subsidiary *income*. Retained earnings in a consolidated position statement does not mean "legally available for the declaration of dividends," unless one assumes that this amount of dividends *could* be distributed if *all* the various companies could so arrange their affairs as to distribute the maximum dividends possible under the legal ceiling of accumulated earnings. The consolidated reports must be read and interpreted with at least the same care as would be required in reading any other set of financial reports.

Summary

Consolidated reports are useful whenever a number of companies, separately organized and operated, form an integrated group with regard to investment, control, or other economic interest. Although the data presented in conventional (legal) or "separate-entity" form could be added together, a certain amount of double counting would result. For instance, the intercompany investments are from the point of view of the group a mere nominal item. The real assets and equities are apart and aside from the intercompany investments. Similarly, such things as intercompany sales and purchases, receivables and payables, incomes and income distributions, dividends declared and received do not really mean anything from the broader view of the consolidation. Therefore, such items are removed from the data, and the combined trial balances are trimmed to take out such interdepartmental items.

Minority interests are established within the legal units, and their rights and equities are determined by those units and the data pertinent to them. Therefore, minority interests in income are determined by the measurements within the firm which has the minority interest, and these are not affected by the consolidation process, although consolidation brings out the position of minority interests more clearly.

Some of the complications of consolidated statements have been purposely omitted from our discussion, but the major items have been discussed and illustrated. In addition, the device of retained earnings allocation was presented to make it easier to determine and to visualize the various interests in multicompany retained earnings.

The reader should now be ready to look at some practical applications of accounting principles and methods to see what overall patterns of financial presentation exist in the world of affairs and to apply what has been described in the preceding pages. The following chapter will consider some typical corporate reports to call attention to the general patterns of practice and the ways in which principles are applied in specific cases. This will also afford an opportunity to discuss some of the major unsolved problems of accounting with respect to price-level changes and other issues.

QUESTIONS

1. What are some of the reasons why business firms combine? What happens when two proprietorships are made into a partnership? (Review Chapter 10, if necessary.) Suppose Adams has a garage with assets: cash, $2,000; inventories, $6,000; tools and equipment, $5,000; and current debts, $7,000. He suggests a partnership arrangement between him and Baskin, who operates an automobile service station with assets: cash, $1,000; inventory, $7,000; land, $6,000; building, $14,000; lifts and pumps, $8,000; current debts, $1,000; mortgage on building, $9,000.

    a) What issues would these prospective parties discuss in trying to negotiate a combination?

    b) Are these issues the same or different from those which involve the combination of The Friendly Finance Corporation and Computer Services, Inc.?

2. Underlying every accounting activity is a concept of entity, i.e., a notion of what constitutes the activity or unit for which the accounting statements are prepared. What can happen when two companies combine with respect to the entity for which accounting is done? Do the old entities disappear to be replaced by a new one or does the notion of entity simply expand to encompass the whole area covered by both firms? What has this to do with pooling versus purchase?

3. What are the objections to effecting a combination by purchase of assets for cash? When Northwest Industries offered Goodrich stockholders 30 percent above the market price for their shares, what financial or other problems do you suppose were faced by Northwest Industries? By Goodrich? Was this really preferable to purchasing Goodrich's assets for cash?

4. In acquiring shares through the market to effect a combination, the text indicates that any excess over the book amounts of net assets would be considered to be goodwill in the acquiring company's investment account. When does this goodwill actually appear in the financial reports? When the acquired company is dissolved, should goodwill be carried indefinitely in the acquiring company's statements? Should it be amortized over some future period as the advantages of the combination are realized? Or should it be immediately written off against the acquiring company's retained earnings since it does not represent more than mere hoped-for advantages from the combination which may or may not materialize. Even then, ought they not be recognized when they do appear rather than when the combination is worked out?

5. If shareholders of two companies agree to exchange shares in some ratio—say, two of acquired company for one of the other—what happens to the valuations of assets held by the acquired company? If the exchange of shares is based on their market values, is it likely that the net stockholder's equity of the acquired company would be exactly equal to the market value of the shares exchanged? What would happen to the retained earnings of the acquired company if the purchase were handled as if the cash raised from selling the acquiring company's stock had been used to buy the shares of the acquired company?

6. What is the concept of a statutory merger and how does it contribute to the notion of a pooling of interests? What have tax considerations to do with the pooling concept? How would the position statement after a pooling be different from one established by purchase?

7. Suppose two companies combine under the "pooling of interests" doctrine just before the close of their fiscal year. What would appear in the report of earnings for that year? (Remember the report goes to both the stockholder groups.) If the pooling of interests concept is valid in preserving the retained earnings balances of both companies, does this not imply that both companies' current earnings must be combined too?

8. Suppose there were some plant assets of Subordinate Company (illustration in text) carried at depreciated cost $100,000. Six months after the pooling has been effected, these plant assets are found to

be unnecessary duplications of Dominant Company's properties and they are sold for $400,000 cash to another corporation. Is this "gain" reportable in the next year's report of earnings? If it is recognized in the next year, how would this be divided among the old and new shareholders? Is this equitable, in view of the fact that Subordinate Company stockholders (5,000 of them) were not aware of the omission of this from the revaluations as negotiated?

9. What are the essential differences between a combination (by purchase or by pooling, stock or cash) and a consolidation? Illustrate by reference to the text illustration of a pooling.

10. Referring to Question 7, how would the answer be different for a consolidation (*a*) if the subsidiary were 100 percent owned and (*b*) if the subsidiary were only 80 percent owned?

11. Suppose the subsidiary were only 60 percent owned and the sale of the unneeded plant occurred in the same way as in Question 8. How would this appear in a consolidated report of earnings? Note the need for reporting minority and majority interest in your answer.

12. Describe the *logical* process of consolidating parent and subsidiary accounting statements. What is meant by elimination? Give examples of eliminations which affect only position statement items; cite the eliminations which affect only items in the earnings report as consolidated.

13. What is meant by consolidated retained earnings? Does this represent total growth in the group of companies since incorporation? Does it represent the amount that could legally be settled by payment of dividends to majority interest stockholders?

14. What are the differences between "consolidated net income" and the sum of the earnings of the constituent companies of a group? Do minority interests in income account for this?

15. What is the concept of intercompany cost, and how does it affect consolidated statements? Does this have anything to do with minority interests on the position statement (as compared to reports of the separate companies)? Does it affect the minority interest in income?

16. What are the disadvantages of consolidated statements from the viewpoint of parent company stockholders? Consider the case of a parent company which operates a chain of supermarkets but which has subsidiaries in fire, life and casualty insurance, food canning, baking and processing, wholesale and retail drug operations, and foreign operations in most of these fields. As an investor, would you be entirely happy with only a single set of consolidated reports?

PROBLEMS

Randall Corporation

Randall Corporation and Smith Company are two companies located in a midwestern city. They sell different lines of products, but they have a similar clientele and cover approximately the same territory. The owners of Smith Company have been in business for a long time; the company has been managed by a local family which has been quite conservative in management, but the company has been quite profitable. However, the present management (and most of the stockholders) are much interested in a proposal made by Randall Corporation to take over the net assets of Smith Company in exchange for 400,000 shares of Randall stock. At the current market price of $9 each, these shares represent about 3.6 million dollars. Smith shares are currently quoted at $60.

The position statements of the two companies are:

ASSETS

	Randall	Smith
Cash in bank..............................	$ 140,000	$ 950,000
Receivables...............................	450,000	730,000
Inventories...............................	580,000	980,000
Unexpired charges........................	25,000	66,500
Total Current Assets...................	$1,195,000	$2,726,500
Plant assets, net of accumulated depreciation......	1,000,000	740,000
Total Assets.......................	$2,195,000	$3,466,500

EQUITIES

	Randall	Smith
Current portion of long-term debt..............	$ 75,000	$ 40,000
Accounts payable...........................	500,000	46,500
Estimated federal taxes payable...............	100,000	200,000
Total Current Debt.....................	$ 675,000	$ 286,500
Long-term debt.............................	150,000	480,000
Total Debt..........................	$ 825,000	$ 766,500
Shareholder Equity:		
Common shares $1 par each.................	$1,270,000	$ 50,000
Retained earnings.........................	100,000	2,650,000
Total Shareholder Equity...............	$1,370,000	$2,700,000
Total Equities......................	$2,195,000	$3,466,500
Market value of inventories....................	$ 600,000	$1,300,000
Market value of plants (net)...................	$1,300,000	$1,240,000
Average earnings per share, last 5 years..........	70¢	$4.00

Required:

1. Prepare the position statement that would result if the exchange of shares were effected and the Randall shares were distributed to Smith stockholders in complete liquidation of that company:

   a) As a purchase, assets of Smith to be taken over at market values.

   b) As a pooling of interests.

2. Alternatively, suppose it is proposed to combine the two companies into an entirely new one to be known as RST Corporation, which will issue 1,000,000 shares of $1 par stock for all the shares of both companies. Present the initial position statement of RST:

    a) Treating the combination as a purchase of assets at market values.

    b) Treating the arrangement as a pooling of interests.

3. How would the shares of RST be divided among the Randall and Smith shareholders?

Boss and Slave Companies

From the data given below, prepare consolidated statements for the year:

Trial Balances, December 31	Boss Co.	Slave Co.	Together
Cost of goods sold...................	$ 420,000	$180,000	$ 600,000
Dividends paid.......................	25,000	12,000	37,000
Expenses............................	125,000	70,000	195,000
Investment in Slave Co. (95%)........	140,000		140,000
Merchandise inventory................	75,000	58,000	133,000
Other assets........................	615,000	300,000	915,000
Total (Debits)..................	$1,400,000	$620,000	$2,020,000
Dividend income, Slave shares........	$ 11,400	. . .	$ 11,400
Liabilities.........................	320,000	185,000	505,000
Sales..............................	600,000	300,000	900,000
Share investments...................	250,000	150,000	400,000
Retained earnings (deficit)..........	218,600	(15,000)	203,600
Total Credits..................	$1,400,000	$620,000	$2,020,000

Boss's investment in Slave Company is carried at cost; it was acquired when Slave Company had retained earnings of $30,000.

During the year Boss purchased goods from Slave amounting to $22,500. The initial inventory had included merchandise acquired by Boss from Slave for $4,500; the final inventory includes $3,600 of such merchandise. The Slave Company prices all of its output (including sales to Boss Company) at a uniform rate of markup. At the end of this year, Boss still owed Slave $10,000 on account of goods purchased during the year.

As an entirely separate problem, suppose that Boss acquires all of Slave's outstanding stock for $200,000, and the assets of Slave were revalued to $70,000 for inventory and $330,000 for the Other Assets. Prepare a merged position statement on a purchase basis. Ignore intercompany transactions.

As another distinct situation, suppose that Boss exchanged 2 Boss Shares for 5 shares of Slave, the market value of Boss shares being $20 and that of Slave shares, $9. Prepare a merged position statement giving effect to a pooling of interests. Ignore intercompany transactions. Compare the three situations, and comment on the results.

Parent Company

The following data are taken from the records of Parent Company and its Subsidiary company:

	Parent	Subsidiary
Common shares outstanding....................	$500,000	$ 50,000
Retained earnings 1/1/ current year............	200,000	100,000
Net income after taxes current year.............	20,000	10,000
Dividends paid, current year...................	15,000	8,000

(1) Investment of Parent in Subsidiary shares represents 90% of the issue, and it was made at a cost of $75,000, when the Subsidiary Company had Retained Earnings of $40,000.

(2) The closing inventory of the Parent Company contains goods purchased from the Subsidiary Company on which Subsidiary had booked a profit of $1,000.

(3) Parent Company income includes $7,200 of Subsidiary dividends received.

Required:

1. Compute the majority interest share of current year income and dividends:

2. Show the Proprietorship section of the Consolidated Balance Sheet as it would appear at the end of this year:

March Investment Company

The March Investment Company, obtained a controlling interest in three operating companies, viz., *A* Company, *B* Company, and *C* Company. The balance sheets of the four companies as at one year after these acquisitions are as follows:

Debits	*March Investment Company*	*A Company*	*B Company*	*C Company*
Investments in other companies:				
A Co.—60% interest (cost $900,000).............	$1,000,000			
B Co.—75% interest at cost.....	600,000			
C Co.—80% interest at cost.....	400,000			
Advances to A Company.........	100,000			
Advances to C Company.........	50,000			
Cash.........................	50,000	$ 100,000	$ 10,000	50,000
Accounts receivable.............		100,000	50,000	100,000
Inventories....................		200,000	100,000	50,000
Plant.........................		1,000,000	600,000	400,000
Deficit.......................			40,000	
Total Debits.............	$2,200,000	$1,400,000	$800,000	$600,000

Credits	March Investment Company	A Company	B Company	C Company
Capital stock..................	$2,000,000	$1,000,000	$800,000	$400,000
March Investment Company......		100,000		50,000
Retained earnings.............	200,000	300,000		150,000
Total Credits.............	$2,200,000	$1,400,000	$800,000	$600,000
Retained earnings analysis:				
Initial balance..................	$ 100,000	$ 200,000	$ 4,000	$100,000
Income:				
6 months to June 30...........		180,000	46,000	25,000
6 months to Dec. 31..........	217,500	220,000	40,000*	25,000
Increase in value of A Co. stock....	100,000			
Dividends paid in January........	217,500*	300,000*	50,000*	
Final Balances............	$ 200,000	$ 300,000	$ 40,000*	$150,000

* Debits

Other Data:

(1)   The March Investment Company has no other source of income than the dividends from the subsidiaries, which have been taken on to its books when received.

(2)   In accordance with a resolution of the Board of Directors of the March Investment Company, the following entry was made on the holding company books at the close of the year.

> Debit Investment in *A* Company............. $100,000
> Credit Retained Earnings.................... $100,000

(3)   The inventories of the *A* Company include $100,000 of goods purchased from *B* Company during the year. The cost of these goods to the *B* Company was $90,000.

(4)   In February, part of the equipment of the *B* Company carried on the books at a cost of $50,000 and Accrued Allowance for Depreciation of $40,000 was destroyed by fire. The only entry made was to credit the Plant Account with the amount of salvage recovery, $5,000.

Required:

Prepare Consolidated Reports for the group.

Popp Company and Subsidiary, Sun Company

From the following information, prepare a consolidated statement of position and a consolidated report of income and retained earnings for the year ended last December 31. Show clearly the computation of both the majority and the minority interests.

POPP CORPORATION AND SUN COMPANY
Trial Balances,
December 31, Last Year

	Popp	Sun	Together
Cash in bank..........................	$ 50,000	$ 20,000	$ 70,000
Accounts receivable (net)..............	90,000	60,000	150,000
Inventories...........................	60,000	30,000	90,000
Investment in Sun Co. (90%)..........	186,000		186,000
Other investments....................	30,000		30,000
Plant and equipment (net).............	700,000	150,000	850,000
Goodwill.............................		10,000	10,000
Cost of goods sold....................	900,000	850,000	1,750,000
Operating expenses...................	110,000	68,000	178,000
Interest charges......................	40,000	1,000	41,000
Income taxes.........................	80,000		80,000
Dividends declared....................	40,000	20,000	60,000
Totals........................	2,286,000	1,209,000	3,495,000
Accounts payable.....................	$ 40,000	$ 25,000	$ 65,000
Notes payable........................		20,000	20,000
Accrued liabilities...................	2,000	4,000	6,000
Dividends payable....................	20,000	10,000	30,000
Preferred stock, Popp................	380,000		380,000
Common stock, Popp.................	500,000		500,000
Paid-In surplus, Popp................	44,000		44,000
Retained earnings, Popp..............	90,000		90,000
Common stock, Sun Co...............		160,000	160,000
Retained earnings, Sun...............		90,000	90,000
Sales revenues.......................	1,200,000	900,000	2,100,000
Interest income......................	10,000		10,000
Totals........................	$2,286,000	$1,209,000	3,495,000

Other Data:
(1) Popp Corporation's investment in Sun Company was made several years ago, when Sun Company's common stock was $160,000 and its retained earnings were $50,000. The $186,000 is the cost of 90% of the Sun Company's outstanding shares.
(2) Dividend declared by Sun Company had neither been received nor recorded by Popp Corporation when the trial balance was taken.
(3) Sales of Popp Corporation include $100,000 sold to Sun Company. One fourth of these goods have not yet been paid for, even though Sun Company has shipped and billed their customers for those goods.
(4) Interest charges of $1,000 shown on Sun Company's trial balance was the amount paid to Popp Corporation on notes payable which have since been paid in full.

Chapter 13

PUBLISHED FINANCIAL REPORTS

In this chapter, we shall review several sets of financial reports to see how the concepts and methods of accounting are actually applied by companies in presenting their reports to the public. An attempt will be made to exhibit a representative collection of such reports for companies in different lines of business; in this way one can gain a broader view of what may be expected in reading such reports. However, it must be borne in mind that every reporting situation is to some extent unique; no two companies ever have precisely the same data to present, the same condition to deal with, or the same demands for information to be met. Financial statements are directed not only to shareholders who have current financial interest in the company but also to the whole field of potential investors who may want to know something of the company's operations. Employees, customers, creditors, competitors, and other people may have a desire to know more or less about the company's activities—its successes and failures, its position, growth, methods of financing, or other indicators of what it has achieved or may be expected to accomplish. There are financial analysts, and there are various government agencies who have specific interests in financial data to be found in corporate reports.

With such a broad audience, the reports can hardly be expected to fit any one need precisely; their general-purpose nature necessarily makes them less than entirely satisfactory for specific uses. Hence, the reports are typically accompanied by explanatory footnotes which help to bridge the gaps in the figures. Typically, a president's letter or other material accompanies the financial reports; all such supplementary information helps one to understand the necessarily condensed pattern of financial reports. Comparison of similar data for two or more successive periods, or relations observed between certain amounts, will nearly always make it easier to draw conclusions about any company's financial reports. The materials presented in this chapter will give the reader a basis for approaching the more difficult problems he will have in reading and interpreting those reports in which he has special interest.

Crown Zellerbach Corporation

The reports of this company appear in Figure 13–1. They include statements of (1) income and income retained in the business, and

FIGURE 13–1

Crown Zellerbach Corporation and Its Subsidiaries

Statements of Income
and Income Retained in the Business, and Other Capital

STATEMENTS OF INCOME	Year Ended December 31, 1968	Year Ended December 31, 1967
Income		
Net sales	$865,470,000	$788,805,000
Other Income:		
From operations	2,681,000	2,338,000
Miscellaneous, net	4,311,000	3,871,000
	872,662,000	795,014,000
Expenses		
Cost of goods sold excluding various taxes ($22,747,000 in 1968, $20,580,000 in 1967)	666,232,000	614,193,000
Selling and administrative costs	77,967,000	72,635,000
Interest on debt	11,836,000	10,828,000
Real and personal property, social security, state income and franchise, use, and occupational taxes	29,087,000	25,462,000
United States and foreign income taxes (note 2)	28,048,000	22,538,000
	813,170,000	745,656,000
Income before extraordinary items	59,492,000	49,358,000
Net gain on sale of timberlands under St. Helens' divestiture and net loss on sale of unprofitable facility, both net of related taxes of $1,973,000	5,820,000	—
Net book value of certain facilities retired during the year, net of related taxes of $2,333,000	—	(2,631,000)
NET INCOME	65,312,000	46,727,000
INCOME RETAINED IN THE BUSINESS		
Balance at the beginning of the year	317,018,000	304,936,000
	382,330,000	351,663,000
Dividends declared:		
Cash dividends:		
On $4.20 cumulative preferred stock	935,000	977,000
On common stock, $2.20 in 1968 and 1967	33,660,000	33,668,000
	34,595,000	34,645,000
Balance at the end of the year (note 8)	$347,735,000	$317,018,000
Income Per Share of Common Stock (Note 1):		
Income before extraordinary items	$3.83	$3.16
Extraordinary items, net of tax	.38	(.17)
Net income	$4.21	$2.99
OTHER CAPITAL		
Balance at the beginning of the year	$ 96,862,000	$ 96,456,000
Proceeds in excess of par value from sale of common stock under Option Plans	1,779,000	46,000
Discount on the purchase and retirement of $4.20 cumulative preferred stock	188,000	267,000
Resulting from sale of shares by a subsidiary	(17,000)	93,000
Excess of cost over net assets of merged company	(2,116,000)	—
	$ 96,696,000	$ 96,862,000

See Notes

other capital; (2) a comparative position statement (balance sheet); (3) a statement of funds; and (4) a set of footnotes and comments. The pages here are reproduced exactly as in the actual report, to preserve the references that are made.

It will be noted that all amounts are rounded to the nearest thousand-dollar figure. Obviously, more refinement in detail would add but little to the information content. Sometimes the last three

FIGURE 13–1 *(Continued)*

Crown Zellerbach Corporation and Its Subsidiaries

Balance Sheets

ASSETS	December 31, 1968	December 31, 1967
Current Assets:		
Cash	$ 21,560,000	$ 21,739,000
Short-term investments	4,449,000	2,775,000
Accounts receivable, net of allowances for losses ($2,330,000 in 1968, $2,269,000 in 1967)	98,009,000	92,013,000
Inventories at lower of cost or market	136,452,000	130,373,000
Prepaid expenses	13,551,000	13,472,000
TOTAL CURRENT ASSETS	274,021,000	260,372,000
Properties, at cost (note 2):		
Buildings, machinery, and equipment	901,622,000	870,658,000
Less allowances for depreciation	375,189,000	347,454,000
	526,433,000	523,204,000
Timberlands, pulp leases, and logging facilities, net of depletion and amortization	92,916,000	89,365,000
Intangibles, principally water power leases and licenses, net of amortization	1,688,000	1,782,000
	621,037,000	614,351,000
Other Assets:		
Investments in affiliated companies (note 3)	26,775,000	22,969,000
Other investments and receivables	15,087,000	15,349,000
Deferred charges	622,000	1,468,000
	42,484,000	39,786,000
	$937,542,000	$914,509,000
LIABILITIES		
Current Liabilities:		
Dividends payable	$ 8,438,000	$ 8,417,000
Trade accounts payable and other liabilities	73,960,000	74,216,000
Long-term debt, installments due within one year (note 4)	4,564,000	5,578,000
Accrued United States income taxes	8,568,000	8,118,000
Accrued Canadian income taxes	6,725,000	3,030,000
TOTAL CURRENT LIABILITIES	102,255,000	99,359,000
Other Liabilities and Reserves:		
Long-term debt, net of installments due within one year (note 4)	217,907,000	231,761,000
Deferred income taxes	60,785,000	57,947,000
Reserve for self-insurance	4,520,000	4,170,000
TOTAL LIABILITIES AND RESERVES	385,467,000	393,237,000
STOCKHOLDERS' EQUITY		
Minority Interest in Canadian subsidiaries	9,092,000	8,346,000
Crown Zellerbach Corporation Stockholders:		
Cumulative preferred stock (note 6):		
No par value $100 liquidation and stated value.		
Authorized 465,116 shares, issuable in series:		
Initial series $4.20 stock, at December 31, 1968 issued and outstanding 218,219 shares	21,822,000	22,528,000
Common stock (note 7):		
$5 par value. Authorized 30,000,000 shares, at December 31, 1968		
issued and outstanding 15,346,094 shares	76,730,000	76,518,000
Other capital (details on page 25)	96,696,000	96,862,000
Income retained in the business (details on page 25)	347,735,000	317,018,000
TOTAL EQUITY — CROWN ZELLERBACH CORPORATION	542,983,000	512,926,000
Total stockholders' equity including minority	552,075,000	521,272,000
	$937,542,000	$914,509,000

See Notes

digits are entirely omitted to achieve even more compactness. But the condensation goes farther than this; some items are not elaborated or explained—in this case, "Other Income" is simply two amounts added to the net sales figure. However, these total only $7.2 million —not a very important fraction of the $865 million sales figure (less than 1 percent). The notion that such relatively small items may be regarded as not material and hence left unexplained (or combined with other items) is common practice in financial reporting. This is to some extent necessary; while the reader is afforded some protection against concealment of *material* information because of the auditing activities performed by the public accounting firms in fi-

FIGURE 13–1 (*Continued*)

Crown Zellerbach Corporation and Its Subsidiaries

Statements of Source and Application of Funds

	Year Ended December 31, 1968	Year Ended December 31, 1967
SOURCE OF FUNDS		
Income (before extraordinary items)	$ 59,492,000	$ 49,358,000
Expenses which did not require current cash outlay:		
Depreciation, amortization and depletion	47,287,000	44,653,000
Net book value of assets sold or abandoned	2,425,000	2,018,000
Provision for deferred income taxes	3,792,000	5,582,000
	112,996,000	101,611,000
Cash flow from operations	10,270,000	
Net proceeds from sales of timberlands under the St. Helens' divestiture and of an unprofitable facility	1,991,000	51,000
Proceeds from sale of common stock under Option Plans	—	30,000,000
Increase in long-term debt	1,629,000	93,000
Reduction of long-term receivables	374,000	955,000
Miscellaneous, net		
	$127,260,000	$132,710,000
APPLICATION OF FUNDS		
Additions to properties	$ 62,397,000	$ 76,737,000
Dividends declared	34,595,000	34,645,000
Long-term debt paid or currently maturing (note 4)	15,192,000	5,793,000
Investments in affiliated companies (note 3)	3,806,000	7,312,000
Preferred stock redemptions (note 6)	518,000	1,096,000
Net increase in working capital	10,752,000	7,127,000
	$127,260,000	$132,710,000

See Notes

Accountants' Report

To the Board of Directors,
Crown Zellerbach Corporation,
San Francisco, California.

We have examined the consolidated financial statements (pages 25 to 29) of Crown Zellerbach Corporation and its Subsidiaries for the year ended December 31, 1968. Our examination was made in accordance with generally accepted auditing standards and accordingly included such tests of the accounting records and such other auditing procedures as we considered necessary in the circumstances. We did not examine the financial statements were examined by Canadian chartered accountants. Limited and its Subsidiaries, which statements were us. Our opinion expressed herein, insofar as it relates to amounts included and reported upon the consolidated financial statements of the company and its subsidiaries for the year ended December 31, 1967.

In our opinion, the above-mentioned financial statements present fairly the consolidated financial position of Crown Zellerbach Corporation and its Subsidiaries at December 31, 1968 and 1967 and the consolidated results of their operations and source and applica- tion of funds for the years then ended, in conformity with generally accepted accounting principles applied on a consistent basis.

Certified Public Accountants

San Francisco, California.
January 22, 1969.

nancial statement preparation, immaterial matters need not be reported in detail. The accountants' certificate, or "opinion" is typically presented with the financial reports. It has here been inset with the statement of funds (on preceding page 311) to conserve space. The accountant also has an interest in seeing that the notes provide essential information about the figures in the report; the statements make reference to the notes in this connection.

Most of the items in the Crown Zellerbach Reports are readily understandable, but some few features deserve mention. The heavy burden of taxation is often highlighted in reports; in this case, even the cost of goods sold is set out to show the tax items separately. The company does include taxes in its manufacturing cost but thinks

FIGURE 13–1 (*Concluded*)

Crown Zellerbach Corporation and Its Subsidiaries

Notes to Financial Statements
for the Year Ended December 31, 1968

1. Basis of Reporting:

The consolidated financial statements include the accounts of Crown Zellerbach Corporation and all of its majority-owned subsidiaries. The amounts included for foreign subsidiaries have been converted to U. S. dollars at appropriate rates of exchange.

Earnings per share are computed on the average number of common shares outstanding during each period.

2. Properties, Depreciation, Depletion and Taxes:

Premises at various locations are leased under long-term agreements with expirations ranging from 1972 to 2028 and, in some instances, with renewal privileges at reduced annual rentals. A subsidiary has four ships under charters which expire in 1977, 1978, 1982 and 1983. The current annual rentals and charter hire under these agreements, exclusive of property taxes and insurance, are approximately $7,834,000; this includes certain premises leased under sale-and-leaseback agreements with rentals aggregating $3,283,000.

The corporation reports depreciation for financial statement purposes on a straight-line basis over the useful lives of all depreciable assets. For federal income tax purposes, depreciation is claimed on accelerated methods and the resulting difference is reflected in the annual provision for deferred income taxes.

The 1968 provision for United States and foreign income taxes consists of:

Taxes currently payable, net of investment tax credit $6,400,000	$24,256,000
Deferred income taxes	3,792,000
	$28,048,000

Depreciation, amortization, and depletion charged to operations was $47,287,000 in 1968 and $44,653,000 in 1967.

3. Investments in Joint Ventures:

The corporation holds 50% equity in the following joint ventures:

St. Francisville Paper Company
Crown Simpson Corporation

Crown Simpson Pulp Company
  (a partnership)
Crown-Van Gelder Papierfabrieken N.V.
Crown-Van Gelder Papier S.A.
Crown-Van Gelder Plastic Film
  Industrie N.V.
Crown Carlton Paper Mills (Pty.) Ltd.
Laja Crown S.A. Papeles Especiales

reflected in the corporation's balance sheet as follows:

Equity investments	$11,202,000
Undistributed earnings	6,315,000
Long-term advances	9,258,000
	$26,775,000

The corporation's share of the earnings of these companies, $3,454,000 in 1968 and $2,354,000 in 1967, is included in miscellaneous other income, net.

4. Long-Term Debt:

Long-term debt totals $222,471,000 of which $4,564,000, maturing within one year, is included in current liabilities. Unsecured notes aggregating $213,813,000 bear interest at rates from 3¼% to 7½%; bonds secured by mortgages totaling $4,875,000 bear interest at rates of 4½% and 5%; deferred payments of Canadian severance taxes amounting to $3,783,000 bear no interest.

Retirements of long-term debt during the next five years will be as follows:

1969	$ 4,600,000
1970	8,400,000
1971	5,200,000*
1972	10,400,000
1973	8,700,000

*In addition, $60,000,000 borrowed under the revolving credit agreement is due no later than December 31, 1971, but may be repaid at any time without penalty or if not repaid will be converted to long-term debt with maturities spread over several years.

5. Pension Plans:

The corporation and its subsidiaries contributed to several pension plans covering substantially all of their eligible employees, including certain employees in foreign countries. The total pension expense for the year was $5,261,000, which includes amortization

of prior service cost. Such prior service costs are being written off over periods ranging from 17 to 30 years. The corporation policy is to fund pension cost accrued.

6. Cumulative Preferred Stock:

The Articles of Incorporation require an annual retirement fund deposit of $530,000 or, in lieu thereof, the application of purchased shares against such requirements at the rate of $102.50 a share. Current purchases of preferred stock have provided for this requirement through July 31, 1972.

There were 218,219 shares of preferred stock outstanding at December 31, 1968, as against 225,279 preferred shares outstanding at December 31, 1967.

7. Common Stock:

Common shares under option at December 31, 1968, and options exercised during the year then ended, were as follows:

Shares under option at Dec. 31, 1968	Shares issued upon exercise of options during the year	Option prices
Option Plan of May 3, 1951:		
57,051	17,988	$48.05
550	—	46.54
Option Plan of February 24, 1966:		
232,285	24,390	$46.19

All options currently granted are fully exercisable.

There were 43,325 additional shares of authorized and unissued common stock reserved for options which may be granted in the future.

There were 15,346,094 shares of common stock outstanding at December 31, 1968, as against 15,303,716 common shares outstanding at December 31, 1967.

8. Income Retained in the Business:

Dividends which can be declared from income retained in the business are restricted under the corporation's Articles of Incorporation and agreements related to long-term debt. There was $109,000,000 available for dividends over the most stringent of these restrictions at December 31, 1968.

shareholders and others should be able to see these clearly; hence the cost of goods sold is "explained" so that the tax amounts may be seen aggregated. This emphasis is also seen in the items reported "net of tax." In the present case, the extraordinary gain from the sale of investments and properties in 1968 and the underdepreciation of assets retired in 1967 are both shown net of taxes. There is also an item in the balance sheet under "Other Liabilities and Reserves" labeled "deferred income taxes." This is an important item, and it requires explanation.

In the first place, association of term "reserve" with liabilities is unfortunate because it suggests something set aside for the future. This is not really the case, for there are no specific assets involved. What is really meant is that there is an obligation which is not an actual liability in a legal sense; however, it does represent a factor which should be kept in mind in interpreting the company's position and results. A better term for "reserve" (if such reserve is not really a legal liability, which it sometimes is) would be "appropriation" or "commitment."

The deferred tax amount reflects the postponement of income taxes. Provisions in the internal revenue code and regulations allow some items to be handled on the tax return in a way which differs from the accounting treatment used for regular financial reports. An example is the use of accelerated depreciation in the tax return; the company may use declining balance, or sum-of-years'-digits depreciation for some assets under specified conditions. If the company follows the straight-line method for its reports, the use of accelerated depreciation in early years of an asset's use will decrease the tax and thus increase net income *after* tax for those years. But, since the asset depreciation cannot be more than the asset's cost, later years' depreciation must be less. The saving from acceleration is therefore regarded by most accountants as merely a postponement of taxes. But while there is no objection to the company's taking advantage of such provisions, the reported income should not be shifted by this process, to inflate early years' income by the tax postponement. Thus, the postponed tax is carried to a special long-term equity account in the early years; when in later years the tax depreciation is less (as it must be), the credit is then applied to reduce the extra tax then recognized. This leaves the reported income after taxes unaffected by the tax postponement. The deferred tax is sometimes regarded as a sort of "interest free loan" which—while not actually negotiated or paid in a literal sense—keeps funds within a business until the tax effect is worked out. But this appears to be a distortion. The only concern is that the shifting of income from tax "savings" could distort after-tax income. A great many financial reports are set up this way to include this as well as other kinds of tax postponement; usually the footnotes indicate the underlying conditions, if they are material.

The effect of deferred income taxes appears in the statement of funds; among the sources added back to net income (to establish the increase in net working capital from regular operations), the provision for deferred income taxes appears along with depreciation and the net book value of assets sold or abandoned. These items are all charges against income which did not affect net working capital. It does appear a bit anomolous that the deferral of income taxes should be a source of funds, but (as explained in Chapter 11) these are not sources but are added back only because the reduction in income resulting from such charges did *not* affect net working capital.

The funds statement also shows the proceeds from the divestiture that was mentioned as an extraordinary gain in the statement of earnings. It is a reasonable inference that the property thus disposed of was a combined net book amount of $2,477,000, but the presentation leaves open to conjecture how much was involved in the divestiture, apart from that related to the "unprofitable facility." This procedure of combining two amounts sometimes serves to omit part of the data from a report. Presumably this was not of material influence, since the accountants did not require disclosure of it. Under the regulatory influence of the Securities and Exchange Commission there is strong pressure to disclose information that would materially affect the statements, especially since the company's reports to the SEC would be required to do so.

In the statement of funds there is also a reference to the exercise of stock options. In order to give management personnel an interest in the future profitability of the company, some key personnel are granted options to purchase shares at a future time, but at a price close to the current market at the date of grant. Then, if the company is profitable and the shares rise in price, the management personnel may share in the market appreciation by exercising the options. While this does not cost the corporation itself anything (indeed, it brings in new capital when the options are exercised), the practice does dilute the equities of other stockholders by allowing the issue of these shares at lower than market prices. Shareholders seldom object to this, however; the management personnel presumably have earned their "bonus" by increasing the company's profitability and the market price of the shares. The practice of granting options to management people is widespread; it does have advantages taxwise, since the gains which managers may realize are capital gains for tax purposes.

Consumers Power Company

This is a relatively small utility company which furnishes electricity, gas, and steam-heating service to the lower peninsula of Michigan. Its reports show, however, those characteristics typical of public utility companies generally (see Figure 13–2). There is a very heavy emphasis upon plant investment, and this is why the statement of funds is oriented in both titles and content to property additions, not to changes in net working capital as in the case with most industrial-commercial firms. Indeed, public utilities (as in this case) often have "deficits" in net working capital.

Depreciation, deferred income taxes, and the investment tax credit constitute a large amount—greater than the net earnings figure in the statement of funds. The investment credit item arises from the fact that, when this report was prepared, the income tax regulations did allow a business taxpayer a credit against income taxes of 7 percent of the cost of asset acquisitions. This credit was intended as an incentive to expansion of plant; the tax reform act of 1969 removed this feature from the tax law. Although the credit was available to the taxpayer in the year of acquiring the asset, accountants viewed this in somewhat the same way as described earlier for "deferred income taxes" arising from difference between tax depreciation and that reported in published statements. The investment credit was thought by many accountants to be amortizable over the life of the asset rather than being allowed to affect the income of only one year. Since this, like the deferred income tax and depreciation, represents a charge against income which does not affect net working capital, the amount must be added back to the net earnings to state properly the working capital increase from operations in the statement of funds. These items may be seen in both the statement of funds and the report of earnings.

The report of earnings shows relatively few expense items, but taxes of all kinds are deducted in calculating net operating income. The sum of taxes, depreciation, and maintenance costs is more than a third of the total operating revenue. Income deductions, in the form of interest, take almost 30 percent of income after taxes. However, there is an item—interest charged to construction—which reduces this effect somewhat. This represents the cost of borrowing funds to finance the construction of utility plant. Since such plants represent large commitments of capital over extended time periods, the interest costs of financing are heavy. In view of the fact that rates are regulated to conform with a fair return on investment, this

FIGURE 13–2

Consumers Power Company

ARTHUR ANDERSEN & CO.

DETROIT, MICHIGAN

To the Board of Directors,
Consumers Power Company:

We have examined the balance sheet of CONSUMERS POWER COMPANY (a Michigan corporation) as of December 31, 1968, and the related statements of income, retained earnings and funds for the year then ended. Our examination was made in accordance with generally accepted auditing standards, and accordingly included such tests of the accounting records and such other auditing procedures as we considered necessary in the circumstances. We have previously examined and reported on the financial statements for the preceding year.

In our opinion, the accompanying balance sheet and statements of income, retained earnings and funds present fairly the financial position of Consumers Power Company as of December 31, 1968, and the results of its operations and source of funds for gross property additions for the year then ended, in conformity with generally accepted accounting principles applied on a basis consistent with that of the preceding year.

Detroit, Michigan,
January 31, 1969.

Arthur Andersen & Co.

STATEMENT OF SOURCE OF FUNDS FOR GROSS PROPERTY ADDITIONS   **CONSUMERS POWER COMPANY**

FOR THE YEARS ENDED DECEMBER 31, 1968 AND 1967

SOURCE OF FUNDS FOR GROSS PROPERTY ADDITIONS:		YEAR ENDED DECEMBER 31	
		1968	1967
Earnings retained in the business:	Net income after dividends on preferred stock	$ 59,009,000	$ 64,956,000
	Less—Dividends on common stock	43,137,000	43,000,000
	Total.	$ 15,872,000	$ 21,956,000
Principal noncash charges:	Depreciation, depletion and amortization	$ 53,285,000	$ 49,743,000
	Deferred income taxes	9,901,000	7,693,000
	Investment tax credit (net)	3,396,000	4,056,000
	Total.	$ 66,582,000	$ 61,492,000
Financing:	Sale of first mortgage bonds	$110,000,000	$ 80,000,000
	Increase (decrease) in notes payable	12,000,000	(16,000,000)
	Retirement of bonds and preferred stock,		
	in accordance with terms of issuance	(6,688,000)	(5,888,000)
	Total.	$115,312,000	$ 58,112,000
Other:	Change in working capital, exclusive of notes		
	payable included in financing	$ 5,862,000	$ (5,386,000)
	Other (net)	4,643,000	4,606,000
		$ 10,505,000	$ (780,000)
	Total.	$208,271,000	$140,780,000
GROSS PROPERTY ADDITIONS		$208,271,000	$140,780,000

( ) Denotes red figure.   The accompanying notes are an integral part of this statement.

financing cost is added to the utility plant costs since it may then be recovered from consumers by way of depreciation or amortization charges—a fairer way of doing this than to absorb such interest as a cost in the year of construction. This procedure is peculiar to utility companies because of the regulation of rates.

The position statement reflects the heavy plant investment; slightly

FIGURE 13–2 (*Continued*)

Consumers Power Company

STATEMENT OF INCOME

FOR THE YEARS ENDED DECEMBER 31, 1968 AND 1967

	YEAR ENDED DECEMBER 31	
	1968	1967
OPERATING REVENUE:		
Electric	$286,245,624	$270,086,001
Gas	217,681,852	205,882,426
Steam heating	1,191,514	1,213,020
Total operating revenue	$505,118,990	$477,181,447
OPERATING EXPENSES AND TAXES:		
Operation—		
Purchased and interchanged power	$ 6,793,357	$ 6,212,512
Fuel consumed in electric generation	56,128,706	52,277,328
Cost of gas sold	93,929,018	85,453,935
Other	89,834,470	86,153,994
Total operation	$246,685,551	$230,097,769
Maintenance	24,685,560	25,125,352
Depreciation and amortization (see Note 7)	48,824,702	45,380,395
General taxes	31,767,807	29,468,285
Federal income taxes	49,260,385	45,486,466
State income taxes	4,859,454	—
Provision for deferred income taxes	9,901,486	7,692,510
Charge equivalent to investment tax credit, net of amortization	3,395,805	4,055,825
Total operating expenses and taxes	$419,380,750	$387,306,602
Net operating income	$ 85,738,240	$ 89,874,845
OTHER INCOME:		
Dividends from Michigan Gas Storage Company	1,029,375	945,000
Other	1,318,981	483,370
Gross income	$ 88,086,596	$ 91,303,215
INCOME DEDUCTIONS:		
Interest on long-term debt	$ 29,043,620	$ 23,571,624
Interest on notes payable	998,123	1,360,651
Interest charged to construction—credit*	4,891,483*	2,555,367*
Other	379,677	402,809
Total income deductions	$ 25,529,937	$ 22,779,717
Net income	$ 62,556,659	$ 68,523,498
DIVIDENDS ON PREFERRED STOCK	3,548,060	3,567,016
Net income after dividends on preferred stock	$ 59,008,599	$ 64,956,482
EARNINGS PER SHARE OF COMMON STOCK		
BASED ON SHARES OUTSTANDING:		
Average during year	$2.60	$2.87
At end of year	$2.59	$2.87

The accompanying notes are an integral part of this statement.

more than 90 percent of the total assets appear as utility plant. The position statement also shows the relatively large debt which is characteristic of utility companies. It will also be noted that some assets are stated at *less* than cost; this arises in part because the utility commissions require that the rate base (the asset investment on which

FIGURE 13–2 (*Continued*)

Consumers Power Company

BALANCE SHEET

AT DECEMBER 31, 1968 AND 1967

		DECEMBER 31	
ASSETS		**1968**	1967
UTILITY PLANT:	At original cost—		
	Electric	$1,253,007,538	$1,123,385,853
	Gas	620,067,956	575,436,343
	Steam heating	4,287,566	3,980,487
	Common to all departments	46,633,978	39,213,861
		$1,923,997,038	$1,742,016,544
	Less—Provision for accrued depreciation	427,774,321	398,061,576
		$1,496,222,717	$1,343,954,968
	Cost in addition to original cost, in process of amortization . . .	85,712	134,068
		$1,496,308,429	$1,344,089,036
OTHER PHYSICAL PROPERTY:	At cost or less—less provision for accrued depreciation of $30,266 in 1968 and $109,668 in 1967	$ 2,920,831	$ 2,195,801
INVESTMENTS:	Common stock of wholly owned subsidiaries, at cost—		
	Michigan Gas Storage Company (see Note 2)	$ 16,205,186	$ 11,250,000
	Northern Michigan Exploration Company	1,500,000	525,000
	Other, at cost or less	876,795	1,112,190
		$ 18,581,981	$ 12,887,190
CURRENT ASSETS:	Cash.	$ 10,338,144	$ 8,169,336
	Accounts receivable, less reserves of $365,600 in 1968 and $351,900 in 1967	42,524,383	39,687,114
	Materials and supplies, at average cost	34,580,535	36,000,087
	Gas in underground storage, at average cost.	15,853,414	14,182,798
	Other	15,412,063	14,806,469
		$ 118,708,539	$ 112,845,804
DEFERRED DEBITS:	Portion of cost of Big Rock Point Nuclear Plant, in process of amortization	$ 3,776,044	$ 4,838,044
	Other	415,663	502,646
		$ 4,191,707	$ 5,340,690
		$1,640,711,487	$1,477,358,521

The accompanying notes are an integral part of this statement.

a fair return is to be earned) must not include more than the cost of the property when it was *first* devoted to public service. Assets acquired from predecessor or absorbed companies must therefore be recorded to separate these cost elements.

The arrangement of the position statement is unusual. It may be true that the utility company is largely a long-term investment structure, and thus it might present its long-term assets and long-term equities at the top of the position statement (in reverse order

FIGURE 13–2 (*Continued*)

Consumers Power Company

		DECEMBER 31	
LIABILITIES		1968	1967
CAPITALIZATION:	Common stockholders' equity— Common stock, authorized 25,000,000 shares, outstanding 22,768,900 shares at $10 par value in 1968 and 22,638,070 shares without par value in 1967 (see Notes 1 and 2)	$ 227,689,000	$ 410,360,158
	Capital in excess of par value (see Notes 1 and 2).	187,654,365	—
	Retained earnings, of which $5,965,035 (equal to $7.50 per share of preferred stock) is not available for payment of cash dividends on common stock	125,503,192	109,631,936
		$ 540,846,557	$ 519,992,094
	Less—Capital stock expense	3,203,150	3,130,299
	Total common stockholders' equity	$ 537,643,407	$ 516,861,795
	Preferred stock, cumulative, $100 par value, authorized 1,500,000 shares (see Notes 1 and 4)	79,533,800	79,962,581
		$ 617,177,207	$ 596,824,376
	Long-term debt (see Note 5).	714,627,900	612,015,900
	Total capitalization	$1,331,805,107	$1,208,840,276
CURRENT LIABILITIES:	Current sinking fund requirement on first mortgage bonds	$ 7,388,000	$ 6,288,000
	Notes payable	36,000,000	24,000,000
	Accounts payable	52,651,947	44,504,365
	Dividends declared on capital stock	11,702,243	11,644,564
	Accrued taxes	45,460,701	45,516,971
	Accrued interest	11,290,952	9,818,744
	Other	8,990,190	7,986,407
		$ 173,484,033	$ 149,759,051
DEFERRED CREDITS:	Investment tax credit, being amortized over life of the related property	$ 18,304,922	$ 14,909,117
	Premium less expenses on outstanding long-term debt, in process of amortization	1,387,234	900,701
	Customers' advances for construction and other	2,909,949	2,406,499
		$ 22,602,105	$ 18,216,317
RESERVES:	Deferred income taxes	$ 94,087,641	$ 84,186,155
	Other	1,937,352	2,066,713
		$ 96,024,993	$ 86,252,868
OTHER:	Contributions in Aid of Construction.	$ 16,795,249	$ 14,290,009
		$1,640,711,487	$1,477,358,521

The accompanying notes are an integral part of this statement.

to what is usually expected); but this is really a reflection of historical inertia. Industrial companies at one time presented position statements in this way, and this is to some extent carried over in this company's reports. But many utility companies now follow the more common arrangement with which the reader is more familiar; only

FIGURE 13–2 (*Concluded*)

Consumers Power Company

STATEMENT OF RETAINED EARNINGS

FOR THE YEARS ENDED DECEMBER 31, 1968 AND 1967

	YEAR ENDED DECEMBER 31	
	1968	1967
RETAINED EARNINGS—Beginning of year	$109,631,936	$180,229,317
ADD—Net income after dividends on preferred stock	59,008,599	64,956,482
	$168,640,535	$245,185,799
DEDUCT:		
Cash dividends on common stock declared in the amount of $1.90 per share in 1968 and 1967 (paid $1.90 per share in 1968 and $1.86 per share in 1967)	43,137,343	42,999,843
Transfer to common stock account representing the fair value at declaration date of 2,056,756 shares issued in connection with 10% common stock dividend . . .	—	92,554,020
RETAINED EARNINGS—End of year (see balance sheet)	$125,503,192	$109,631,936

The accompanying notes are an integral part of this statement.

NOTES TO THE FINANCIAL STATEMENTS

1 On June 6, 1968 the Company changed its state of incorporation from Maine to Michigan by the merger of the Maine corporation into a new Michigan corporation formed for that purpose. On the effective date of the merger, the shares of common and preferred capital stock of the Maine corporation (all of which were without par value) were converted into an equal number of shares of common and preferred capital stock of the Michigan corporation, with the common stock having a par value of $10 per share and the preferred stock having a par value of $100 per share. The amounts by which the common and preferred stock accounts of the Maine corporation exceeded the aggregate par value of the issued shares of common and preferred stock, respectively, of the Michigan corporation, totaling $184,007,479, are included in capital in excess of par value in the accompanying balance sheet. Other than the foregoing, there were no changes in the recorded amounts of assets, liabilities and retained earnings of the Company as a result of the merger.

2 On October 1, 1968 the Company acquired 37,500 shares of common stock (the entire minority interest) of Michigan Gas Storage Company from Panhandle Eastern Pipe Line Company in exchange for 130,830 shares of common stock of the Company. This additional investment was recorded at the approximate market value ($4,955,186) of the common stock issued of which $1,308,300, representing the par value of the shares issued, was credited to the common stock account and $3,646,886 was credited to capital in excess of par value.

3 The Company has a trusteed noncontributory pension plan under which full-time regular employees within specified age limits and periods of service are qualified to participate. The contributions to the plan of $6,749,000 in 1968 and $6,200,000 in 1967 were charged to various operating, construction and other accounts. The 1968 contribution includes current service costs, interest on unfunded prior service costs and amortization of prior service costs of $343,715. The unfunded prior service cost at July 1, 1968 amounted to $4,430,783.

	REDEMPTION PRICE PER SHARE	DECEMBER 31	
		1968	1967
4 Preferred stock is represented by:			
$4.50—547,788 shares outstanding	$110.00	$54,778,800	$54,778,800
$4.52—147,550 shares outstanding	$104.725	14,755,000	15,155,000
$4.16—100,000 shares outstanding	$103.25	10,000,000	10,000,000
Premium on preferred stock		—	28,781
Total preferred stock		$79,533,800	$79,962,581

The Company is required to endeavor to purchase and retire annually 4,000 shares of the $4.52 Preferred Stock at a price per share not to exceed $102.725 plus accrued dividends.

a few still retain the older form of presentation. However, there are two other items in the position statement which require comment. The first is the use of deferred credits as a caption to set out the investment credit, unamortized premium on bonds payable, and customer advances for construction. The distinction between this and the reserve caption which is mostly deferred income taxes is really not very clear. One other unusual item in this statement is "Contributions in Aid of Construction" which represents grants or cost sharing arrangements entered into with outside organizations such as government agencies. This is a special kind of investment equity which is permanent capital, but not shareholder equity; hence it is reported separately.

The notes to these financial statements are typical; the principal item of interest here is the fact that a fully owned subsidiary is carried as an investment, not consolidated. This is in part explained by the special nature of the subsidiary company and in part by the small size and probable immateriality of the subsidiary company's operations.

Columbus-Founders Savings and Loan Association

This set of reports (Figure 13–3) is an example of another specialized industry situation and a somewhat different kind of format. The position statement shows none of the classification of assets and equities that would be expected in industrial or commercial companies. This is because, like most other financial institutions, the savings and loan association does not have the characteristic conversion-cycle pattern that underlies the current asset classification. In the present case, the principal asset is Loans Receivable—nearly 90 percent of the asset total. The only other asset greater than 2 percent of total assets is United States Government Obligations, carried obviously to provide a ready source of funds to meet withdrawals if needed.

The equities side of the position statement shows what may appear to be a large amount of liabilities; but this is also characteristic of financial institutions which collect individuals' savings for investment. Regulatory restrictions make the shareholder equities somewhat different from commercial and industrial practice. This, plus the effects of the merger (which appear in various places in the set of reports) is the reason for the Statement of Stockholders' Equity specially prepared for this association.

FIGURE 13–3

Columbus-Founders Savings and Loan Association and Subsidiaries

Consolidated Statement of Financial Condition

December 31, 1969 with comparative figures for 1968 (Note 1).

ASSETS	1969	1968
Cash	$ 858,216	545,283
United States Government obligations, at amortized cost (Market: 1969, $8,800,000; 1968, $12,404,800)	9,924,074	12,930,401
Other investments, at cost (Market: 1969, $547,800; 1968, $64,800)	561,704	76,607
Loans receivable (Note 2)	178,396,077	169,963,826
Accrued interest receivable	697,761	704,718
Real estate acquired in settlement of loans (Note 3)	2,314,321	2,551,602
Real estate purchased for development and sale (Note 4)	3,683,020	4,383,036
Property and equipment at cost, less accumulated depreciation of: 1969, $805,642; 1968, $694,274 (Note 5)	3,050,644	2,837,224
Investment in stock of the Federal Home Loan Bank of San Francisco, at cost (Note 6)	2,807,400	2,485,000
Prepayment to Federal Savings and Loan Insurance Corporation— Secondary Reserve	3,543,118	3,151,997
Prepaid expenses and other assets	406,825	412,893
Merger settlement receivable (Notes 1 and 7)	1,336,146	798,947
	$207,579,306	200,841,534

See accompanying notes to financial statements.

FIGURE 13–3 (*Continued*)

Columbus-Founders Savings and Loan Association and Subsidiaries

LIABILITIES AND STOCKHOLDERS' EQUITY	1969	1968
Savings accounts	$156,143,546	161,842,168
Advances from Federal Home Loan Bank (Note 6)	33,088,500	21,452,500
Loans in process	518,451	778.634
Accounts payable and accrued expenses	2,051,275	2,002,267
Accrued taxes on income (Note 8)	541,472	730,979
Total Liabilities	192,343,244	186,806,548
Deferred loan fees	206,902	156,582
Interest collected in advance	87,978	162,088
Subordinated notes payable (Note 9)	4,000,000	4,000,000
Stockholders' equity: (Note 8) Capital stock $1.00 par value per share. Authorized 5,000,000 shares; issued 1,516,589 (Note 1)	1,516,589	1,516,589
Additional paid in capital	330,320	330,320
General reserves (Note 10)	7,756,028	7,267,693
Specific reserves	356	5,625
Undivided profits	1,337,889	596,089
Total Stockholders' Equity	10,941,182	9,716,316
	$207,579,306	200,841,534

See accompanying notes to financial statements.

FIGURE 13–3 (*Continued*)

Columbus-Founders Savings and Loan Association and Subsidiaries

CONSOLIDATED STATEMENT OF INCOME AND EXPENSE	Year ended December 31, 1969 with comparative figures for 1968 (Note 1)			
	1969	Per Share	1968	Per Share
INCOME:				
Interest on real estate loans	$12,499,545		11,587,006	
Loan origination fees and other fees	688,673		811,518	
Interest and dividends on investments	1,082,722		956,832	
Income (Loss) from real estate acquired for investment, net of losses of: 1969, $327,441; 1968, $107,880	(66,395)		110,469	
Other income	150,767		223,221	
	14,355,312		13,689,046	
EXPENSES:				
General and administrative expenses (Notes 5 and 11)	2,379,120		2,413,809	
Interest on savings accounts	8,130,942		8,007,545	
Interest on borrowed money	2,128,313		1,161,800	
Losses on loans and real estate acquired in settlement of loans, net	569,210		555,314	
Taxes on income (Note 8)	103,742		291,302	
	13,311,327		12,429,770	
Income from operations, combined	1,043,985		1,259,276	
Income from operations applicable to purchase portion of Guarantee and Standard Savings and Loan Associations (Note 1)			(298,951)	
Income from operations	1,043,985	0.67	960,325	0.62
Loss on sale of securities, net of related taxes of $77,322	(204,660)	(0.13)		
Income before recoveries	839,325			
Recoveries under merger agreement (Notes 1 and 7)	537,200	0.35		
Net Income	$ 1,376,525	0.89	960,325	0.62

See accompanying notes to financial statements.

FIGURE 13–3 (*Continued*)

Columbus-Founders Savings and Loan Association and Subsidiaries

CONSOLIDATED STATEMENT OF STOCKHOLDERS' EQUITY						Year ended December 31, 1969
	Capital Stock	Paid in Surplus	General Reserves	Specific Reserves	Undivided Profits	Treasury Stock
As reported, December 31, 1968						
Columbus-Founders	$1,149,000	239,600	5,348,647	5,625	602,649	170,584
Guarantee	215,000	417,300	834,391	681,324	(307,647)	
Standard	289,600	593,862	1,084,655	562,735	1,116,408	
Combined	1,653,600	1,250,762	7,267,693	1,249,684	1,411,410	170,584
Adjustment to effect merger (Note 1)	(137,011)	(920,442)		(1,244,059)	(1,813,747)	(170,584)
Reversal of Prior Years' Losses (Note 1)					998,426	
December 31, 1968, as adjusted . .	1,516,589	330,320	7,267,693	5,625	596,089	
Net income					1,376,525	
Cash dividends ($0.10 per share) . .					(151,659)	
Transfers (Note 10)			488,335	(5,269)	(483,066)	
December 31, 1969	$1,516,589	330,320	7,756,028	356	1,337,889	NONE

See accompanying notes to financial statements.

NOTES TO FINANCIAL STATEMENTS	Year ended December 31, 1969

NOTE 1: Principles of Consolidation and Related Matters

The financial statements include the accounts of the Association and its subsidiaries. On June 30, 1969, the Association acquired all the outstanding stock of Guarantee Savings and Loan Association of Yolo (Guarantee Savings) and Standard Savings and Loan Association (Standard Savings) in exchange for 422,655 shares of Association stock (of which 30,066 have been deferred for future issue) and the assumption of bank debt in an aggregate amount of $4,000,000. These associations were then merged into the Association. In accordance with the terms of the merger agreement, this transaction was effective as of December 31, 1968, and was recorded as a purchase to the extent of shares acquired for the assumption of bank debt and as a pooling of interests as to the shares exchanged.

The financial statements of the preceding year have been restated to include Guarantee Savings and Standard Savings. The statement of consolidated earnings for 1968 reflects the elimination of the net income applicable to the purchase portion of the transaction prior to the effective date of the acquisition. The statement of stockholders' equity reflects the net entries necessary to effect the merger as of December 31, 1968. The valuation allowances of Standard Savings and Guarantee Savings, established prior to merger, have been restored to

undivided profits, net of $110,936 which will be borne by the Association, as a reversal of prior years' losses.

Per share data have been computed on the basis of 1,546,655 shares which includes 30,066 "deferred shares", mentioned above.

NOTE 2: Loans Receivable

The Association's net investment in loans as of December 31, 1969, is summarized as follows:

Loan Secured by Real Estate	
Dwellings, not more than four units . . .	$138,514,086
Dwellings, over four units	27,809,195
Commercial property loans	9,200,545
Land loans	2,500,787
	178,024,613
Less allowance for losses	552,845
Total loans secured by real estate . .	177,471,768
Unsecured loans	94,200
Loans secured by savings accounts	830,109
Total loans receivable	$178,396,077

Certain of the Association's real estate loans are pledged as

(Continued on next page)

FIGURE 13–3 (*Continued*)

Columbus-Founders Savings and Loan Association and Subsidiaries

NOTES TO FINANCIAL STATEMENTS   (continued)   **Year ended December 31, 1969**

collateral for borrowings from the Federal Home Loan Bank of San Francisco as set forth in Note 6.

Included in the above summary are loans which were made to finance the sale of property formerly held for investment (Section 6705 loans) in the amount of $270,939. Such loans are secured by land or dwellings of not more than four units.

Also included in the above summary are loans made to facilitate sale of foreclosed real estate in the aggregate amount of $4,176,200. Such loans are secured primarily by single-family dwellings.

At December 31, 1969, there were 123 loans with aggregate net unpaid principal balances of $2,397,193, which were 90 days or more contractually delinquent.

It is anticipated that losses will result on the ultimate disposition of loans acquired from the merged associations, Guarantee Savings and Standard Savings; accordingly, an allowance for losses in the amount of $536,945 has been established. Any adjustments to this allowance for loss will be offset by a charge or credit to the settlements of merger (See Note 7).

NOTE 3: Real Estate Acquired in Settlement of Loans

Real estate acquired in settlement of loans is stated at net realizable value and consists of the following as of December 31, 1969:

	Number	Cost
Dwellings, not more than four units .	66	$ 740,986
Dwellings, over four units	3	244,254
Improved building lots	43	897,925
Other land	5	319,465
Commercial	5	612,305
	122	2,814,935
Allowance for losses		500,614
		$2,314,321

Of the above total, $2,016,224 represents real estate acquired from the merged associations, Standard Savings and Guarantee Savings, against which an allowance for losses of $479,294 has been established. Any adjustment of the allowance for losses will be offset by a charge or credit to the settlements of merger (See Note 7).

NOTE 4: Real Estate Purchased for Development and Sale

Real estate purchased for development and sale consists of the following as of December 31, 1969:

	Cost of Investment	Allowance for Losses	Net
Unimproved land . . .	$1,223,639	307,860	915,779
Improved building lots .	632,318	5,240	627,078
Land under development:			
By Association . . .	510,818		510,818
Under joint venture agreement . .	961,025		961,025
Office building, net of reserve for depreciation $32,000	748,320	80,000	668,320
	$4,076,120	393,100	3,683,020

Land under development by the Association represents the cost of two projects involving the construction of single-family homes.

In addition, projects are being developed under a joint venture agreement with a general contractor involving the construction of single-family homes and fourplex dwelling units whereby the Association furnishes funds and the general contractor provides construction supervision.

Of the above total, $3,282,401 was acquired as a result of the merger with Standard Savings and Guarantee Savings and against which an allowance for losses in the amount of $393,100 has been established. Any adjustments to this allowance for losses will be offset by a charge or credit to the settlements of merger (See Note 7).

NOTE 5: Property and Equipment

Property and equipment is summarized as follows:

	Cost	Estimated Useful Life
Buildings	$1,974,756	40 - 50 years
Leasehold Improvements . .	72,594	Life of Lease
Furniture and equipment . .	885,184	3 - 20 years
	2,932,534	
Less accumulated depreciation .	805,642	
	2,126,892	
Land	923,752	
	$3,050,644	

Depreciation is computed by the straight-line method. Depreciation expense for 1969 is $159,690.

NOTE 6: Advances from the Federal Home Loan Bank

The advances from the Federal Home Loan Bank of San Francisco as of December 31, 1969, are categorized as follows:

Withdrawal allowances	$22,113,863
Loan expansion advances	8,974,637
Special advances	2,000,000
Total advances	$33,088,500

The interest rate on withdrawal advances and loan expansion advances at December 31, 1969 was 7¼% per annum. The interest rate on such notes is subject to change on 15 days written notice from the Federal Home Loan Bank and was raised to 7¾%, effective March 15, 1970.

The Association has pledged 5,335 real estate loans with net principal balances of approximately $62 million and the Association's investment in stock of the Federal Home Loan Bank of San Francisco to secure these borrowings.

Withdrawal advances are obtained from the Federal Home Loan Bank to meet savings withdrawals. These notes are written as five-year, interest-only notes with special provision that principal reduction will be accomplished by applying proceeds from loan principal amortization and loan payoffs arising from the former Standard Savings' and Guarantee Savings' loan portfolios, in addition to any net savings increases arising from the operations of the Concord Branch and Woodland Branch (formerly Standard Savings and Guarantee Savings.

(Continued on next page)

FIGURE 13–3 (*Continued*)

Columbus-Founders Savings and Loan Association and Subsidiaries

NOTES TO FINANCIAL STATEMENTS (continued)

respectively). It is anticipated that principal reductions would amount to approximately $300,000 per month or $3,600,000 annually.

Loan expansion advances have scheduled maturity dates from January 6, 1970, to October 1, 1970, and are payable in quarterly installments.

Special advances of $1,000,000 each are payable on November 25, 1974, and August 25, 1974, respectively, and have stated interest rates of 8¼% and 7.8%.

NOTE 7: Merger Settlement Receivable

Under the terms of the Agreement Providing for the Merger of Guarantee Savings and Standard Savings into the Association, the net worth of the two merged associations was determined assuming 100% collectibility of all assets. To indemnify the Association against possible losses which may result from the realization of such assets, the Association was given a lien on 367,589 shares issued and deposited into escrow for a five-year period ending December 31, 1973 ("escrowed shares") and also on 30,066 shares which may be issued at that time ("deferred shares"). The former stockholders of Guarantee Savings and Standard Savings are to be charged for net losses on loans and real estate, expenses of carrying real estate, excess cost of borrowing to replace savings withdrawals, etc., and are to be given credit for differences in portfolio yields, etc. In addition, the Association will give the selling stockholders credit equal to 10% of the net losses charged to the settlement account in an aggregate amount not to exceed $200,000. These items are recorded on the books of the Association as merger settlement receivables. At the end of the five-year period, the Association will have the right to offset any receivable balance in the settlement account against the deferred shares and the escrowed shares on the basis of the then book value, or, at the option of the former stockholders of Guarantee Savings and Standard Savings, receive cash in an amount equal to the receivable balance. It is the opinion of management that the deferred shares and escrowed shares should be adequate to cover any balance due the Association at the end of the five-year escrow period.

At any time during the escrow period, escrowed stock may be withdrawn by the substitution of cash in an amount equal to the then current book value of the Association's capital stock. It is anticipated that the settlement account will be satisfied by the substitution of cash if the market value of the Association's capital stock is in excess of the book value at the time of substitution, which was the case at December 31, 1969.

The merger settlement receivable as of December 31, 1969, in the amount of $1,336,146 represents settlements for the current year as specified above in an amount of $254,779 plus an amount of $1,280,846 ($998,426 at December 31, 1968) representing allowances for estimated future losses on loans and real estate acquired from the two associations, reduced by $199,479 established as a reserve for deferred shares.

Under a separate agreement, the bank has further indemnified the Association by agreeing that if any balance due remains in the settlement account after the application of cash or cancellation of shares, such balance due may be offset against the unpaid balance of the note due the bank. (See Note 9.)

NOTE 8: Taxes on Income

Taxes on income include Federal income tax and California franchise tax.

Under the Internal Revenue Code, the Association is allowed a special bad debt deduction related to additions to tax bad debt reserves established for the purposes of absorbing losses which can be in an amount equal to the greater of 60% of taxable income before such bad debt deduction or an amount sufficient to increase the reserve for loan losses to 3% of outstanding qualifying real property loans. Through the use of the 3% method, the Association will show a net operating loss on the current Federal income tax return. The tax loss will be used in part to recover taxes paid in the three preceding years and the balance will be available to carry forward to future years.

Taxes on income which are currently payable amount to $31,000 in 1969 and $155,000 in 1968. The difference between these amounts and those reflected in the consolidated statement of income and expense represent deferred taxes arising from various timing differences in reporting items of income and expense (primarily loan fees) for financial statements versus tax returns.

The earnings of Standard and Guarantee Savings were included in the consolidated Federal income tax returns of their parent companies for the year 1968 and for the six months ended June 30, 1969, and offset in part against losses of other members of such consolidated groups. Had such associations followed the practice of filing their respective Federal tax returns on a separate basis and taking the maximum bad debt deduction allowable, they would have accrued taxes of approximately $96,000 for the six months ended June 30, 1969, and $89,000 for 1968.

Stockholders' equity includes approximately $8,570,000 which constitutes actual or anticipated additions to the bad debt reserve for income tax purposes and, therefore, may be subject to tax if removed from such status.

The Tax Reform Act of 1969 has for taxable years beginning after July 12, 1969, limited the method of computing the additions to tax bad debt reserves to a percentage of taxable income and reduces the allowable percentage from 60% to 40% ratably over the next ten years.

Tax returns of the Association for the year ended December 31, 1966, and subsequent years (as are the returns of Standard Savings for the year ended December 31, 1967 and 1968 and the six months ended June 30, 1969, and the returns of Guarantee Savings for the years ended December 31, 1966, 1967, and 1968 and the six months ended June 30, 1969) are subject to review by the taxing authorities.

Accrued taxes on income as shown on the consolidated statement of financial condition in 1969 include an estimated deferred tax liability of $731,000 and are reduced by recoverable taxes of $211,310. Accrued taxes for 1968 include a deferred tax liability of $667,000.

NOTE 9: Subordinated Notes Payable

The subordinated notes payable represent unsecured obligations of the Association and the unpaid portion thereof is subordinated to and ranked subsequent to all claims of the hold-

(Continued on next page)

FIGURE 13–3 *(Concluded)*

Columbus-Founders Savings and Loan Association and Subsidiaries

---

NOTES TO FINANCIAL STATEMENTS (continued)

---

ers of investment certificates or savings accounts and to claims of the Federal Savings and Loan Insurance Corporation and the Federal Home Loan Bank of San Francisco.

The principal amount of the notes is payable to a bank in the following manner:

No part of the principal shall become due and payable, except at the election of the Association prior to June 30, 1970. For the next five consecutive years, annual principal payments of $200,000 each shall be made. Thereafter, annual principal payments in an amount equal to 50% of the net earnings (but not less than $200,000 nor more than $400,000 in any one year) shall be made.

Upon maturity, June 30, 1980, the entire unpaid balance of principal, together with any accrued unpaid interest, shall become due and payable.

Interest is payable quarterly at the prime rate of interest charged by the bank at the beginning of the quarter, which was 8.5% at December 31, 1969.

The notes are further conditioned to the right of the Association to offset the unpaid principal balance against unsatisfied amounts due the Association in the settlement account as described more fully in Note 7. In addition, the settlement account is to be charged for all interest paid in excess of 6% per annum.

NOTE 10: General Reserves

The Rules and Regulations for Insurance of Accounts provide that, as a condition of insurance by the Federal Savings and Loan Insurance Corporation, associations are required to establish and maintain a Federal insurance reserve which is available only to cover possible losses. In this connection, the Association has designated a part of its general reserves as its Federal insurance reserve. Through December 31, 1969, the transfer requirements to the Federal insurance reserve have been satisfied as computed in the semiannual reports to the Federal Home Loan Bank Board.

NOTE 11: Retirement Income Plan

The Association has established a retirement income plan which covers substantially all of its eligible employees. Expenses of the plan amounted to $31,037 for 1969.

The Association's policy is to fund the accrued cost of the retirement plan including amortization of unfunded past service benefits. At December 31, 1969, unfunded past service benefits amounted to $91,152 which is being amortized over a ten-year period.

NOTE 12: Qualified Stock Option Plan

On February 25, 1970, the Association adopted a qualified stock option plan subject to the approval by the stockholders of the Association at the next annual meeting to be held on April 6, 1970 and the Association's obtaining a favorable tax ruling. The plan provides for the authorization of stock options not to exceed 75,000 shares of guarantee capital stock which will be granted to participants selected by a committee of the Board of Directors from among the full-time executive officers and branch managers, provided, however, that no participant be allowed to purchase more than 10,000 shares in the aggregate or own stock in excess of 5% of the total outstanding stock.

The option price shall be not less than 100% of the fair market value on the date the option is granted. No option will be exercisable for longer than five years from the date the option is granted.

NOTE 13: Compliance with Supervisory Agency Rules

The Association is subject to the rules and regulations of both Federal and state supervisory agencies. Each of these agencies performs an annual examination and requires periodic reports to determine compliance with these rules and regulations. At December 31, 1969, the Association was in compliance with the various rules and regulations in all material respects.

Accountants' Report

PEAT, MARWICK, MITCHELL & CO.

CERTIFIED PUBLIC ACCOUNTANTS

601 CALIFORNIA STREET

SAN FRANCISCO, CALIFORNIA 94108

The Board of Directors,
Columbus-Founders Savings and Loan Association:

We have examined the consolidated statement of financial condition of Columbus-Founders Savings and Loan Association and subsidiaries as of December 31, 1969 and the related statements of income and expense and of stockholders' equity for the year then ended. Our examination was made in accordance with generally accepted auditing standards, and accordingly included such tests of the accounting records and such other auditing procedures as we considered necessary in the circumstances.

In our opinion, the accompanying consolidated statement of financial condition and statements of income and expense and of stockholders' equity present fairly the financial position of Columbus-Founders Savings and Loan Association and subsidiaries at December 31, 1969 and the results of their operations for the year then ended, in conformity with generally accepted accounting principles applied on a basis consistent with that of the preceding year.

Peat, Marwick, Mitchell & Co.

March 12, 1970

While the character of the savings and loan business makes this set of reports of interest, this interest is heightened by the portrayal of the merger. The last item among the assets refers to a special arrangement for settling equities when their values are not easily determinable at the time of merger. The Statement of Income and Expense shows part of the 1968 income excluded because it was applicable to purchased rather than pooled shares. The extensive footnotes give much detail about the essentials of the merger, but they cannot be expected to tell the whole story. This was presented in the proxy statement for the stockholders' meeting of June 27, 1969, and ran to almost a hundred pages. Some idea of the complicating factors may be had from a careful reading of footnote 8 which refers to income tax issues related to these reports.

Stone & Webster, Incorporated

The position statement of this company (on page 330) indicates something of the wide range of activities encompassed by its operations. The assets do include the usual cash, accounts receivable, inventories, and such, but there are also marketable securities incident to investment banking operations, unbilled charges on construction contracts, natural gas, oil properties and other mineral interests, cold storage plant, office building and other real estate. In addition to the typical equities found on industrial or commercial balance sheets, we find here advance payments by clients, clients' funds held under construction contracts, and deferred profit on installment sales.

Slightly more than 8 percent of the outstanding common shares have been reacquired by the company. Note D indicates that 149,-600 shares were reacquired during 1969, and 111,451 shares were used to acquire two added subsidiaries. This resulted in a credit to common stock issued of $1,093,000—the amount by which market value of these shares exceeded the cost of acquiring them; but the excess of the market value of the shares over the underlying assets of these companies was $2,252,000. The acquired companies are included in the consolidation, in conformity with standard practice.

The statement of income and expense exhibits this company's long-standing practice of reporting the gross earnings of each of its major divisions. This is commendable; however, some analysts would like to see the costs reported in the same mold, to measure divisional profitability. Aside from indicating the cost of gas purchased for resale, the company does not allocate the costs to the divisions. This is well within conventional norms: there is no requirement as yet generally recognized for detailed divisional earnings in published reports.

Most of the other data in the report and in the accompanying notes are self-explanatory. There is some evidence that the company is ready for opportunities to expand if they arise. The note about

FIGURE 13-4

Stone & Webster, Incorporated and Consolidated Subsidiaries

CONSOLIDATED BALANCE SHEET

ASSETS

	December 31, 1969	December 31, 1968
Current Assets:		
Cash	$ 7,290,000	$ 7,686,000
U. S. Government Securities and Bank Certificates of Deposit	3,740,000	0,515,000
Securities incident to investment banking business, at cost .	10,817,000	16,532,000
Total based on market quotations: $10,566,000 at December 31, 1969 and $16,945,000 at December 31, 1968.		
Includes securities, carried at $6,522,000 at December 31, 1969 and $12,731,000 at December 31, 1968, pledged as collateral for bank loans.		
Accounts, Notes and Interest Receivable	37,562,000	38,238,000
Includes $29,666,000 at December 31, 1969 and $30,848,000 at December 31, 1968 incident to the investment banking business.		
Unbilled Charges under Contracts	4,104,000	3,656,000
Materials and Supplies, at cost	214,000	238,000
Total Current Assets	63,727,000	74,865,000
Clients' Funds Held under Construction Contracts (per contra) .	795,000	798,000
Investments in Unconsolidated Subsidiaries, at cost (Note A) . .	754,000	567,000
Other Investment Securities, at cost	9,600,000	9,630,000
Total based on market quotations: $77,138,000 at December 31, 1969 and $98,692,000 at December 31, 1968 (no allowance made for taxes on unrealized appreciation).		
Long-Term Receivable, less amount included under Current Assets	3,389,000	3,944,000
From sale of natural gas interest, due in varying amounts from 1971 to 1980.		
Natural Gas and Oil Properties and Other Mineral Interests . . .	11,593,000	11,630,000
At cost, less accumulated depreciation and depletion of $8,769,000 at December 31, 1969 and $8,402,000 at December 31, 1968.		
Cold Storage Plant and Equipment	5,628,000	5,520,000
At cost, less accumulated depreciation of $808,000 at December 31, 1969 and $661,000 at December 31, 1968.		
Office Building and Other Property	3,927,000	3,226,000
Building at less than cost, other property at cost, less accumulated depreciation of $4,379,000 at December 31, 1969 and $4,220,000 at December 31, 1968.		
Furniture and Equipment	1,636,000	1,300,000
At cost, less accumulated depreciation of $2,491,000 at December 31, 1969 and $2,121,000 at December 31, 1968.		
Other Assets and Deferred Charges	5,191,000	2,013,000
Includes, at December 31, 1969, $2,262,000 cost in excess of equity of firms acquired; none at December 31, 1968 (Note D).		
	$106,240,000	$113,493,000

See Notes to Financial Statements.

Treasury shares suggests that the company may continue to acquire such shares for purposes of acquisitions; but there is authorization for 2 million shares of preferred stock, and an additional 5 million common shares. Thus the directors may be in a position to move quickly to raise funds if it becomes desirable to do so. Note E gives information about the decline in one part of earnings from construction and engineering services; these amounts are swamped by the other business in that area as reported in the earnings statement. The note about stock options is of interest mostly because of the small amounts

FIGURE 13–4 (*Continued*)

Stone & Webster, Incorporated and Consolidated Subsidiaries

LIABILITIES AND STOCKHOLDERS' EQUITY

Current Liabilities:	December 31, 1969	December 31, 1968
Notes Payable (bank loans)	$ 6,138,000	$ 11,850,000
Indebtedness of investment banking subsidiary, with securities pledged as collateral.		
Accounts Payable	24,821,000	27,200,000
Includes $22,872,000 at December 31, 1969 and $25,182,000 at December 31, 1968 incident to the investment banking business.		
Dividends Declared	1,869,000	1,887,000
Advance Payments by Clients	1,827,000	1,646,000
Long-Term Debt (payments due within one year)	171,000	165,000
Accrued Federal, State and Other Taxes	2,344,000	2,422,000
Other Accrued Liabilities	3,216,000	2,832,000
Total Current Liabilities	40,386,000	48,002,000
Clients' Funds Held under Construction Contracts (per contra) .	795,000	798,000
Long-Term Debt of Commercial Cold Storage, Inc. (a subsidiary), less amount shown under Current Liabilities	1,458,000	1,629,000
Due in varying amounts from 1971 to 1978, and bearing interest at various rates.		
Deferred Profit	3,867,000	4,412,000
From sale of natural gas interest, being taken into earnings on installment basis.		
Deferred Federal Taxes on Income	1,452,000	1,318,000
Stockholders' Equity:		
Preferred Stock	—	—
Authorized, 2,000,000 shares of no par value; none issued. (Note B).		
Common Stock, carried at	7,874,000	6,778,000
Authorized, 10,000,000 shares of $1 par value; issued, 4,287,502 shares at December 31, 1969 and 4,287,402 shares at December 31, 1968, including shares held in treasury. (Notes B, C and D).		
Capital in Excess of Carrying Value of Common Stock	8,927,000	8,927,000
Retained Earnings	53,467,000	50,858,000
	70,268,000	66,563,000
Less Common Stock in Treasury, at cost	11,986,000	9,229,000
352,715 shares at December 31, 1969 and 314,556 shares at December 31, 1968. (Note D).		
Total Stockholders' Equity	58,282,000	57,334,000
	$106,240,000	$113,493,000

involved, and the fact that all options expire sometime in early 1970. There are data to indicate that the company is amortizing past service credits for pensions over a 20-year period, and that the contributions to the trustee have been increased in the past year. The note concerning leases merely states the aggregate annual rentals and indicates the term of the longest lease to be 25 years from the end of 1969.

FIGURE 13–4 (*Continued*)

Stone & Webster, Incorporated and Consolidated Subsidiaries

CONSOLIDATED STATEMENT OF INCOME AND RETAINED EARNINGS

	Year Ended December 31, 1969	Year Ended December 31, 1968
Gross Earnings:		
Engineering and construction services (Note E)	$25,258,000	$21,232,000
Consulting and other services	4,006,000	1,719,000
Securities underwriting and trading, and other income incident to investment banking business	10,928,000	7,361,000
Natural gas and oil sales, profit and other income from mineral interests	9,929,000	9,501,000
Cold storage and related activities	1,611,000	1,438,000
Dividends and interest	5,499,000	5,566,000
Includes dividends from unconsolidated subsidiaries (foreign): $606,000 in 1969 and $631,000 in 1968.		
Profits on investment securities	218,000	660,000
Rents	1,278,000	1,240,000
Other	13,000	8,000
Total	59,420,000	51,725,000
Operating and General Expenses	39,244,000	32,152,000
Includes cost of gas purchased for resale of $5,905,000 in 1969 and $5,535,000 in 1968.		
Provision for Federal Taxes on Income	5,550,000	4,884,000
Other Taxes	2,492,000	2,450,000
Provision for Depreciation and Depletion (Note F)	1,294,000	1,219,000
Interest and Amortization of Debt Expense	708,000	464,000
Total	49,288,000	41,169,000
Net Income (per share*: $2.55 in 1969; $2.63 in 1968)	10,132,000	10,556,000
Retained Earnings at beginning of year	50,858,000	47,619,000
Total	60,990,000	58,175,000
Dividends Declared	7,523,000	7,317,000
Per share:		
1969: 47½¢ each paid on May 1, August 1 and November 1, 1969; 47½¢ payable on February 2, 1970.		
1968: 45¢ each paid on May 1, August 1 and November 1, 1968; 47½¢ paid on February 1, 1969.		
Retained Earnings at end of year	$53,467,000	$50,858,000

* *Per share figures based on average number of shares outstanding during each period.*

See Notes to Financial Statements.

This is typical disclosure; the capitalization of leaseholds is not yet a widespread practice. The final note concerning pending litigation is a reassurance rather than factual information, but this is as it must be.

The reader will have noted that this set of reports does not include a statement of funds. This is a little unusual, for a great many companies are including the statement of funds as a part of the report.

FIGURE 13–4 (*Concluded*)

Stone & Webster, Incorporated and Consolidated Subsidiaries

NOTES TO FINANCIAL STATEMENTS

(A) The consolidated financial statements include the accounts of subsidiaries of Stone & Webster, Incorporated, other than foreign subsidiaries and certain subsidiaries organized for foreign activities. The net assets applicable to the investments in the unconsolidated subsidiaries, as shown by their balance sheets, exceeded the aggregate amount at which such investments are carried by approximately $1,650,000 at December 31, 1969 ($1,095,000 at December 31, 1968), based on appropriate rates of exchange where foreign currencies are involved. Such excess represents undistributed earnings of the unconsolidated subsidiaries since acquisition.

(B) At the Annual Meeting on May 8, 1969, the stockholders approved the amendment of the Corporation's Certificate of Incorporation to increase the authorized capital stock from 5,000,000 shares, $1 par value per share (all of which was, prior to such date, designated as "Capital Stock") to 12,000,000 shares consisting of: (a) 2,000,000 shares of Preferred Stock, without par value, to be issuable in series and having such terms as shall be fixed by the Board of Directors; and (b) 10,000,000 shares of Common Stock, $1 par value per share, with each of the previously authorized 5,000,000 shares of Capital Stock to be automatically changed into one share of Common Stock authorized by such amendment.

(C) Under the Stock Option Plan for certain officers and employees of the Corporation and its subsidiaries which was approved by the stockholders in 1958, the period for granting options expired in 1965. During 1969 an option previously granted in respect of 100 shares was exercised at $33.25 per share. At the year-end, options covering 3,800 shares were outstanding at a price of $33.25 per share as compared with outstanding options covering 3,900 shares at the beginning of the year at $33.25 per share. All of the options outstanding at the year-end expire April 21, 1970.

(D) The Corporation purchased 149,600 shares of its Common Stock for a total cost of $6,262,489 in 1969 and 86,924 shares at a cost of $3,460,394 in 1968 which were added to its holdings of Treasury Stock. During 1969 a total of 111,451 shares of Treasury Stock was issued in connection with the acquisition of two firms in the investment banking business. The excess of the market value of the shares issued over the equity of the businesses acquired, $2,252,000, is included in Other Assets and Deferred Charges. Common Stock has been credited with $1,093,000, representing the excess of the market

value of the Treasury Stock issued over the related cost thereof. The Corporation has continued and may continue, from time to time, to purchase additional shares of its Common Stock, for possible acquisitions, use in employee savings plan, and for other corporate purposes, on the New York Stock Exchange, or otherwise.

(E) Gross earnings from engineering and construction services include, generally on a percentage of completion basis, fees earned on agency contracts and the excess of revenues ($5,142,000 in 1969 and $14,654,000 in 1968) over direct construction costs ($3,160,000 in 1969 and $11,308,000 in 1968) on non-agency contracts. Such revenues and costs are exclusive of expenditures made directly by clients.

(F) Depreciation generally is provided on a straight-line basis at rates adequate to depreciate the applicable assets over their estimated useful lives. Depreciation expense for 1969 was $1,084,000 and $1,020,000 for 1968. At December 31, 1969 depreciable assets were carried at $15,986,000 after deducting accumulated depreciation.

(G) The Corporation and its principal subsidiaries, the accounts of which are included in the consolidated financial statements, have a retirement plan covering executive, administrative, technical and clerical employees. The Plan was amended in 1969, effective in 1970, so as to improve generally the relationship between retirement benefits and salary. Total retirement expense for 1969 was $1,344,000, as compared with $1,213,000 for 1968. Said amounts include amortization for the respective years of the unfunded balance of prior service cost as of January 1, 1967 over a period of 20 years. Contributions to the trust fund under the plan totaled $1,294,000 in 1969 and $1,213,000 in 1968. It is estimated that retirement expense in 1970 will approximate $1,500,000.

(H) Subsidiary companies are committed for annual rentals approximating $1,600,000 under long-term leases, the longest of which extends to 1995.

(I) Stone & Webster Engineering Corporation, a subsidiary, has been named a defendant, along with others, in legal actions claiming damages in connection with construction projects. Counsel and management believe, on the basis of their examination and consideration of these matters, that these actions will not result in payment of amounts which would have a material effect on the financial statements.

REPORT OF CERTIFIED PUBLIC ACCOUNTANTS

To the Board of Directors of
Stone & Webster, Incorporated:

We have examined the consolidated balance sheet of Stone & Webster, Incorporated and Consolidated Subsidiaries as of December 31, 1969 and the related consolidated statement of income and retained earnings for the year then ended. Our examination was made in accordance with generally accepted auditing standards, and accordingly included such tests of the accounting records and such other auditing procedures as we considered necessary in the circumstances. We previously examined and reported upon the consolidated financial statements of the Corporation for the year 1968.

In our opinion, the aforementioned financial statements present fairly the consolidated financial position of Stone & Webster, Incorporated and Consolidated Subsidiaries at December 31, 1969 and 1968, and the results of their operations for the years then ended, in conformity with generally accepted accounting principles applied on a consistent basis.

LYBRAND, ROSS BROS. & MONTGOMERY

New York, February 17, 1970

But this is not mandatory, and the company evidently views the statement of funds as unnecessary, on the ground that the major fund flows are adequately reflected in the statement of income and the appended notes.

R. H. Macy and Co., Inc.

This set of statements (Figure 13–5) has a number of interesting features. The statement of earnings covers a 52-week year, ending August 2, 1969; but August 3, 1968, closed a 53-week year. This is necessary because the company uses a full number of weeks in a year; since the calendar actually contains 2¼ days more than 52 weeks, it is necessary once in a while to use a long year to keep the closing date somewhere near the end of July. A 52-week year lends itself easily to division into quarters (13 weeks each) or into 4-week periods for internal reporting. In some businesses the days of the week are quite different in significance; a year with a fractional week at the end may be quite different from another one with a different fraction. This calendar pattern is not common practice; but it is used by a fair number of companies.

The expense data for Macy's are highly condensed. Taxes (other than income taxes), rent, depreciation, and maintenance repairs are the only separate items; cost of goods sold and all other expenses are combined. This is no doubt done to avoid showing gross merchandise profit margins. However, a bit more detail appears in the notes. Income from retail operations is separated from "nontrading" sources. Federal income taxes (in 1969, more than 50 percent of before-tax income) are explained by a footnote which gives details of deferred tax transactions.

The other interesting feature of this report is the presentation of "diluted" earnings per share. This is explained in the notes, but it may be observed that this is the result of action by the American Institute of CPAs (which was mentioned in Chapter 12) to require such treatment for convertible securities which may have a claim on common stock equity. The effect in the present case is not large, but it is required to be handled in this way.

Macy sets up the retained earnings data in a separate report. This serves to emphasize current year figures and to separate dividends from the earnings report. There is also a prior year correction item with respect to Lifo inventory procedure. This is to some extent

FIGURE 13–5

R. H. Macy & Co., Inc., and Consolidated Subsidiaries

CONSOLIDATED STATEMENT OF EARNINGS

	Fiscal year ended	
	August 2, 1969 (52 weeks)	August 3, 1968 (53 weeks)
Net Retail Sales (including licensed departments)	$878,479,652	$824,812,625
Costs and Expenses of Retail Operations:		
Cost of goods sold and expenses,* exclusive of items listed below	762,802,287	720,126,302
Taxes, except Federal income taxes	21,467,617	18,703,953
Rent expense — net	14,649,510	14,510,567
Depreciation (straight-line method)	12,702,677	11,479,256
Maintenance and repairs	6,769,564	6,923,472
	818,391,655	771,743,550
Income from Retail Operations	60,087,997	53,069,075
Income from non-trading sources — net	2,427,263	2,104,380
	62,515,260	55,173,455
Interest expense, less interest income of $1,358,277 and $1,813,200	13,714,576	11,886,817
Earnings before Federal Income Taxes	48,800,684	43,286,638
Federal Income Taxes (Note 3)	24,435,000	21,326,000
Net Earnings	$ 24,365,684	$ 21,960,638
Primary Earnings per Share (Note 1)	$2.53	$2.32
Fully Diluted Earnings per Share (Note 1)	$2.29	$2.09

CONSOLIDATED EARNINGS REINVESTED IN THE BUSINESS

	Fiscal year ended	
	August 2, 1969 (52 weeks)	August 3, 1968 (53 weeks)
Balance, beginning of year	$116,177,641	$103,157,193
Net earnings for the year	24,365,684	21,960,638
Amounts applicable to prior years resulting from change in inventory basis	114,033	24,481
	140,657,358	125,142,312
Cash Dividends Declared:		
Cumulative preferred shares, 4¼% Series A	678,342	678,342
Cumulative preferred shares, 4% Series B	400,000	400,000
Common shares —		
$0.20 per share quarterly	—	1,789,528
$0.22½ per share quarterly	2,056,625	6,096,801
$0.25 per share quarterly	6,911,904	—
	10,046,871	8,964,671
Balance, end of year	$130,610,487	$116,177,641

See notes to financial statements

* The following note appeared in the 1967 reports:

The Corporation has heretofore stated its merchandise inventories at Lifo (last-in, first-out) cost, as determined by the retail inventory method, using 1941 as the base year. That Lifo basis, however, had not been allowed to the Corporation for income tax purposes. As of the beginning of the year ended July 29, 1967, the Corporation decided (1) to adopt the Lifo method for Federal income tax purposes for about 40% of the total inventory using 1966 as the base year, and (2) to use the lower of Fifo (first-in, first-out) cost or market, as determined by the retail inventory method, for the balance of the inventory. To conform to the tax basis, the Corporation has revised the computations for financial statement purposes to use 1966 as the base year, rather than 1941, for those inventories which continue to be stated at Lifo cost. The change in the Lifo base year for a portion of the inventory plus the change to a Fifo basis for the balance, resulted in an increase of $15,831,000 in the inventory as of the beginning of the year ended July 29, 1967. That amount, less all applicable income taxes of $7,989,000, has added $7,842,000 to earnings reinvested in the business. The changes referred to above did not materially affect the net earnings for the year ended July 29, 1967.

That portion of the inventory on the Lifo basis as of July 29, 1967, is approximately at the lower of Fifo cost or market, as determined by the retail inventory method.

FIGURE 13–5 (*Continued*)

R. H. Macy & Co., Inc., and Consolidated Subsidiaries

**CONSOLIDATED
STATEMENT OF
FINANCIAL CONDITION**

ASSETS

	August 2, 1969	August 3, 1968
Current Assets:		
Cash	$ 25,698,723	$ 20,354,850
Marketable securities, at amortized cost (approximate market)	19,599,097	41,956,151
Customers' accounts receivable, per statement	68,499,784	62,060,029
Other receivables	8,417,606	8,358,950
Merchandise inventories (Note 2)	120,500,825	105,530,176
Prepaid expenses and supplies	8,387,224	7,905,847
Total current assets	251,103,259	246,166,003
Other Assets:		
Investment in Macy Credit Corp., at equity, per statement	23,299,497	21,354,066
Investments in and advances to affiliated shopping centers	7,933,223	1,949,209
Miscellaneous, including unamortized deferred charges of $3,873,416 and $3,418,256	6,972,267	7,664,978
	38,204,987	30,968,253
Property and Equipment:		
Land	36,751,924	36,415,329
Buildings and improvements on owned properties	100,367,725	93,277,634
Buildings and improvements on leased properties and leaseholds	58,153,193	57,780,964
Fixtures and equipment	100,488,251	93,829,874
Construction in progress	21,140,175	12,666,779
	316,901,268	293,970,580
Accumulated depreciation	75,461,135	72,664,483
	241,440,133	221,306,097
Goodwill and Other Intangible Assets — at cost, less accumulated amortization of $2,119,681 and $2,036,365	571,629	654,945
	$531,320,008	$499,095,298

See notes to financial statements

FIGURE 13–5 (*Continued*)

R. H. Macy & Co., Inc., and Consolidated Subsidiaries

LIABILITIES AND INVESTMENT OF SHAREHOLDERS

	August 2, 1969	August 3, 1968
Current Liabilities:		
Accounts payable and accrued liabilities	$ 93,869,725	$ 81,008,816
Federal income taxes (Note 3)		
Current	4,801,498	4,647,143
Deferred	32,216,746	28,735,739
Long-term debt due within one year	4,407,809	4,661,114
Total current liabilities	135,295,778	119,052,812
Deferred Credits:		
Deferred Federal and state taxes (Note 3)	28,483,534	24,091,677
Deferred investment credit ($5,052,652 and $4,401,074) and unamortized capital gains on sales and leasebacks	8,150,543	7,599,978
Deferred contingent compensation and pension funding (Note 3)	3,808,611	4,674,364
	40,442,688	36,366,019
Long-Term Debt, due after one year, per statement		
R. H. Macy & Co., Inc.	52,803,482	57,644,783
Real estate subsidiaries	82,909,437	85,939,687
	135,712,919	143,584,470
Investment of Shareholders:		
Cumulative preferred shares, 500,000 authorized; par value $100 each—		
4¼% Series A—165,600 shares issued; 5,990 in treasury; 159,610 outstanding, callable at $107.50 each	15,961,000	15,961,000
4% Series B—100,000 shares issued and outstanding; annual sinking fund payments of 20% from 1971 to 1975	10,000,000	10,000,000
Preference shares, $5.00 par value per share— 1,000,000 authorized and unissued	—	—
Common shares, $0.25 par value, assigned value $3.75 per share — 20,000,000 authorized; 9,342,777 and 9,132,291 issued; 15,756 in treasury; leaving 9,327,021 and 9,116,535 outstanding (Notes 4 and 5)	34,976,329	34,187,006
Additional paid-in capital, per statement	28,320,807	23,766,350
Earnings reinvested in the business, per statement at August 2, 1969, $78,100,000 is not distributable to common shareholders under terms of long-term debt agreements	130,610,487	116,177,641
Total investment of shareholders	219,868,623	200,091,997
	$531,320,008	$499,095,298

FIGURE 13–5 *(Continued)*

R. H. Macy & Co., Inc., and Consolidated Subsidiaries

		August 2, 1969	August 3, 1968
CONSOLIDATED CUSTOMERS' ACCOUNTS RECEIVABLE	Total customers' receivables — principally deferred payment accounts	$218,394,709	$200,047,385
	Deduct accounts sold without recourse (net of Corporation's equity) and unremitted collections thereon to be applied against accounts contracted to be sold	144,409,925	132,623,356
		73,984,784	67,424,029
	Less estimated uncollectible amounts	5,485,000	5,364,000
	Customers' accounts — net	$ 68,499,784	$ 62,060,029

		August 2, 1969	August 3, 1968
CONSOLIDATED LONG-TERM DEBT (Amounts due within one year included in current liabilities)	**R. H. Macy & Co., Inc.:**		
	Twenty-Five Year 2⅞% Sinking Fund Debentures, due November 1972; annual sinking fund of $800,000	$ 7,600,000	$ 8,400,000
	3¾% Promissory Notes, $750,000 due annually, balance due January 1973	6,000,000	6,750,000
	5% Convertible Subordinated Debentures, due November 1992; annual sinking fund of $875,000 from 1978 (Note 4)	22,341,600	22,357,900
	4¼% Convertible Subordinated Debentures, due June 1990; annual sinking fund of $863,000 from 1983 (Note 4)	15,027,900	18,832,600
	5% Convertible Subordinated Debentures, due February 1977 (Note 4)	411,100	447,600
	Other long-term debt	1,422,882	856,683
		52,803,482	57,644,783
	Real Estate Subsidiaries:		
	Mortgage and other secured notes (Note 6)	82,389,102	85,046,346
	Other long-term debt	520,335	893,341
		82,909,437	85,939,687
		$135,712,919	$143,584,470

See notes to financial statements

FIGURE 13–5 (*Continued*)

R. H. Macy & Co., Inc., and Consolidated Subsidiaries

		Fiscal year ended	
		August 2, 1969 (52 weeks)	August 3, 1968 (53 weeks)
CONSOLIDATED ADDITIONAL PAID-IN CAPITAL	**Balance,** beginning of year	$23,766,350	$22,254,042
	**Reversal of inferred debt discount attributable to the conversion feature of convertible debentures	—	(2,185,280)
	Proceeds received over assigned value of 78,699 and 70,534 common shares issued under options	1,255,155	1,028,425
	Credit from conversions of debentures into 131,787 and 115,149 common shares	3,299,302	2,669,163
	Balance, end of year	$28,320,807	$23,766,350

		Fiscal year ended	
		August 2, 1969 (52 weeks)	August 3, 1968 (53 weeks)
CONSOLIDATED STATEMENT OF SOURCE AND APPLICATION OF FUNDS	**Source of Funds:**		
	Net earnings	$24,365,684	$21,960,638
	Non-cash items —		
	Depreciation*	13,249,228	11,998,784
	Increase in deferred Federal and state taxes	4,391,857	2,876,776
	Other	371,706	1,747,529
		42,378,475	38,583,727
	Additions to long-term debt	540,000	33,728,255
	Sales of property	1,221,411	3,278,823
	Proceeds from sales of common shares under options	1,550,277	1,292,928
	Miscellaneous — net	315,337	621,929
	Decrease (increase) in working capital	11,305,710	(24,613,563)
		$57,311,210	$52,892,099
	Application of Funds:		
	Additions to property (including investments in and advances to affiliated shopping centers)	$40,764,857	$37,492,741
	Dividends on common and preferred shares	10,046,871	8,964,671
	Reduction in previously existing long-term debt†	4,554,051	4,680,498
	Increase in equity in Macy Credit Corp.	1,945,431	1,754,189
		$57,311,210	$52,892,099

* Includes $546,551 and $519,528 of shopping center subsidiaries' depreciation charged to Income from non-trading sources in the Consolidated Statement of Earnings.

† Excludes conversions of debentures.

See notes to financial statements

** The previous year's reports included the following note:

The inferred value attributable to the conversion feature of convertible debt issued in July 1965 was accounted for in the year ended July 29, 1967 in accordance with an opinion issued in December 1966 by the Accounting Principles Board of the American Institute of C.P.A.'s. That board has recently proposed to reverse its opinion and the Internal Revenue Service has also recently proposed that the amortization of such inferred value would not be deductible. Accordingly, the Corporation has reversed the inferred value previously recorded.

NOTES TO FINANCIAL STATEMENTS

1 Primary earnings per share were computed by dividing net earnings, less dividends on preferred shares, by the weighted average number of common shares outstanding during the year. Fully diluted earnings per share assume full conversion of debentures and exercise of stock options at the beginning of the year (or later date of issuance).

2 Merchandise inventories are determined by the retail inventory method, using Lifo (last-in, first-out) cost for about 48% (at August 2, 1969) of the total inventory, and the lower of Fifo (first-in, first-out) cost or market for the balance of the inventory. That portion of the inventory on the Lifo basis as of August 2, 1969 is stated at $2,173,346 less than it would have been if the Fifo basis had been used.

3 Federal income taxes for fiscal years through July 31, 1965 have been settled; tax returns for later years are subject to audit by the Internal Revenue Service.

Federal income tax provisions for the fiscal years 1969 and 1968 include deferred taxes of $5,694,000 and $5,334,500, respectively. Such deferred Federal income taxes result primarily from the use, for tax purposes, of accelerated depreciation methods and of the installment method of accounting for deferred payment sales. The portion thereof resulting from the latter is included with current liabilities. Federal income tax provisions have been reduced by $490,000 and $370,000 for the fiscal years 1969 and 1968, respectively, for amortization of accumulated investment credits over the useful lives of the related equipment.

As now required, taxes previously deducted from deferred contingent compensation and pension funding have been included in deferred taxes. Figures at August 3, 1968 have been restated to be comparable.

4 The conversion prices of the three issues of outstanding convertible subordinated debentures and the number of common shares reserved at August 2, 1969 for such conversions are as follows:

	Conversion price	Number of shares reserved
5%, due 1977	$ 8.00	51,388
4¼%, due 1990	30.00	500,931
5%, due 1992	36.00	620,600
		1,172,919

5 The Corporation's Employee Stock Option Plans provide, as to grants prior to January 1, 1964, for 10-year options exercisable in nine installments and, as to grants after that date, for 5-year options exercisable in four installments, commencing, in each instance, 18 months from grant dates.

The changes during the year in the number of shares subject to outstanding options were as follows:

Outstanding at August 3, 1968	491,346
Granted ($31.50 to $39.25 per share)	31,000
Exercised ($9.41 to $26.75 per share)	(78,699)
Canceled	(22,950)
Outstanding at August 2, 1969	420,697
Exercisable at August 2, 1969	157,997

Options outstanding at the year-end are exercisable

at $10.31 to $39.25 per share, representing 100% of market price on dates of grant.

Unoptioned shares available for issuance under the Plans were:

August 3, 1968	298,800
August 2, 1969	290,750

6 Approximately $3,000,000 of the mortgage and other secured notes of the real estate subsidiaries at August 2, 1969 is payable annually for the next five years, and the balance through 1998. This indebtedness bears interest at the following rates: 3%, $1,669,217; 4⅛%–4⅞%, $16,969,667; 5%–5⅞%, $49,441,159; 6%–6¾%, $14,309,059.

7 The Corporation has non-contributory pension plans covering substantially all employees. For the year ended August 2, 1969, the total pension expense was $3,715,238, which included current service costs and provision for prior service costs (being amortized over a 20-year period). At the year-end, the total liability for prior service was $12,418,235.

The retirement system for employees, which includes all pension plans and the profit sharing plan, had net assets of $65,323,000 at July 31, 1969. The assets of the pension plans at that date exceeded the actuarially computed value of vested benefits.

8 Costs and expenses of retail operations are reported to the Securities and Exchange Commission in accordance with its requirements as follows:

	Fiscal year ended	
	August 2, 1969 (52 weeks)	August 3, 1968 (53 weeks)
Cost of goods sold, including occupancy and buying costs	$650,702,300	$613,146,836
Selling, publicity, general, and administrative expenses	162,115,073	153,675,841
Provision for doubtful accounts	5,574,282	4,920,873
	$818,391,655	$771,743,550

9 The earnings before Federal income taxes of Macy Credit Corp. represent intercompany profits ($4,122,431 and $3,564,189 for 1969 and 1968, respectively) and are applied in consolidation to reduce the related intercompany interest expense. Such subsidiary's Federal income taxes are included in consolidated Federal income taxes; accordingly, its net earnings of $1,945,431 and $1,754,189 for 1969 and 1968, respectively, are included in consolidated net earnings for the respective periods.

10 Under leases of more than three years from August 2, 1969, average minimum annual rentals on a consolidated basis by five-year periods for the succeeding 20 years are approximately $12,500,000 in 1970-1974, $10,900,000 in 1975-1979, $9,400,000 in 1980-1984, and $8,300,000 in 1985-1989. In addition, in certain instances, there are payable real estate and personal property taxes, other expenses, and additional amounts based on percentages of sales. The leases provide for varying lease periods, including renewal privileges up to 2084. Taxes incurred under leases are included with other taxes in the statement of earnings.

FIGURE 13–5 (*Continued*)

R. H. Macy & Co., Inc., and Consolidated Subsidiaries

MACY CREDIT CORP. —
STATEMENT OF
FINANCIAL CONDITION

ASSETS

	August 2, 1969	August 3, 1968
Current Assets:		
Cash	$ 619,617	$ 672,306
Customers' deferred payment accounts of R. H. Macy & Co., Inc., purchased without recourse, less estimated uncollectible amounts of $1,620,597 and $1,447,117	160,439,122	143,264,606
Prepaid expenses and other assets	824,949	448,160
Total current assets	161,883,688	144,385,072
Unamortized Debt Expense	314,390	337,140
	$162,198,078	$144,722,212

LIABILITIES AND INVESTMENT OF R. H. MACY & CO., INC.

Current Liabilities:		
Notes payable	$ 96,011,000	$ 82,190,000
Portion of purchase price of customers' deferred payment accounts withheld pending collection, less allowance for estimated uncollectible amounts shown above	14,585,375	13,024,055
Accrued interest and other liabilities	802,206	654,091
Total current liabilities	111,398,581	95,868,146
Long-Term Debt:		
4¾% Debentures, due November 1981	20,000,000	20,000,000
4⅞% Subordinated Debentures, due June 1985	7,500,000	7,500,000
	27,500,000	27,500,000
Investment of R. H. Macy & Co., Inc.:		
Capital stock, $100 par value — 200,000 shares authorized; 100,000 shares issued and outstanding	10,000,000	10,000,000
Earnings reinvested —		
Balance, beginning of year	11,354,066	9,599,877
Net earnings	1,945,431	1,754,189
Balance, end of year	13,299,497	11,354,066
Total investment	23,299,497	21,354,066
	$162,198,078	$144,722,212

NOTE:

Under the 4¾% Debentures Indenture, Macy Credit Corp. may not declare dividends or acquire its capital stock if, after giving effect to such transactions, current assets (as defined) are not at least equal to 120% of total liabilities (as defined). At August 2, 1969, earnings were not restricted under these provisions.

FIGURE 13–5 (*Concluded*)

R. H. Macy & Co., Inc., and Consolidated Subsidiaries

INDEPENDENT
AUDITORS'
REPORT

To the Board of Directors and Shareholders of R. H. Macy & Co., Inc.:

We have examined the consolidated statement of financial condition of R. H. Macy & Co., Inc. and consolidated subsidiaries as of August 2, 1969, and the related statements of earnings, earnings reinvested in the business and source and application of funds for the fiscal year (52 weeks) then ended. We have also examined the statement of financial condition of Macy Credit Corp. as of August 2, 1969. Our examinations were made in accordance with generally accepted auditing standards, and accordingly included such tests of the accounting records and such other auditing procedures as we considered necessary in the circumstances.

In our opinion, the financial statements referred to above present fairly the consolidated financial position of R. H. Macy & Co., Inc. and consolidated subsidiaries at August 2, 1969, and the consolidated results of their operations and the source and application of funds for the fiscal year (52 weeks) then ended, as well as the financial position of Macy Credit Corp. at August 2, 1969, in conformity with generally accepted accounting principles applied on a basis consistent with that of the preceding year.

Touche Ross & Co.

Certified Public Accountants

80 Pine Street, New York, N.Y. 10005
September 30, 1969

clarified by the notes of the 1967 report, which are reproduced on page 335. (Lifo will be considered in Chapter 14.)

The position statement is not too unusual in form and arrangement, but it does call attention to the presence in the organization of Macy Credit Corporation. This subsidiary company (not consolidated, but reported on an "equity" accounting basis) holds some of R. H. Macy's deferred payment accounts, operating as a finance company. Details of customer accounts are given in a separate schedule, and the entire statement of position for the Credit Corporation (including the net earnings figure for 1969) are reported in a separate tabulation on page 341.

Along with the analysis of customer receivables (page 338) is a detailed statement of outstanding long-term debt which shows interest rates and maturity dates. The long-term debt schedule calls attention to note 4 which gives details as to conversion features; these we noted in the computation of "diluted earnings per share" in the report of earnings.

The statement of funds is conventional; perhaps the only comment called for is to note the handling of a "decrease in net working capital" as a source of funds. This requires a negative amount in the comparative figure for 1968, which was an *increase* in net working capital, here shown as a "red" item. No particular significance need be attached to this, except that a careless reader might think the working capital position was *improved* in 1969 simply because of the arrangement of items. (See page 339).

The rest of the material in the 1969 Macy report is self-explanatory. Some of the complexity of this set of financial data arises from the nature of the enterprise. It is not simply a department store, but a company which has widely dispersed interests (Macy's, California, is one subsidiary); the reports present an extremely complex set of operations in a relatively concise fashion; the initiated reader can gain much information from a careful reading and analysis of these data.

Summary Observations on Financial Reporting Practice

Every company must be to some extent its own judge of how the data concerning its activities will be released to the public. This, in effect, means that the financial statements are management's responsibility as much as they are that of the accountant. It is true that the public auditor cannot usurp the basic position of managers in presenting the results of operations. But the accountant does in his certificate take responsibility for the overall fairness and reliability of the data presented, within the limits of his professional position. That is, the accountant who audits and reviews the financial reports puts a mark of approval on them by stating his opinion based on generally accepted principles and procedures. Of course, the public accountant may have some influence on the company's own accounting executives when they consider how the financial data are to be reported.

There are other controls on reporting practices, such as the rules of the stock exchanges on which the company's shares may be listed, and the rules of the Securities and Exchange Commission. There are state regulatory agencies which are concerned with similar problems in intrastate security offerings. The rules of agencies such as these are specific and well oriented in the main, but they cannot cover every detail or all alternative procedures in financial reporting. In the last analysis, management and its accounting staff must take much responsibility for the content and presentation of financial data about the firm.

There are some specific issues of financial reporting that will concern us in the rest of this chapter, and these will be treated in general terms rather than by specific company illustration. These issues are, nevertheless, of considerable importance to the user of financial data. There is an established set of techniques for reducing financial information to a more manageable level, systematizing and condensing the material, and applying certain kinds of tests to help interpret it. From this it may be easier to draw more extensive conclusions, using relationships or trends observable in the reports. This set of techniques may be applied to several companies' reports and by facilitating comparison increase their usefulness. The rest of this chapter is concerned with such techniques.

STATEMENT ANALYSIS

It is a difficult task for the reader to visualize clearly the impact of an entire period's operations upon a business enterprise. The financial statements themselves are complex because they cover many facets of company operations that have to be assimilated into an overall impression or evaluation. Even so, the data are extensive, and there is often a real need to pull together and to analyze the array of the information contained in a set of reports.

One aspect of this has already been discussed in the funds statement that was described in an earlier chapter. The financing operations of a company are better understood if they are brought out into a separate tabulation and tied in to some reasonably clear conception of financial status. The funds statement does not report everything that has happened in a business firm, but it does focus attention on the in and out flow of resources associated with the financing side of the business. In effect, this report emphasizes certain items in the overall chain of events over the year to make clearer the way in which capital needs were met, or how available resources were employed.

Common Size Statements

A similar effect may be had by other analytical techniques, one of the simplest of which is the reduction of financial data in specific reports to what might be called "standard size," "common-size" or "percentage" forms. The complex six- and nine-digit amounts in an earnings statement, for instance, are not easy to comprehend in their raw form. If the earnings statement is reduced to a percentage basis by dividing each item in the report by the revenue figure, it is much easier to follow and understand. The relation between $719,486,327 in revenue and an expense item of $80,582,469 is not nearly so easy to see as when revenue is expressed as 100 percent, and the expense item becomes (after dividing by the revenue figure) 11.2 percent. Reducing the details in report of earnings to percentages makes their interpretation much more easy and positive.

This kind of simplification of data may also be applied to the fund statement, using as the 100 percent base, the total or gross fund flow; or it may be worked out by using some other figure as a base, such as the amount of net working capital at the beginning of the year. Recasting financial reports in this way is perhaps the easiest way for the reader to form general impressions of the overall trend of events in relation to each other.

The common size or percentage transformation process may also be applied to the statement of position, using as the 100 percent base the total assets (or for those statements arranged in that way) the "total net working capital and other assets." The general financial structure may be more easily seen when its parts are expressed as parts of 100 percent.

What can be done for the position statement as a whole on the asset side may also be done on the equity side. But this can also be done for whatever parts of the overall position statement that show complexity. In the usual situation the detailed current assets (or the net working capital items) may be expressed as percentages of related subtotals with good effect.

By such means as these, the whole set of financial reports may be restated in more easily intelligible terms, and the reader can gain a much clearer impression of what the reports are intended to convey.

Ratio Analysis

All the percentages set up by means of the "common size statement" approach are ratios—ratios of parts to respective wholes, however these are defined. But is it possible also to set up relationships between items that are not mere parts of a set of data; perhaps one of the most significant of these is a computation that uses one item from the earnings statement and one from the position of the firm: for example, the ratio or net income to total shareholder equity. This is a reflection (from the viewpoint of the shareholder rather than for the firm as a whole) of the "rate of return on invest-ment." As such, this ratio reflects the financial productivity of the company so far as the shareholder sees it for the current period.

Another important overall measure related to the return on in-vestment is the rate of net income to sales revenue. This is an indica-tion of profitability in current period terms, for it reflects the amount of gross value of product that remains after current period costs are deducted. This ratio would vary considerably among com-panies, especially where the relative turnover of investment was different. Ten percent net income to sales revenue may produce either a large or small return on investment. If the capital investment is large relative to sales (the capital turnover or ratio of sales to investment is small), the return on investment would be relatively less. The relationship is:

$$\frac{\text{Income}}{\text{Sales}} \times \frac{\text{Sales}}{\text{Investment}} = \frac{\text{Income}}{\text{Investment}}$$

These ratios summarize rather broadly the overall profit pattern, but they leave much unsaid because other factors are also impor-tant in the overall picture. There are two broad classes of ratios: one set which arises from the matching of related items within a given position statement, and another set that is devised by cross-referencing data from the position statement to the report of earn-ings, and vice versa.

Position Statement Ratios

Obviously, every percentage computation involved in reducing the position statement to "common size" represents a ratio of that item to its total. There are, however, at least five additional ratios that are generally considered useful. These are discussed separately (though briefly) below.

The "Current" Ratio: Current Assets to Current Debt. Some people regard this as a classic item in the ratio analysis scheme, for it has been used for a long time to indicate financial solvency. It does show in a limited way the ability of a firm to pay its debts as they mature without depending upon profits from new sales. Current assets are generally of such character as to be capable of conversion into cash (and normally are so converted) in short periods. But the limitation of the current ratio as a measure of financial solvency is easily seen in the case of public utility companies where the ratio would often be less than 1 to 1 (see the Consumers Power Report earlier in this chapter).

The "Acid Test" Ratio: Current Money Claims, Divided by Current Debt. This is, in a sense, an extension of the "current" ratio, since the ability of the firm to pay debts without any action other than collection of its receivables is measured by this ratio. Again, it must be applied to different businesses with care, for conditions in specific industries make for variations in this ratio.

"Inventory Position Index": Inventory Divided by Receivables. One of the ways in which companies may get themselves into financial tangles is to allow inventory to accumulate to levels not justified by the size of the firm or the amount of business it does. One way to test for this kind of imbalance is to compare the amount of inventory with the amounts due from customers; the idea is that there should be a kind of balance between these two elements. However, this balance may be high or low without indicating of itself any good or bad condition. Interpretation is likely to be improved by considering other measures, such as inventory turnover, the percentage of inventory to net working capital, or the ratio of inventory to current payables. Few ratios are good or bad in themselves. No matter what level of a ratio appears in a given case, it should be viewed in relation to all the other available information.

Other Working Capital Ratios. The importance of net working capital balances is reflected in other ratios used by analysts. The ratio of long-term debt to net working capital is thought by some to indicate a relative balance which is of importance. Net working capital divided by total assets is another measure of relative liquidity which is sometimes useful.

Plant Assets to Shareholder Equities. Based on an implicitly appealing theory that the company's plant ought to be financed by shareholder money, this ratio is a kind of "balance indicator" in financial relationships. If the plant investment is greater than the shareholder equities, it is obvious that some other kind of financing has been used to supplement shareholders' contributions (and retained earnings) in the financing of plant assets. Whether or not this is undesirable depends upon the nature of the business. For one thing, there are income tax advantages to debt financing (see Chapter 10). Further, there are many cases in which it is advantageous to borrow money at lower rates of interest than those funds will earn in the operations of the firm. For this reason many public utilities follow the practice of financing plant through the use of bonds or mortgages with relatively low rates of interest. The stable nature of the utility company's operations makes the investment in that company's bonds less risky to the bondholder; utility company earnings seldom fluctuate so much that they are unable to make interest payments when they are due, and the business is usually so highly predictable that the principal payments are also no great problem. Thus the company may borrow, say, a million dollars, at 8 percent, on which it may be able to earn 10 percent in its operations. The extra 2 percent ($20,000) is an additional return to the shareholders; this serves to increase the rate of return on the common stock.

However, other companies may have entirely different risk patterns or debt structures, and the ratio of plant to share equity would, therefore, have to be interpreted in different context.

Shareholder Equity Divided by Debt.   This is another phase of the financial structure which in some cases reflects a kind of balance that is of interest. Given a certain risk situation, the capital used in the enterprise ought to be kept in some fairly definite bounds as to the two major sources of funds, shareholder equities and debts. This relationship is sometimes used to test the kind of financial stringency that arises from too heavy a debt burden. Obviously, companies may vary widely as to the applicability of such a test, even though the ratio and its changes over time may indicate something of the general position and trend of financial structure.

Shareholder Equity Divided by Number of Shares.   This is often not regarded as a ratio but treated as an absolute measure of stockholder position; it is called "book value per share" by some accountants and investors. However, other accountants object (including the author) to the implication of value to *any* accounting measure. The results of accounting do not give values because the accounting process does not encompass the future expectations that are an essential part of any value. The objection just voiced is to some extent overcome if it be clearly understood that value is used in the generic and mathematical sense of "amount" or "quantity." However, it is just as well to refer to this measure as the book equity per share (the ratio of shareholder equity to the number of outstanding shares) and avoid confusing terminology. As a digression, it may be noted that there is a practice of referring to shareholder equities (in total) as the net worth of the firm; this is an even more distorting and misleading use of language, for accounting does not measure the "worth" of anything. The accountant may use estimates of worth (quantified in the cost data, or in the revenue data of the firm) as measures of the service potentials implicit and underlying the financial data, but it is the measured aspect of cost or bargained price that makes such estimates useful, not their relation to some judgment of "value" or "worth."

Turnovers; Ratios Involving Earnings Statement and Position Items. The relationships measured by the ratios thus far described are all of the nature of balance in a structure represented by position statement items. An entirely different variety of measures is afforded by approaching the question of relationships via the matching of operating earnings statement data with elements of financial position. Such ratios are generically to be regarded as turnovers, since they reflect the number of times a given level of investment may be put through a cycle of activity. Capital thus turned over in short periods of time (or more times per given period) is more productive than similar amounts turned over less frequently. However, extremely high turnovers may indicate strain; too small an inventory investment may actually *reduce* sales if needed items are not available to fill orders.

The basic ratio of this class is merchandise turnover, the merchandise cost of goods sold in a period divided by the average inventory investment during that period. Of course, the typical reports do not give average inventory, but this may be inferred from taking the midpoint between the beginning and the ending inventory amounts. A company with a merchandise cost of goods sold of $750,000, an inventory at the beginning of the year of $130,000, and one at the year-end amounting to $170,000 has a merchandise (inventory) turnover of five times per year.

$$\$750,000 \left/ \left(\frac{\$130,000 + 170,000}{2} \right) \right. = 5$$

In some cases, the merchandise cost of goods sold does not appear in the reports as a specific figure; then the analyst will use sales in place of the merchandise cost of goods sold. This produces a slight upward bias, but it is still useful to measure the productivity of inventory investment.

Sales Divided by Receivables. This ratio is an indicator of the effectiveness of collection procedures. If the collection of customer accounts is slower, the amount of current receivables will be larger relative to the sales; the decline in the ratio will then indicate the lowered efficiency of receivables investment.

Another way to measure this set of relationships is to compute the average collection period. This is obtained by dividing the amount of outstanding receivables at year-end by the average daily sales on credit for the year. The result is an index of sluggishness in collections. However, again it is important to note that what may be sluggish collection in one company may not be so in another; it may even vary for the same company as conditions change. This measure indicates only a relative condition or relationship which may be subject to further interpretation.

Sales Divided by Shareholder Equity.   This measure of volume of business done with respect to shareholders' current investment is another kind of turnover—even though shareholder investment is not a definable section of assets. The amount of business done by a firm ought to bear some relationship to the amount of share capital employed, and changes in this relationship may indicate a shift in a fundamental operating pattern. The shareholder equity in this ratio must, of course, be the midpoint between the beginning and end of the year amounts, for the same reasons as mentioned under merchandise turnover.

Sales Divided by Plant Investment.   This, like other measures of turnover, is an index of the effectiveness of plant investment. For a given size of plant, the company might be expected to maintain some level of sales; an extension of plant investment without a commensurate increase in the volume of business indicates less effectiveness in the use of plant facilities. However, it should also be observed that the inverse effect may also raise doubts. A consistent and drastic increase in sales volume without somewhat the same increase in plant assets may indicate an overstraining of plant facilities (by multishift operations, by crowding, or by "rushing through" production) which may have bad effects on the level of product quality, or may indicate the imminence of lost sales and poor customer relations because of inadequate or old equipment. This reverse effect, in which the ratio may indicate stress at either high or low levels, is also true with other ratios that have been mentioned. A too high inventory turnover may have the same effect as an overstressed plant turnover; more money receivables than current debt may actually mean (if carried too far) an inability or unwillingness to invest funds, and a resulting loss of earnings that might otherwise have been had. No ratio is an absolute measure; each must be interpreted in the light of surrounding conditions.

Index Analysis

Another way to approach the problem of interpreting financial reports is to relate the report items to each other over a time period, thus reviewing trends or shifts in patterns over the period. This is done by selecting a base year—say, five years ago—and expressing each financial statement item as a percentage or index related to the base year amount. Thus, if sales were $20 million five years ago and then moved to $26 million, $33 million, $41 million, and $37 million, the "index of sales" would be, for the five years, 100, 103, 165, 205, and 185 percent. Much of the complexity of a set of reports may be cleared away by this procedure. This may, of course, be applied to every item in every kind of report. It is possible, when index numbers have been calculated, to observe ratio analysis patterns without making specific calculations, since the indexes are easier to compare than the raw data would be. A sales index increasing at a steady rate and accompanied by a similarly increasing receivables index indicates a relatively unchanging sales-receivables ratio. Indexes focus attention on the changes in a given item over a period of time, and they therefore show a good deal more than does the ratio analysis of the reports of a single period. Neither approach, however, is complete in itself; each adds something to the understanding gained by the use of the other. A single year is not enough of a view to make a reasoned projection of probable future activities and results; reviewing the patterns over several years gives a clearer idea as to how and when the observable conditions arose and permits a better understanding as to how the course of the future may run. Thus, indexes over a period of time add to the pattern of interpretation achieved by ratio analysis.

It is possible also to set *ratios* in series over a period of years so to emphasize the changes in the indicated relationships over the period. This often improves interpretation; for instance, conclusions about a plant turnover ratio may be much more dependable if they are based on a review of the ratio over a five-year period. The analyst will use the various approaches and methods as they may be needed to clarify the situation which confronts him.

All analytical procedures, however, are based on the data as reported, and every attempt at analysis must be viewed as limited by the completeness and dependability of those data. Some of the limitations of financial reports need to be stated at this point to emphasize the partial and conventionalized nature of the information presented in such reports.

Limitations of Financial Reports

Financial statements as prepared by accountants are by far the best means thus far devised to present the overall results of business operations. They are widely used by those who need to evaluate those results, and the purposes to be served by financial reports are important and useful purposes. Yet, it must be recognized that the information which can be conveyed by any set of financial reports is, no matter how carefully prepared, not complete. Perhaps the most important weakness arises from the very fact that financial statements are used for so many things.

General-Purpose versus Special-Purpose Statements

The kinds of accounting reports thus far studied are prepared for the enterprise as a whole, and they have been set up in such form as to be *generally* useful. That is, the kind of information presented through accounting reports has been gathered and presented without any specific aim in mind other than giving an overall summary of what has happened in the operations of the period, and how those events have affected the results and position of the firm. The reports we have been working with are intended for no single or special evaluation; they have been set up so that all the financial information available would be summarized into a systematic aggregate. The vast arrays of data that actually exist in the firm have been boiled down to put them into a condensed and assimilable form. Further, they have been set up in such a way as to be suitable for publication. The information in the typical corporate position statement, earnings reports, and fund statement is aimed at the general consumer of such information. Whether the reader is a present shareholder, a prospective investor, a creditor, customer, employee, or other kind of interested party, these reports are expected to give the entire picture of the results and position of the firm in a concise and objective form.

This generalization and summary of data can be a source of trouble. Many analysts object to the relative paucity of detail in published reports. But these details are in some cases too close to the internal decisions of management for release to the general public.

Unfortunately, neither the accountant nor the management has any control over the uses to which the published reports will be put. Therefore, it is not possible to make much of an attempt to fit the presentation to the needs of any single reader. Even within groups of people interested in financial reports (such as the common stockholders of a given company), there are sufficient differences in viewpoint, objectives, and position that no one report presentation will meet the needs of all individuals. Since the financial reports of large companies (and those of many smaller companies as well) may fall into the area of public domain by publication and distribution, it is easy to see how the accountant may try to present data so as to be objective rather than particularly useful for specified purposes.

Even though the techniques of financial analysis may aid the interpretation of financial reports by stressing financial relationships and trends, those techniques cannot add material to that which appears in the reports themselves. Whatever limitations there are in the reports themselves must still affect the ratios, indexes, and other derivations.

Importance of Nonfinancial Data

It is easy to overlook the fact that no one technique of communication is likely to cover all the demands of a situation. The emphasis that has been given here to the financial aspects of reporting has, no doubt, tended to overshadow the fact that much pertinent information about a company is of nonfinancial nature. The number of employees, the geographical and other distributions of customers, and similar statistical data may be of real significance in determining the kind and amount of progress made by a company. Further, there are data that are neither financial nor statistical but really qualitative in nature, such as the patterns of product development, programs of developing managerial personnel, relations between the company and its competitors and suppliers—such data may reveal important aspects of what is being accomplished and where the company stands, even though numbers do not adequately describe the situation. There is still good reason for a president's letter to accompany the financial reports; some facets of aims and operations need to be expressed, and plans may be an important key to understanding of results. Despite the importance of financial measurements in conveying information about the company in concrete and objective language, it should be remembered that not everything can be quantified in terms of dollars and cents. Conditions, circumstances, objectives, and alternatives are always important; such information must be taken into account to supplement the financial and other quantitative data.

Historical Emphasis

In addition to the fact that financial reports are general-purpose compilations that exclude nonfinancial and nonquantitative information, it should be kept in mind that financial reports are essentially historical in nature. This is exactly the way in which they are prepared, and it is the way in which we have viewed them in this book. There is no need for us to be unduly concerned by the historical orientation of such reports. However, the point should be made that information about the past is not in itself basic or significant. Historical data are useful primarily in making decisions that concern the future. Thus, all financial reports (or any other historical data, for that matter) should be viewed as having their primary usefulness in mirroring the future. It is true that no historical report ever states the future as such, for the repetitions of history are seldom apparent in business. However, we can use historical data with appropriate adjustment to form a judgment of what may be expected. It is in this sense that we use past or current data for decision purposes; adjustments to reflect future considerations are part of the process of analysis and judgment. History must be taken as history, adjusted as necessary, to provide a basis for judgment as to the future. Financial reports thus need to be leavened with interpretations and extentions; they are not directly useful in projections unless the historical horizon is recognized and provided for.

Price Changes

One aspect of financial reports that may have an important bearing on their use is the fact that they do not reflect current prices as they are conventionally prepared. The problem of prices and the way they behave is, of course, one of the most intricate and the most intriguing of all business problems. The fact that financial reports are expressed in terms of money and that the financial transactions tend to be measured in "price aggregates" means that every financial amount is colored to some extent by a price factor; each amount is the result of some physical quantity being multiplied by a price.

Price changes are sufficiently important to be given separate treatment according to the problems with which they are associated. Those aspects of price that have to do with the marketing of products or that have to do with the interpretations of cost for managerial purposes had best be considered with respect to the management problems that they reflect. The problem of price change associated with the financial reports for the enterprise, however, does deserve some attention at this point. Since this is a departure from current practice involving some special issues, the subject is treated in the following chapter.

QUESTIONS

1. The reports that have been presented in this chapter are typical of current practice. How much of the information contained in such reports do you think most investors read? Understand? What implications are there for the communication of financial information to the "general public"? Does this affect the accountant's position in the preparation of such statements?

2. Financial reports are frequently described as being presentations of the management of the subject companies. What has the accountant to do, then, with the content and presentation of such reports?

3. Much emphasis is placed by some financial analysts (and others) upon the "rate of return" based on current market prices of shares. Is this logically sound and in keeping with what appears in financial statements? Does the notion implied here make better sense by using the concept of the market price as a multiple of earnings per share? What logical difficulty is involved in using accounting figures as a determinant of market value of shares?

4. How different are the reports of companies in various industries? Give examples of these differences observable in the reports presented in the text. Do these differences arise from variations in accounting principles and procedures or from other factors? What other factors?

5. One of the ways to gain better understanding of financial reports is to employ various kinds of analytical techniques. Distinguish between the following approaches:
   a) Common size statements.
   b) Ratio analysis.
   c) Index analysis.

6. List the ratios which you think are most useful in measuring solvency. Should these ratios be comparable between firms in the same industry—say, steel production, furniture manufacturing, railroads,

bus lines, airlines, steamship companies? How does one define an industry for such purposes?

7. What ratios indicate the two basic factors which determine net return on total investment? What other ratios could be said to underlie these two, indicating the reasons for their level and changes over time?

8. What ratios tend to reflect relative overall stability (balance) in the position of the firm as regard to asset and equity structures? What would be the merit of comparing these ratios over time?

9. What is turnover? Should inventory turnover be higher for a retail store as compared to a wholesale trading firm or a manufacturer? Why? Would turnover be higher in a meat market than for a carpet and floor covering retailer? Why? How may inventory turnover be increased? What would a very high merchandise turnover (say, 25 times a year in a men's clothing store) indicate?

10. What are the limitations on the use of analytical devices and supplementary calculations based on financial reports? How much do these affect the validity of relationships such as have been discussed here?

11. Select a company whose securities are listed on an organized stock exchange; find the salient financial data in a financial reports manual (such as Poor's) or in copies of the actual company reports, and compute a set of ratios and indexes covering a five-year period. With a report, present the results of your work and draw conclusions as to the financial effectiveness of the company's operations.

12. Select two companies in comparable lines of business and prepare an evaluation of their reports over the past three years and compare their operations for their effectiveness and desirability as an investment medium. Would an analysis such as this be more suitable for such purposes than to consider one company in greater detail for a longer period?

13. What, in your opinion, are the basic problems of communication in financial reporting—assuming that there is no substantial change in prices and that accounting procedures themselves are not *purposely* misused to distort income and position? In other words, if we required absolutely uniform accounting procedures (whatever that may mean) and could keep prices from changing over time, what communication problems would still remain?

PROBLEMS

Mill Valley Lumber and Supply Company

At the end of last year, the financial reports of this company, attested by its certified public accountant, were as follows:

Statements of Position

	Four Years Ago		Current Year	
ASSETS				
Cash in bank....................		$ 28,000		$ 7,100
Accounts receivable (net)........		170,100		236,800
Inventory (Fifo cost)............		157,200		246,100
Total Current Assets........		$ 355,300		$ 490,000
Plant and equipment cost.........	$ 67,100		$ 84,800	
Accumulated depreciation......	18,200	48,900	36,100	48,700
Other assets (investments).......		18,500		23,700
Total Assets.............		$ 422,700		$ 562,400
EQUITIES				
Current debt—trade notes payable.....................		. . .		$ 14,800
Trade accounts payable..........		$ 61,700		125,700
Bank loans.....................		25,000		60,000
Other current debt..............		18,300		26,100
Total Current Debt........		$ 105,000		$ 226,600
Mortgage notes on plant and equipment..................		16,200		9,600
Common stock.................		200,000		200,000
Retained earnings..............		101,500		126,200
Total Equities...........		$ 422,700		$ 562,400

Statements of Earnings

	Four Years Ago		Current Year	
Sales revenues (net, after un-collectibles, etc.)..............		$1,583,600		$1,932,700
Merchandise costs:				
Initial inventory..............	$ 148,800		$ 237,900	
Purchases...................	1,344,300		1,688,900	
Gross cost..................	$1,493,100		$1,926,800	
Closing inventory............	157,200		246,100	
Cost of goods sold............		1,335,900		1,680,700
Merchandise margin...........		$ 247,700		$ 252,000
Other expenses: salaries and wages......................	$ 99,900		$ 100,600	
Millwork and delivery costs.....	99,564		98,000	
Other items (note)...........	16,836	216,300	34,100	232,700
Net operating margin...........		$ 31,400		$ 19,300
Miscellaneous income...........	$ 2,000		$ 1,500	
Interest charges................	3,800		4,400	
Net charges....................		1,800		2,900
Net Earnings for the Year........		$ 29,600		$ 16,400

(Note): Other items include federal income taxes at current rates, and depreciation charges. There have been no retirements of plant and equipment, and no dividends have been paid.

Required:

Make an analysis of these reports, using ratios, percentages, or derived statements. Write a short report of your work and your conclusions.

Chapter 14

ACCOUNTING FOR PRICE CHANGES

Conventional accounting takes notice of price changes only when they are directly associated with transactions or conditions. In Chapter 13, there were instances of the use of last-in, first-out inventory costing, and we discussed earlier the reporting of inventory "price losses" when the replacement costs of an inventory was less than the historical cost. But the problem of price changes and their effects is sufficiently important to warrant a more detailed treatment, which is attempted in this chapter.

Flow Assumptions in Cost Assignment

The best place to begin with price change problems is with inventory procedure—not only because inventory costs are large in amount for many firms but because this is a place where price changes necessarily get into the accounting record and must be dealt with, somehow.

Theoretically, every unit in inventory has been acquired at some specific cost, and when it is sold, the cost of that unit ought to be carried to the Cost of Goods Sold account. This is attempted in some situations, such as retail furniture or piano establishments. Each item of merchandise may be marked with the cost of acquiring it (even though the marking may have to be in code); thus, when a particular instrument or piece of furniture is sold, the cost of goods sold is a matter of precise record. But the great bulk of inventories consist of items that are alike, and they are not readily marked in such a way as to trace their individual costs. Hence there must be some means of assigning costs without specifically identifying them; this is found in the "flow" assumption.

The flow of costs through inventory into cost of goods sold may be viewed in three ways: first-in, first-out; last-in, first-out; or some kind of average. First-in, first-out assumes that the oldest costs should be assigned to the first goods sold; last-in, first-out assumes that the most recent costs ought to be assigned first; an averaging approach assumes that costs should be commingled and every unit sold or used during a month or other period should be costed at the same amount.

Fifo, Lifo, and Average Methods

The effects of these assumptions may be clearer if we first note that an inventory is carried to absorb differences between the rate of use and the rate of acquiring goods. It is thus a buffer or cushion between usage and acquisition, and its presence allows a lag between the two flows. If there is a change in price and we assume a first-in, first-out flow of costs, the presence of inventory creates a lag between the actual price change and its appearance in operating charges. If the inventory is constant at 1,000 units and we use 10 units per day, the change in price will not appear in operating costs until 100 days have elapsed. Under a last-in, first-out assumption, this lag does not exist, for the next issue of materials after a price change will carry the new price. Under an averaging procedure, the effect of the price change will depend upon how often and in what way the average is computed; but the price change will not appear specifically because it will be merged with other data which will dampen its effect. Thus, it is seen that first-in, first-out pricing tends to have costs lag behind so that operations are charged with older costs than those current when reports are prepared; last-in, first-out tends to yield more current figures for operating charges, and averaging is somewhat between.

Holding Gains

This is only part of the story, however; there is also the matter of the inventory asset balance. First-in, first-out tends to state inventories more nearly at current prices, while last-in, first-out tends to leave the oldest prices in the inventory. Thus, both procedures are unsatisfactory in that they allow the older, noncurrent prices to appear either in inventory or in the operating costs; if one desires a current figure for the position statement, there is a correspondingly uncurrent cost of goods used, and vice versa. Averaging is something of a compromise but is even less interpretable, unless one can reconstruct the averaging process and restate the figures in some way.

Taking the view that the position statement is of less importance than the report of earnings, some companies have employed last-in, first-out procedures to reduce "price profits" in periods of rising prices. If the higher prices are carried promptly into operating costs, the holding gain that shows in higher inventory under first-in, first-out will instead be deducted from sales as cost of current operations.[1] This is particularly advantageous for tax purposes, when taxes approximate half the corporate income. It is not hard to see why a company might use a last-in, first-out procedure under such conditions.

Some accountants have felt that this holding gain should not be included in income for other reasons. Although the items in inventory are constantly in a state of flow, the general level of inventory changes only slowly; and the amount of price gain produced by the increased money value assigned to inventory is really frozen in the sense that inventory quantities are seldom if ever drastically reduced to make even part of the price gain available as a "realized" profit. The crux of the matter is that the price effects in inventory position are carried into current income of the period by the use of first-in, first-out procedure; but the effect of last-in, first-out calculations is to leave the inventory stated at an amount which conceals the price gain in a lower inventory and prevents this important fact from being revealed. One proposed solution to this dilemma is to use last-in, first-out to compute cost of goods sold or usage and then to write up the inventory to the first-in, first-out level, reporting this write-up as a holding gain arising from inventory price change. This proposal has not gained much acceptance in practice.

---

[1] What has been said about the pattern of cost flow in a period of rising prices would also apply in the opposite manner during a period of falling prices. Thus, it may be argued that first-in, first-out produces greater fluctuations in income over the business cycles; or from another point of view, the effect of last-in, first-out is to "conceal" those fluctuations.

Current Costs and Lifo

It should be carefully noted that the reference to current prices in any comparison of these inventory calculations is somewhat oblique. Price changes are likely to be quite independent of individual purchases, and the record of purchases cannot be expected to be current if purchases are made only at intervals. To really get current prices into the financial data flow, they would have to be recognized specifically. To illustrate, if a company had acquired inventory at $10, $12, and $14, the sale of one unit would be reported as $10 under first-in, first-out; $14 under last-in, first-out; and $12 on an average basis. But if these items were held until the price had risen to $15, the current cost would not appear in the accounts, and even last-in, first-out procedure would not really achieve its purported aim. Rigid emphasis upon recorded events does not produce measures of independent phenomena. To meet this complication, one would have to price every issue from inventory at the price quoted at that instant, which is generally objected to on practical grounds. There is one other difficulty to be recognized in the attempt to measure price effects by last-in, first-out procedures. This is, that the quantity level of inventory does not remain absolutely constant. So long as inventory quantities do not fall, last-in, first-out does put the more current figures into the costs of operation. But if physical level of the inventory declines in quantity so as to exhaust the most recent level of prices, the next layer of issue prices may be quite *un*current. Suppose a company starts with an inventory of 1,000 units which it has acquired at current prices at $10 each. Under last-in, first-out, purchases which are costed out to operations may be made at increasingly higher prices until in a later year the price being paid for such items is $15. If the amount currently sold does not exceed the amount purchased in that year, the unit charge to operations is $15; but if any more units are issued, they will be costed at $10, and $5 of price profit will thus appear in the income of that period. Thus, a reduction of inventory below the base quantity may bring very old costs into the income calculation. This may cause problems in taxes, as well as in financial reporting, unless those low-priced units are replaced before the end of the fiscal period. If the replacement is made at $15, Lifo will put the $15 into cost of goods sold. But if the replacement is made after the close of the period, the $15 item will establish a new "layer" of inventory cost.

Replacement Costs and Net Realizable Values

The departure from a cost basis of accounting can go further than a mere recognition of replacement costs. It is quite possible to argue that economic income arises from the processes of production and merchandising rather than from sales and that the sale, as signaled by delivery of goods or service, is a secondary rather than the primary aspect of revenue recognition. Those who take this position would show inventories at their "net realizable value"—the revenue to be obtained on delivery, less the costs incident to delivery and collection efforts. This would serve to report all income from the sale as soon as production was completed. Most accountants reject this notion in view of the uncertainties involved. They feel that revenue comes into being (is "realized") only after the act of delivery, from which an enforceable claim for payment arises.

It is not altogether clear as to how far the application of net realizable values to inventories would go in practice. While it is perhaps easy to establish the net realizable value of a finished goods inventory by subtracting the costs of selling and delivery from expected sales price, it is less simple to arrive at the net realizable amount for work in process. The costs of completion for goods being completed may be estimated, and this subtracted from the realizable value for finished goods; but how far back in the production process can this be continued? Conceivably, the process might be carried to the beginning of the productive process to the acquisition of materials; but no advocate for this has appeared.

The principal gain from the use of net realizable values would be that the holding gains in inventory would be measured in terms of the external price situation. For internal costing purposes, it is doubtful that the net realizable value approach could be applied with real advantage. Except in the form of the "lower of cost or market" notion, net realizable value is applied to inventories mostly to deal with obsolete or otherwise unusual inventory situations.

Standard Cost Approaches

Still another proposal to deal with inventory problems is the use of a standard or rationally expected cost. For any given product or process it is possible to state—after careful study—what it *ought* to cost. From a technical viewpoint, this is a matter of specifying the activities to be carried out, the kinds of tools and equipment to be used, and the personal skills that must be applied. If current prices are applied to the technical coefficients, the result is a projected cost, at a stated level of efficiency and prices. If such a cost were established at the beginning of each year, it could serve as a measuring stick for variations during the period. Most of these "variances" would relate to the internal efficiency of operations—we leave them to those who discuss the problem of cost control. But some of them could show how much actual prices moved away from the norms established in the standard. To illustrate, suppose the standard cost of an item of materials is $10 per unit. An inventory at the beginning of the year would be priced at that figure, say, 1,000 units at $10 or $10,000. If issues from stores are always priced at the standard price, the inventory balance will always be stated at the actual quantities times the standard price. Purchases of more of this material—say, 40,000 units—would be added to inventory at the standard price, but credited to Accounts Payable at the actual prices, $404,000. The $4,000 difference would be the amount of price deviation from the standard of $5 per unit. At the end of the year, a new standard would be established with a view toward next year's activities, say $10.15 per unit. The closing inventory (if there had been 38,000 units issued during the year) would show 3,000 units and $30,000. The effect of the new standard on the final inventory would be to increase it to $30,450 (3,000 × $10.15). Thus the effect of price increases for this material during the year would be summarized as $4,000 from the recorded variance, less $450 to be added to the final inventory, a net of $3,550. An attempt to divide this further (as between the initial inventory and the purchases of the current year) would require records to be maintained showing the cost of the material at the dates of issue. Probably this is an unnecessary refinement.

Evaluation of Inventory Accounting for Price Changes

There is considerable variety in the methods of accounting for inventories. Probably about a third of all business firms use first-in, first-out procedures, only slightly less employ last-in, first-out—probably for tax reasons more than anything else. But a quarter of the firms utilize some form of average to trace costs into operations; the remaining firms (about 10 percent) divide into two groups: the first half employs standard cost, and the rest follow various other methods. It is interesting to note that practically none of these methods make any real attempt to isolate holding gains; even when the methods in use would lend themselves to such a measurement, it is seldom that the price gain in inventory is specifically reported.

The wide variations in inventory procedure are to some extent the result of habit; the principle of consistency in accounting would frown upon changes in inventory or other methods of accounting. But variations in inventory procedure are also the result of differences in the nature of the materials or products, the frequency and extent of price-fluctuations, the pattern of established industry practices, and the extent of competition. And the income tax law is a very important factor when tax rates are high and prices change rapidly.

Long-Term Assets and Appraisals

Fixed asset costs affect the costs of operation over many more years than do inventory costs. During those longer periods, price changes can become more extensive. Fixed assets are acquired in bigger packages less evenly spread through time; yet their aggregate amount may be greater than inventories in large-scale companies. Perhaps even more important is the fact that individuality of design and usage, as well as the effects of technological change, tend to make plant and equipment items quite highly specialized. For such assets, current market prices are likely to refer to items of very different nature than those now owned, and the determination of specific replacement costs is difficult, if not impossible.

For these reasons it is not uncommon to see adjustments brought about by appraisals of fixed assets to recognize the effect of higher or lower *reproduction* costs. An example or two will make clearer the way in which such figures are established.

Suppose a company has owned a piece of land on which it hoped to build a larger plant some day. The land was bought 10 years ago for $20,000 but is now considered to be worth much more. A reputable appraiser states the value of the land as $30,000. In preparing financial reports for credit purposes, the company may wish to reflect this new and higher value.

The first question that arises is whether the indicated write-up represents income, and the answer is clear that it is not. Income arises from a transaction in which the bargained price received is greater than the costs that are released. The holding gain represents an appreciation in value which has not been realized in an exchange transaction. Some accountants would prefer not to recognize this at all, especially since the land was not held for resale; in addition, the write-up will not affect future operations since the land is not depreciable but has an indefinite service life.

There is, however, the fact that the amount of capital (in money terms) now represented by the land is greater than the records and reports show. Even though the land is not being used, the amount of alternative funds it represents would be more realistically stated by adjusting the carrying amount to the higher level, the credit being carried to a "capital adjustment" account:

Land Appreciation...................................... 10,000
    Capital Adjustment, Revaluation of Land..............   10,000

The Land Appreciation account is an adjunct to the Land account in which the cost was recorded; the use of an adjunct preserves the cost figure, along with the current value addition. The Capital Adjustment account represents an addition to the invested capital of the firm; it would appear in a position statement along with Additional Paid-In Capital and Common Stock accounts. Since the land is not depreciable, the recording of this appraisal would have no bearing on past, current, or future income.

The Effect of Price Shifts on Depreciation

A somewhat different question arises when the item that has been appraised is a depreciable asset, a building or equipment. Here there is an additional reason to record the change in amount of the asset because the depreciation of the asset (services provided by the asset for the benefit of operations in specified periods) should be higher if the asset really represents more dollars of investment. Over a period of years, the changes in price of items of equipment may make a considerable difference in the costs of operation, especially if replacement prices are increasing steadily.

By way of example, assume that a company has a machine used for manufacturing which cost $20,000 10 years ago and which has been depreciated at 5 percent per year. The replacement prices of similar machines are now around $38,000; machines exactly like the one in use are offered for sale in the used-machine market for $18,000. Depreciation on the old machine is still charged at $1,000 per year, despite the fact that such a machine cannot be leased on a 10-year basis for less than twice this amount. An engineer examines the machine and reports that it is in excellent condition, easily good for another 10 years of use, and the equivalent of these offered in the market for $18,000. The appraisal could be entered as follows:

```
Machinery Appreciation............................ 16,000
    Accumulated Depreciation of Machinery..............        8,000
    Capital Adjustment—Revaluation of Machinery........        8,000
```

The rationale underlying the $16,000 write-up of machinery is that if a 10-year expected life represents $18,000, the amount of adjustment to the original cost should be to raise it from $20,000 to $36,-000, the implied cost of replacing the machine as new. The current price of "similar" machines is evidence to support this. The reason for not using the $38,000 price of new (similar) equipment is that the similarity may not be close enough to justify a new design price for the existing equipment. From this point on, the depreciation charge would be $1,800 per year; in fact the $8,000 credit to accumulated depreciation is the result of figuring depreciation at $800 more per year for the 10 years elapsed to date. Capital adjustment from revaluation of machinery is carried into the position statement along with that set up earlier for the land revaluation, as another addition to invested capital.

Errors in Past Depreciation

There are occasions when the situation is complicated not only by changes in the replacement cost of the asset but also by errors in depreciation. A plant building which cost $50,000 and has been depreciated at 2.5 percent per year for 10 years would have a net book value of $37,500 (cost, $50,000 less 25 percent, or $12,500, accumulated depreciation). If this building is appraised at a sound value of $40,000, one might think that this "current" valuation would indicate a new reproduction cost of $53,333 ($\frac{4}{3} \times 40,000$) since the $40,000 is presumably based on one-fourth expiration to date. But the appraisal should also review the condition of the building and its probable future service life. If the appraiser had indicated that $2,000 of repairs are necessary to put the building into such condition that would justify the valuation of $40,000, and that the expected future life was 20 years, this would be reason to record the following adjustments, even if the change in price were ignored:

(1)
```
Retained Earnings........................................ 2,000
    Appropriation for Deferred Maintenance.................        2,000
    To record the undermaintenance of the plant building, which
    should have been treated as expense to prior years.
```

Another adjustment would be made as follows:

(2)

Retained Earnings	4,167	
Accumulated Depreciation of Buildings		4,167

To correct accumulated depreciation for the changed use-life
expectancy of the building from 20 to 30 years.

The charge should have been calculated at $3\frac{1}{3}$ percent per year
instead of $2\frac{1}{2}$ percent over a 10-year period, an understatement of
$\frac{5}{6}$ percent per year; or $8\frac{1}{3}$ percent of cost, cumulative to date. This
adjustment makes total accumulated depreciation to date of the
building one third of the total cost or $16,667.

The appraisal then could be recorded:

Building Appreciation	10,000	
Accumulated Depreciation of Building		3,333
Capital Adjustment for Revaluation of Building		6,667

This entry recognizes that the $40,000 appraisal covers two-thirds
of the reproduction cost, new, because the building is 10 years old
and will remain in service for 20 years more; total life is thus 30
years. If the appraisal adds $10,000 or one fifth of the cost of the
asset to show reproduction cost new, the accumulated depreciation
of $16,667 as adjusted ought to be increased also by one fifth of the
book amount. This is $3,333; the effect of the higher valuation
carries the rest of the increase in the carrying amount of the building ($6,667) into the Capital Adjustment account.

These calculations could be arranged systematically as follows:

		Cost	Cost with Adjusted Use-Life	Appraisal	Mainte- nance
Gross amount	(a)	$50,000	$50,000	③ $60,000	⑥ $2,000
Accumulated depreciation	(b)	12,500	④ 16,667	② 20,000	
Net account	(c)	37,500	⑤ 33,333	① 40,000	

This table would be made up by first entering the data in the Cost
column—these are the figures now in the accounts. The other figures would be put into the tableau in the order of the circled numbers, under the following reasoning:

The sound value per appraisal is $40,000① which covers 20 years
of expected use-life. Since 10 years have elapsed, the accumulated
depreciation to date is $20,000② and the gross reproduction cost
is $60,000③. The accumulated depreciation now on the books is in-
adequate because it ought to be one-third of the gross cost (20/60)
instead of only one-fourth of it (12.5/50). The correct figure would
be $16,667④ and the net carrying value on the changed use-life

would be $33,333⑤. The total charge to retained earnings needed to state depreciation and maintenance to date is $4,167 + $2,000, the former being credited to accumulated depreciation and the latter to Appropriation for Undermaintenance⑥. The entries could be written up easily after this analysis.

Overall Changes in the General Price Level

One of the reasons for accountants' reservations about treating the recognition of price changes as profit or income is that a change in price is often associated with other price changes, and it is not easy to see what the effect of a change in one price is without checking other data to interpret it. To illustrate, suppose a company regularly uses a material in its operations which has cost $3.00 per pound; it is used in solution at the rate of $1/10$ pound per gallon of water. A substitute material sells regularly for 30 cents a gallon, already diluted to the proper strength. Now if the price of the regularly used material increases to $3.10 per pound, it appears advantageous (assuming water cost is negligible) to use the substitute. Would it be correct to say that the higher price quoted for the material in inventory justifies the recognition of a profit? Certainly the regular material is no more valuable than its substitute; the $3.10 price actually would mean that the regular material would be supplanted by the substitute. Under these conditions, the write-up ought not to be made; it could hardly be considered as a gain in any sense.

Now, if the price of the *substitute* had changed, we might have the same real effect on decision without ever raising the issue of gain or loss from price changes. Suppose that instead of the price of the regular material increasing, it had remained unchanged at $3.00 per pound. The price of the substitute, however, declined to 29 cents per gallon. We would have a similar reason to prefer the substitute, but no basis for a price gain. Indeed, we ought to consider writing down the regular material inventory to $2.90 per pound, since the substitute would do the same work, and the regular material has cost more than we should have spent for it.

Lastly, consider what happens if the price of the substitute rises. This makes the regular material relatively more desirable, even though its price is unchanged. And, although we could not write-up the inventory of regular material because its price did not change, we would nevertheless be better off than before since its *relative* price advantage is greater than before.

All of this is groundwork to show that the change in any price has to be interpreted in relation to other price changes. This is not only because goods are substitutes for each other but because money is substitutable for any and all goods and services offered in the market. Money is a general purchasing power which takes its meaning from the wide range of items for which it may be exchanged. Hence any dollar measurement must be viewed in terms of the set of prices current when that dollar amount was established. Thus when over some extended period the whole level of prices undergoes a change of substantial amount, the dollar figures need restatement to preserve their meaning. This restatement is typically referred to as making a general price level adjustment, "correcting for the change in the value of the monetary unit" or simply common-dollar reporting.

Basis for Measuring General Price Level Changes

In the situation of changing price levels, the amount of adjustment is established by the use of a general price index, such as the wholesale commodity index in the GNP Deflator; there are a number of such indexes that are satisfactory measures of general price level changes, and their technical features are beyond the scope of our present interest. But every dollar amount has a special significance expressed by the index number level when the dollar amount is established; thus an expenditure of $1,000 for merchandise when the price index stands at 105 has a different meaning from that attached to it when the price index stands at 110. To establish the meaning of $1,000, index 105, in terms of a situation index 110, we must divide the amount by 105, and multiply the result by 110. Our $1,000 expenditure made when the index stood at 105 is $1,047.62 for index 110 ($1,000/1.05 = $952.38; $952.38 × 110 = $1,047.62). The general approach to price level adjustments is to divide by the index value current at the time of record and multiply by the index at the time of reporting to show all transactions in terms of the current price level—i.e., in "common" dollars.

Take, as an illustration, the set of conventional reports in Figures 14–1A, 14–1B, and 14–1C; these reports are made up of various dollar amounts, but the dollar items are representative of different price levels, as shown in the notes following the statement of funds. These price level data are not very helpful in the form of notes; we need to put them into the financial figures in some way if we are to see what they mean.

Some of the figures in conventional statement actually appear in

FIGURE 14–1A

INFLATED SPECIALTY COMPANY

Comparative Position Data at Beginning and End of Year

	January 1	December 31	Change
Cash and receivables........................	$120,000	$160,000	$ 40,000
Inventories, first-in, first-out cost.............	180,000	187,000	7,000
Current Assets........................	$300,000	$347,000	$ 47,000
Less current payables........................	96,000	108,000	12,000
Net working capital........................	$204,000	$239,000	$ 35,000
Plant and equipment (net)...................	240,000	246,000	6,000
Total Net Working Capital and Other Assets........................	$444,000	$485,000	$ 41,000
Long-Term Equities:			
Long-term debt........................	$135,000	$142,000	$ 7,000
Common shares........................	297,000	300,000	3,000
Retained earnings........................	12,000	43,000	31,000
Total Long-Term Equities...........	$444,000	$485,000	$ 41,000

terms of current prices. Monetary assets stated at the close of the period mean what money is supposed to mean—dollars to purchase things at current prices. But the balances of these items at the beginning of the year are not stated in the same kind of dollars; they must be adjusted to current levels.[2]

We cannot really compare any dollar amounts unless they are all adjusted to mean what dollars mean at the end of the period when we read the reports. Even cash balances are not comparable

FIGURE 14–1B

INFLATED SPECIALTY COMPANY

Current Year Earnings
Year Ended 12/31/–

Sales revenue..		$1,057,000
Expense:		
Cost of goods sold................................	$810,000	
Selling expense....................................	154,000	
Depreciation......................................	24,000	$ 988,000
Operating net margin....................................		$ 69,000
Income taxes..	$ 22,000	
Dividends (paid December 21)........................	16,000	$ 38,000
Net Earnings Retained for the Year.....................		$ 31,000

---

[2] Before we attempt any such computations, it may be noted that the price indexes have been set up to make arithmetic simpler. By using indexes of 80, 90, 100, 110, and 120, we make it easier to see what kinds of adjustments are needed. The relative amounts of these adjustments are unrealistic—prices hardly ever rise 20 percent in one year. But the *amounts* of the changes are less important than the effects they have in this illustration.

FIGURE 14–1C

INFLATED SPECIALTY COMPANY

Statement of Funds

Net working capital, January 1.............		$204,000
Add:		
Operating net margin..................	$69,000	
Depreciation.........................	24,000	93,000
New funded debt......................		$ 7,000
Common shares issued 12/31/–...........		3,000
Total................................		$307,000
Less:		
Plant additions (12/31/–)..............	$30,000	
Income taxes.........................	22,000	
Dividends paid (12/31/–)..............	16,000	68,000
Net Working Capital December 31........		$239,000

Index numbers of general prices, beginning of year, 100; and end of year, 120.
Index number at date of incorporation and acquisition of plant, 80.
Sales revenue, current year, $182,000 (index 100); $315,000 (index 105); $560,000 (index 112).
Cost of goods sold:
  $180,000 (index 100) + $306,000 (index 102) + $324,000 (index 108). Closing inventory, $187,000; index 110.
"Average" index over the year for expense and tax conversions, 110.

unless they pertain to the same price level. This is because—although the holding of dollars while prices rise does not change the *number* of dollars—their purchasing power is different. Thus, the same $100 is simply viewed in terms of the new price level as "dollars," but we automatically interpret dollars as *current* dollars—which, in fact, is the only kind of dollars that we can use. Since the dollars of a year ago bought more than they do when prices have risen, we need to adjust their initial amounts to agree with the current situation. Thus, all monetary items, as at the beginning of the year (cash, accounts receivable, and debt figures for long term as well as current debt), need to be restated in terms of the price changes that have occurred.

On the other hand, nonmonetary assets and equities do not have the automatic shift in interpretation that occurs with current dollar claims and debts. Therefore *both* the beginning and the ending balances of nonmonetary assets and equities must be adjusted, for such items are conventionally recorded in terms of the price level at which they were first recognized, no matter how long they have been carried on the books. The inventory that appears in the position statement is presented in terms of dollar cost, part of which may be different in meaning, because the components were acquired at different dates. A Fifo inventory is higher than the corresponding Lifo inventory when prices have risen—merely because the prices shown in the final Fifo inventory are more recent than those in the Lifo inventory. Thus, the use of Lifo does not reflect price level changes, except for putting somewhat more recent prices into the income statement. Neither does Fifo reflect price level changes except that the more recent prices are kept out of the cost of goods sold, which buries part of the price change in the reported earnings. This same "burying" is done in Lifo by the reduction of closing inventory, and neither method compensates or reports price

FIGURE 14–2A

INFLATED SPECIALTY COMPANY

Index Number Adjusted Position Data, at December 31

	Last Year	Current Year	Change
Cash and receivables.....................	$144,000	$160,000	$16,000
Inventories (first-in, first-out)..............	216,000	204,000	12,000*
Current Assets......................	$360,000	$364,000	$ 4,000
Current payables........................	115,200	108,000	7,200*
Net working capital.....................	$244,800	$256,000	$11,200
Plant and equipment (net)................	360,000	354,000	6,000*
Total Net Working Capital and Other Assets...........................	$604,800	$610,000	$ 5,200*
Long-Term Equities:			
Long-term debt.......................	$162,000	$142,000	$20,000*
Common shares.......................	445,500	448,500	3,000
Retained earnings (books)..............	12,000	43,000	31,000
Capital adjustment, price level changes.....	14,700*	23,500*	8,800*
Total Long-Term Equities.............	$604,800	$610,000	$ 5,200*

* Deduction

changes fully. To reflect price changes in inventory we need to adjust the initial as well as the final amounts, taking them from the price levels at which they were recorded to the current one. In the illustration before us, this would mean dividing the initial inventory by 100 (assuming the Fifo inventory costs were *current* at that time) and multiplying by 120 to state those costs in end-of-year dollars. Also, the *final* inventory requires adjustment because it was acquired when the price level was 110; the indicated adjustment is 120/110, in this case increasing the final inventory of $187,000 to $204,000. The adjustments we have made to cash, receivables, debts, and inventories are reflected in the index-number-adjusted position statement, Figure 14–2A.

For reasons already given, it is necessary to adjust other figures in the position statement. The initial plant and equipment was conventionally $240,000, but the cost was incurred when the price level was 80; therefore, it is restated to 120/80 ($240,000) or $360,000. The specific equities (those other than retained earnings) which appeared at the beginning of the year are also converted to the 120-index price level. For funded debt the computation is $135,000 (120/100) = $162,000. Common shares were issued when the price index was 80; therefore they are converted as $297,000 × 120/80 or $445,500. The Retained Earnings balance of $12,000 is left unadjusted, for the entire effect of position restatement should appear separately as a specific adjustment to the stock equity—not merely buried in Retained Earnings. This balancing figure, which is the net effect of all the adjustments we have made, is $14,700 debit, as may be seen in Figure 14–2A, first column.

The meaning of this debit balance is that the total effect of inflation up to the beginning of this year was a net decline in equivalent purchasing power of the capital invested and retained in the business. This decline amounts to $14,700. That is, it required that many more dollars to balance the price equivalents in the position statement at the 120 price index.

The *end* of year position statement balances for plant and equipment are composite. There is an initial cost of equipment (price level 80) amounting to $240,000, less $24,000 depreciation. This $216,000 is multiplied by 120/80 to make it $324,000, and the $30,000 plant additions at the end of the year (index 120/120) are added to give $354,000 in the adjusted position statement. The long-term debt is at 120/120; it is payable in current dollars—$135,000 +$7,000 addition during the year.

Common share investment at the end of the year is also a composite —$297,000 converted at 120/80 ($445,500) plus $3,000 of new issues on December 31, index 120/120. The total of $448,500 appears as the final amount. The retained earnings figure is left unchanged so that the whole set of price change adjustments will be reflected in the balancing figure. The capital adjustment for price level shifts (which, at the beginning of the year was $14,700) is now seen to be $23,500 at the end of the year. The net debit change in this account of $8,800 is the aggregate capital shrinkage from price level changes that have occurred over the year.

This price level shrinkage may be explained by operating reports, just as conventional changes are detailed in ordinary earnings and fund flow reports. To accomplish this, the reported figures in those statements must be adjusted for price changes as was done with balance sheet items. Computations to restate the earnings report data for the year are shown within the price-adjusted earnings report in Figure 14–2B.

This report shows an income $32,600 less than the conventional one; there is a net loss of $1,600 instead of a gain of $31,000. But this does not agree with the price level shrinkage as shown by the position statement, an $8,800 decline. There must be some other

FIGURE 14–2B

INFLATED SPECIALTY COMPANY

Index Number Adjusted Earnings Report
Year Ended 12/31/–

	Books	Index	Adjusted	Net Changes
Sales revenue..................	$ 182,000	120/100	$ 218,400	$ 36,400
	315,000	120/105	360,000	45,000
	560,000	120/112	600,000	40,000
Total Revenue.............	$1,057,000		$1,178,400	$121,400
Cost of goods sold.............	$ 180,000	120/100	$ 216,000	$ 36,000
	306,000	120/102	360,000	54,000
	324,000	120/108	360,000	26,000
Total Cost of Goods Sold.....	$ 810,000		$ 936,000	$126,000
Selling expense................	$ 154,000	120/110	168,000	14,000
Depreciation..................	24,000	120/80	36,000	12,000
Total Expense..............	$ 988,000		$1,140,000	$152,000
Operating net margin...........	$ 69,000		$ 38,400	$ 30,600*
Federal income tax charges.......	22,000	120/110	24,000	2,000
Dividends declared.............	16,000	120/120	16,000	—
Net Income or Loss.............	$ 31,000		$ 1,600*	$ 32,600*

   * Deduction

price level effect(s) which amount to the difference between $32,-600 and $8,800. The price level effects that have not yet been identified arise from holding or owing dollars while prices change. Part of the effect of price level change upon monetary assets and equities will be seen if we prepare a statement of funds in terms of the index-number adjusted data, as in Figure 14–2C.

The conventional columns in this statement of funds are exactly as shown in Figure 14–1C and require no comment. In the index number adjusted columns the figures for operating net margin and depreciation charges are from the adjusted income statement, Figure 14–2B, as are the adjusted income taxes. The additions to long-term debt and common stock were stated at index 120 because these transactions occurred December 31; the same is true of the plant additions and the dividends.

But if we compare the long-term debt increase with the change in that item in the adjusted position statement, we note that the position statement change is $20,000 decline instead of the $7,000 increase which did occur; further, the amount of net working capital at December 31 is $256,000 in the position statement, but $259,200 in the statement of funds. These two items are effects of holding dollar

FIGURE 14–2C

INFLATED SPECIALTY COMPANY

Index Number Adjusted Statement of Funds
Year Ended 12/31/–

	Conventional from Figure 14–1C		Index Number Adjusted	
Net working capital beginning........		$204,000		$244,800
Operating net margin..............	$69,000		$38,400	
Depreciation charges..............	24,000	93,000	36,000	74,400
New long-term debt..............	$ 7,000		$ 7,000	
New common shares issued..........	3,000	10,000	3,000	10,000
Total......................		$307,000		$329,200
Deduct:				
Plant additions, 12/31/–..........	$30,000		$30,000	
Income taxes..................	22,000		24,000	
Dividends declared..............	16,000	68,000	16,000	70,000
Net Working Capital End of Year.....		$239,000		$259,200

assets or debt while prices changed. They are explained separately, below.

The best way to see what happened to the long-term debt position is to recall what we did when we arranged the position statement to reflect the price change. We looked back (at the end of the year) to the initial position; the nominal debt of $135,000 was seen to have supplied the same financial effect as would require $162,000 in end of year dollars. The operations during the year had the use of those funds, despite the fact that this creditor needs to be paid only 135,000 "dollars" regardless of the price level. The difference of $27,000 is the advantage from borrowing at a low price level but repaying at a higher one, settling the obligation in "cheaper" dollars of purchasing power. This gain does not affect the net working capital directly, and it cannot appear in the statement of funds, so we shall have to report it in some other way, as will be explained later.

The other price level adjustment appeared as a difference between the net working capital as computed in the statement of funds
and the net working capital figure shown by the position statement.
This is a $3,200 decline in net working capital ($256,000 less
$259,200). This item is similar to the long-term debt situation just
described; but it applies to current position, and it represents not
only the effect of borrowing during periods of changing prices but
also the effect of holding dollar claims (the reverse of borrowing)
during such a period. A loss of this kind should be expected here, for
the company had an initial current position of $144,000 cash and
receivables and only $115,200 of current debt; at the end of the year
the position was similar with even more cash and receivables
($160,000) as compared to less current debt ($108,000). Holding
net dollar claims produces a loss, just as maintaining a net debt position produces a gain in a rising price situation.

The $3,200 difference could be "explained" by tabulating indi-
vidual items that show how the price level adjusted fund-statement is
different from the conventional one:

Initial net working capital greater	$40,800	
Final net working capital greater		$17,000
Net operating margin greater		30,600
Depreciation greater	12,000	
Income taxes greater		2,000
Net difference		3,200
Total	$52,800	$52,800

But the change really comes about in a more detailed way. Details
of a computation to verify this are given in Figure 14–3.

The detailed analysis given in Figure 14–3 is not essential to the
overall reporting of price changes, but it does "prove" the figure
which must be added to the statement of funds; showing the reduction in net working capital from price changes indicates how many
added dollars were required to maintain the effective current position.

Summary of Price Level Changes

Our discussion has preserved in all of the illustrations those figures
which would appear in conventional operating reports. Both the
earnings and the funds reports show both the conventional and the
price adjusted figures. The position statement, too, separated the

FIGURE 14–3

INFLATED SPECIALTY COMPANY

Net Working Capital Dollar Gains and Losses
Effects of Holding Cash and Receivables, and Current Debt
in a Period in Which Prices Shift Upward

	Nominal		Index Adjusted
Cash and receivables:			
Initial balance..................	$ 120,000	× 120/100	$ 144,000
Sales revenues.................	1,057,000	(see earnings	1,178,400
Total......................	$1,177,000	report)	$1,322,400
Routine payments (below)..........	$ 981,000	× 120/110	$1,070,200
Dividends.......................	16,000	(end of year)	16,000
Debt retirement..................	20,000	(end of year)	20,000
Total Disbursements..........	$1,017,000		$1,106,200
Final balances...................	$ 160,000		$ 216,200
Loss, holding cash..............			56,200
Total Accounted For.........	$ 160,000		$ 160,000
Payables:			
Initial balances:.................	$ 96,000	× 120/100	$ 115,200
Merchandise acquired $306 + $324		(360 + 360	
+ $187 (000)................	817,000	+ 204(000)*	924,000
		position reports	
Selling expenses................	154,000	× 120/110	168,000
Income taxes..................	22,000	× 120/110	24,000
Total......................	$1,089,000		$1,231,200
Routine payments (to balance)......	$ 981,000	× 120/110	$1,070,200
Final balances...................	$ 108,000		161,000
Gain, carrying debt.............			53,000
Total Accounted For.........	$ 108,000		$ 108,000

Summary

Gain, carrying debt...........................	$53,000
Loss, holding dollar claims.....................	57,200
Net Loss on Current Position...................	$ 3,200

* See earnings report and position statement Figures 14–2A and 14–2B.

effect of price level change from the retained earnings equity; the price adjusted position statement showed a separate item for capital adjustment, price level changes. Some accountants would not bother to maintain such distinctions. But it should be obvious that the really important thing about price level adjustments is to show specifically what the change in price level has done to the conventional measurement of income. Another reason for separating price level adjustment effects is that no index is more than an approximate measure of price level change; actually, it is a different kind of data which most accounting procedures do not recognize. The author thinks it better accounting to report in such a way that one can see in the reports what has been adjusted, and how.

Assuming that the reported conventional earnings of $31,000 would be added to the beginning retained earnings balance to produce the $43,000 conventional equity element in the position statement, we could summarize the price level adjustments in a separate report shown in Figure 14–4.

Preparing such a statement as Figure 14–4 has the effect of giving a quick summary view of what inflation has done to the operations and position of the firm. The details may be traced back into the operating reports if desired, or the reader may focus his attention on

FIGURE 14-4

INFLATED SPECIALTY COMPANY
Summary of Price Level Adjustments
Year Ended 12/31/–

Price level adjustments applicable to current earnings, per Figure 14–2B	$32,600 Loss
Reduction of net working capital from holding net dollar claims	3,200 Loss
Total	$35,800
Deduct gain from carrying long-term debt	27,000 Gain
Net decrease in equity from price level adjustments during the year	$ 8,800 Loss
Add price level losses from prior years	14,700 Loss
Ending balance, Capital Adjustment, Price Level Changes	$23,500 Loss

conventional figures in those reports. The really essential point in all this is that the price changes are separated because they are largely independent of the actions or decisions of the management and thus ought to be reported apart from those actions which management did control.

Conclusion

The procedures described above are admittedly a bit more complex than those underlying conventional reports. These procedures have not yet been widely adopted in the United States. But some such pattern of adjustments *is* used in some other countries, and the increasing effect of inflation has already produced more than passing interest in such procedures here. The basic reason for non-adoption of these methods is not that they take more time and effort but rather that the readers of such financial reports would need to be educated to these presentations. Many people regard recorded dollars as "facts"; to tamper with "facts" is to create confusion by adding a mysterious new element into the report pattern.

But perhaps the really most widely advanced reason for failure to accept full index-number adjustments in reports is that the two most important price effects can be to some extent "taken care of" within the limits of conventional accounting. The first of these has to do with inventories, as we have suggested; however, price adjustments in inventories are largely offset within or between adjacent years (except for Lifo which does not show inventory appreciation). In the case discussed here, the initial inventory adjustment of $36,000 was partially offset by the final inventory write-up of $17,000. While these amounts are large, this is only because of the violent movements introduced by our selection of "arithmetically simple" index numbers; the point is, that the only effect on income is the *net* of the two inventory adjustments for any year.

The other salient price effect is in the area of plant and equipment figures. Here, the depreciation charge is the principal factor for any given year's income. Price changes can be reflected by adjusting the historical costs by appraisal when that seems really essential. While this is a specific rather than a general price level adjustment, it may for practical purposes substitute for the index number corrections. Some accountants distinguish between price *level* adjustments, and specific asset price changes on the ground that the former reflects neither gain nor loss, being rather a change in the "value of money." Measuring the difference between the general price level adjustment and the specific price change may be regarded as a refinement, which is designed to measure a real gain or loss from speculation in that particular asset, over and above the general price level shift. This refinement is largely academic in view of the current attitude toward price level adjustments.

Of course, none of this meets the real argument that price level changes are an inherent part of economic life and that accounting measurements would be more meaningful if restated in terms of current prices. However, the validity of this argument has not yet moved those who prepare and authorize the publication of financial reports to change reporting practices. And until these people are impressed with the importance to common-dollar reporting, we are not likely to see such reports used in practice.

QUESTIONS

1. What is the reason for emphasis upon prices in economic affairs? Has this anything to do with the measurement of income?

2. Among the short-run influences of price change which affect income is the matter of how price change affects inventories. What is meant by a flow assumption in this connection?

3. What lag in the effects of price changes is created by a first-in, first-out assumption of cost flow? What happens to this if turnover of the inventory increases or decreases? Does the same thing happen if turnover increases or decreases with a last-in, first-out inventory pricing method?

4. In a period of falling prices, the effect of the last-in, first-out and the first-in, first-out procedures is reversed, i.e., last-in produces lower expense charges and higher inventory amounts than would be had by first-in procedures. Is there a similar reversal of the effects of turnover? Why or why not?

5. What is the merit of using last-in, first-out to establish cost of goods sold or usage and then using the first-in, first-out procedure to set up the final inventory balance? Does this put both the cost of goods sold or used and the closing inventory on a strictly current cost basis? Why?

6. What peculiarly of last-in, first-out procedure is met when the physical level of inventory declines? An initial inventory of 1,000 units at $10 is increased by 400 units at a price of $11, then decreased by 500 units. What is the cost of goods sold on a Fifo basis? on a Lifo basis? What happens to the inventory if after the foregoing, 200 units are acquired at $13? What effect might this have on taxable income measured via Lifo?

7. What is the difference between Lifo accounting and a replacement cost method? Illustrate from the data given in Question 6. Current price quotations at the time of the issue of 500 units was $12, and current price at the end of the period was $14.

8. Why is the use of net realizable values not a solution to the inventory pricing problem?

9. When an asset is appraised, why is the credit necessary to record the appraisal carried to a "Capital Adjustment" account? In the case of a depreciable asset, can an appraisal be recorded without some adjustment to Accumulated Depreciation?

10. Why does an appraisal sometimes indicate a different use-life expectancy than that suggested by the remaining undepreciated cost? What procedure is employed to separate the change in life expectancy from the price change in recording an appraisal?

11. When the appraisal or write-up has been recorded, is depreciation still recorded on a cost basis? Why?

12. What happens to the Capital Adjustment account over the remaining life of the asset whose appraisal is there reflected? What happens when that asset is disposed of?

13. Why is the change in the general price level different from the price change for a specific asset? Is there a good reason for recognizing both kinds of change? If only one adjustment for price change is feasible (for "practical" reasons) should it be made in terms of specific asset price adjustments or a thorough going general index adjustment?

14. When the general price level adjustment is made to a set of financial statements, what difference is there between monetary assets and debts, and nonmonetary assets? What is the purpose of the account labeled Capital Adjustment, Price Level Changes?

15. When price level adjusted reports are presented, what changes are there in the report of earnings as compared to the conventional earnings statement? Does this price level adjusted earnings report include all the effects of price level adjustments? Does a price level adjusted statement of funds include any price change effects other than those in the price level adjusted earnings report? Why is it desirable to prepare an additional summary statement of price level adjustments?

16. Do you think there is a good reason to include current price effects in all accounting reports (*a*) to reflect specific price changes, (*b*) to reflect general price level changes, or (*c*) both? What conditions would affect your decision?

PROBLEMS

Heier, Lore, Price Company

One inventory item used by this company at the end of last year consisted of 5,000 units, at an actual purchase cost of $30 each. The currently quoted replacement price of the item at that time was $28. The company was considering whether to change its inventory method from first-in, first-out to a last-in, first-out basis. But it was also suggested that a standard cost basis or a moving average procedure could be used.

Under Lifo, according to tax rules, there could be no write-down of inventory to market at any time, and the cost of goods sold would have to be computed by subtracting the end-of-year Lifo inventory figure from the total charges to inventory during the year—not by detailing specific purchases and sales. The moving average procedure would price out each issue according to an average price recomputed for all goods on hand after recording each purchase. Standard cost would be $31 throughout the year.

During this year, the company completed four purchases and four sales of this item, the units purchased at the beginning of each quarter, and the sales at the end of each quarter follow:

| | Purchases | | Sales |
Quarter	Units	Price	(Units)
First....................	14,000	$29	15,000
Second.................	24,000	$31	18,000
Third.................	10,000	$33	12,000
Fourth.................	18,000	$34	20,000

Required:

1. State the cost of goods sold and the closing inventory under each of the four methods.
2. Write the entries for the transactions under the standard cost procedure.
3. Compute the holding gain on 5,000 units held over the year—
   a) as included in cost of goods sold via Fifo.
   b) as deducted from total charges, via end of year Lifo (more than one answer).
   c) as it would be computed using market prices beginning and end of year.

Magnus Manufacturing Company

At the end of last year the officers of this company decided to embark on an extensive expansion; it hoped to raise a considerable amount of new capital. At that time, however, its financial reports reflected only the historical costs of long-term assets that had been acquired some years before, when price levels were considerably lower. In order to present a more current picture of the company assets, the Universal Appraisal Company was engaged to make a survey of the company's properties to restate assets in more current terms.

Data from certain sections of the appraisal company's report dated January 2, this year, are given below:

(1) *Plant Site.* The land cost $40,000 25 years ago; it consists of a 15-acre tract, of which about half is still vacant. In view of recent sales

of similar properties in the vicinity, the tract is considered to be worth $75,000 in the current market.

(2) *Buildings.* Construction cost in December, 25 years ago, was $180,000. When these buildings were completed they were expected to have a useful life of 50 years; accumulated depreciation to the end of last year is thus $90,000. The survey indicates that about $5,000 of maintenance work needs to be done on these buildings. Reproduction cost new at January 1, this year, would be $330,000; the buildings have an indicated service life of 35 years from the beginning of this year.

(3) *Machinery.* Original cost, January 2, nine years ago, was $240,000. Depreciation has been charged at 8 percent per year. Rehabilitation and overhauling costs of $13,000 were charged against the accumulated depreciation account two years ago. Present net sound value, $154,000; estimated service life from January 2, this year, is seven years.

(4) *Equipment.* Purchased January 2, 16 years ago, for $90,000. Items of this same kind are no longer available in the market, but equipment to render the same service is now available at approximately $60,000 installed. Service life of the old equipment was originally taken as 30 years, but it is now considered to be only 9 years from January 2, this year. The service life for equivalent items of present-day design is 25 years overall.

Required:

Prepare entries to give effect to the appraisal company's report and to record depreciation for the current year.

Capital Corporation

A machine used in the plant of Capital Corporation cost $41,600 installed on January 1, 1962. The company recorded depreciation at 10% of the gross cost per year up to and including the year ended December 31, 1969. On January 6, 1970, the company was informed by the American Appraisal Company that this machine when appraised by them at December 31, 1969, had a net sound value of $20,000, and an estimated remaining life of five years from that date. In addition, they pointed out that some minor parts needed replacement and these would cost $700 installed; the appraisal value had not been reduced for these repairs. Set up entries to give effect to the appraisal company's report.

On December 31, 1970, the Capital Corporation decided to accept an offer of $17,000 cash for this machine, which was no longer needed. Depreciation for 1970 had not been recorded; make entries necessary to show depreciation and the disposal of the machine.

Assuming that we could obtain valid appraisals of all long term assets, would procedures such as those you used immediately above for all such assets give adequate accounting for changes in price levels? Why or why not?

OOO Meye Company

Position Statement

	Last Year	This Year
Cash and receivables....	$ 40,000	$ 98,000
Inventory...	50,000	29,000
Plant (net)...	360,000	333,000
Total...	$450,000	$460,000

	Last Year	This Year
Current debt...	$ 30,000	$ 28,300
Common stock...	378,000	378,000
Retained earnings...	42,000	53,700
Total...	$450,000	$460,000

Statement of Earnings

Sales revenue...		$189,000
Inventory...	$ 50,000	
Purchases...	126,000	
Total...	$176,000	
Inventory...	29,000	147,000
		$ 42,000
Depreciation...		27,000
Net income...		$ 15,000
Tax...		3,300
Net Income Retained...		$ 11,700

Beginning index, 100; ending index, 110; index average for year, 105; index at incorporation, 90. All plant assets were acquired at incorporation.

Required:

Use these data to prepare an index-number-adjusted position statement and appropriately related reports for this firm.

Buena Vista Homes, Incorporated

An apartment building was constructed 20 years ago, when the price-level stood at index 80. The building was financed by a twenty year mortgage for $40,000; the rest of the building cost was covered by common stock subscriptions. At the end of the twentieth year, the following conventional reports were presented. They were entirely correct according to accepted accounting principles.

BUENA VISTA HOMES, INCORPORATED

Position Statement at End of Years 19 and 20

ASSETS

	12/31/19	*12/31/20*
Cash in bank.................	$ 5,000	$ 6,250
Building cost.................	80,000	80,000
Accumulated depreciation...........	40,000*	44,000*
Total Assets...............	$45,000	$42,250

EQUITIES

	12/31/19	*12/31/20*
Current debt.................	nil	nil
Mortgage payable...............	$ 4,000	nil
Common stock.................	40,000	$40,000
Retained earnings...............	1,000	2,250
Total Equities...............	$45,000	$42,250

* Deduction

During the 20th year, revenues had been $105,000, cash payments for expenses were $99,750, and depreciation was $4,000. Net income was $1,250 before income taxes, but income taxes are ignored for our purposes.

Recognizing that the price level stood at 100 at the end of year 19, and at 110 for the end of year 20, the average level being 105 for the year, the following price-level adjusted reports were set up:

BUENA VISTA HOMES, INCORPORATED

Price-level Adjusted Position Statement at End of Years 19 and 20

ASSETS

	12/31/19	*12/31/20*
Cash in bank.................	$ 5,500	$ 6,250
Building.................	110,000	110,000
Accumulated depreciation........	55,000*	60,500*
Total Assets............	60,500	55,750

EQUITIES

	12/31/19	*12/31/20*
Mortgage payable...............	$ 5,500	nil
Common stock.................	55,000	$55,000
Retained earnings...............	1,000	2,250
Price-level adjustment...........	1,000*	1,500*
Total Equities............	$60,500	$55,750

BUENA VISTA HOMES, INCORPORATED

Price-Adjusted Statement of Earnings Year End 12/31/20

Revenue ($105,000 × 110/105)...................	$110,000
Expenses (cash), (99,750 × 110/105)..............	104,500
Depreciation (4,000 × 110/80)....................	5,500
Net Income before Taxes on Income...............	nil

* Deduction

When these reports (all of the above) were shown to the stockholders, several questions were raised. Since you have learned about such things, they expect you to answer.

Required:

Answer the following questions.

1. In the adjusted position statement for year 19, there is an equity deduction of $1,000. What is this, and why is it separated from the Retained Earnings?

2. This $1,000 debit item referred to in Q1 has increased by $500 during year 20. Evidently there was a further price level loss in year 20. The $1,250 earnings wiped out by price adjustments cannot be this difference; if it is part of it, how is the other $750 accounted for?

3. In the year 19 position statement, the mortgage appears as $5,500. The amount paid on the mortgage was $4,000, because the cash account shows this: $5,000 + $105,000 less $99,750 left $10,250; the final balance of $6,250 permits only $4,000 payment to have occurred. To whom do we owe the other $1,500, or who got it if we don't owe it?

4. Over twenty years, the company has owned nothing besides small cash balances and the building. In a period of rising prices real estate grows in value, and this is shown in the statements. Further, the building has been financed in part by debt, and debtors gain in periods of rising price levels. How, then, can we have a cumulative loss from price level changes, and no profit this last year, even though our cash increased after we paid off the final installment on the mortgage?

Broken Arms Hotel

At December 31, this year, the comparative position statement of the Broken Arms Hotel Co. was as follows:

BROKEN ARMS HOTEL COMPANY
Position Statement at December 31, 1968 and 69

ASSETS

	Last Year	This Year
Cash and receivables................	$ 5,000	$ 11,980
Land and building..................	$102,000	$102,000
Accumulated depreciation...........	51,000*	55,080*
Total Assets................	$ 56,000	$ 58,900

EQUITIES

	Last Year	This Year
Mortgage payable..................	$15,300	$10,200
Common stock.....................	20,400	20,400
Retained earnings.................	20,300	28,300
Total Equities...............	$56,000	$58,900

* Deduction.

The earnings for this year were: Gross Rental Revenue, $26,520, less Payroll Expense $11,220, Depreciation Expense $4,080, Interest Charges $1,020 and Income Taxes Charge $2,200; a net of $8,000. Some of the directors are concerned about the effect of price level change over the past 25 years, and ask you to indicate what effect would be seen if the statements were expressed in common dollars.

You find that the price index 25 years ago when the firm was established was 51, as compared to 100 at the beginning of this year. The stock was issued, and the building and mortgage were acquired at the time of incorporation. The index at December 31, 1969 is 105, and the average price index over the year was 102. Interest was paid monthly, but the indicated mortgage reduction, as well as the income tax, are paid at the end of each year.

Required:
Set up the price-adjusted statements.

Inflationary Sales Company

Prepare financial reports to reflect price level changes, and reconcile the differences between conventional and price adjusted reports.

Conventional Position Statements

		Last Year 12/31/		This Year 12/31/
Cash in bank....................		$20,000		$ 9,500
Accounts receivable.............		22,000		74,500
Inventories (Fifo cost)...........		40,000		82,000
Total Current Assets........		$82,000		$166,000
Current liabilities...............		40,000		103,000
Net working capital.............		$42,000		$ 63,000
Fixed assets................... $66,000			$66,000	
Less: Accumulated depreciation...................... 22,000		44,000	24,100	41,900
Total Working Capital and Other Assets........		$86,000		$104,900
Stockholder equities common stock......................		$30,000		$ 30,000
Retained earnings..............		56,000		74,900
Total Stockholder Equities...............		$86,000		$104,900

Transactions for the current year included the following:
(1) Sales, on account, at regular prices, $105,000.
(2) Merchandise cost of goods sold, $84,000.
(3) Collections from customers, $52,500.
(4) Purchases of merchandise, on account, $126,000.

(5) Payments on accounts payable, $63,000.
(6) Depreciation, $2,100.

There were no expenses other than merchandise costs and depreciation. This company uses Fifo to account for merchandise costs.

An index of the general price level (fictitious) was:

January 1, 1954..................... Index, 55
December 31, last year.............. Index, 100
December 31, this year.............. Index, 110

All fixed assets were acquired January 1, 1950, at incorporation.

Transactions that spread over the year are assumed to have ocurred at the average index level of 105 (average of 100 and 110).

The Eldorado Company

The position statement given below is conventional. The numbers in parentheses are the index of the general price-level when those amounts first appeared in the company records—the date of acquisition or contract. Current index is 108.

Position Statement at December 31, Current Year

ASSETS			EQUITIES		
Cash in bank.............	(108)	$ 40,000	Current debt.............	(108)	$344,540
Accounts receivable.......	(105)	231,000			
Notes receivable..........	(107)	10,807	30 Year 5% bonds		
Inventory, new mdse......	(104)	251,992	($300,000 face)........	(85)	258,400
Returned mdse...........	(106)	2,166	Total debt........		$602,940
Total current assets.....		$535,965			
			Common stock, no par		
Long-term investments....	(90)	$ 63,000	(10,000 shares)........	(78)	390,000
Land..................	(78)	85,800	Retained earnings........		67,825
Plant and equipment......	(80)	376,000	Total share equity......		$457,825
Total long-term assets..		$ 524,800			
Total Assets.......		$1,060,765	Total Equities.......		$1,060,765

The following additional data are available:

New merchandise inventory replacement cost, $261,000. Returned merchandise will sell for $2,880, but refinishing will cost $159. Long-term investments are currently quoted at $76,550. Net appraisal values of land, $115,000; of plant, $508,000. Long-term debt quoted at 108¼, yield rate 4½ percent. The common stock is quoted at 67.

Required:

Set up what you think is the most useful report(s) to meet the needs of people interested in this company.

INDEX TO PROBLEMS

TOPIC INDEX

*This book has been set in 11 point and 10
point Janson, leaded 2 points. Chapter numbers are in 12 point and 36 point Ultra
Bodoni, and chapter titles are in 18 point
Caledonia. The size of the type page is 27
by 46 picas.*